# THE MOTHERLESS OVEN

Rob Davis

SELF
MADE
HERO

BETTER SORRY THAN SAFE.

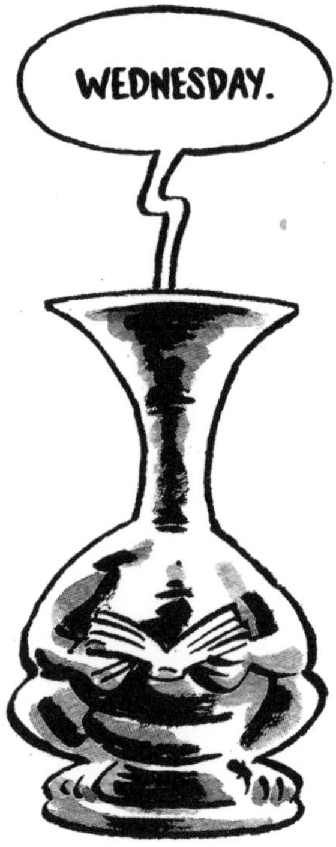
WEDNESDAY.

THE WEATHER CLOCK SAID,

KNIFE O'CLOCK.

SO I CHAINED DAD UP
IN THE SHED.

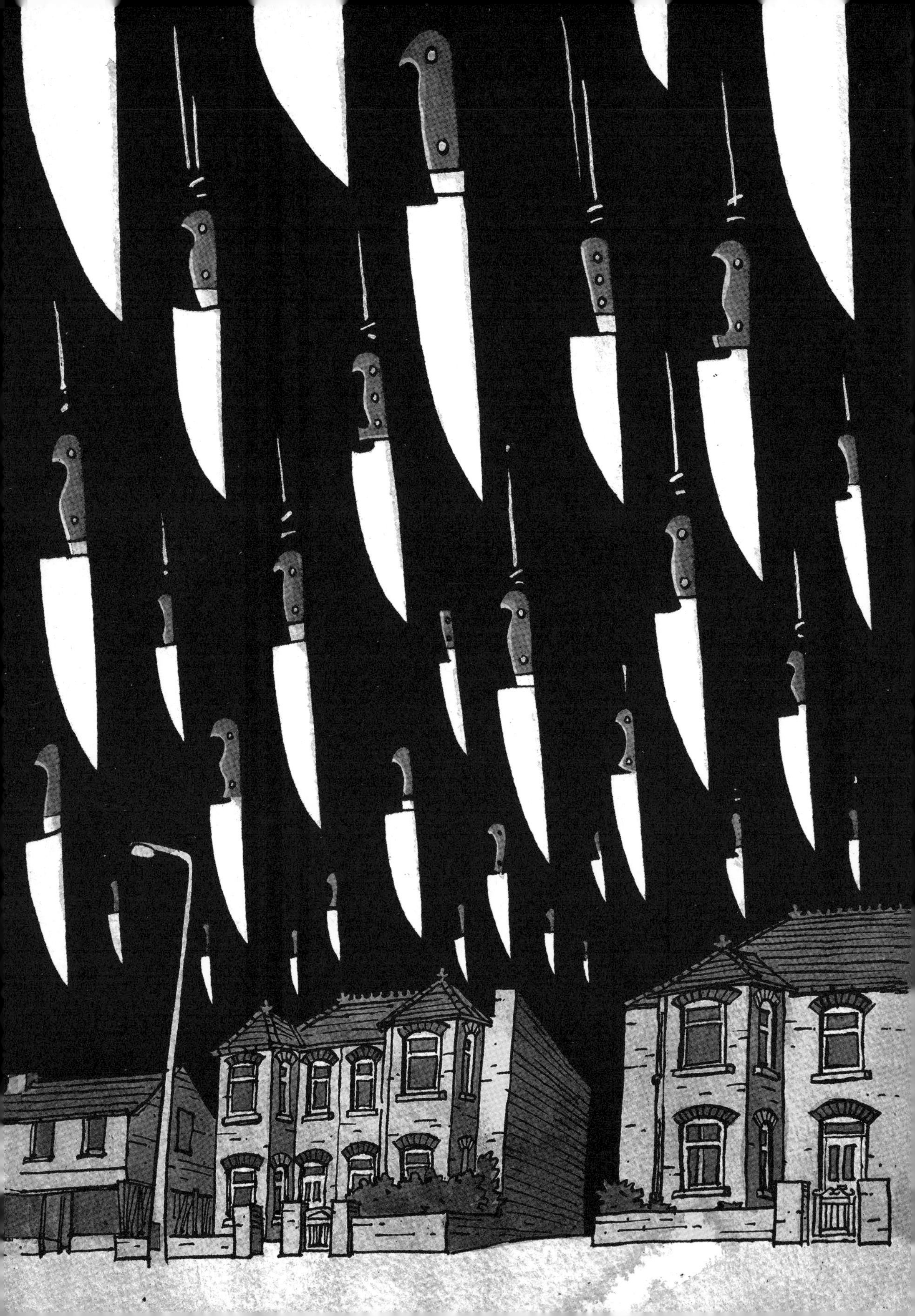

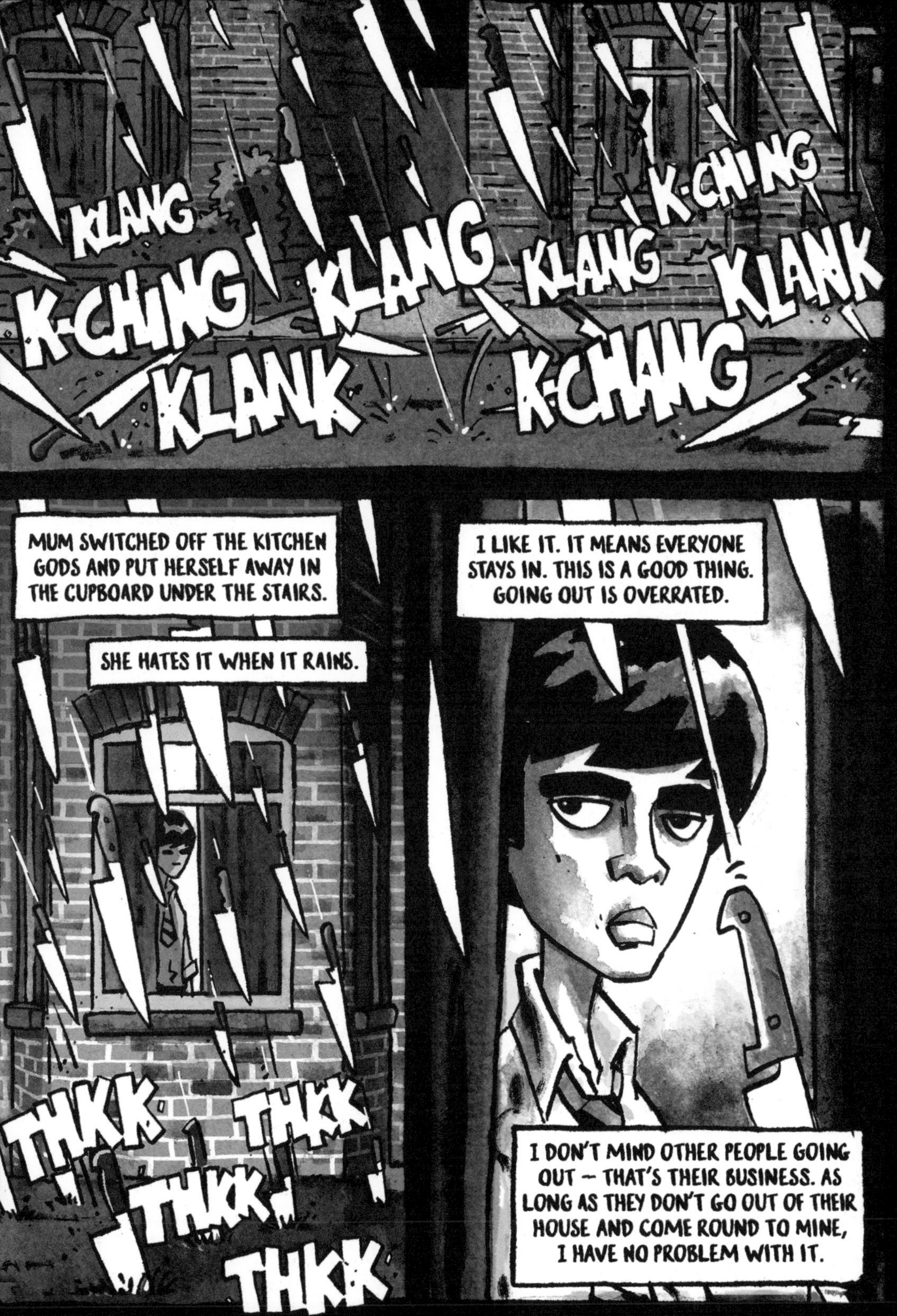
KLANG
K-CHING
KLANG
KLANK
KLANG
K-CHING
KLANK
K-CHANG
MUM SWITCHED OFF THE KITCHEN GODS AND PUT HERSELF AWAY IN THE CUPBOARD UNDER THE STAIRS.
SHE HATES IT WHEN IT RAINS.
THKK
THKK
THKK
THKK
I LIKE IT. IT MEANS EVERYONE STAYS IN. THIS IS A GOOD THING. GOING OUT IS OVERRATED.
I DON'T MIND OTHER PEOPLE GOING OUT – THAT'S THEIR BUSINESS. AS LONG AS THEY DON'T GO OUT OF THEIR HOUSE AND COME ROUND TO MINE, I HAVE NO PROBLEM WITH IT.

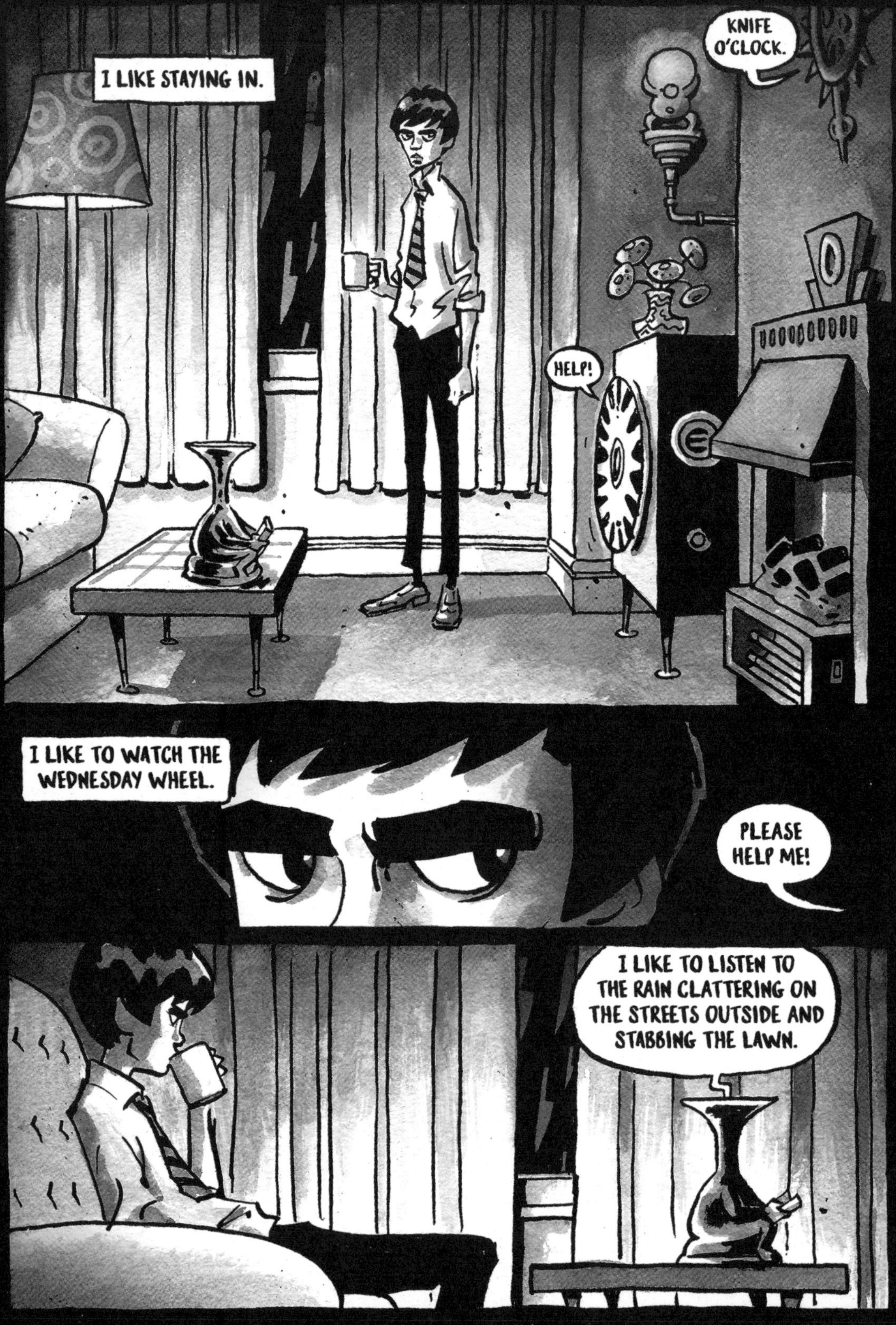
I LIKE STAYING IN.
KNIFE O'CLOCK.
HELP!
I LIKE TO WATCH THE WEDNESDAY WHEEL.
PLEASE HELP ME!
I LIKE TO LISTEN TO THE RAIN CLATTERING ON THE STREETS OUTSIDE AND STABBING THE LAWN.

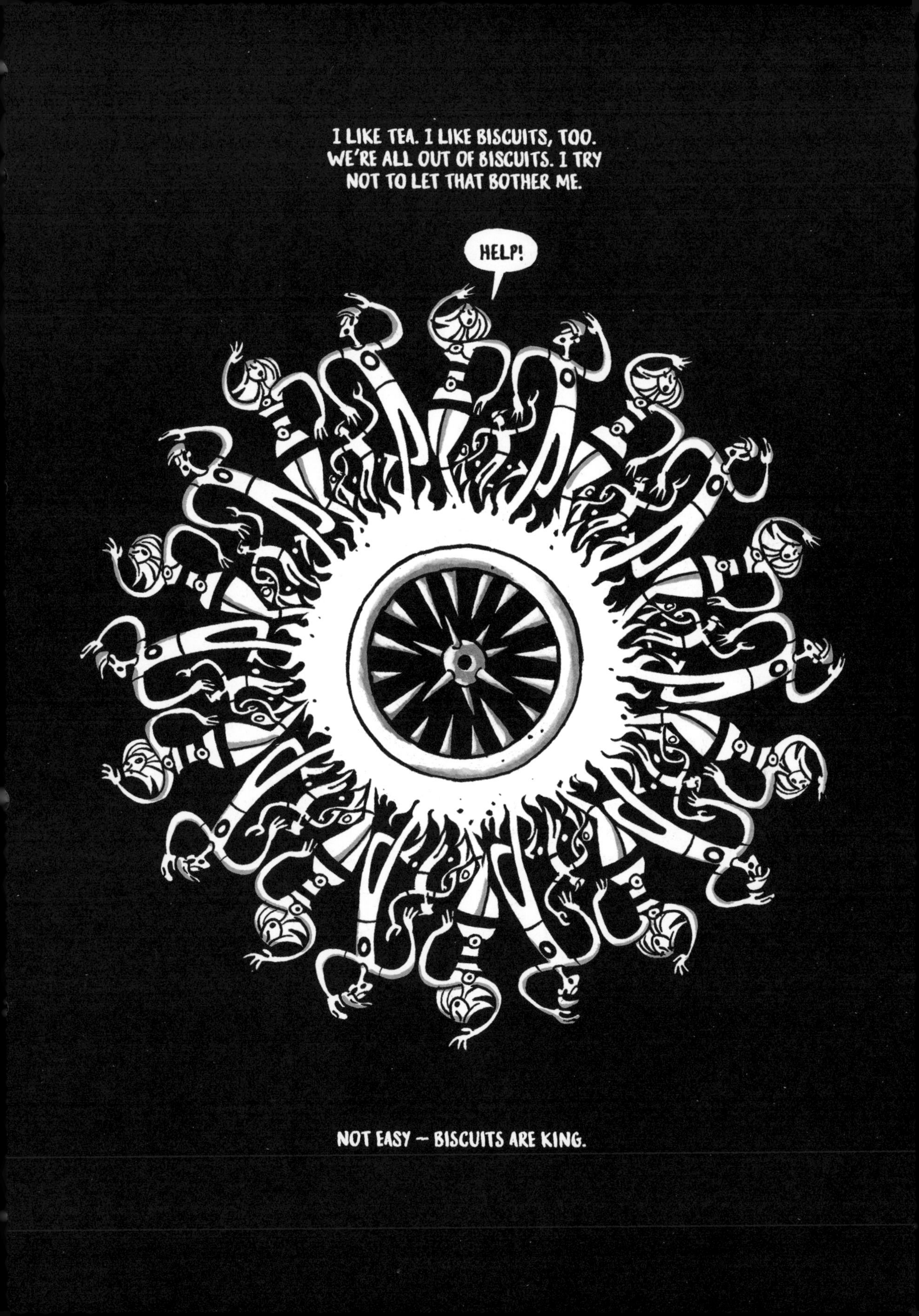
I LIKE TEA. I LIKE BISCUITS, TOO. WE'RE ALL OUT OF BISCUITS. I TRY NOT TO LET THAT BOTHER ME.
HELP!
NOT EASY – BISCUITS ARE KING.

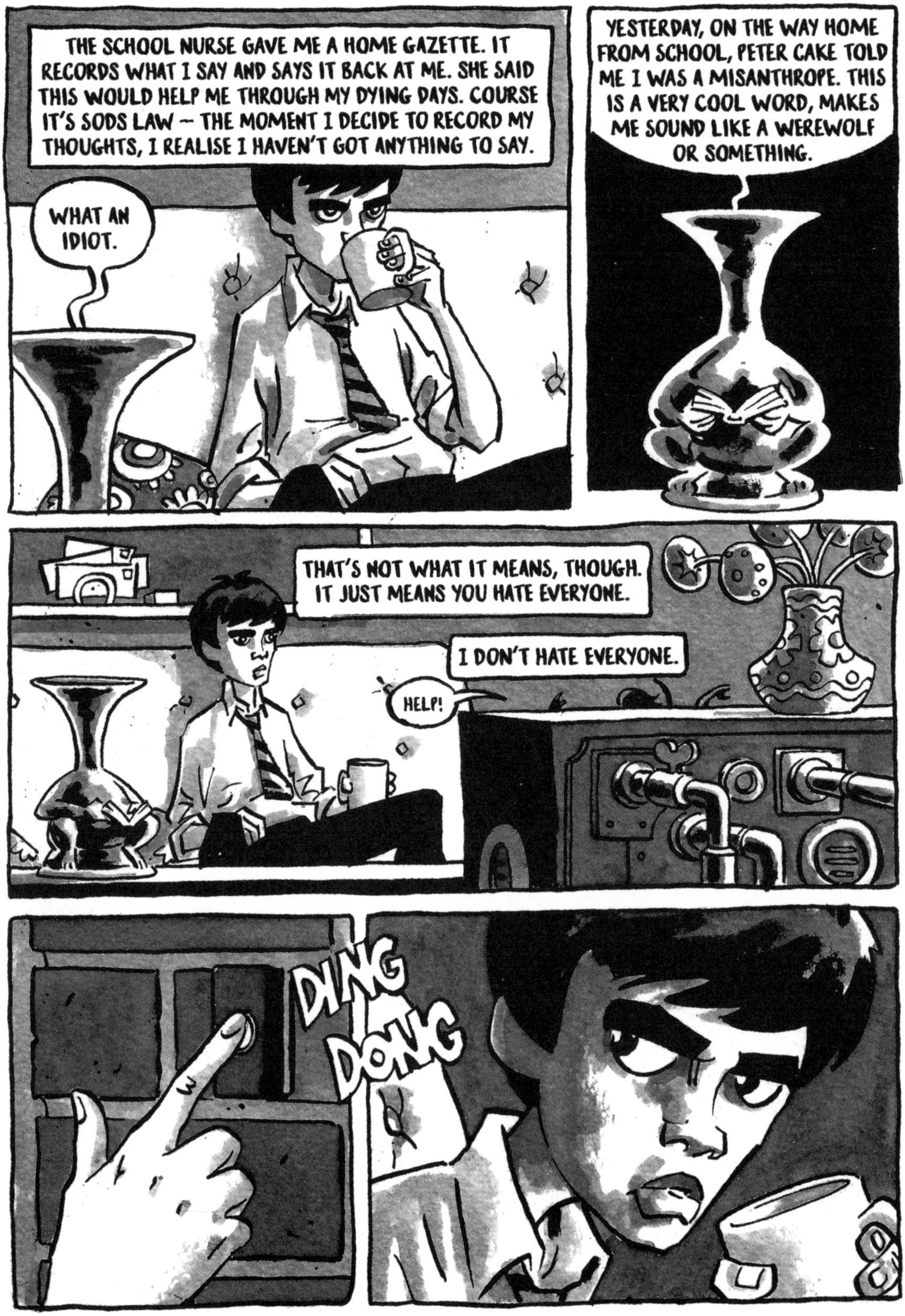
THE SCHOOL NURSE GAVE ME A HOME GAZETTE. IT RECORDS WHAT I SAY AND SAYS IT BACK AT ME. SHE SAID THIS WOULD HELP ME THROUGH MY DYING DAYS. COURSE IT'S SODS LAW – THE MOMENT I DECIDE TO RECORD MY THOUGHTS, I REALISE I HAVEN'T GOT ANYTHING TO SAY.
WHAT AN IDIOT.
YESTERDAY, ON THE WAY HOME FROM SCHOOL, PETER CAKE TOLD ME I WAS A MISANTHROPE. THIS IS A VERY COOL WORD, MAKES ME SOUND LIKE A WEREWOLF OR SOMETHING.
THAT'S NOT WHAT IT MEANS, THOUGH. IT JUST MEANS YOU HATE EVERYONE.
I DON'T HATE EVERYONE.
HELP!
DING
DONG

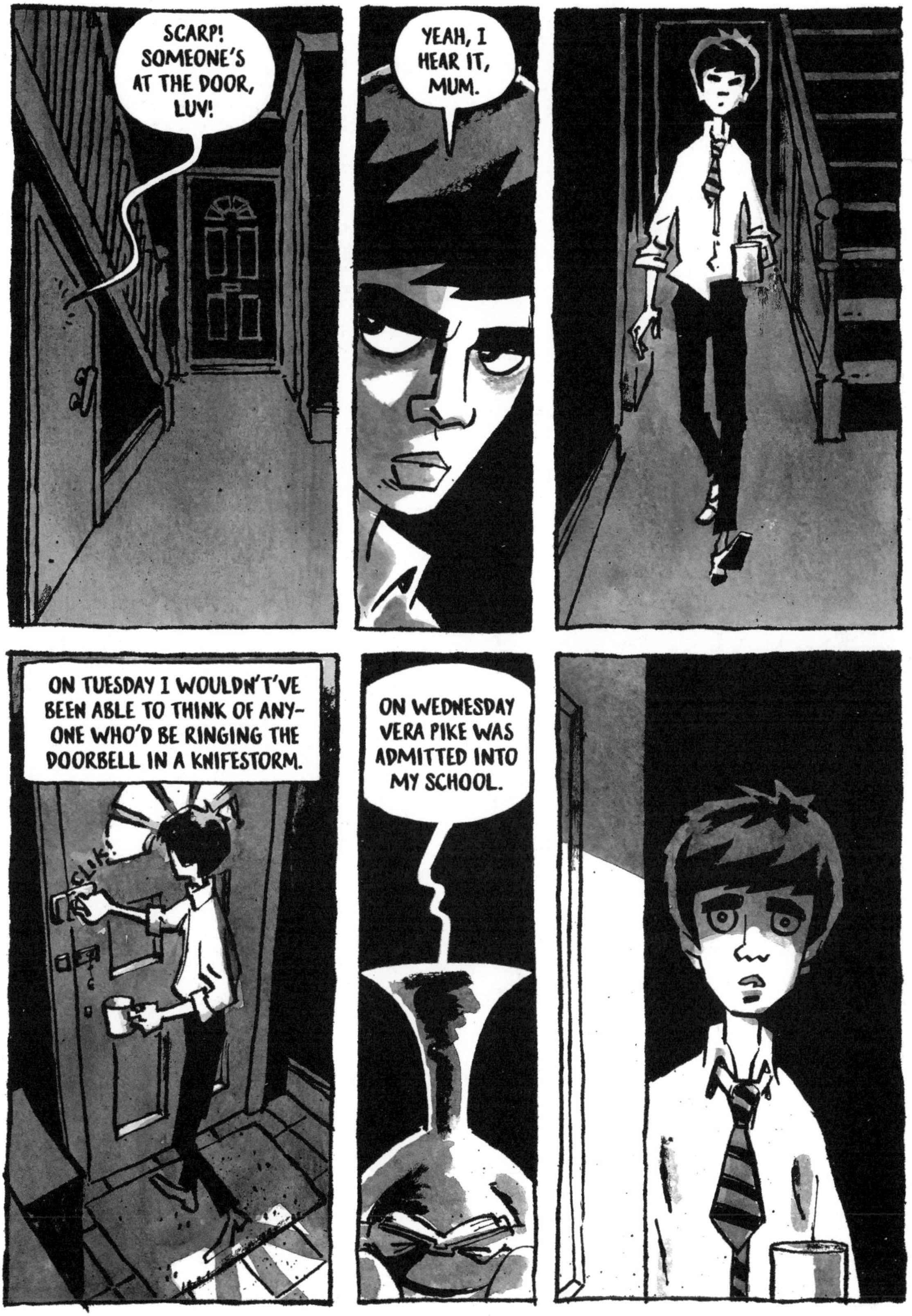
SCARP! SOMEONE'S AT THE DOOR, LUV!
YEAH, I HEAR IT, MUM.
ON TUESDAY I WOULDN'T'VE BEEN ABLE TO THINK OF ANY-ONE WHO'D BE RINGING THE DOORBELL IN A KNIFESTORM.
CLIK!
ON WEDNESDAY VERA PIKE WAS ADMITTED INTO MY SCHOOL.

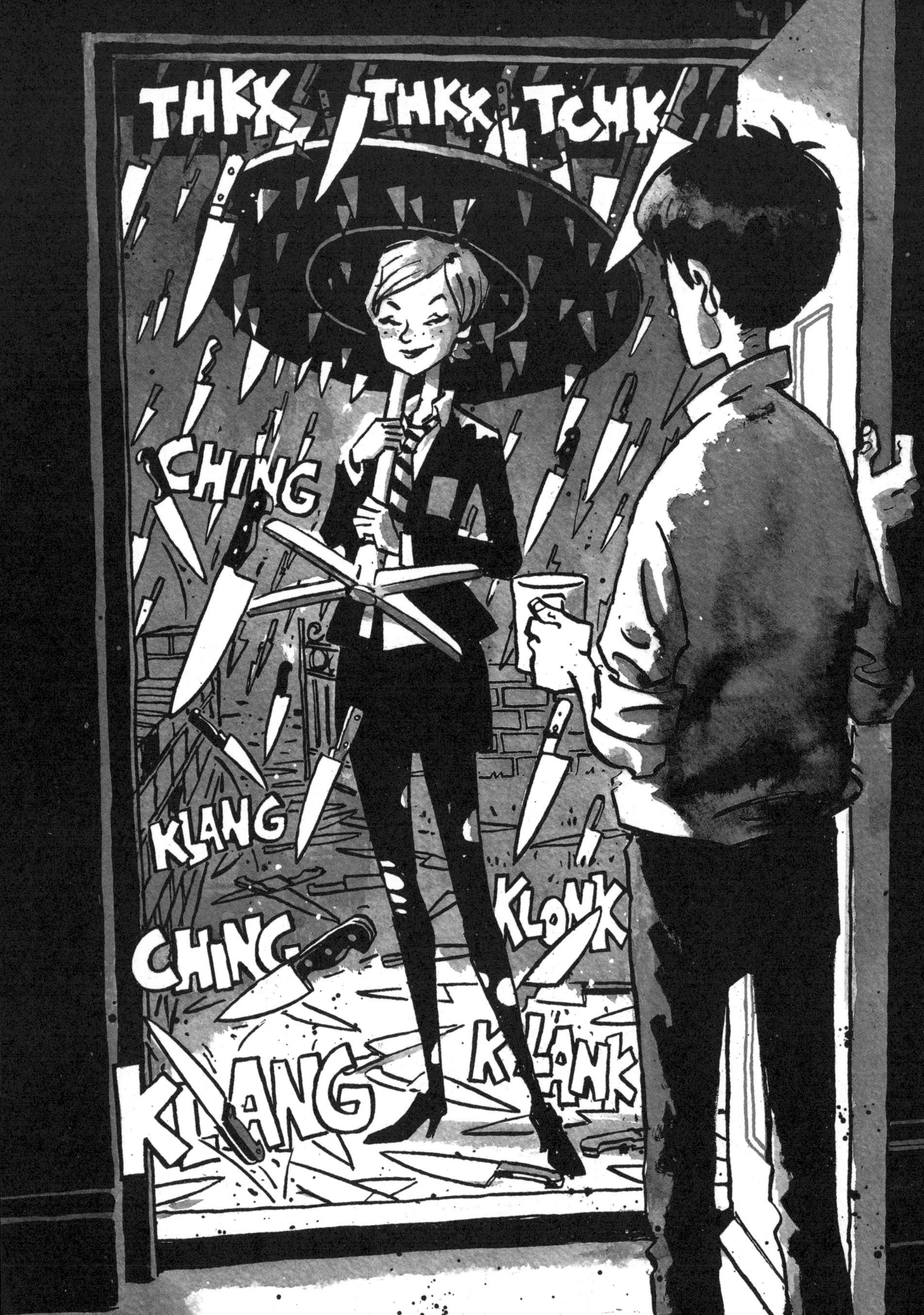
THKK
THKK
TCHK
CHING
KLANG
CHING
KLONK
KLANG
KLANK

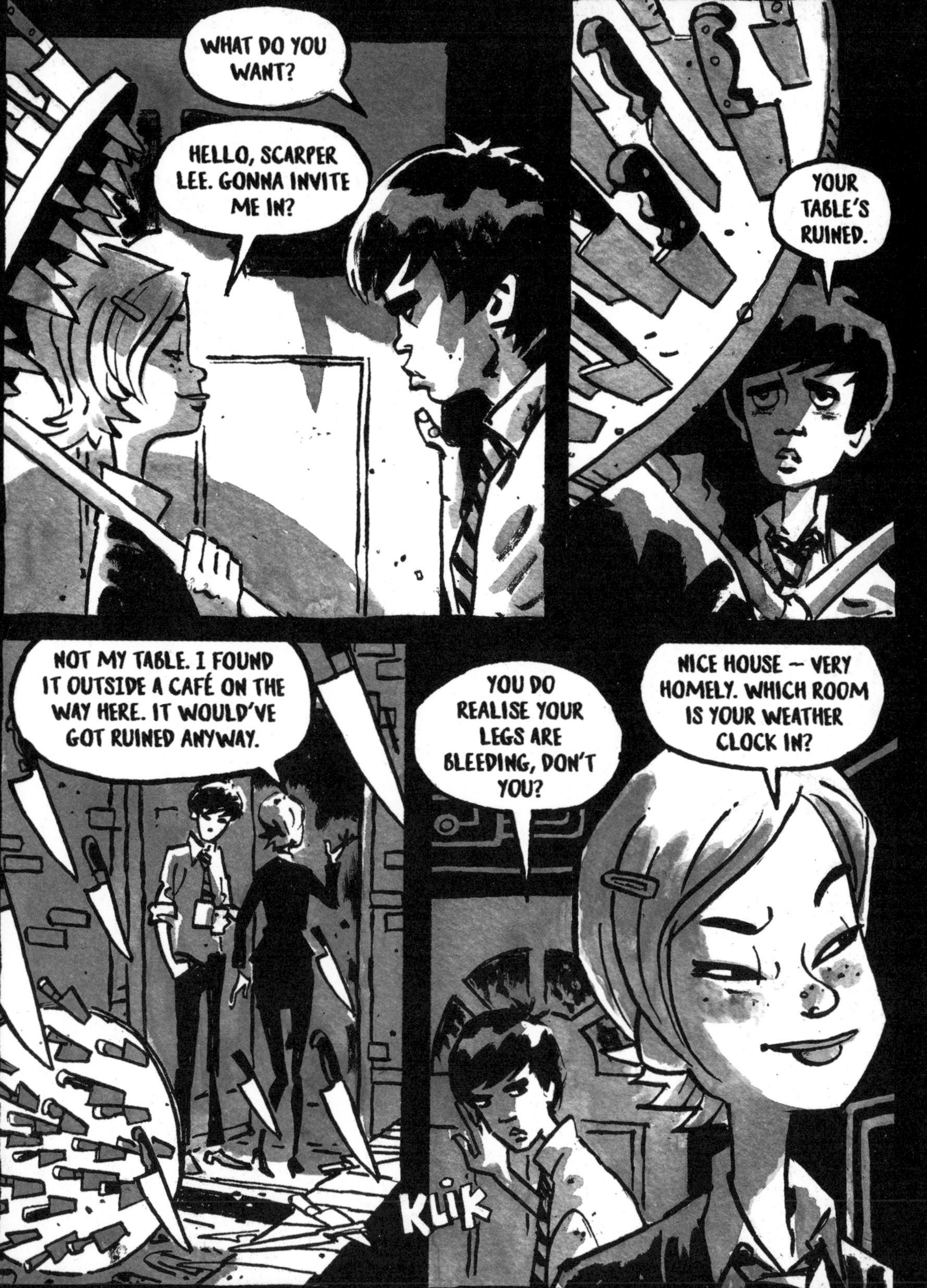
WHAT DO YOU WANT?
HELLO, SCARPER LEE. GONNA INVITE ME IN?
YOUR TABLE'S RUINED.
NOT MY TABLE. I FOUND IT OUTSIDE A CAFÉ ON THE WAY HERE. IT WOULD'VE GOT RUINED ANYWAY.
YOU DO REALISE YOUR LEGS ARE BLEEDING, DON'T YOU?
NICE HOUSE — VERY HOMELY. WHICH ROOM IS YOUR WEATHER CLOCK IN?
KLIK

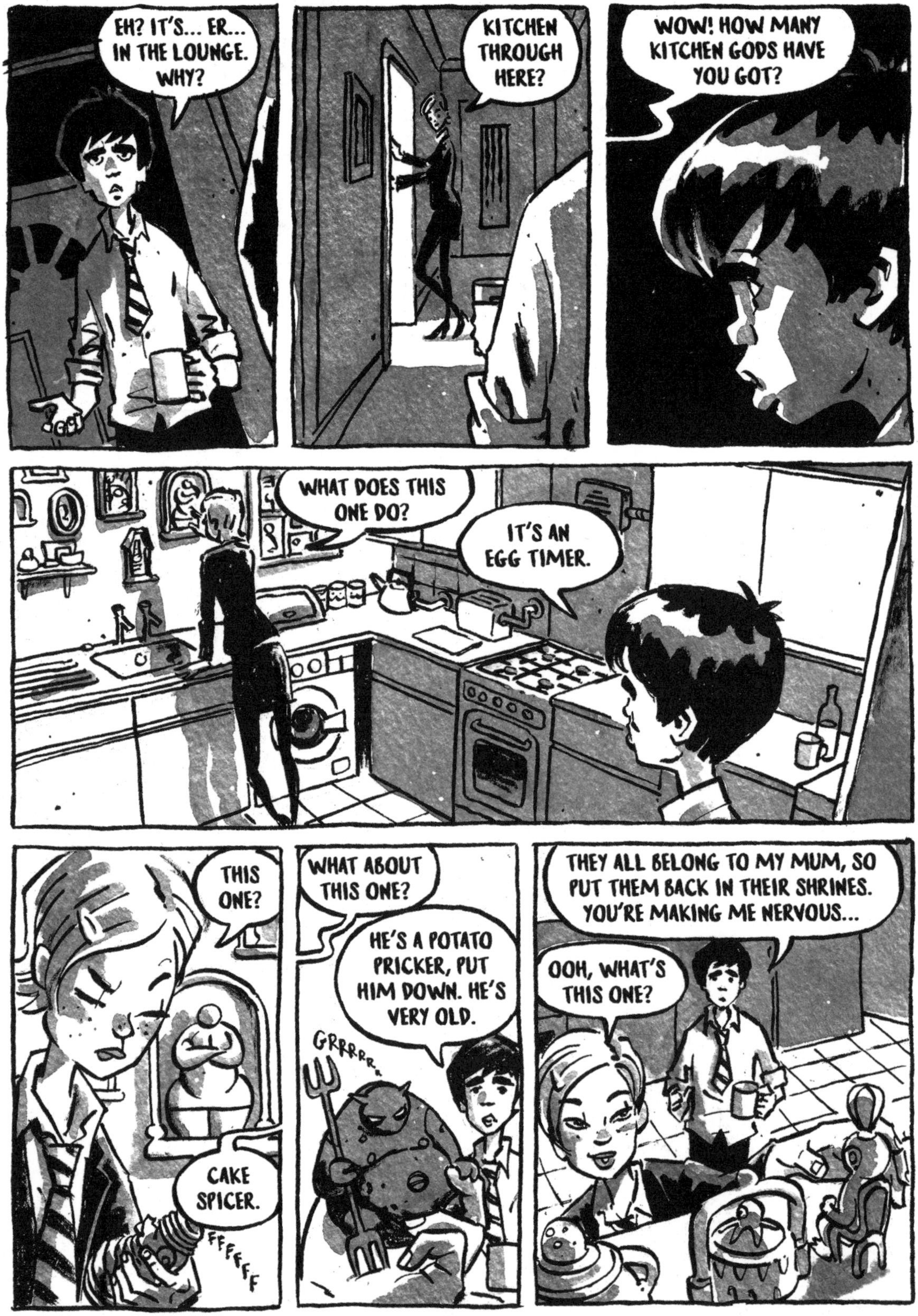
EH? IT'S... ER... IN THE LOUNGE. WHY?
KITCHEN THROUGH HERE?
WOW! HOW MANY KITCHEN GODS HAVE YOU GOT?
WHAT DOES THIS ONE DO?
IT'S AN EGG TIMER.
THIS ONE?
CAKE SPICER.
FFFFFFF
WHAT ABOUT THIS ONE?
HE'S A POTATO PRICKER, PUT HIM DOWN. HE'S VERY OLD.
GRRRRRR
THEY ALL BELONG TO MY MUM, SO PUT THEM BACK IN THEIR SHRINES. YOU'RE MAKING ME NERVOUS...
OOH, WHAT'S THIS ONE?

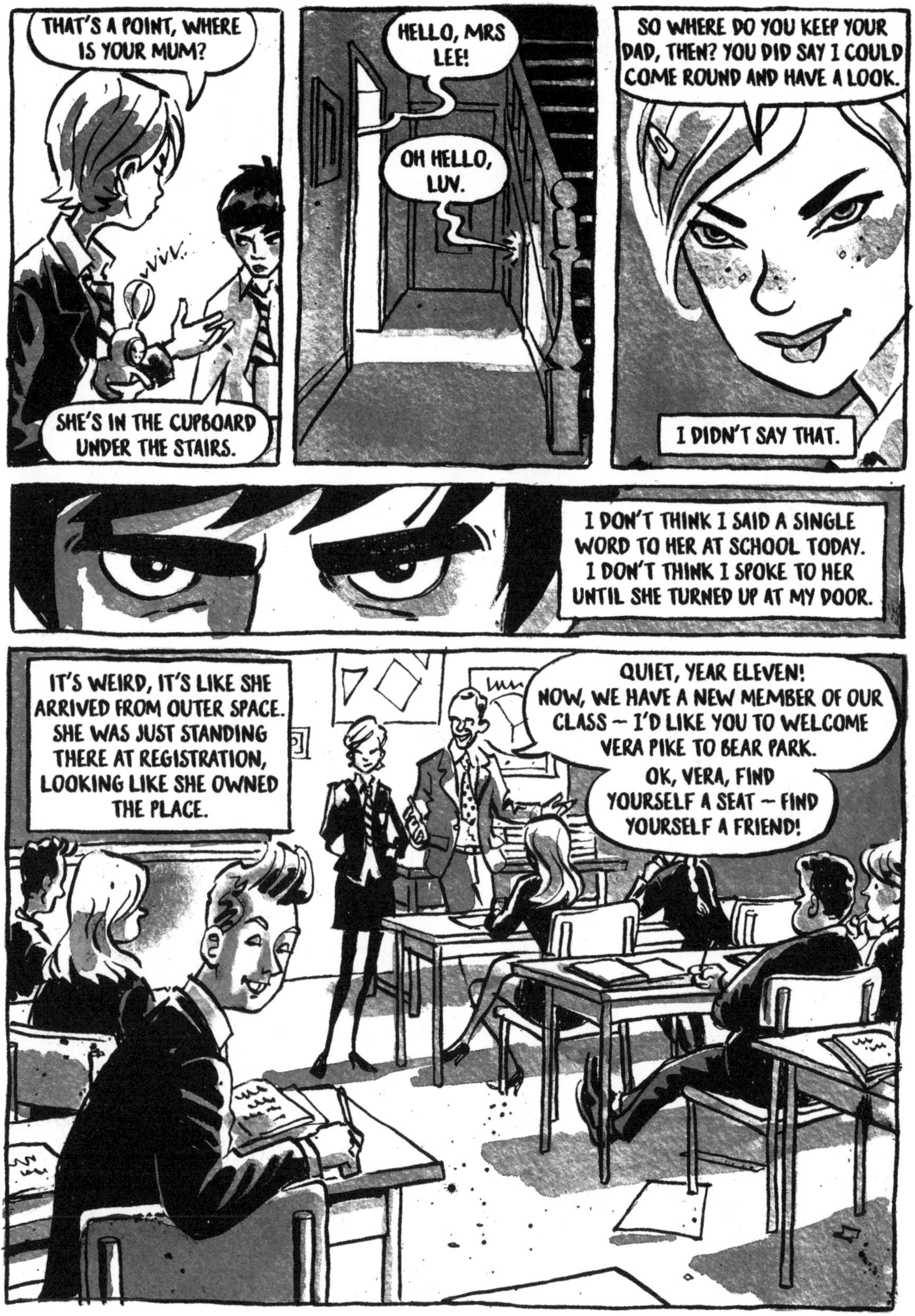
THAT'S A POINT, WHERE IS YOUR MUM?
SHE'S IN THE CUPBOARD UNDER THE STAIRS.
HELLO, MRS LEE!
OH HELLO, LUV.
SO WHERE DO YOU KEEP YOUR DAD, THEN? YOU DID SAY I COULD COME ROUND AND HAVE A LOOK.
I DIDN'T SAY THAT.
I DON'T THINK I SAID A SINGLE WORD TO HER AT SCHOOL TODAY. I DON'T THINK I SPOKE TO HER UNTIL SHE TURNED UP AT MY DOOR.
IT'S WEIRD, IT'S LIKE SHE ARRIVED FROM OUTER SPACE. SHE WAS JUST STANDING THERE AT REGISTRATION, LOOKING LIKE SHE OWNED THE PLACE.
QUIET, YEAR ELEVEN! NOW, WE HAVE A NEW MEMBER OF OUR CLASS – I'D LIKE YOU TO WELCOME VERA PIKE TO BEAR PARK.
OK, VERA, FIND YOURSELF A SEAT – FIND YOURSELF A FRIEND!

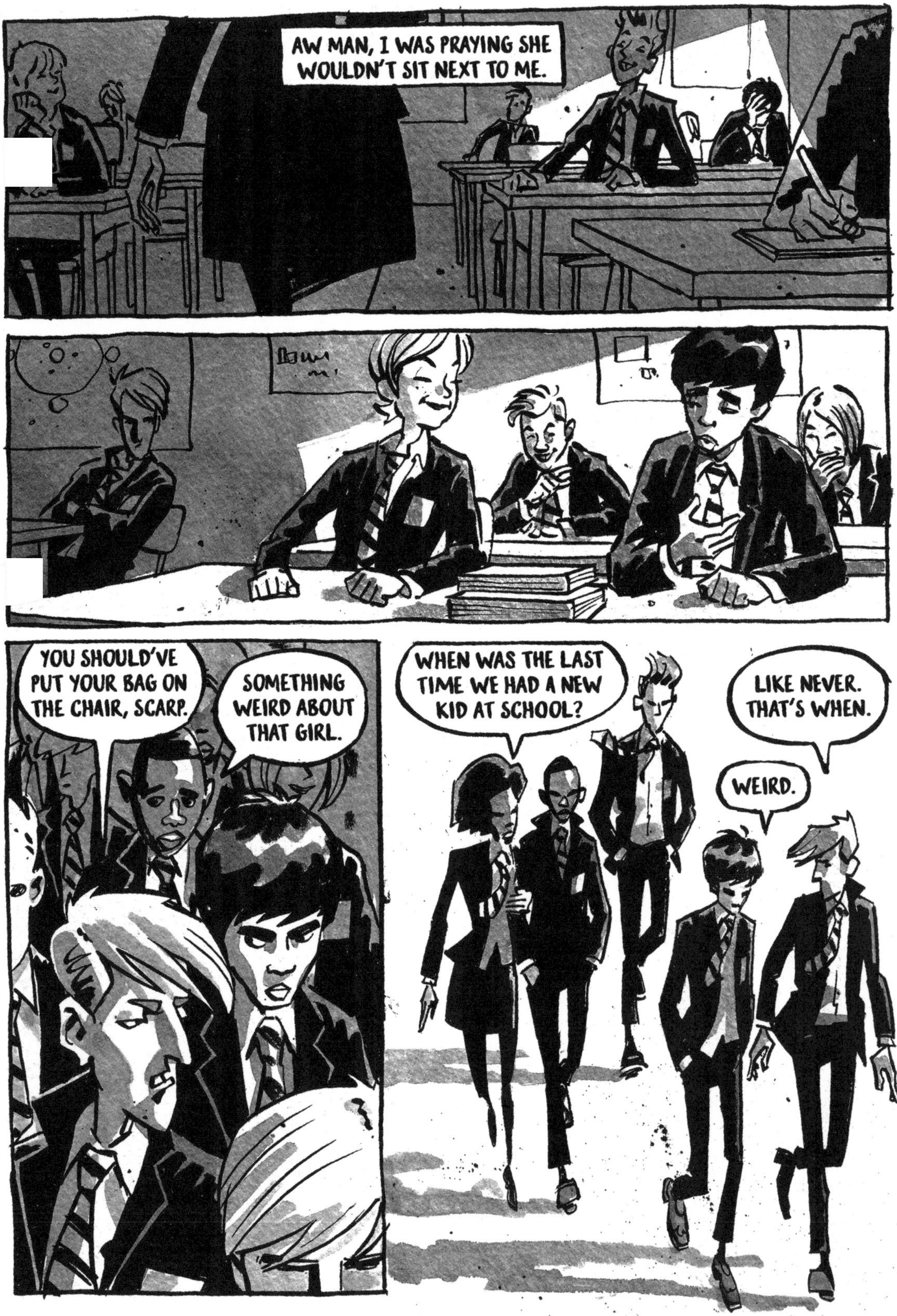
AW MAN, I WAS PRAYING SHE WOULDN'T SIT NEXT TO ME.
YOU SHOULD'VE PUT YOUR BAG ON THE CHAIR, SCARP.
SOMETHING WEIRD ABOUT THAT GIRL.
WHEN WAS THE LAST TIME WE HAD A NEW KID AT SCHOOL?
LIKE NEVER. THAT'S WHEN.
WEIRD.

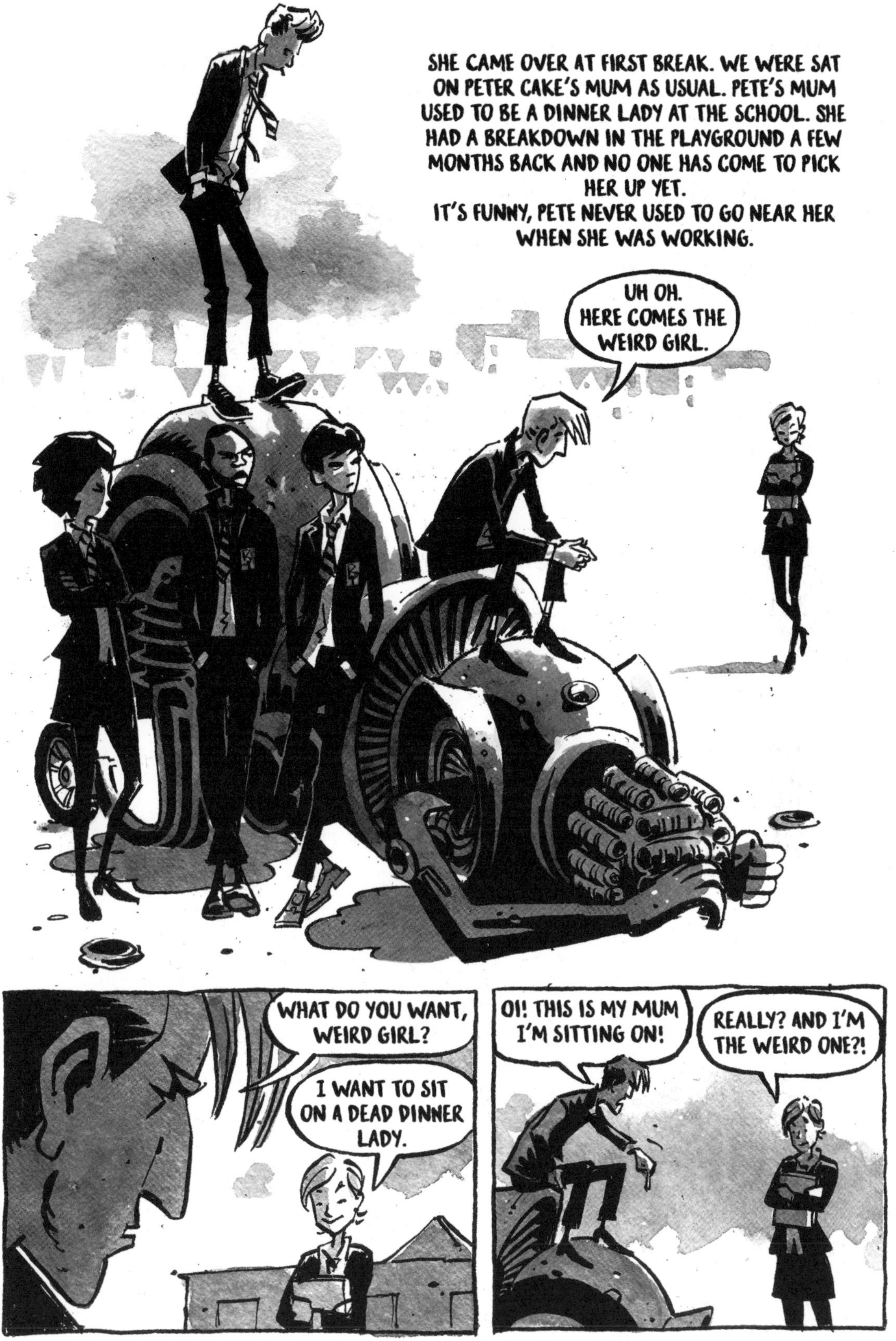
SHE CAME OVER AT FIRST BREAK. WE WERE SAT ON PETER CAKE'S MUM AS USUAL. PETE'S MUM USED TO BE A DINNER LADY AT THE SCHOOL. SHE HAD A BREAKDOWN IN THE PLAYGROUND A FEW MONTHS BACK AND NO ONE HAS COME TO PICK HER UP YET.
IT'S FUNNY, PETE NEVER USED TO GO NEAR HER WHEN SHE WAS WORKING.
UH OH. HERE COMES THE WEIRD GIRL.
WHAT DO YOU WANT, WEIRD GIRL?
I WANT TO SIT ON A DEAD DINNER LADY.
OI! THIS IS MY MUM I'M SITTING ON!
REALLY? AND I'M THE WEIRD ONE?!

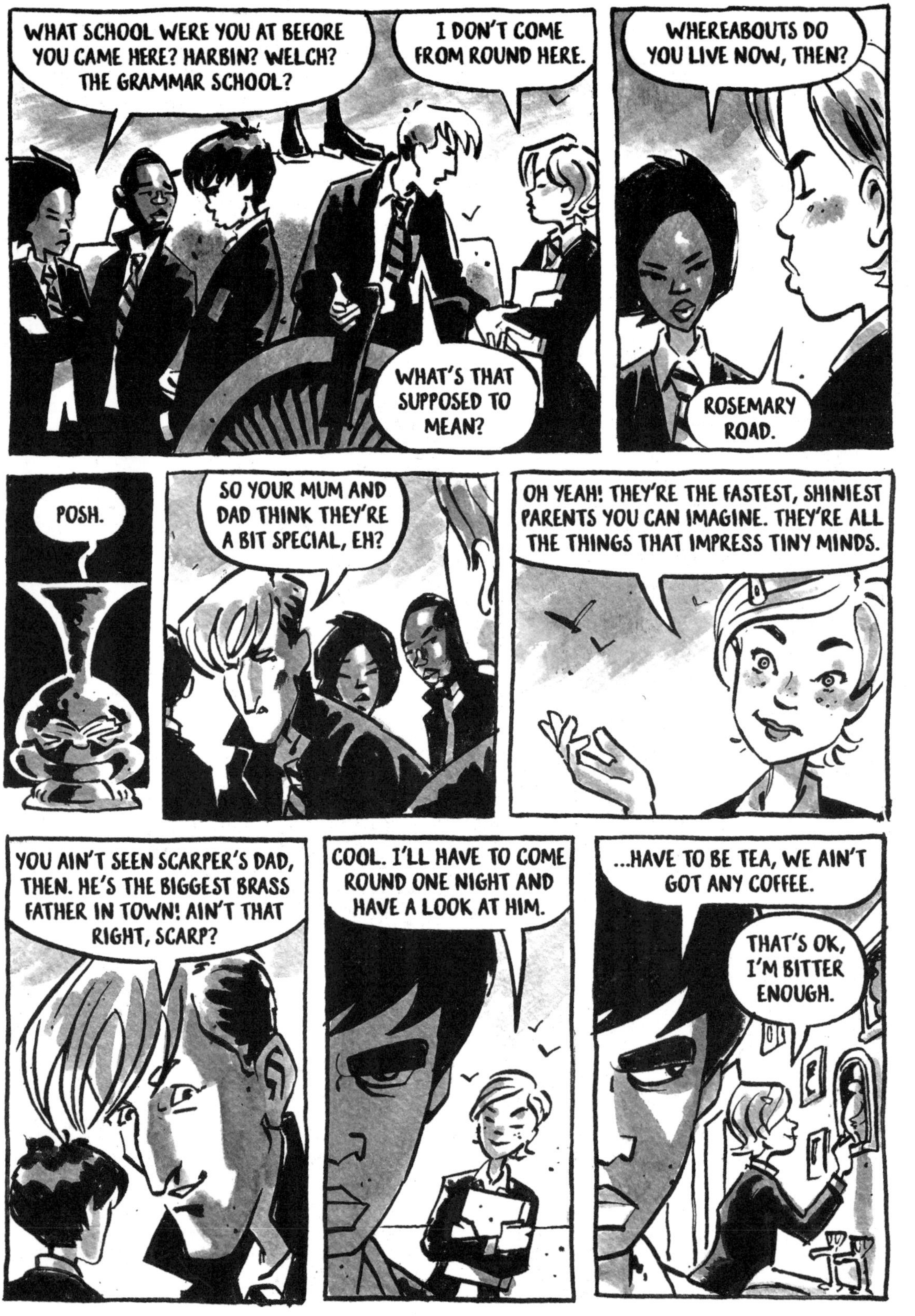
WHAT SCHOOL WERE YOU AT BEFORE YOU CAME HERE? HARBIN? WELCH? THE GRAMMAR SCHOOL?
I DON'T COME FROM ROUND HERE.
WHAT'S THAT SUPPOSED TO MEAN?
WHEREABOUTS DO YOU LIVE NOW, THEN?
ROSEMARY ROAD.
POSH.
SO YOUR MUM AND DAD THINK THEY'RE A BIT SPECIAL, EH?
OH YEAH! THEY'RE THE FASTEST, SHINIEST PARENTS YOU CAN IMAGINE. THEY'RE ALL THE THINGS THAT IMPRESS TINY MINDS.
YOU AIN'T SEEN SCARPER'S DAD, THEN. HE'S THE BIGGEST BRASS FATHER IN TOWN! AIN'T THAT RIGHT, SCARP?
COOL. I'LL HAVE TO COME ROUND ONE NIGHT AND HAVE A LOOK AT HIM.
...HAVE TO BE TEA, WE AIN'T GOT ANY COFFEE.
THAT'S OK, I'M BITTER ENOUGH.

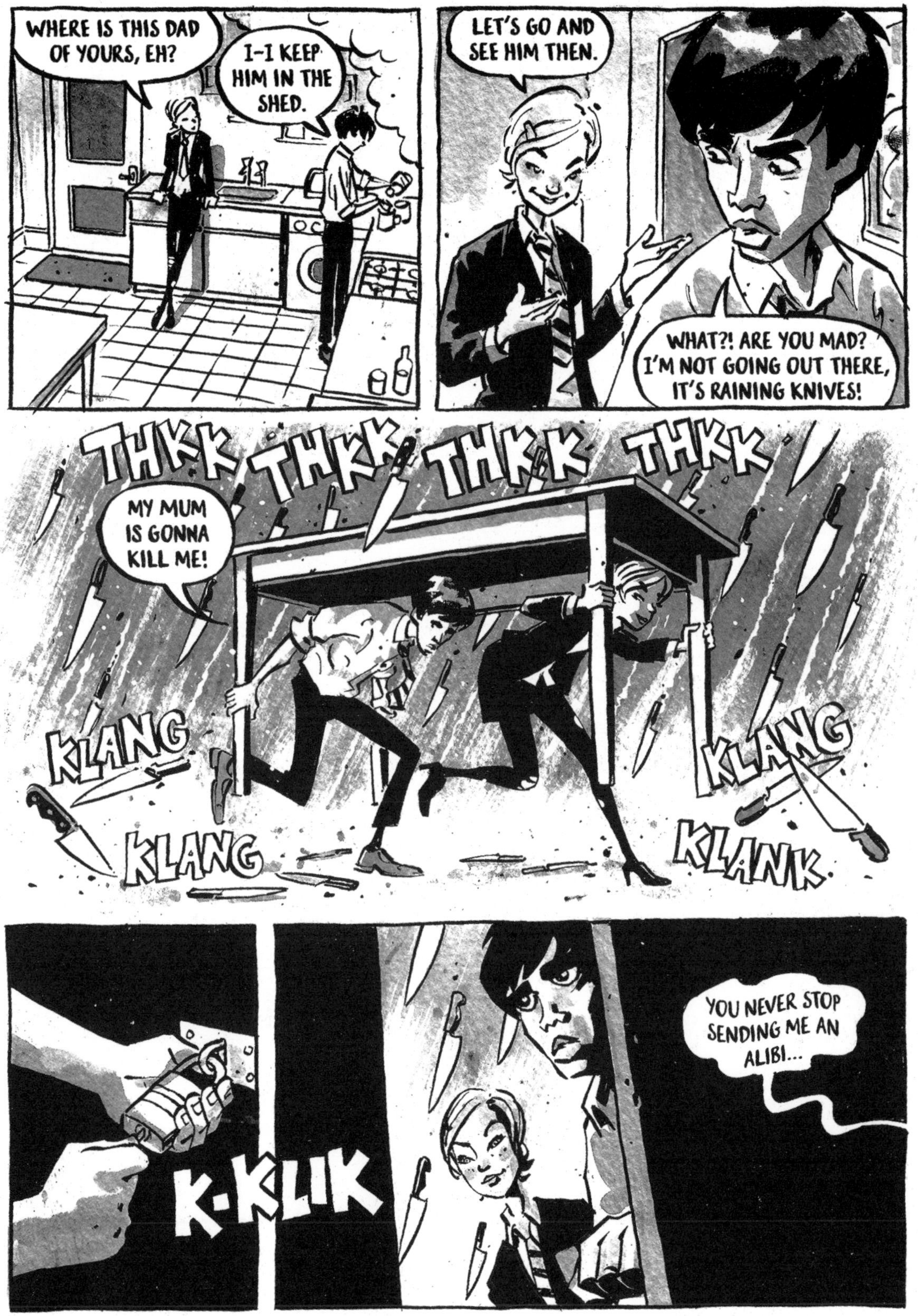
WHERE IS THIS DAD OF YOURS, EH?
I-I KEEP HIM IN THE SHED.
LET'S GO AND SEE HIM THEN.
WHAT?! ARE YOU MAD? I'M NOT GOING OUT THERE, IT'S RAINING KNIVES!
THKK THKK THKK THKK
MY MUM IS GONNA KILL ME!
KLANG
KLANG
KLANG
KLANK
K-KLIK
YOU NEVER STOP SENDING ME AN ALIBI...

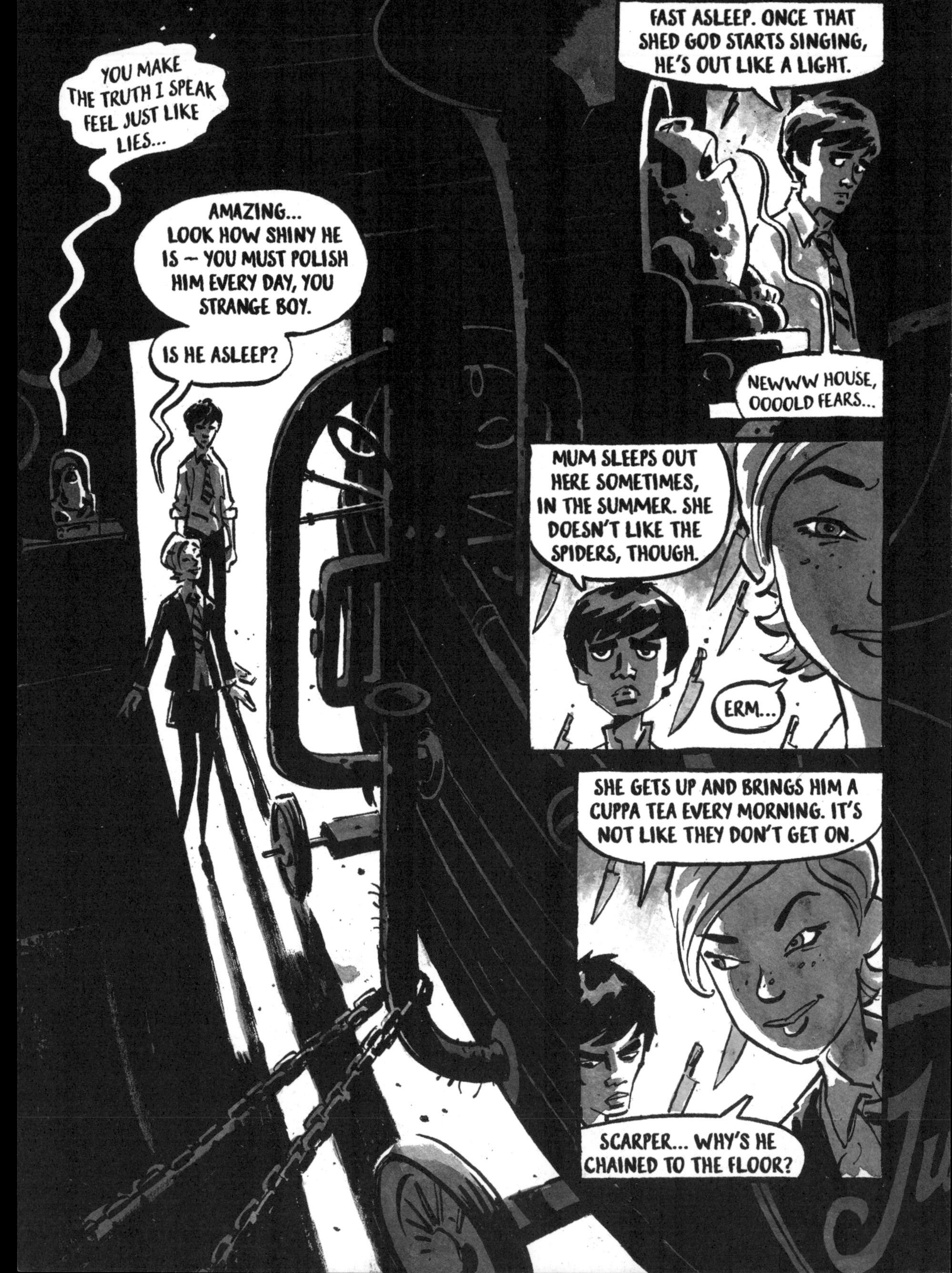
YOU MAKE THE TRUTH I SPEAK FEEL JUST LIKE LIES...
AMAZING... LOOK HOW SHINY HE IS – YOU MUST POLISH HIM EVERY DAY, YOU STRANGE BOY.
IS HE ASLEEP?
FAST ASLEEP. ONCE THAT SHED GOD STARTS SINGING, HE'S OUT LIKE A LIGHT.
NEWWW HOUSE, OOOOLD FEARS...
MUM SLEEPS OUT HERE SOMETIMES, IN THE SUMMER. SHE DOESN'T LIKE THE SPIDERS, THOUGH.
ERM...
SHE GETS UP AND BRINGS HIM A CUPPA TEA EVERY MORNING. IT'S NOT LIKE THEY DON'T GET ON.
SCARPER... WHY'S HE CHAINED TO THE FLOOR?

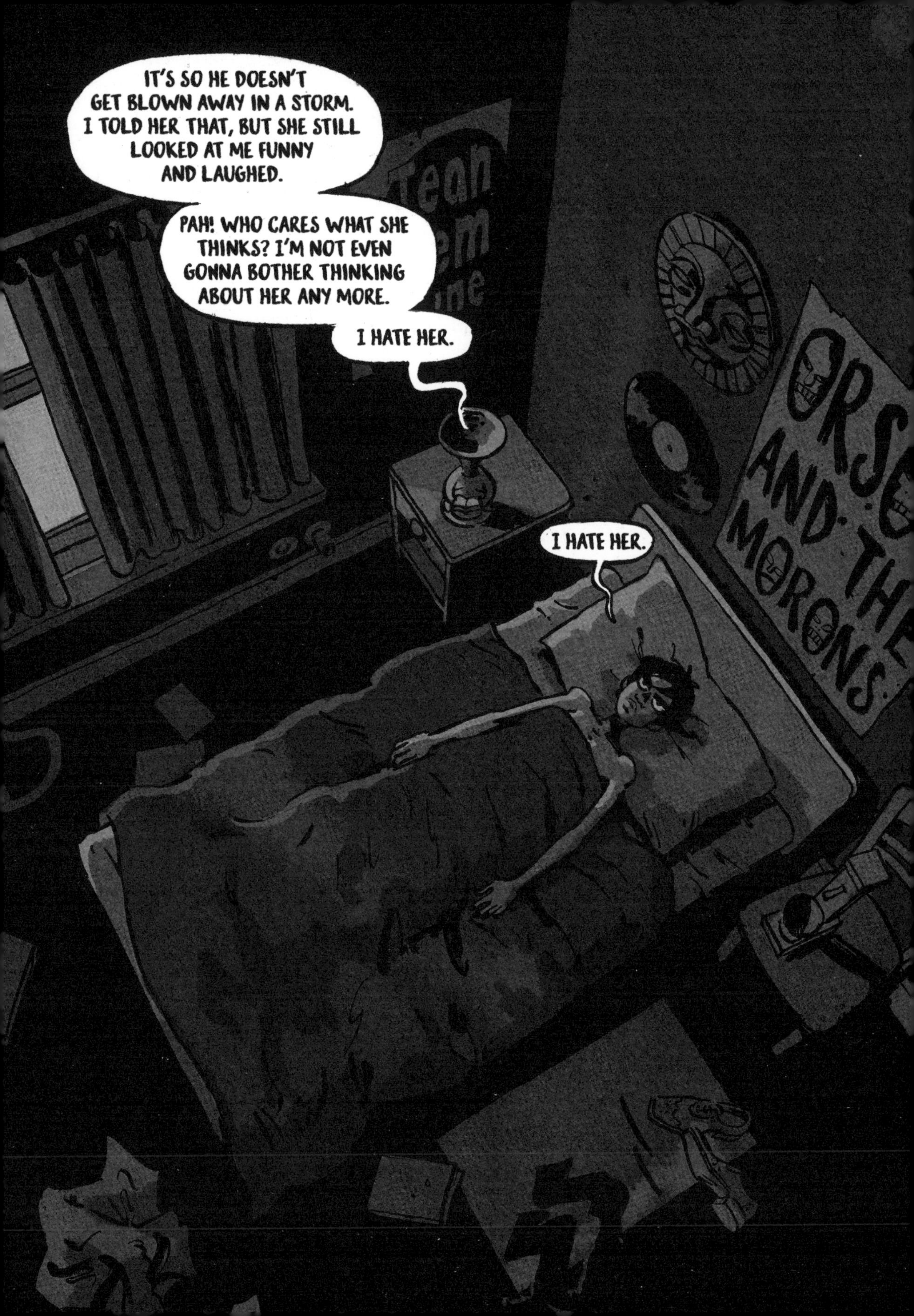
IT'S SO HE DOESN'T GET BLOWN AWAY IN A STORM. I TOLD HER THAT, BUT SHE STILL LOOKED AT ME FUNNY AND LAUGHED.
PAH! WHO CARES WHAT SHE THINKS? I'M NOT EVEN GONNA BOTHER THINKING ABOUT HER ANY MORE.
I HATE HER.
I HATE HER.
ORSE AND THE MORONS

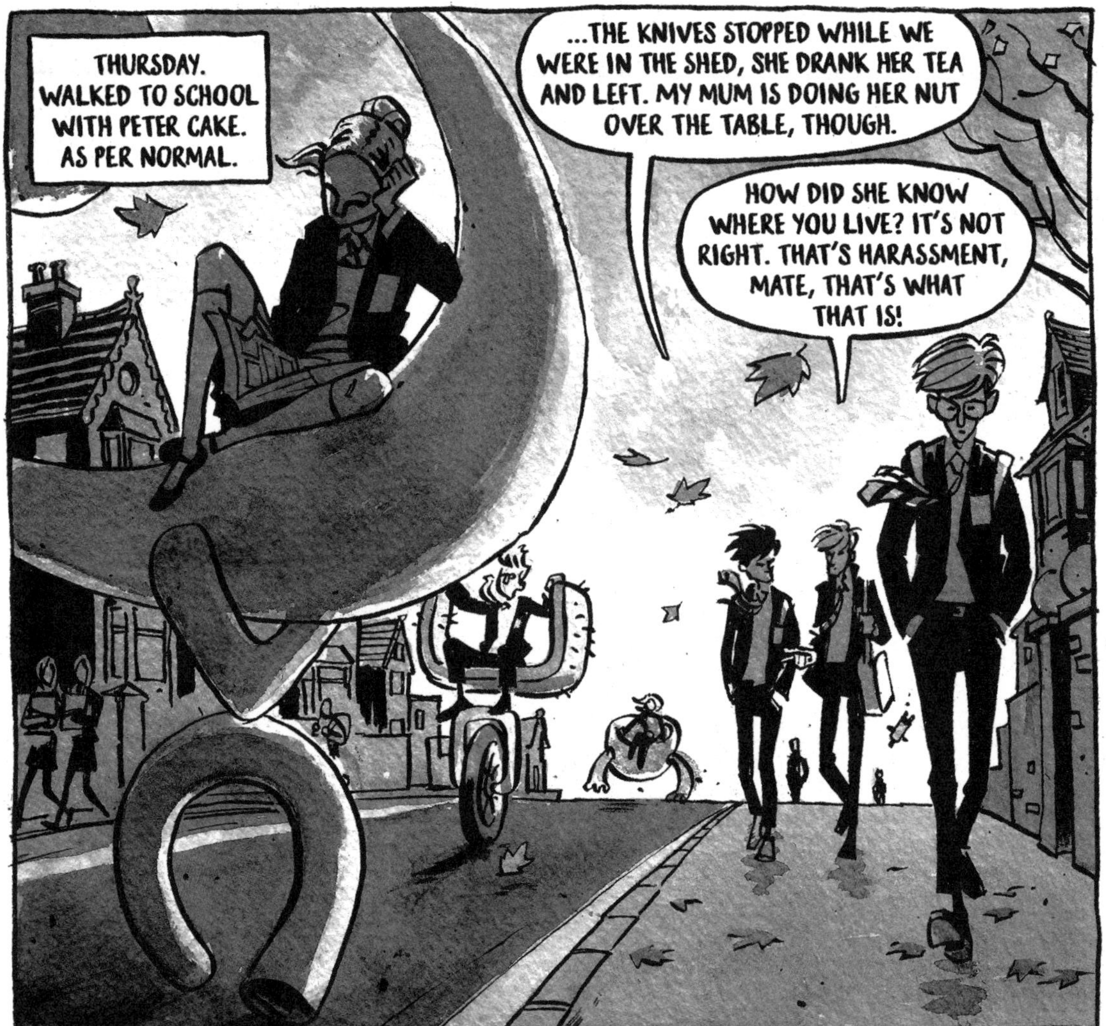
THURSDAY. WALKED TO SCHOOL WITH PETER CAKE. AS PER NORMAL.
...THE KNIVES STOPPED WHILE WE WERE IN THE SHED, SHE DRANK HER TEA AND LEFT. MY MUM IS DOING HER NUT OVER THE TABLE, THOUGH.
HOW DID SHE KNOW WHERE YOU LIVE? IT'S NOT RIGHT. THAT'S HARASSMENT, MATE, THAT'S WHAT THAT IS!

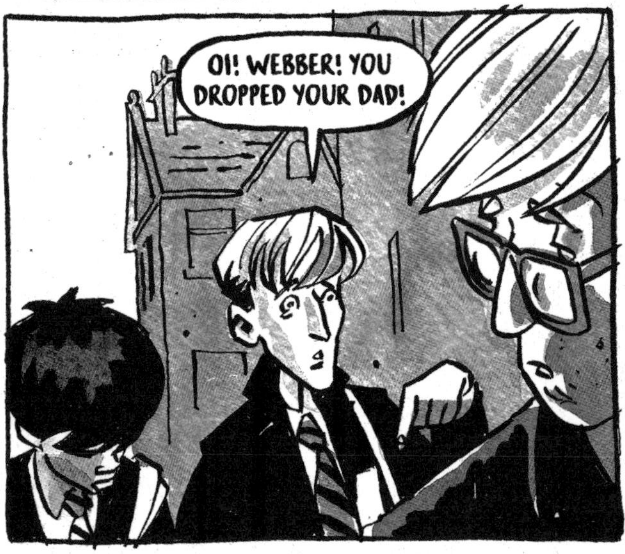
OI! WEBBER! YOU DROPPED YOUR DAD!

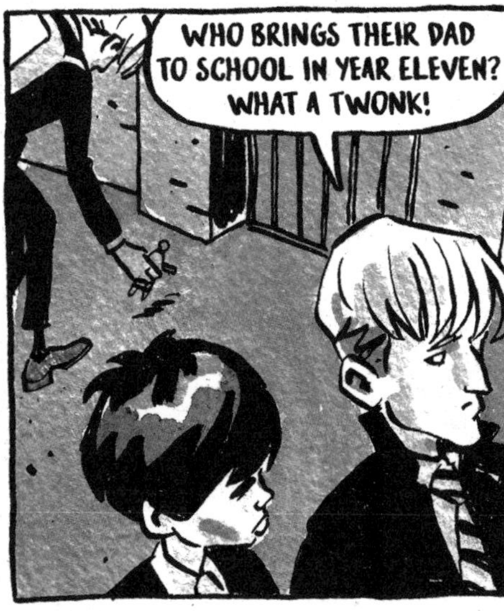
WHO BRINGS THEIR DAD TO SCHOOL IN YEAR ELEVEN? WHAT A TWONK!

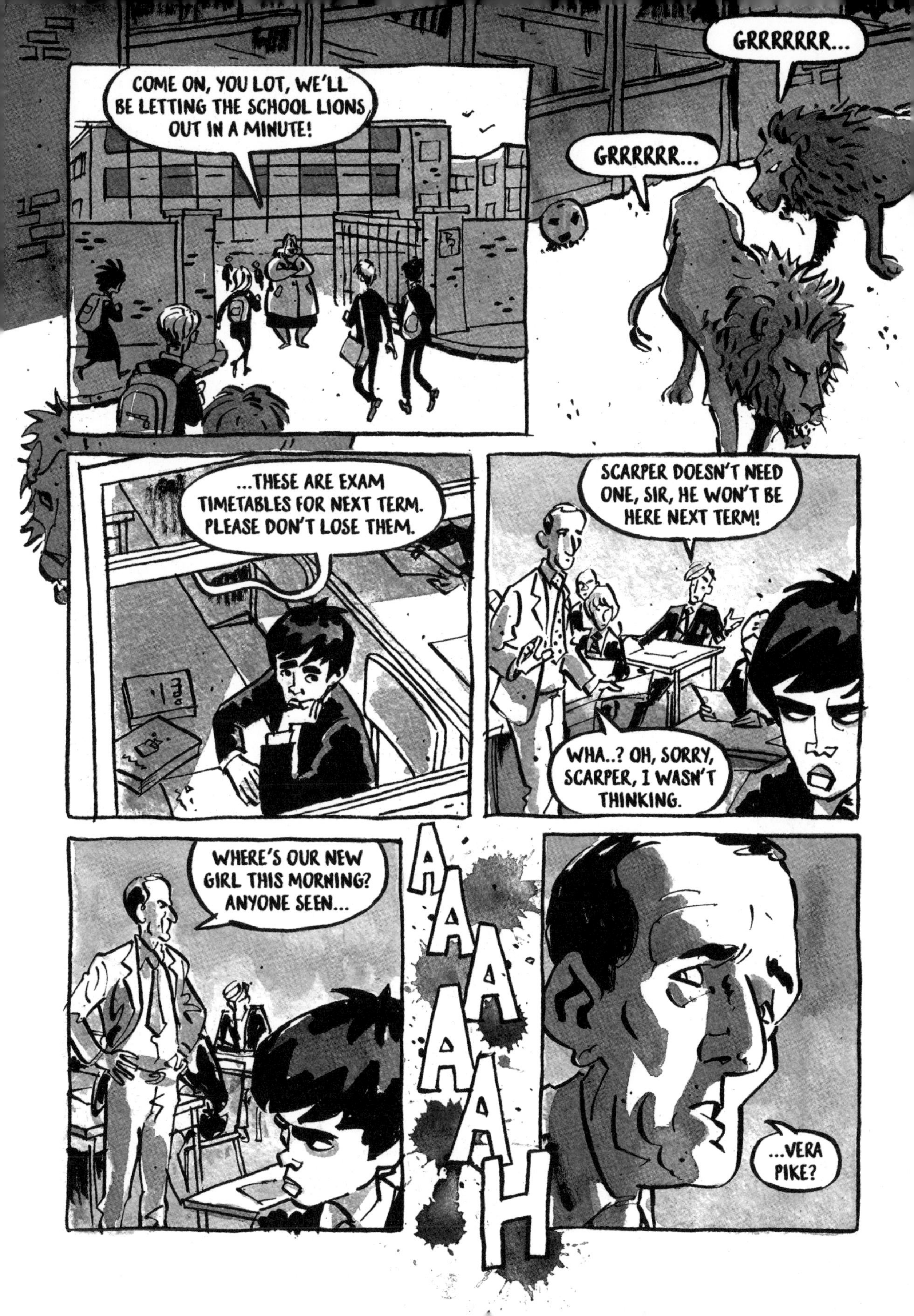
COME ON, YOU LOT, WE'LL BE LETTING THE SCHOOL LIONS OUT IN A MINUTE!
GRRRRRRR...
GRRRRRR...
...THESE ARE EXAM TIMETABLES FOR NEXT TERM. PLEASE DON'T LOSE THEM.
SCARPER DOESN'T NEED ONE, SIR, HE WON'T BE HERE NEXT TERM!
WHA..? OH, SORRY, SCARPER, I WASN'T THINKING.
WHERE'S OUR NEW GIRL THIS MORNING? ANYONE SEEN...
AAAAAAAAH
...VERA PIKE?

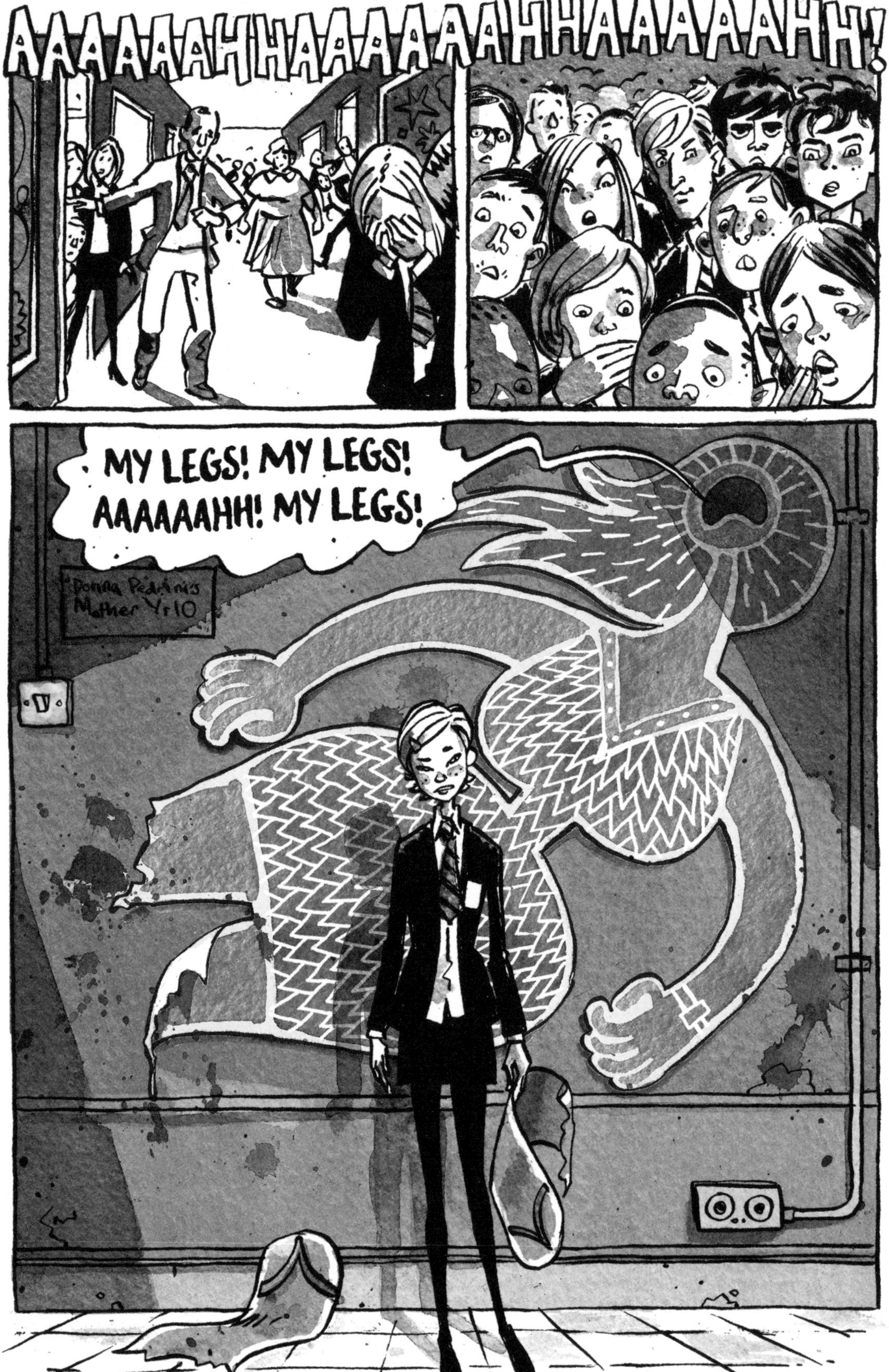
AAAAAAHHAAAAAAAHHAAAAAAHH!
MY LEGS! MY LEGS! AAAAAAHH! MY LEGS!
Donna Pedrini's Mother Yr10

AAAAAAHH!

RIGHT, EVERYONE BACK TO YOUR CLASSES!

WHAT HAPPENED, DID YOU SEE IT?

YEAH, SHE RIPPED DONNA'S MUM'S LEGS OFF!

DONNA DIDN'T DO NOTHING TO DESERVE IT.

DONNA GOES, 'HI, YOU'RE NEW. HAVE YOU SEEN MY MUM?' AND THE NEW GIRL JUST GOES 'HMMPH' AND RIPS HER LEGS OFF!

WILL HER MUM DIE?

I RECKON. MOTHER PAPER BLEEDS REALLY BAD.

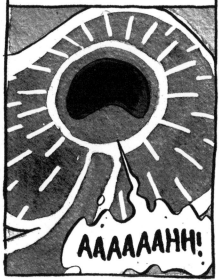

I DUNNO WHY THE SCHOOL PUT DONNA PEDRINI'S MUM ON DISPLAY. STUPID IDEA IN THE FIRST PLACE. AND SHE NEVER STOPPED TALKING ABOUT HERSELF, EVEN IF NO ONE WAS THERE TO LISTEN.

AAAAAAHH!

NOW NO ONE CAN IGNORE HER. OR VERA.

TOTALLY BANJO.

HMMM...

THEY COULDN'T STOP HER SCREAMING AND THEY COULDN'T GET HER DOWN FROM THE WALL. IN THE END, THE NOISE WAS SO BAD WE GOT SENT HOME EARLY FROM SCHOOL.

AAAAAAHH!

-G-DNNK!-

AAAAAAHH!

CALM Y'SELF, MRS PEDRINI, I'M TRYING TO STAPLE THEM BACK ON.

AAAAAAAAAHH!

OH, SCARPER, HOW ARE YOU GETTING ON WITH THAT HOME GAZETTE?

UM, YEAH, FINE.

AW, THAT'S GOOD. JUST KEEP TELLING IT ALL YOUR WOES.

A HOME GAZETTE?! YOU KIDDIN' ME?

MATE, THAT IS NOT GOOD. I KEEP TELLING YOU, JUST PLAY IT LIKE EVERYTHING'S NORMAL, DON'T DRAW ATTENTION TO YOURSELF.

YOU THINK I WANT ATTENTION? EVERYBODY KNOWS WHEN MY DEATHDAY IS, GETTING A HOME GAZETTE OFF THE SCHOOL NURSE IS TOTALLY NORMAL!

I'M NOT SAYING THAT, I JUST... HEY! THERE SHE IS — THERE'S PIKE!

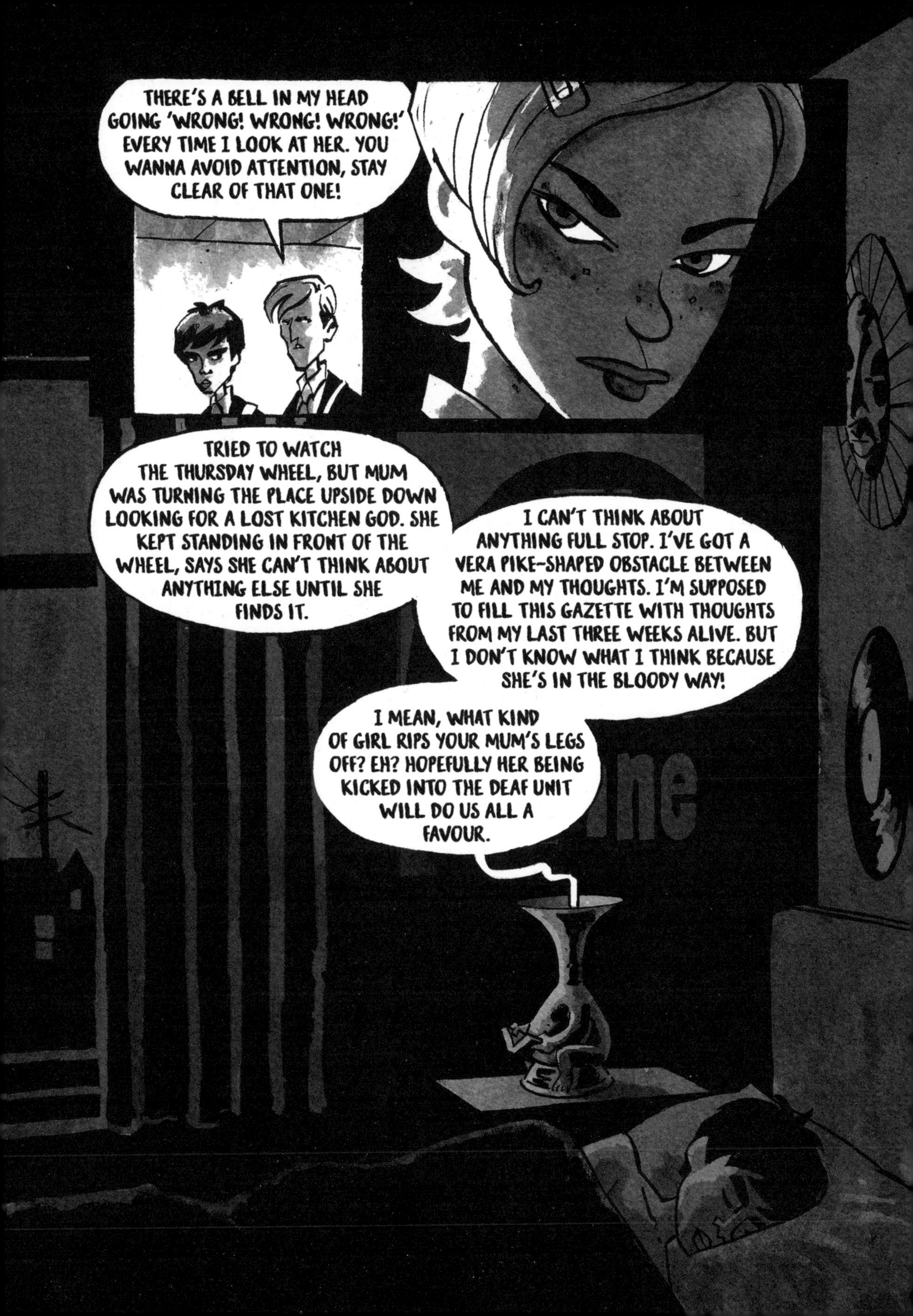
THERE'S A BELL IN MY HEAD GOING 'WRONG! WRONG! WRONG!' EVERY TIME I LOOK AT HER. YOU WANNA AVOID ATTENTION, STAY CLEAR OF THAT ONE!
TRIED TO WATCH THE THURSDAY WHEEL, BUT MUM WAS TURNING THE PLACE UPSIDE DOWN LOOKING FOR A LOST KITCHEN GOD. SHE KEPT STANDING IN FRONT OF THE WHEEL, SAYS SHE CAN'T THINK ABOUT ANYTHING ELSE UNTIL SHE FINDS IT.
I CAN'T THINK ABOUT ANYTHING FULL STOP. I'VE GOT A VERA PIKE-SHAPED OBSTACLE BETWEEN ME AND MY THOUGHTS. I'M SUPPOSED TO FILL THIS GAZETTE WITH THOUGHTS FROM MY LAST THREE WEEKS ALIVE. BUT I DON'T KNOW WHAT I THINK BECAUSE SHE'S IN THE BLOODY WAY!
I MEAN, WHAT KIND OF GIRL RIPS YOUR MUM'S LEGS OFF? EH? HOPEFULLY HER BEING KICKED INTO THE DEAF UNIT WILL DO US ALL A FAVOUR.

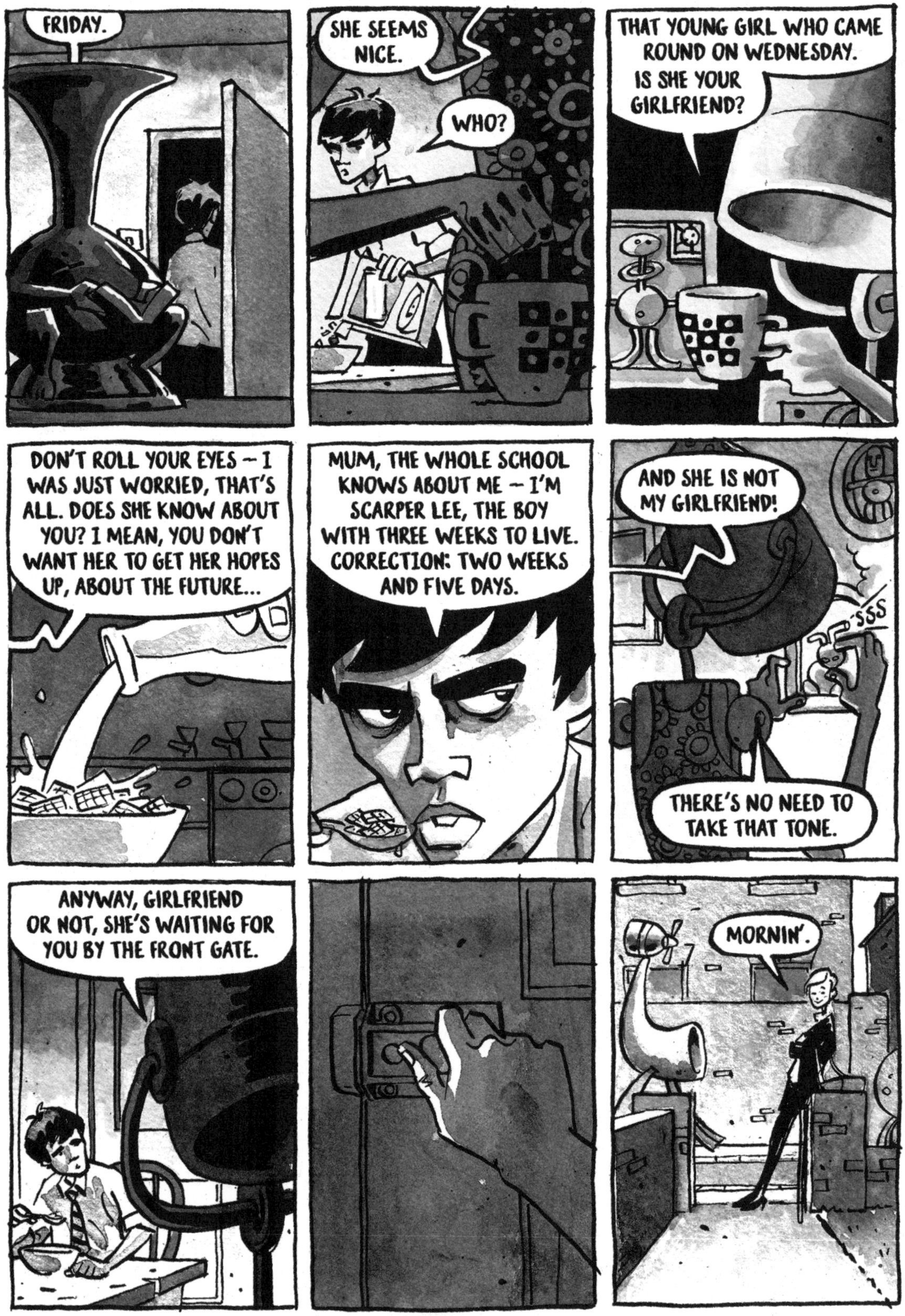
FRIDAY.
SHE SEEMS NICE.
WHO?
THAT YOUNG GIRL WHO CAME ROUND ON WEDNESDAY. IS SHE YOUR GIRLFRIEND?
DON'T ROLL YOUR EYES – I WAS JUST WORRIED, THAT'S ALL. DOES SHE KNOW ABOUT YOU? I MEAN, YOU DON'T WANT HER TO GET HER HOPES UP, ABOUT THE FUTURE...
MUM, THE WHOLE SCHOOL KNOWS ABOUT ME – I'M SCARPER LEE, THE BOY WITH THREE WEEKS TO LIVE. CORRECTION: TWO WEEKS AND FIVE DAYS.
AND SHE IS NOT MY GIRLFRIEND!
SSS
THERE'S NO NEED TO TAKE THAT TONE.
ANYWAY, GIRLFRIEND OR NOT, SHE'S WAITING FOR YOU BY THE FRONT GATE.
MORNIN'.

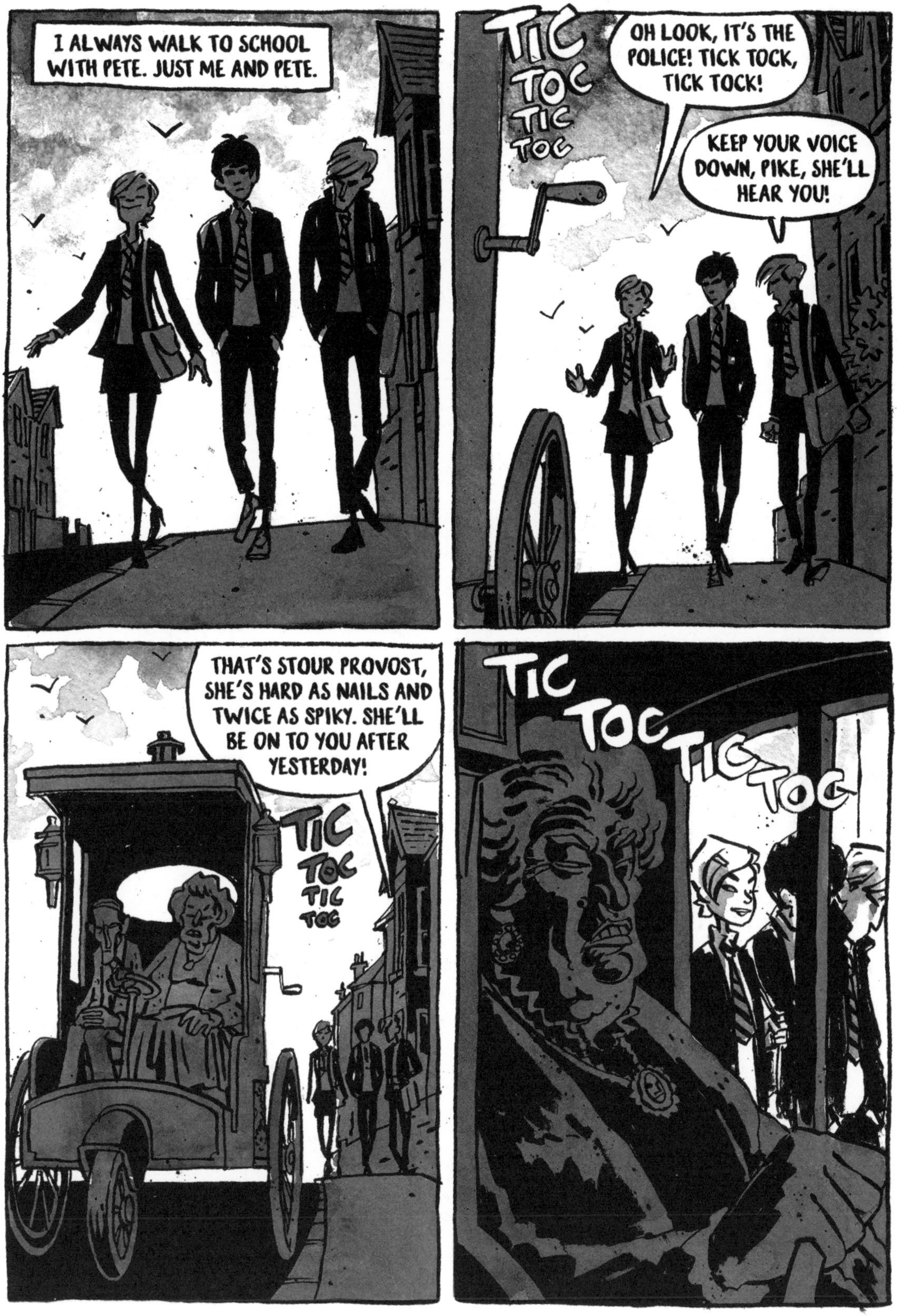
I ALWAYS WALK TO SCHOOL WITH PETE. JUST ME AND PETE.
TIC TOC TIC TOC
OH LOOK, IT'S THE POLICE! TICK TOCK, TICK TOCK!
KEEP YOUR VOICE DOWN, PIKE, SHE'LL HEAR YOU!
THAT'S STOUR PROVOST, SHE'S HARD AS NAILS AND TWICE AS SPIKY. SHE'LL BE ON TO YOU AFTER YESTERDAY!
TIC TOC TIC TOC
TIC TOC TIC TOC

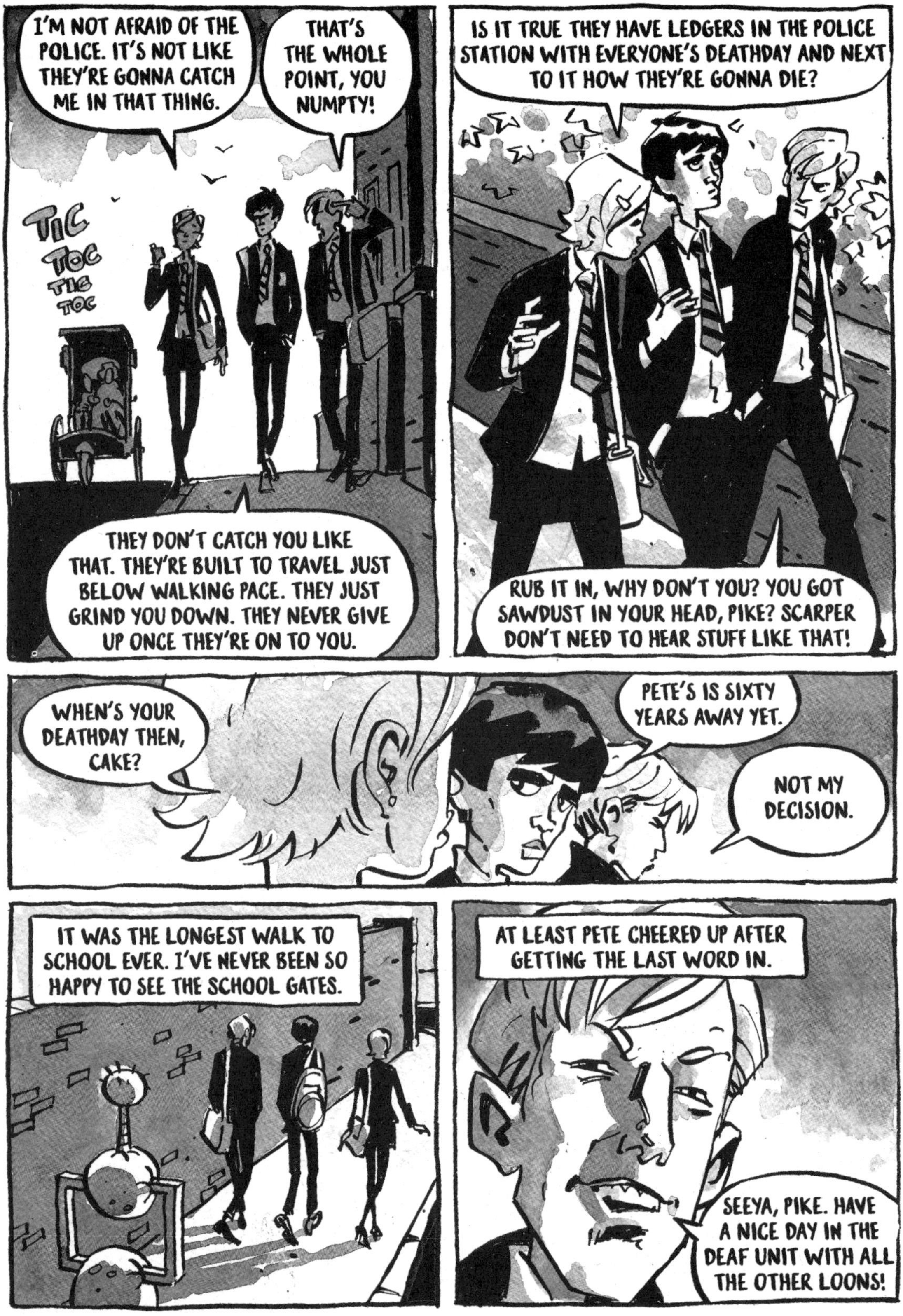
I'M NOT AFRAID OF THE POLICE. IT'S NOT LIKE THEY'RE GONNA CATCH ME IN THAT THING.
THAT'S THE WHOLE POINT, YOU NUMPTY!
TIC TOC TIC TOC
THEY DON'T CATCH YOU LIKE THAT. THEY'RE BUILT TO TRAVEL JUST BELOW WALKING PACE. THEY JUST GRIND YOU DOWN. THEY NEVER GIVE UP ONCE THEY'RE ON TO YOU.
IS IT TRUE THEY HAVE LEDGERS IN THE POLICE STATION WITH EVERYONE'S DEATHDAY AND NEXT TO IT HOW THEY'RE GONNA DIE?
RUB IT IN, WHY DON'T YOU? YOU GOT SAWDUST IN YOUR HEAD, PIKE? SCARPER DON'T NEED TO HEAR STUFF LIKE THAT!
WHEN'S YOUR DEATHDAY THEN, CAKE?
PETE'S IS SIXTY YEARS AWAY YET.
NOT MY DECISION.
IT WAS THE LONGEST WALK TO SCHOOL EVER. I'VE NEVER BEEN SO HAPPY TO SEE THE SCHOOL GATES.
AT LEAST PETE CHEERED UP AFTER GETTING THE LAST WORD IN.
SEEYA, PIKE. HAVE A NICE DAY IN THE DEAF UNIT WITH ALL THE OTHER LOONS!

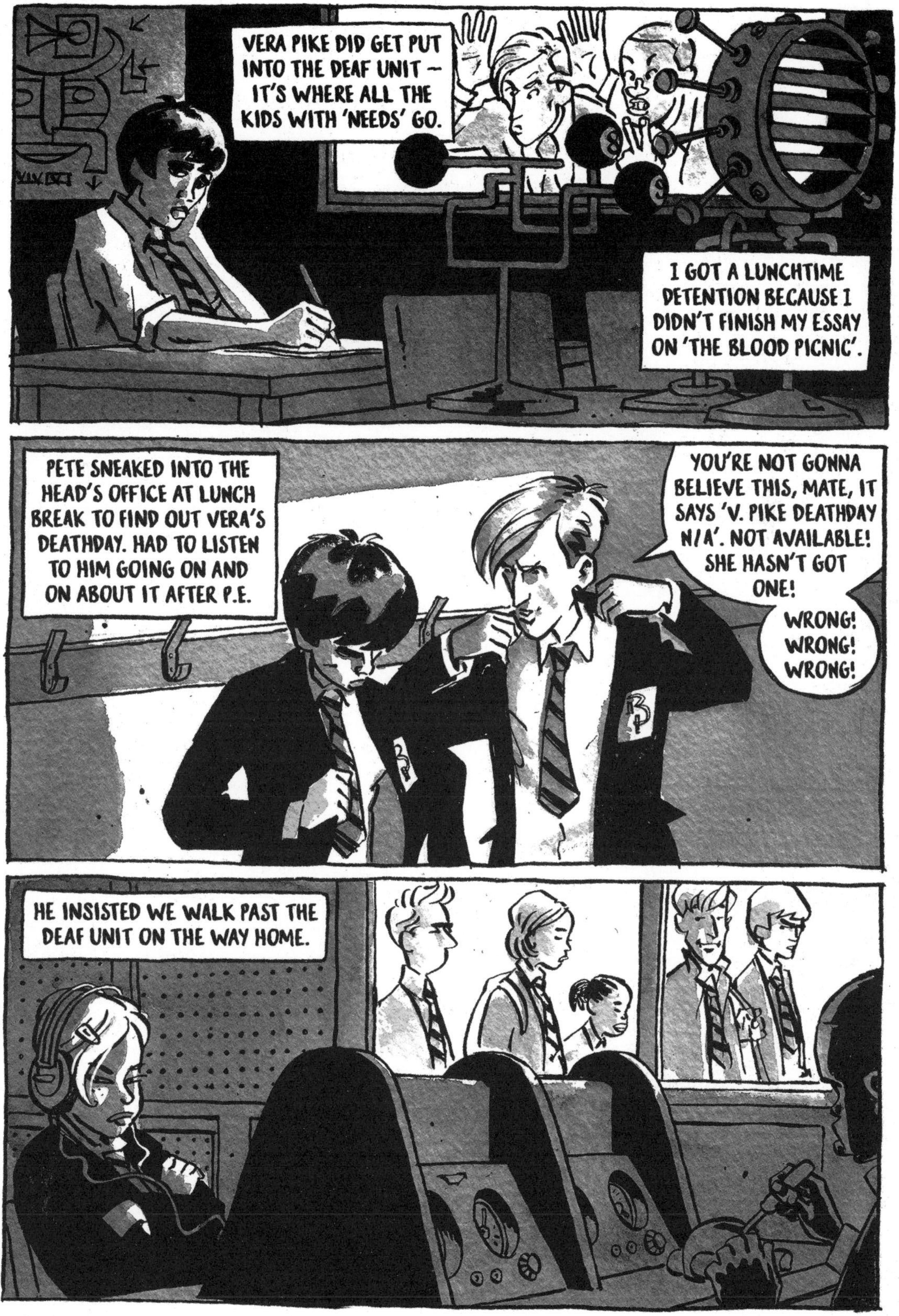
VERA PIKE DID GET PUT INTO THE DEAF UNIT – IT'S WHERE ALL THE KIDS WITH 'NEEDS' GO.
I GOT A LUNCHTIME DETENTION BECAUSE I DIDN'T FINISH MY ESSAY ON 'THE BLOOD PICNIC'.
PETE SNEAKED INTO THE HEAD'S OFFICE AT LUNCH BREAK TO FIND OUT VERA'S DEATHDAY. HAD TO LISTEN TO HIM GOING ON AND ON ABOUT IT AFTER P.E.
YOU'RE NOT GONNA BELIEVE THIS, MATE, IT SAYS 'V. PIKE DEATHDAY N/A'. NOT AVAILABLE! SHE HASN'T GOT ONE!
WRONG! WRONG! WRONG!
HE INSISTED WE WALK PAST THE DEAF UNIT ON THE WAY HOME.

MUM WAS STILL LOOKING FOR HER MISSING GOD, SO
TEA WAS LATE. I ATE MINE IN FRONT OF THE FRIDAY WHEEL.
THE FRIDAY WHEEL IS THE BEST WHEEL OF THE WEEK.

NOT THAT I COULD HEAR ANY OF IT.
A COUPLE OF LOCAL BANDS WERE TORTURING
THEIR PARENTS OUTSIDE — RACING THEM UP AND
DOWN THE MAIN ROAD AT FULL THROTTLE.

FRIDAY IS ANOTHER GOOD NIGHT TO STAY IN.

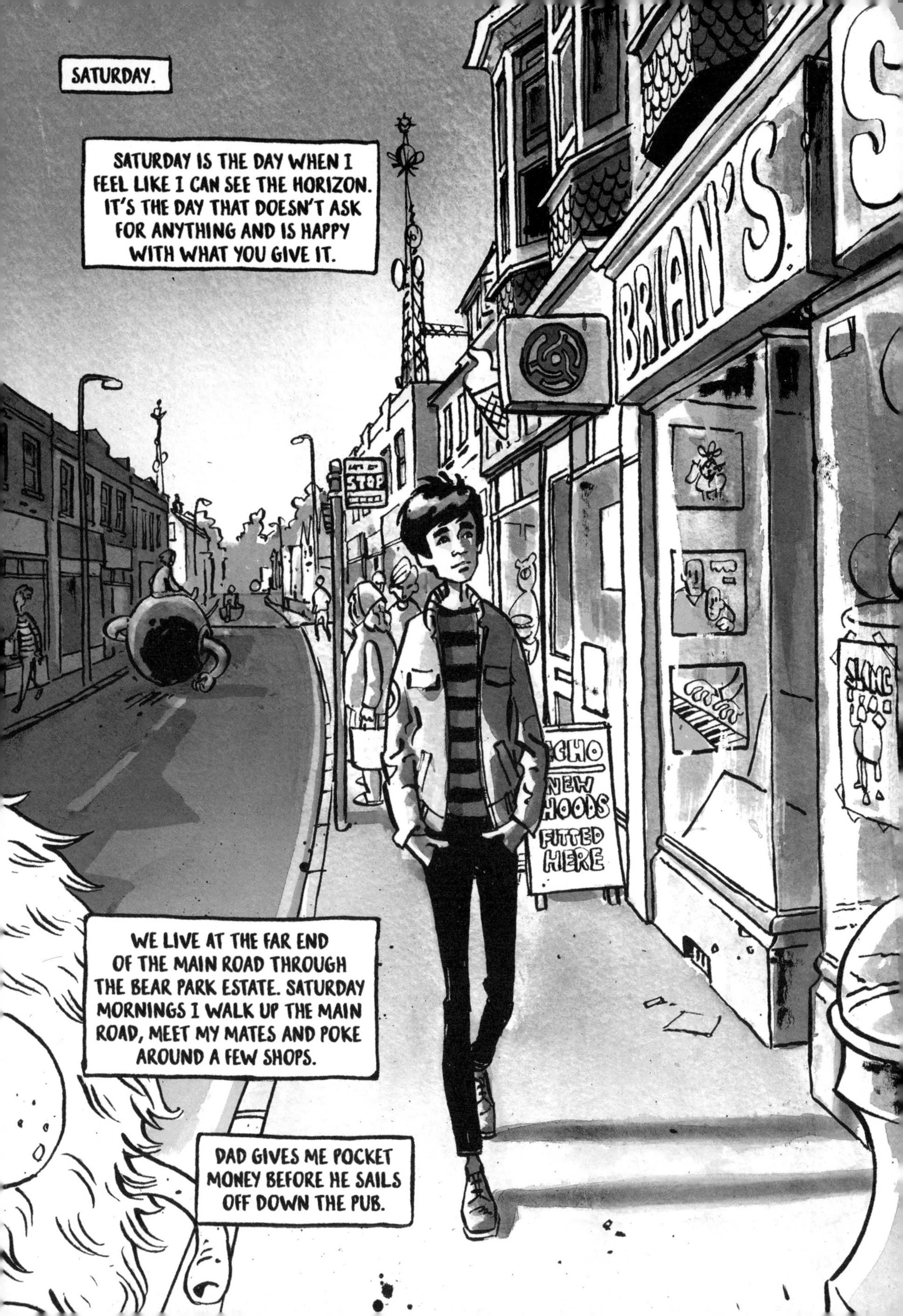
SATURDAY.
SATURDAY IS THE DAY WHEN I FEEL LIKE I CAN SEE THE HORIZON. IT'S THE DAY THAT DOESN'T ASK FOR ANYTHING AND IS HAPPY WITH WHAT YOU GIVE IT.
BRIAN'S
STOP
FITTED HERE
WE LIVE AT THE FAR END OF THE MAIN ROAD THROUGH THE BEAR PARK ESTATE. SATURDAY MORNINGS I WALK UP THE MAIN ROAD, MEET MY MATES AND POKE AROUND A FEW SHOPS.
DAD GIVES ME POCKET MONEY BEFORE HE SAILS OFF DOWN THE PUB.

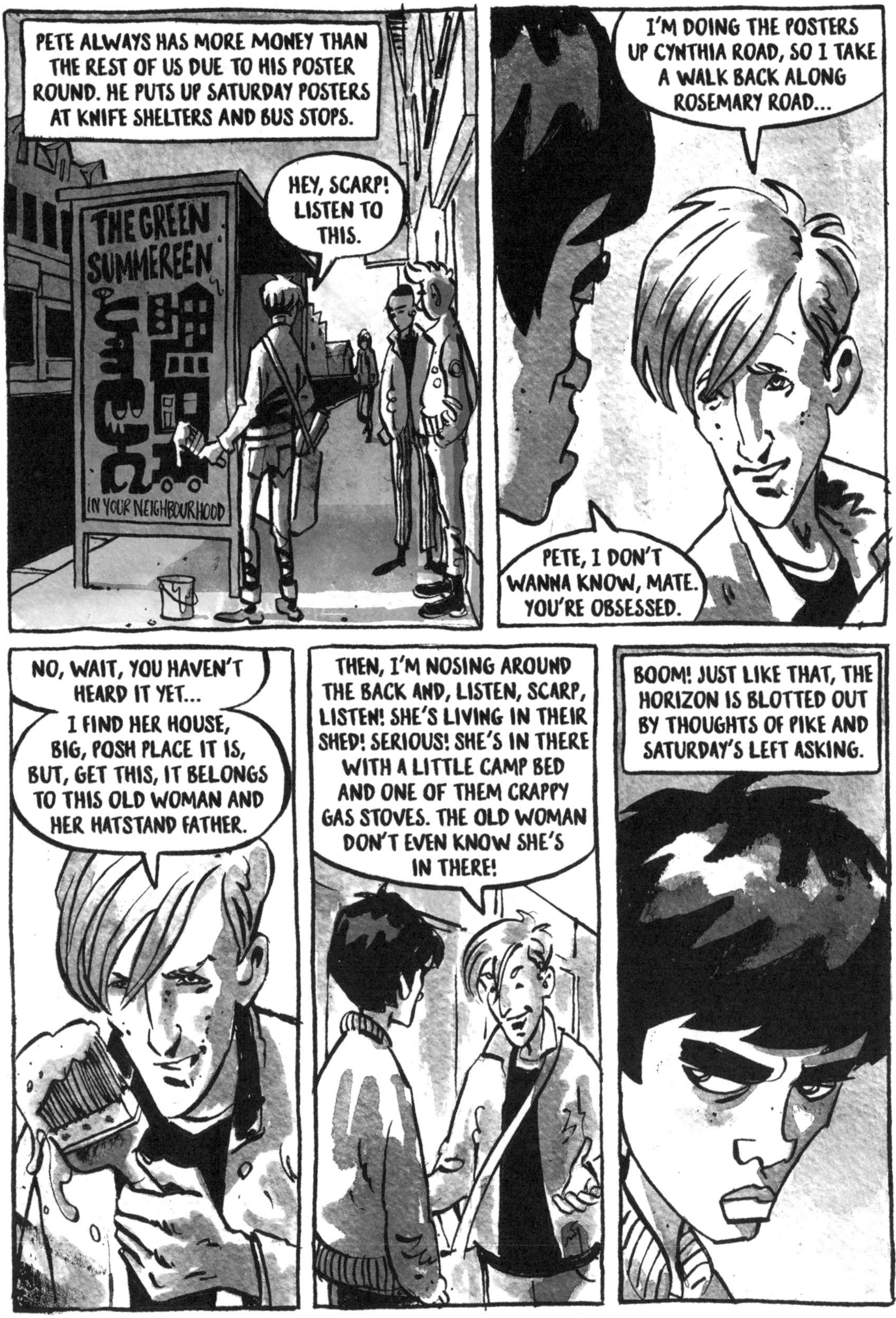
PETE ALWAYS HAS MORE MONEY THAN THE REST OF US DUE TO HIS POSTER ROUND. HE PUTS UP SATURDAY POSTERS AT KNIFE SHELTERS AND BUS STOPS.
HEY, SCARP! LISTEN TO THIS.
THE GREEN SUMMEREEN
IN YOUR NEIGHBOURHOOD
I'M DOING THE POSTERS UP CYNTHIA ROAD, SO I TAKE A WALK BACK ALONG ROSEMARY ROAD...
PETE, I DON'T WANNA KNOW, MATE. YOU'RE OBSESSED.
NO, WAIT, YOU HAVEN'T HEARD IT YET...
I FIND HER HOUSE, BIG, POSH PLACE IT IS, BUT, GET THIS, IT BELONGS TO THIS OLD WOMAN AND HER HATSTAND FATHER.
THEN, I'M NOSING AROUND THE BACK AND, LISTEN, SCARP, LISTEN! SHE'S LIVING IN THEIR SHED! SERIOUS! SHE'S IN THERE WITH A LITTLE CAMP BED AND ONE OF THEM CRAPPY GAS STOVES. THE OLD WOMAN DON'T EVEN KNOW SHE'S IN THERE!
BOOM! JUST LIKE THAT, THE HORIZON IS BLOTTED OUT BY THOUGHTS OF PIKE AND SATURDAY'S LEFT ASKING.

SATURDAY HAS A QUESTION.

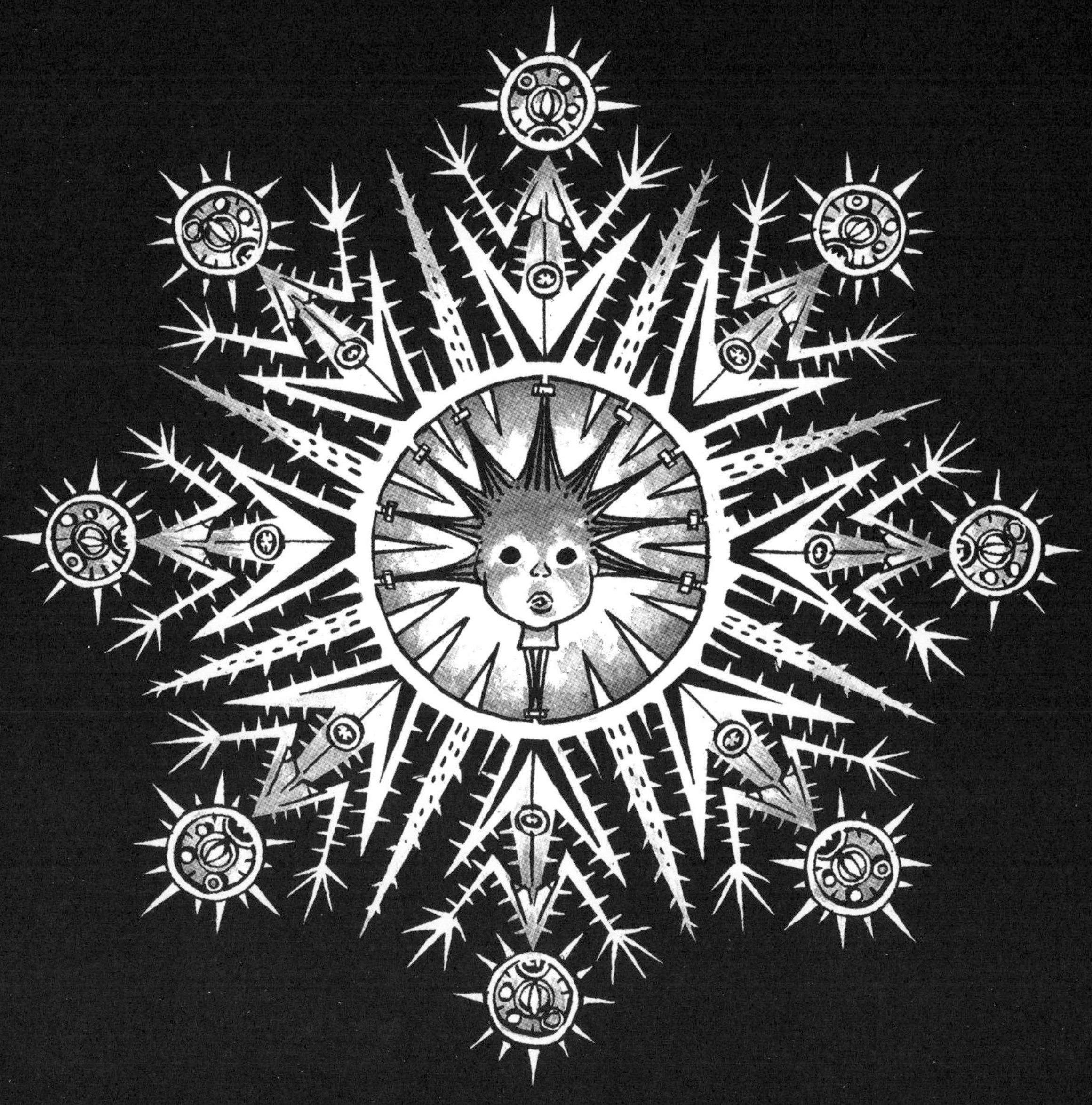

WHO THE HELL IS VERA PIKE?

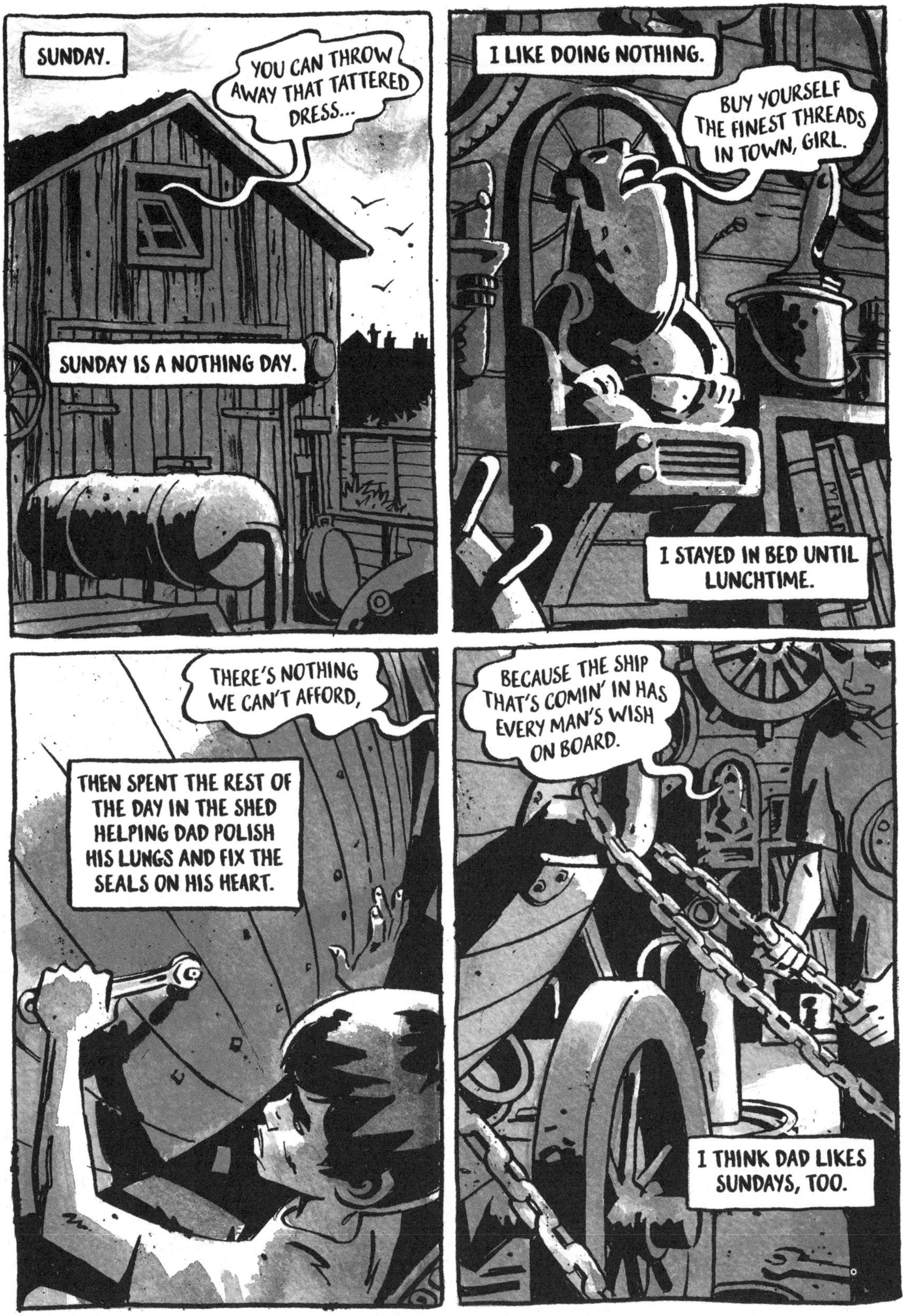
SUNDAY.
YOU CAN THROW AWAY THAT TATTERED DRESS...
SUNDAY IS A NOTHING DAY.
I LIKE DOING NOTHING.
BUY YOURSELF THE FINEST THREADS IN TOWN, GIRL.
I STAYED IN BED UNTIL LUNCHTIME.
THERE'S NOTHING WE CAN'T AFFORD,
THEN SPENT THE REST OF THE DAY IN THE SHED HELPING DAD POLISH HIS LUNGS AND FIX THE SEALS ON HIS HEART.
BECAUSE THE SHIP THAT'S COMIN' IN HAS EVERY MAN'S WISH ON BOARD.
I THINK DAD LIKES SUNDAYS, TOO.

THAT EVENING, ME AND MUM ATE
TRIANGLE SANDWICHES AND WATCHED
THE SUNDAY WHEEL.

THE SUNDAY WHEEL IS A BIT BORING.
WE ONLY WATCH IT BECAUSE IT'S ON.

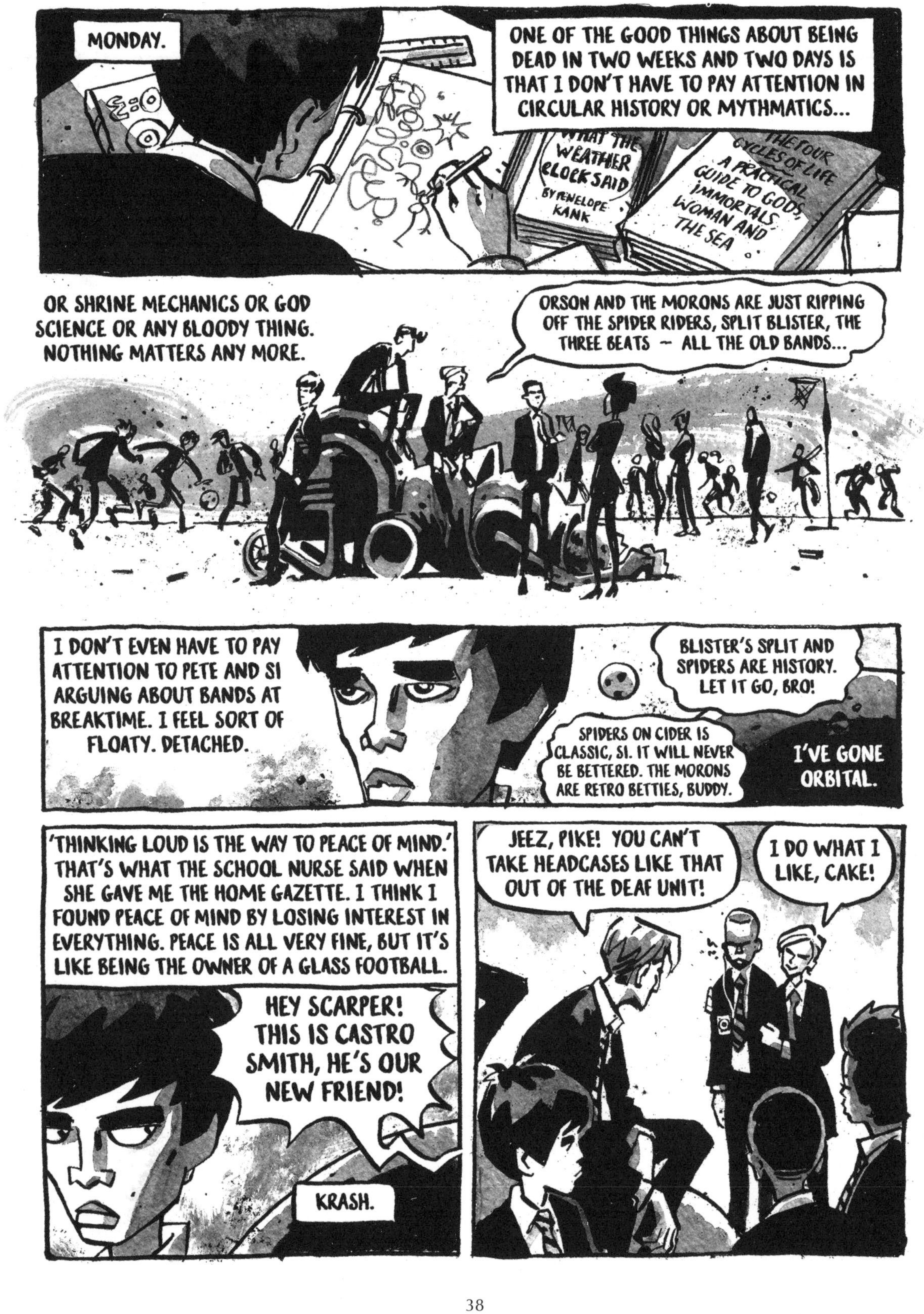
MONDAY.
ONE OF THE GOOD THINGS ABOUT BEING DEAD IN TWO WEEKS AND TWO DAYS IS THAT I DON'T HAVE TO PAY ATTENTION IN CIRCULAR HISTORY OR MYTHMATICS...
WHAT THE WEATHER CLOCK SAID BY PENELOPE KANK
THE FOUR CYCLES OF LIFE A PRACTICAL GUIDE TO GODS, IMMORTALS, WOMAN AND THE SEA
OR SHRINE MECHANICS OR GOD SCIENCE OR ANY BLOODY THING. NOTHING MATTERS ANY MORE.
ORSON AND THE MORONS ARE JUST RIPPING OFF THE SPIDER RIDERS, SPLIT BLISTER, THE THREE BEATS – ALL THE OLD BANDS...
I DON'T EVEN HAVE TO PAY ATTENTION TO PETE AND SI ARGUING ABOUT BANDS AT BREAKTIME. I FEEL SORT OF FLOATY. DETACHED.
BLISTER'S SPLIT AND SPIDERS ARE HISTORY. LET IT GO, BRO!
SPIDERS ON CIDER IS CLASSIC, SI. IT WILL NEVER BE BETTERED. THE MORONS ARE RETRO BETTIES, BUDDY.
I'VE GONE ORBITAL.
'THINKING LOUD IS THE WAY TO PEACE OF MIND.' THAT'S WHAT THE SCHOOL NURSE SAID WHEN SHE GAVE ME THE HOME GAZETTE. I THINK I FOUND PEACE OF MIND BY LOSING INTEREST IN EVERYTHING. PEACE IS ALL VERY FINE, BUT IT'S LIKE BEING THE OWNER OF A GLASS FOOTBALL.
HEY SCARPER! THIS IS CASTRO SMITH, HE'S OUR NEW FRIEND!
KRASH.
JEEZ, PIKE! YOU CAN'T TAKE HEADCASES LIKE THAT OUT OF THE DEAF UNIT!
I DO WHAT I LIKE, CAKE!

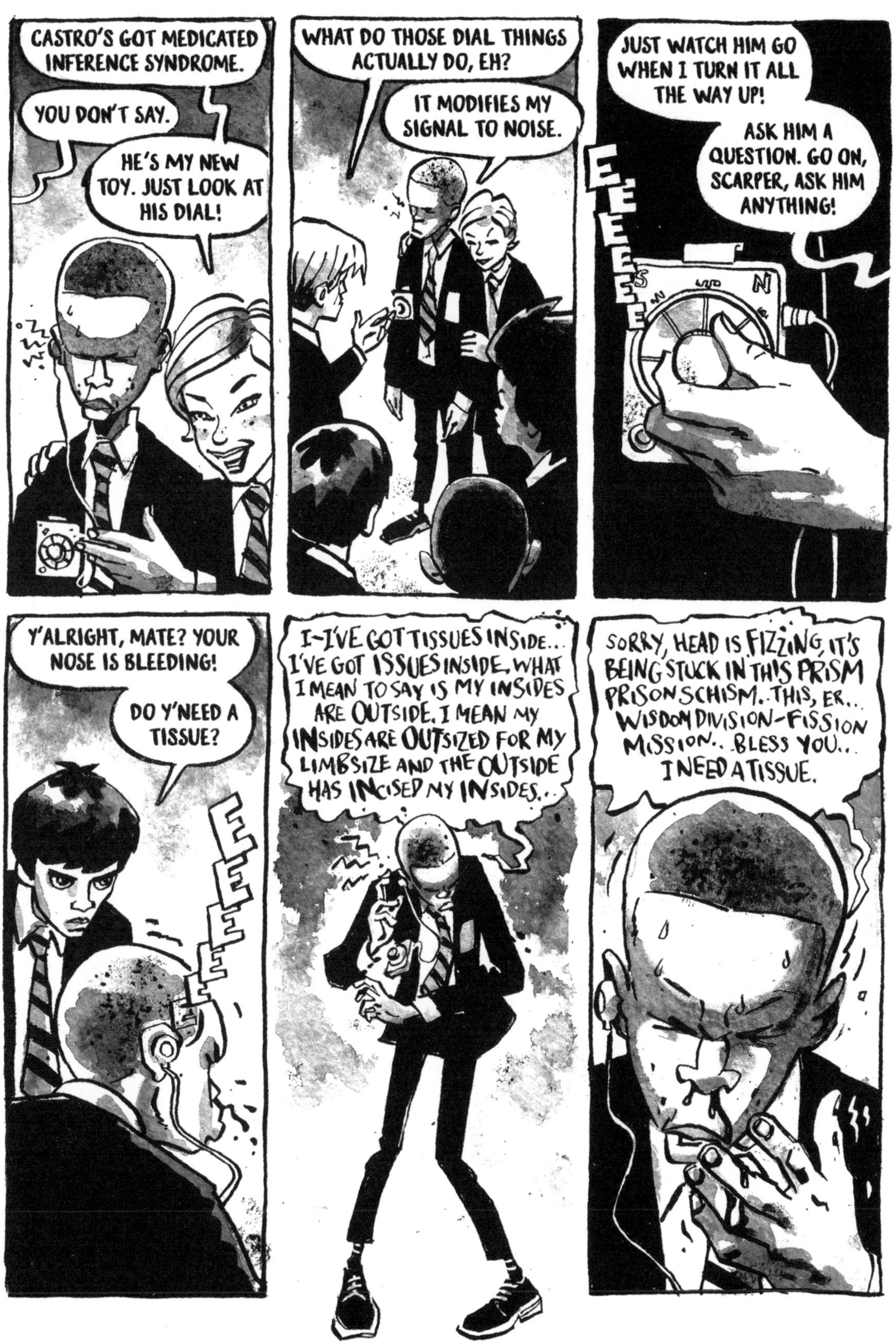
CASTRO'S GOT MEDICATED INFERENCE SYNDROME.
YOU DON'T SAY.
HE'S MY NEW TOY. JUST LOOK AT HIS DIAL!
WHAT DO THOSE DIAL THINGS ACTUALLY DO, EH?
IT MODIFIES MY SIGNAL TO NOISE.
JUST WATCH HIM GO WHEN I TURN IT ALL THE WAY UP!
ASK HIM A QUESTION. GO ON, SCARPER, ASK HIM ANYTHING!
EEEEEEE
Y'ALRIGHT, MATE? YOUR NOSE IS BLEEDING!
DO Y'NEED A TISSUE?
EEEEEE
I-I'VE GOT TISSUES INSIDE... I'VE GOT ISSUES INSIDE, WHAT I MEAN TO SAY IS MY INSIDES ARE OUTSIDE. I MEAN MY INSIDES ARE OUTSIZED FOR MY LIMBSIZE AND THE OUTSIDE HAS INCISED MY INSIDES...
SORRY, HEAD IS FIZZING, IT'S BEING STUCK IN THIS PRISM PRISON SCHISM.. THIS, ER... WISDOM DIVISION-FISSION MISSION.. BLESS YOU... I NEED A TISSUE.

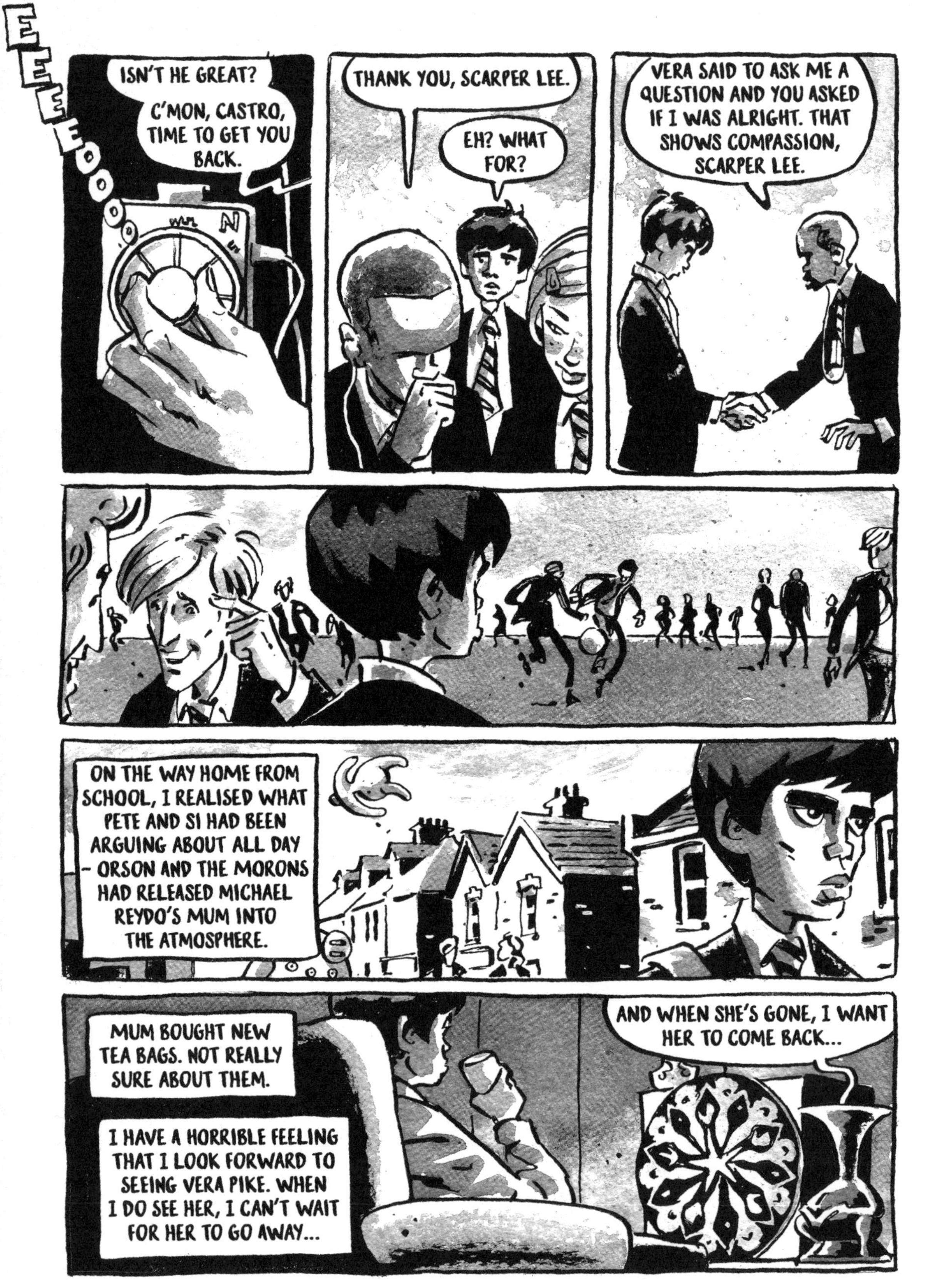
EEEEEOOOOO
ISN'T HE GREAT?
C'MON, CASTRO, TIME TO GET YOU BACK.
THANK YOU, SCARPER LEE.
EH? WHAT FOR?
VERA SAID TO ASK ME A QUESTION AND YOU ASKED IF I WAS ALRIGHT. THAT SHOWS COMPASSION, SCARPER LEE.
ON THE WAY HOME FROM SCHOOL, I REALISED WHAT PETE AND SI HAD BEEN ARGUING ABOUT ALL DAY – ORSON AND THE MORONS HAD RELEASED MICHAEL REYDO'S MUM INTO THE ATMOSPHERE.
MUM BOUGHT NEW TEA BAGS. NOT REALLY SURE ABOUT THEM.
I HAVE A HORRIBLE FEELING THAT I LOOK FORWARD TO SEEING VERA PIKE. WHEN I DO SEE HER, I CAN'T WAIT FOR HER TO GO AWAY...
AND WHEN SHE'S GONE, I WANT HER TO COME BACK...

IT'S LIKE THE SEA, THE THING THAT
PULLS YOU IN PUSHES YOU AWAY.

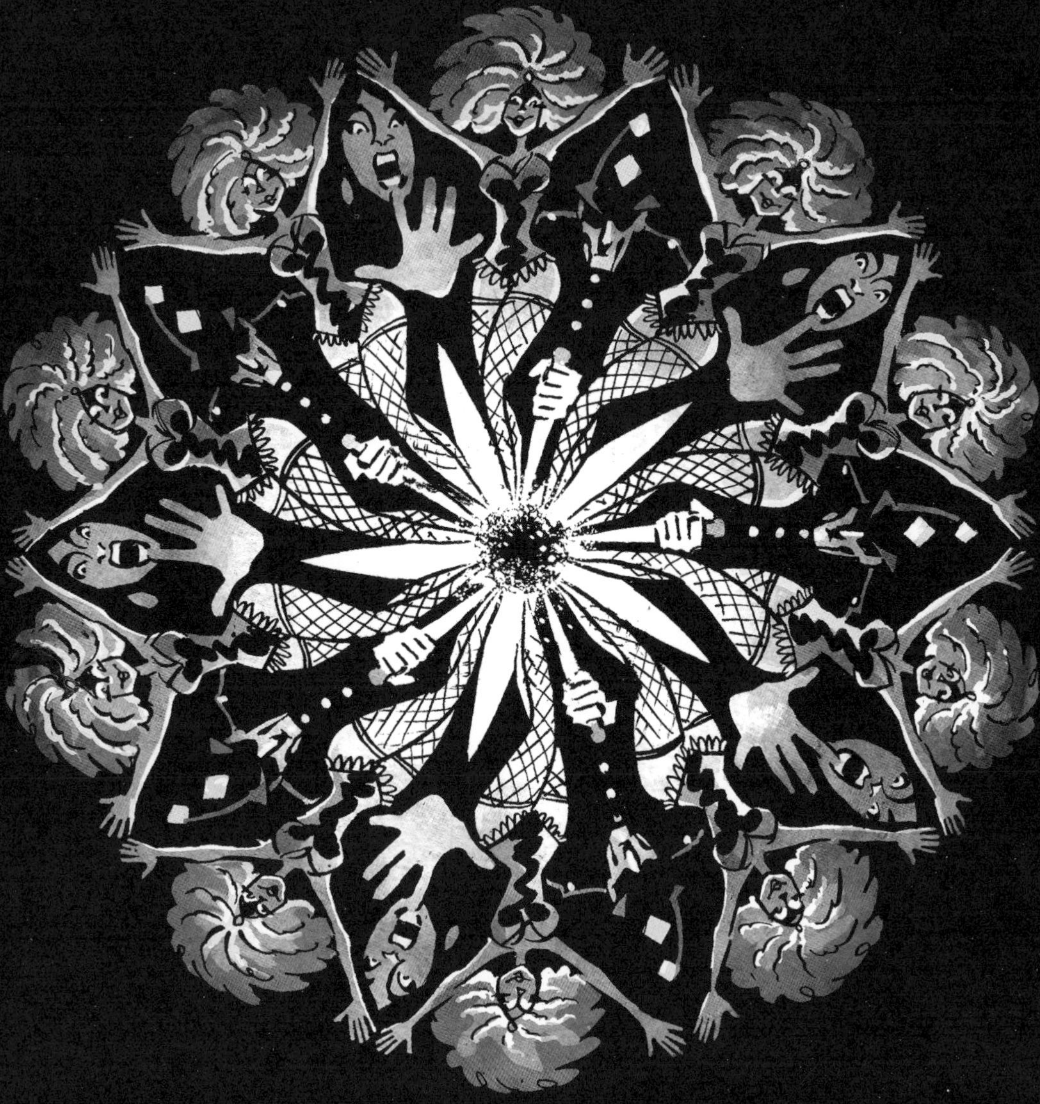

AND I'M LOOKING AT THE HOME GAZETTE, AT
THE WAY IT SUCKS IN MY WORDS AS I BLOW THEM
OUT. THEN IT BLOWS THEM BACK OUT AGAIN...

THE THING THAT PULLS YOU
IN PUSHES YOU AWAY.

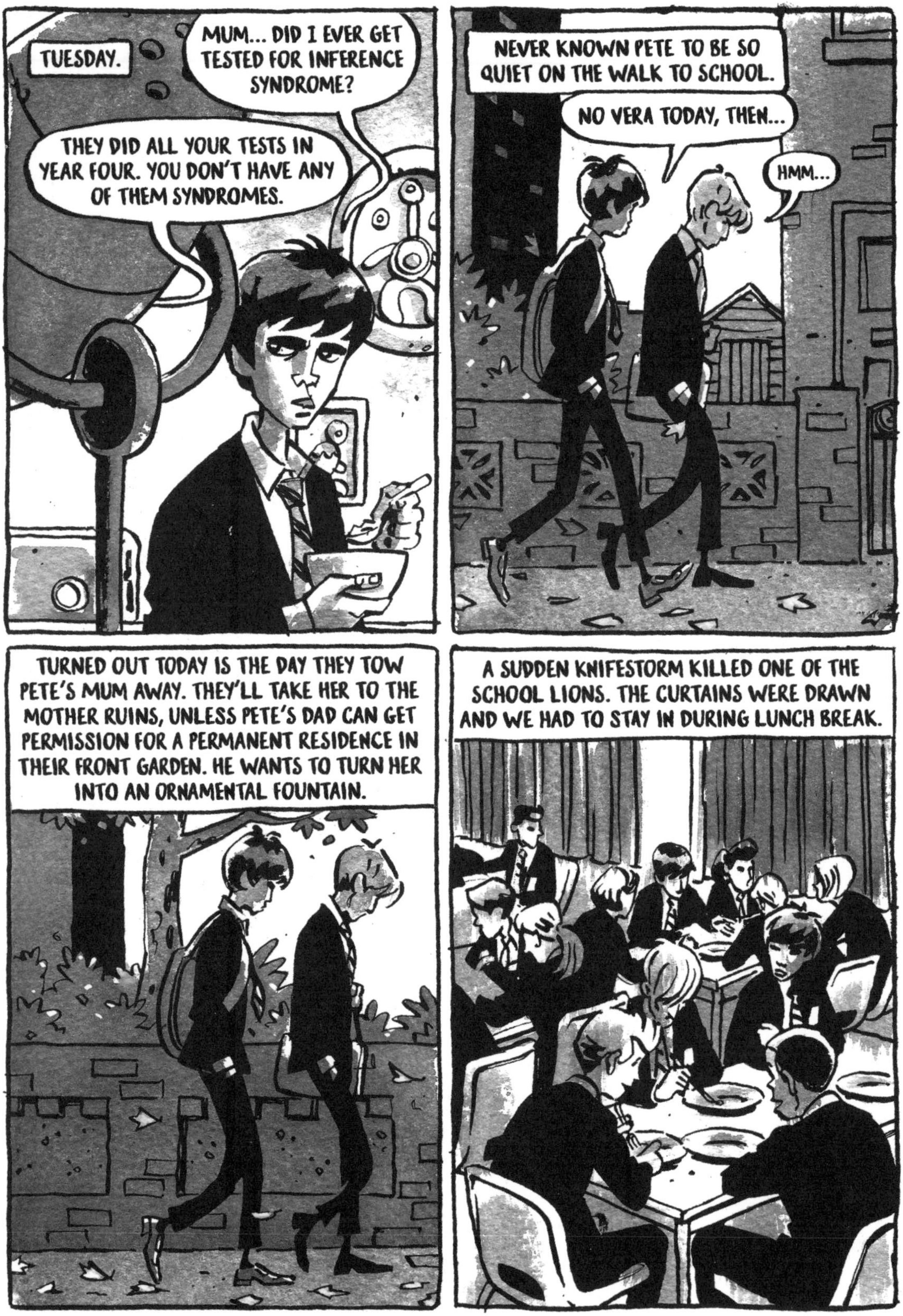
TUESDAY.
MUM... DID I EVER GET TESTED FOR INFERENCE SYNDROME?
THEY DID ALL YOUR TESTS IN YEAR FOUR. YOU DON'T HAVE ANY OF THEM SYNDROMES.
NEVER KNOWN PETE TO BE SO QUIET ON THE WALK TO SCHOOL.
NO VERA TODAY, THEN...
HMM...
TURNED OUT TODAY IS THE DAY THEY TOW PETE'S MUM AWAY. THEY'LL TAKE HER TO THE MOTHER RUINS, UNLESS PETE'S DAD CAN GET PERMISSION FOR A PERMANENT RESIDENCE IN THEIR FRONT GARDEN. HE WANTS TO TURN HER INTO AN ORNAMENTAL FOUNTAIN.
A SUDDEN KNIFESTORM KILLED ONE OF THE SCHOOL LIONS. THE CURTAINS WERE DRAWN AND WE HAD TO STAY IN DURING LUNCH BREAK.

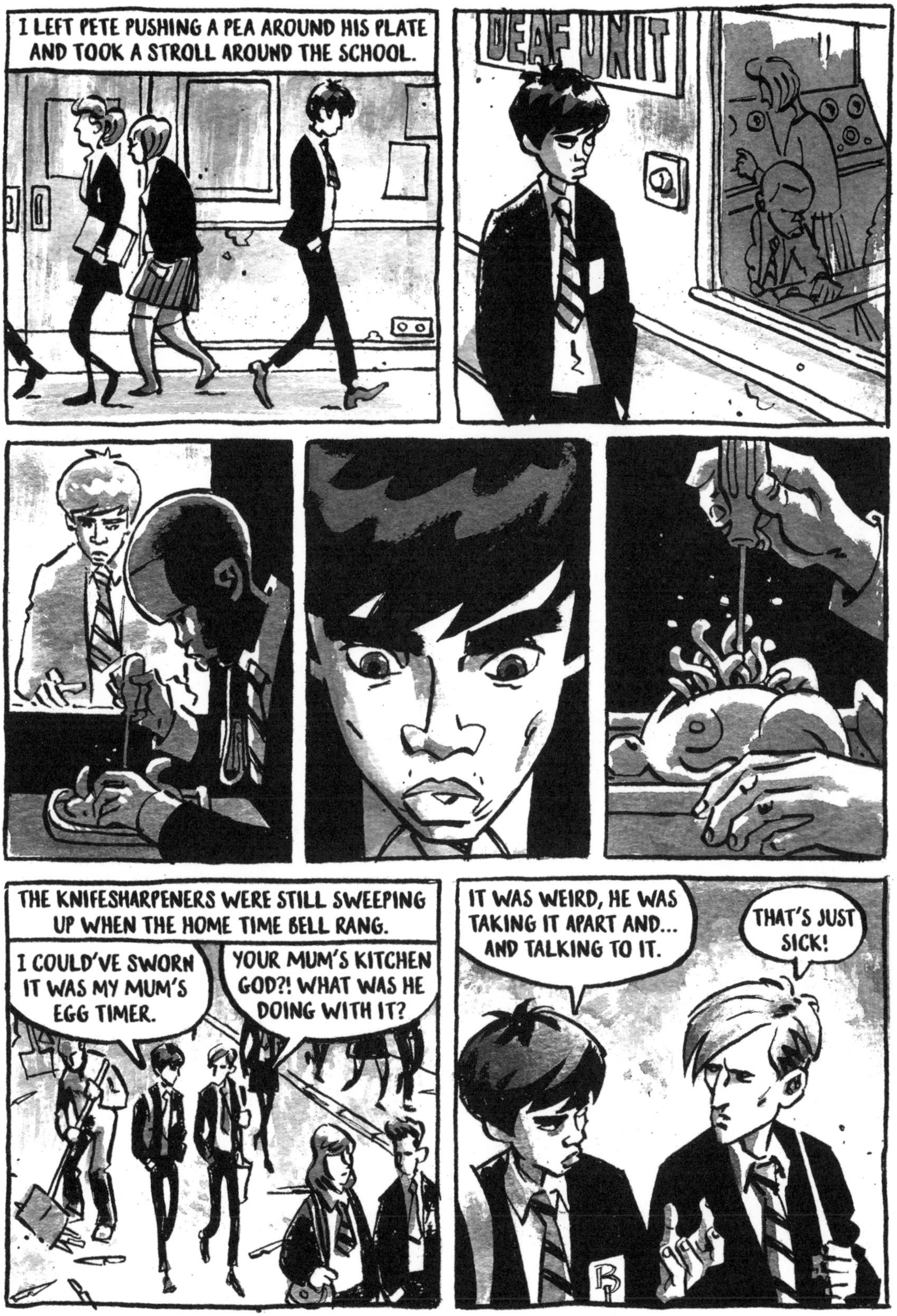
I LEFT PETE PUSHING A PEA AROUND HIS PLATE AND TOOK A STROLL AROUND THE SCHOOL.
DEAF UNIT
THE KNIFESHARPENERS WERE STILL SWEEPING UP WHEN THE HOME TIME BELL RANG.
I COULD'VE SWORN IT WAS MY MUM'S EGG TIMER.
YOUR MUM'S KITCHEN GOD?! WHAT WAS HE DOING WITH IT?
IT WAS WEIRD, HE WAS TAKING IT APART AND... AND TALKING TO IT.
THAT'S JUST SICK!

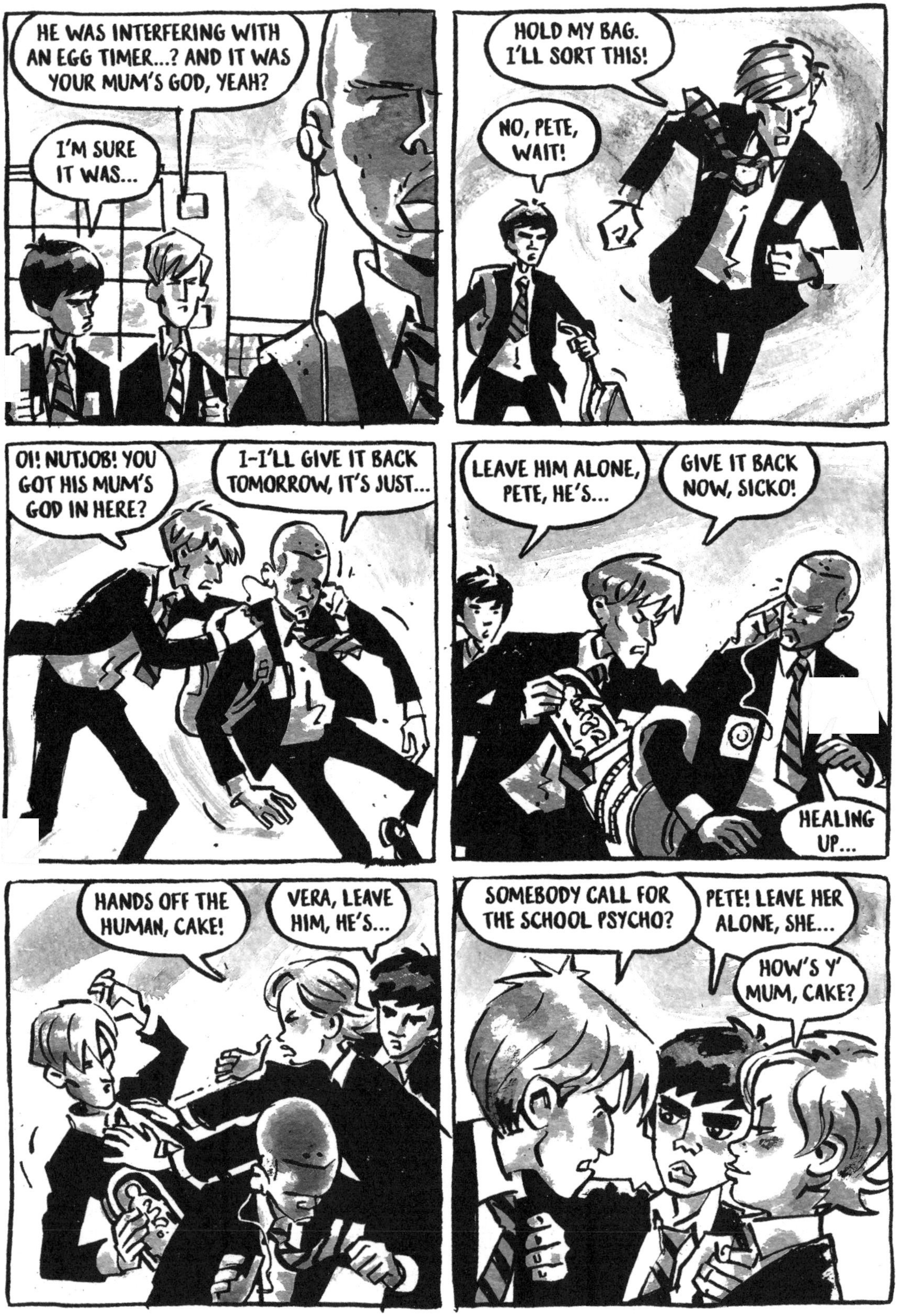
HE WAS INTERFERING WITH AN EGG TIMER...? AND IT WAS YOUR MUM'S GOD, YEAH?
I'M SURE IT WAS...
HOLD MY BAG. I'LL SORT THIS!
NO, PETE, WAIT!
OI! NUTJOB! YOU GOT HIS MUM'S GOD IN HERE?
I-I'LL GIVE IT BACK TOMORROW, IT'S JUST...
LEAVE HIM ALONE, PETE, HE'S...
GIVE IT BACK NOW, SICKO!
HEALING UP...
HANDS OFF THE HUMAN, CAKE!
VERA, LEAVE HIM, HE'S...
SOMEBODY CALL FOR THE SCHOOL PSYCHO?
PETE! LEAVE HER ALONE, SHE...
HOW'S Y' MUM, CAKE?

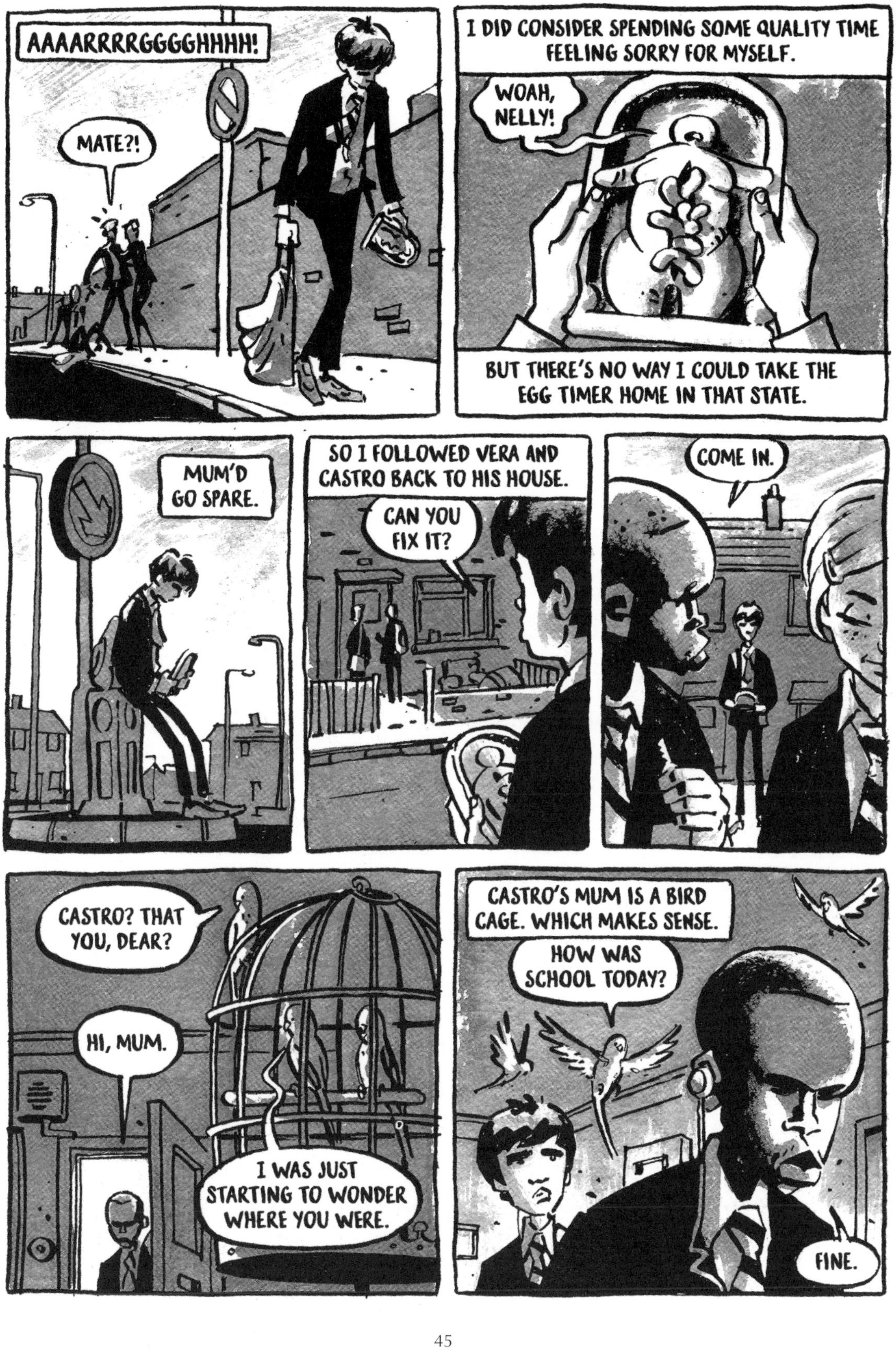
AAAARRRRGGGGHHHH!
MATE?!
I DID CONSIDER SPENDING SOME QUALITY TIME FEELING SORRY FOR MYSELF.
WOAH, NELLY!
BUT THERE'S NO WAY I COULD TAKE THE EGG TIMER HOME IN THAT STATE.
MUM'D GO SPARE.
SO I FOLLOWED VERA AND CASTRO BACK TO HIS HOUSE.
CAN YOU FIX IT?
COME IN.
CASTRO? THAT YOU, DEAR?
HI, MUM.
I WAS JUST STARTING TO WONDER WHERE YOU WERE.
CASTRO'S MUM IS A BIRD CAGE. WHICH MAKES SENSE.
HOW WAS SCHOOL TODAY?
FINE.

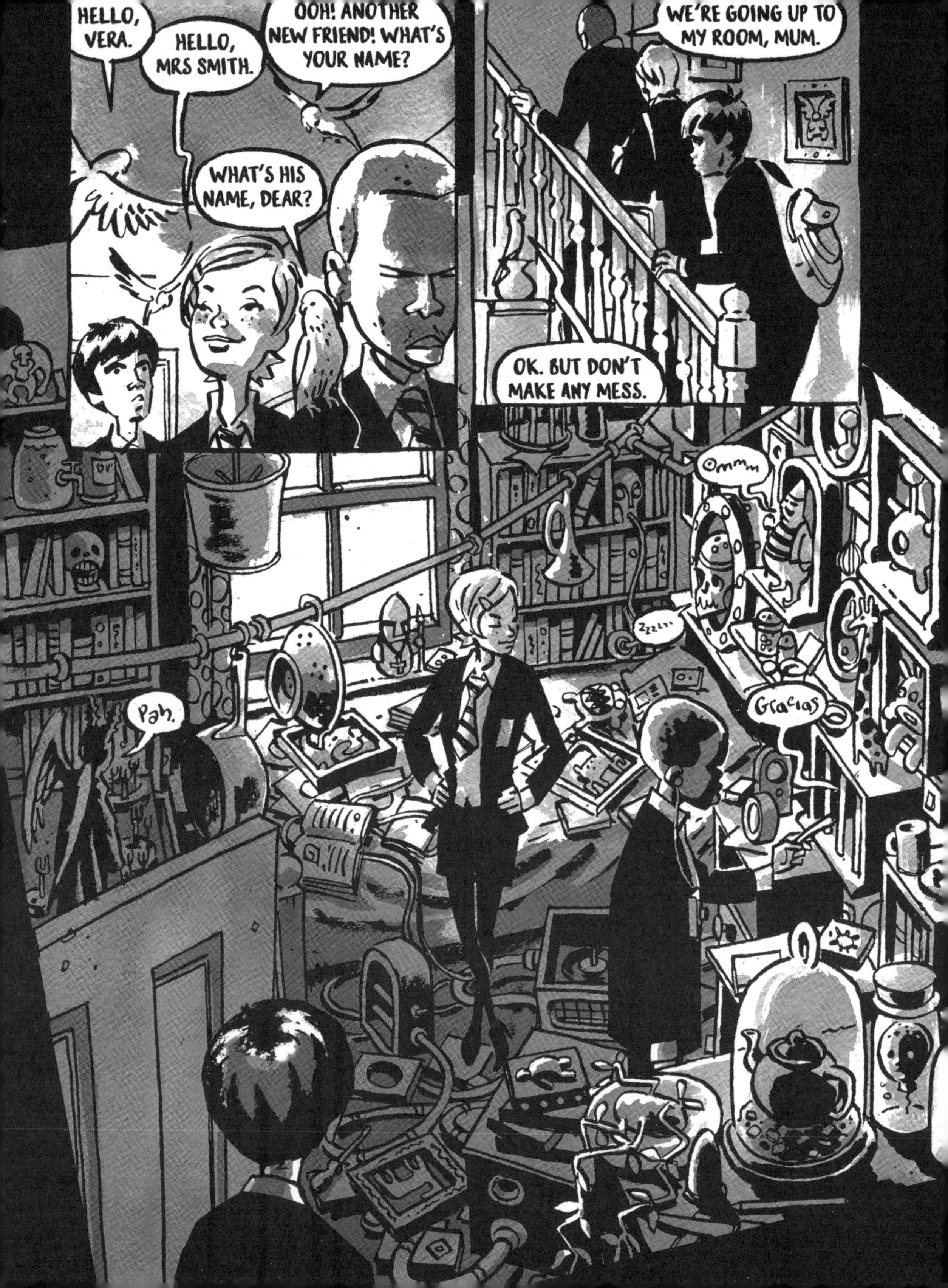
HELLO, VERA.
HELLO, MRS SMITH.
OOH! ANOTHER NEW FRIEND! WHAT'S YOUR NAME?
WHAT'S HIS NAME, DEAR?
WE'RE GOING UP TO MY ROOM, MUM.
OK. BUT DON'T MAKE ANY MESS.
Ommm
Zzzz
Pah.
Gracias

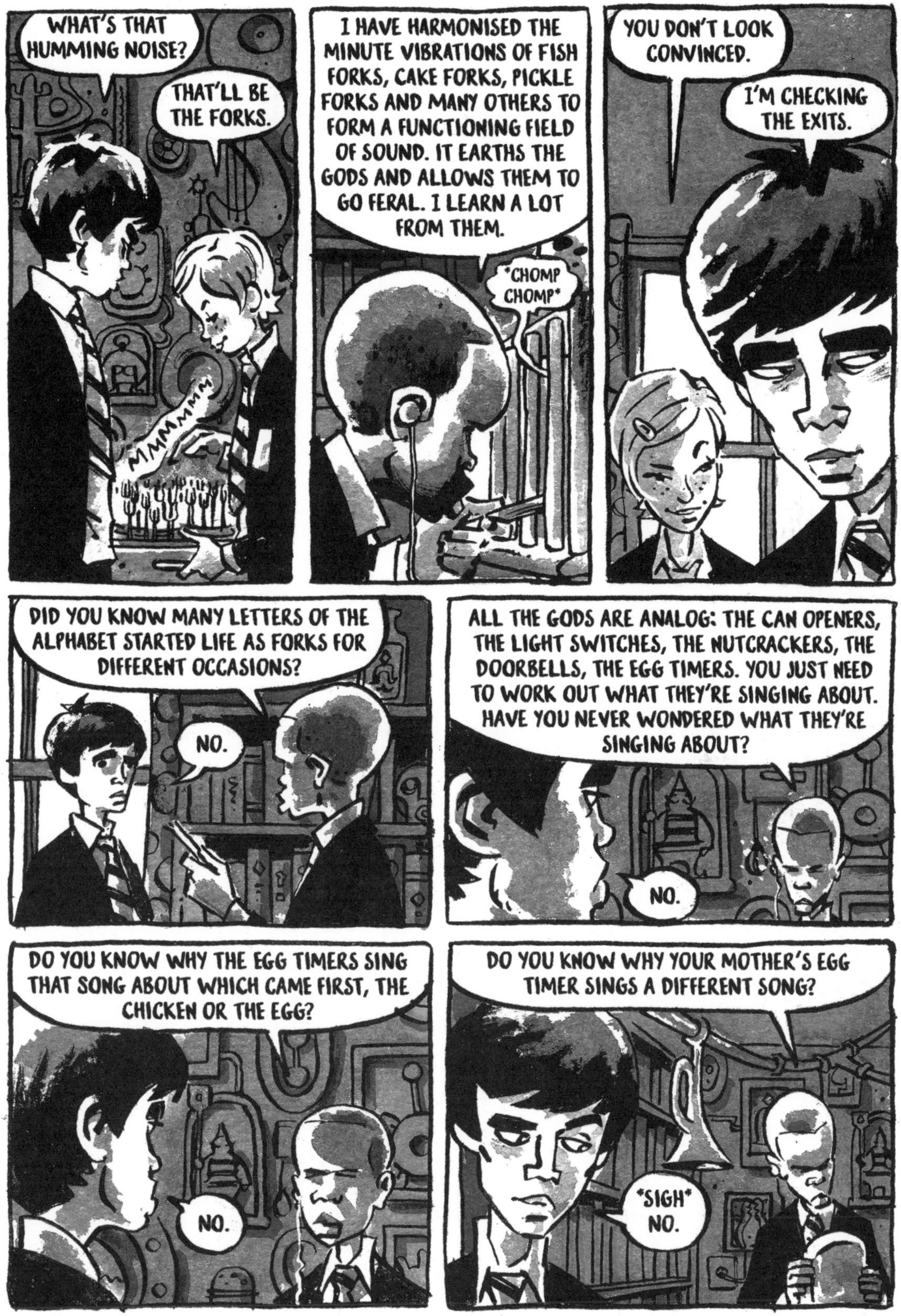
WHAT'S THAT HUMMING NOISE?
THAT'LL BE THE FORKS.
MMMMMM
I HAVE HARMONISED THE MINUTE VIBRATIONS OF FISH FORKS, CAKE FORKS, PICKLE FORKS AND MANY OTHERS TO FORM A FUNCTIONING FIELD OF SOUND. IT EARTHS THE GODS AND ALLOWS THEM TO GO FERAL. I LEARN A LOT FROM THEM.
*CHOMP CHOMP*
YOU DON'T LOOK CONVINCED.
I'M CHECKING THE EXITS.
DID YOU KNOW MANY LETTERS OF THE ALPHABET STARTED LIFE AS FORKS FOR DIFFERENT OCCASIONS?
NO.
ALL THE GODS ARE ANALOG: THE CAN OPENERS, THE LIGHT SWITCHES, THE NUTCRACKERS, THE DOORBELLS, THE EGG TIMERS. YOU JUST NEED TO WORK OUT WHAT THEY'RE SINGING ABOUT. HAVE YOU NEVER WONDERED WHAT THEY'RE SINGING ABOUT?
NO.
DO YOU KNOW WHY THE EGG TIMERS SING THAT SONG ABOUT WHICH CAME FIRST, THE CHICKEN OR THE EGG?
NO.
DO YOU KNOW WHY YOUR MOTHER'S EGG TIMER SINGS A DIFFERENT SONG?
*SIGH* NO.

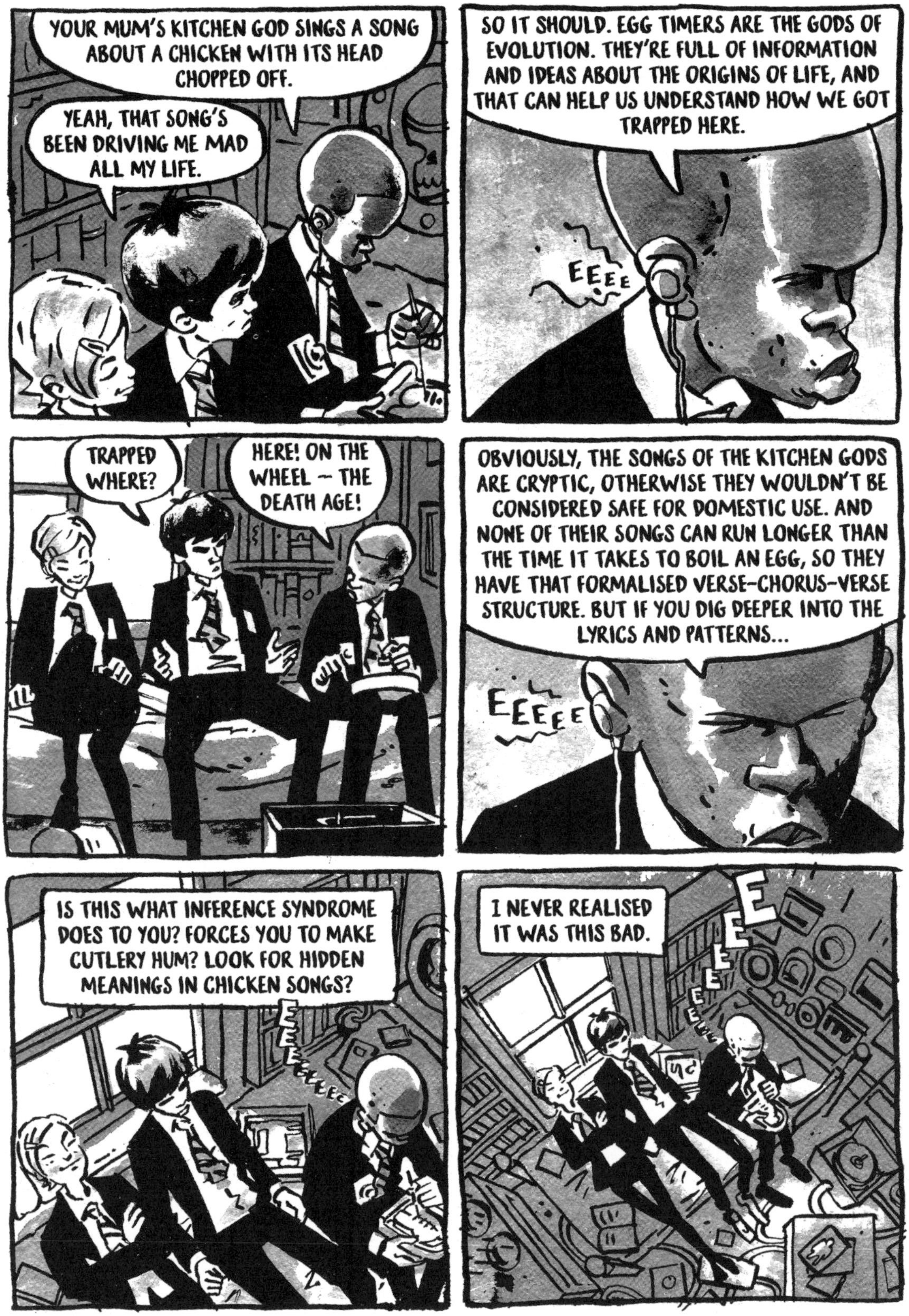

YOUR MUM'S KITCHEN GOD SINGS A SONG ABOUT A CHICKEN WITH ITS HEAD CHOPPED OFF.
YEAH, THAT SONG'S BEEN DRIVING ME MAD ALL MY LIFE.
SO IT SHOULD. EGG TIMERS ARE THE GODS OF EVOLUTION. THEY'RE FULL OF INFORMATION AND IDEAS ABOUT THE ORIGINS OF LIFE, AND THAT CAN HELP US UNDERSTAND HOW WE GOT TRAPPED HERE.
EEEE
TRAPPED WHERE?
HERE! ON THE WHEEL — THE DEATH AGE!
OBVIOUSLY, THE SONGS OF THE KITCHEN GODS ARE CRYPTIC, OTHERWISE THEY WOULDN'T BE CONSIDERED SAFE FOR DOMESTIC USE. AND NONE OF THEIR SONGS CAN RUN LONGER THAN THE TIME IT TAKES TO BOIL AN EGG, SO THEY HAVE THAT FORMALISED VERSE-CHORUS-VERSE STRUCTURE. BUT IF YOU DIG DEEPER INTO THE LYRICS AND PATTERNS...
EEEEE
IS THIS WHAT INFERENCE SYNDROME DOES TO YOU? FORCES YOU TO MAKE CUTLERY HUM? LOOK FOR HIDDEN MEANINGS IN CHICKEN SONGS?
I NEVER REALISED IT WAS THIS BAD.

I LISTENED TO FORKS. I LISTENED TO KETTLES, ALARM CLOCKS, LIGHT SWITCHES, COFFEE POTS AND CASTRO SMITH. AS I SAT THERE ON THE BED, SQUASHED BETWEEN THEM, IT FELT LIKE EVERYTHING WAS COMING TOGETHER AND I WAS COMING APART.

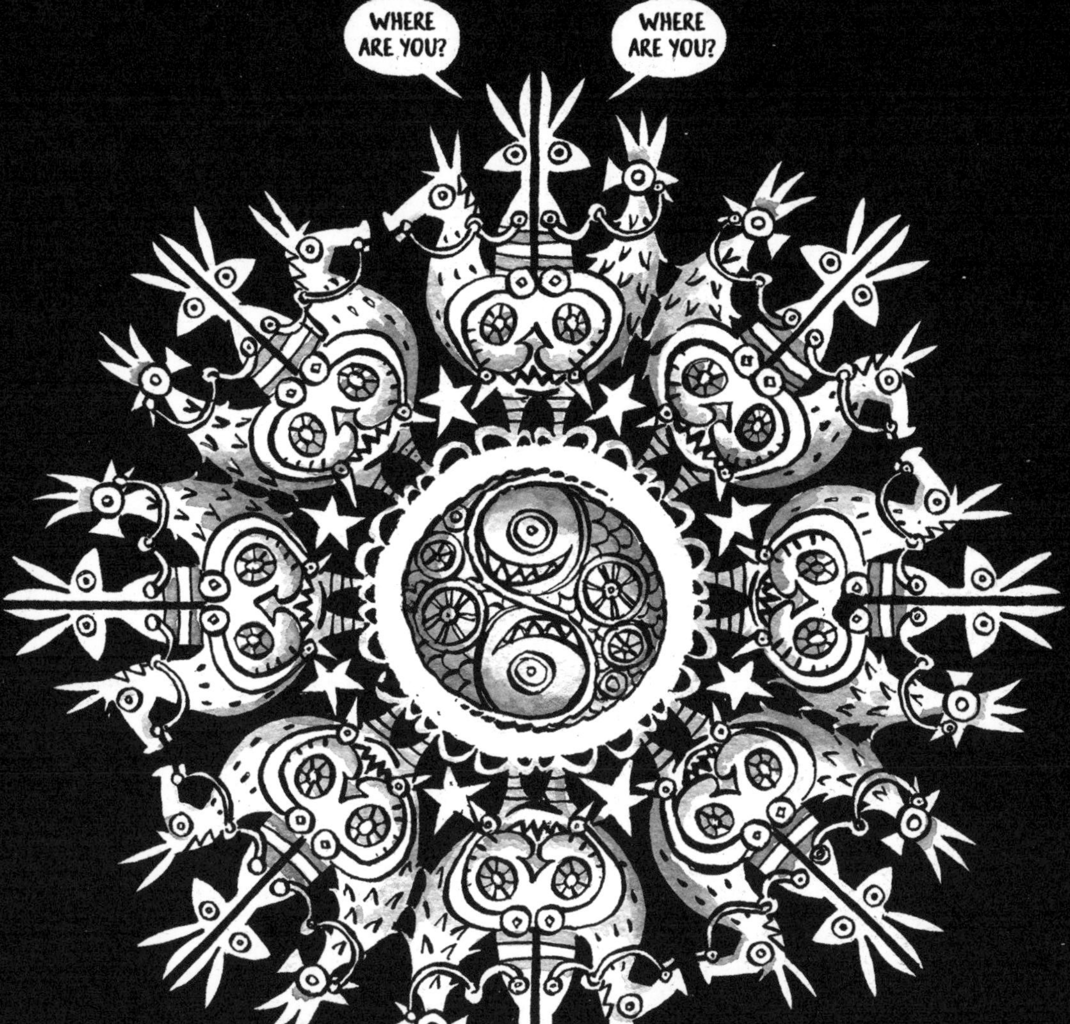
WHERE ARE YOU?
WHERE ARE YOU?

SOME IMPORTANT LITTLE BOLT THAT HELD MY TWO HALVES TOGETHER DROPPED OUT AND ONE HALF OF ME FLOATED AWAY OVER THE ROOFTOPS, LIKE MICHAEL REYDO'S MUM. THINGS LOOKED DIFFERENT ON THE WALK HOME. OPENING THE FRONT DOOR, THE HALL LOOKED UNFAMILIAR. MUM LOOKED AT ME ODD, THE LIGHTS SEEMED BRIGHTER, TEA TASTED STRANGE AND THE TUESDAY WHEEL STARTED MAKING SENSE. I HAD ENTERED THE WORLD OF WRONG.

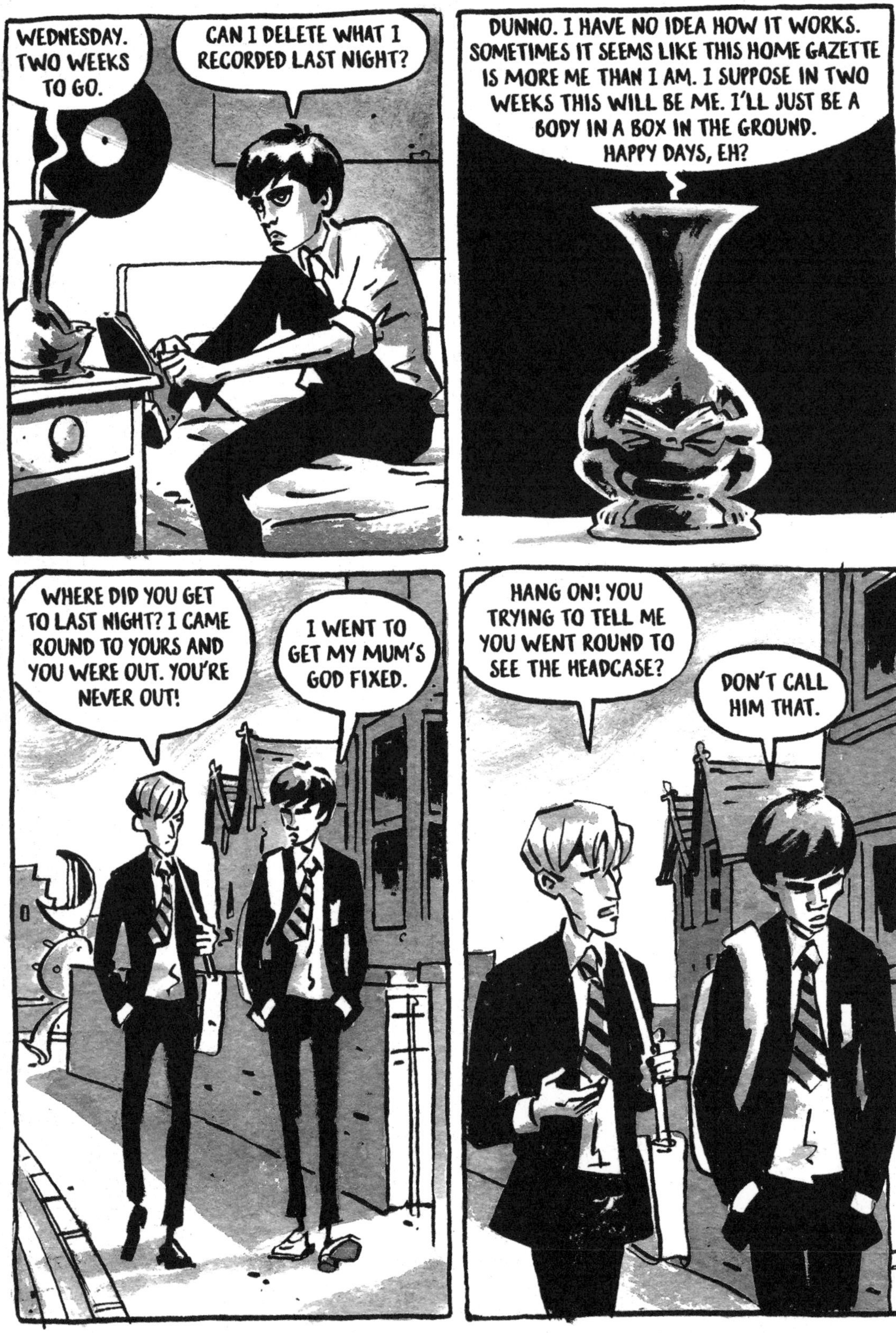
WEDNESDAY. TWO WEEKS TO GO.
CAN I DELETE WHAT I RECORDED LAST NIGHT?
DUNNO. I HAVE NO IDEA HOW IT WORKS. SOMETIMES IT SEEMS LIKE THIS HOME GAZETTE IS MORE ME THAN I AM. I SUPPOSE IN TWO WEEKS THIS WILL BE ME. I'LL JUST BE A BODY IN A BOX IN THE GROUND. HAPPY DAYS, EH?
WHERE DID YOU GET TO LAST NIGHT? I CAME ROUND TO YOURS AND YOU WERE OUT. YOU'RE NEVER OUT!
I WENT TO GET MY MUM'S GOD FIXED.
HANG ON! YOU TRYING TO TELL ME YOU WENT ROUND TO SEE THE HEADCASE?
DON'T CALL HIM THAT.

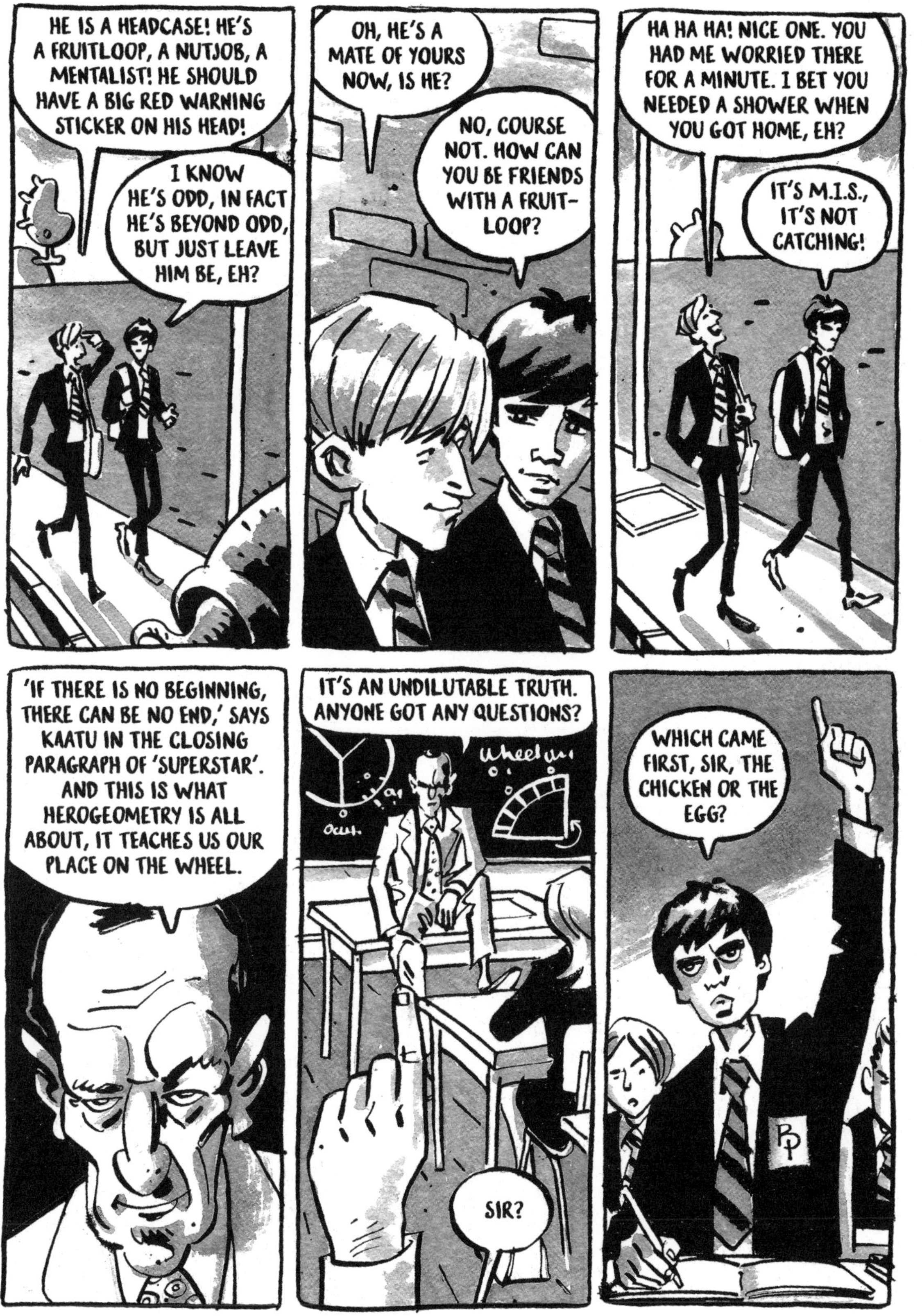
HE IS A HEADCASE! HE'S A FRUITLOOP, A NUTJOB, A MENTALIST! HE SHOULD HAVE A BIG RED WARNING STICKER ON HIS HEAD!
I KNOW HE'S ODD, IN FACT HE'S BEYOND ODD, BUT JUST LEAVE HIM BE, EH?
OH, HE'S A MATE OF YOURS NOW, IS HE?
NO, COURSE NOT. HOW CAN YOU BE FRIENDS WITH A FRUIT-LOOP?
HA HA HA! NICE ONE. YOU HAD ME WORRIED THERE FOR A MINUTE. I BET YOU NEEDED A SHOWER WHEN YOU GOT HOME, EH?
IT'S M.I.S., IT'S NOT CATCHING!
'IF THERE IS NO BEGINNING, THERE CAN BE NO END,' SAYS KAATU IN THE CLOSING PARAGRAPH OF 'SUPERSTAR'. AND THIS IS WHAT HEROGEOMETRY IS ALL ABOUT, IT TEACHES US OUR PLACE ON THE WHEEL.
IT'S AN UNDILUTABLE TRUTH. ANYONE GOT ANY QUESTIONS?
SIR?
WHICH CAME FIRST, SIR, THE CHICKEN OR THE EGG?

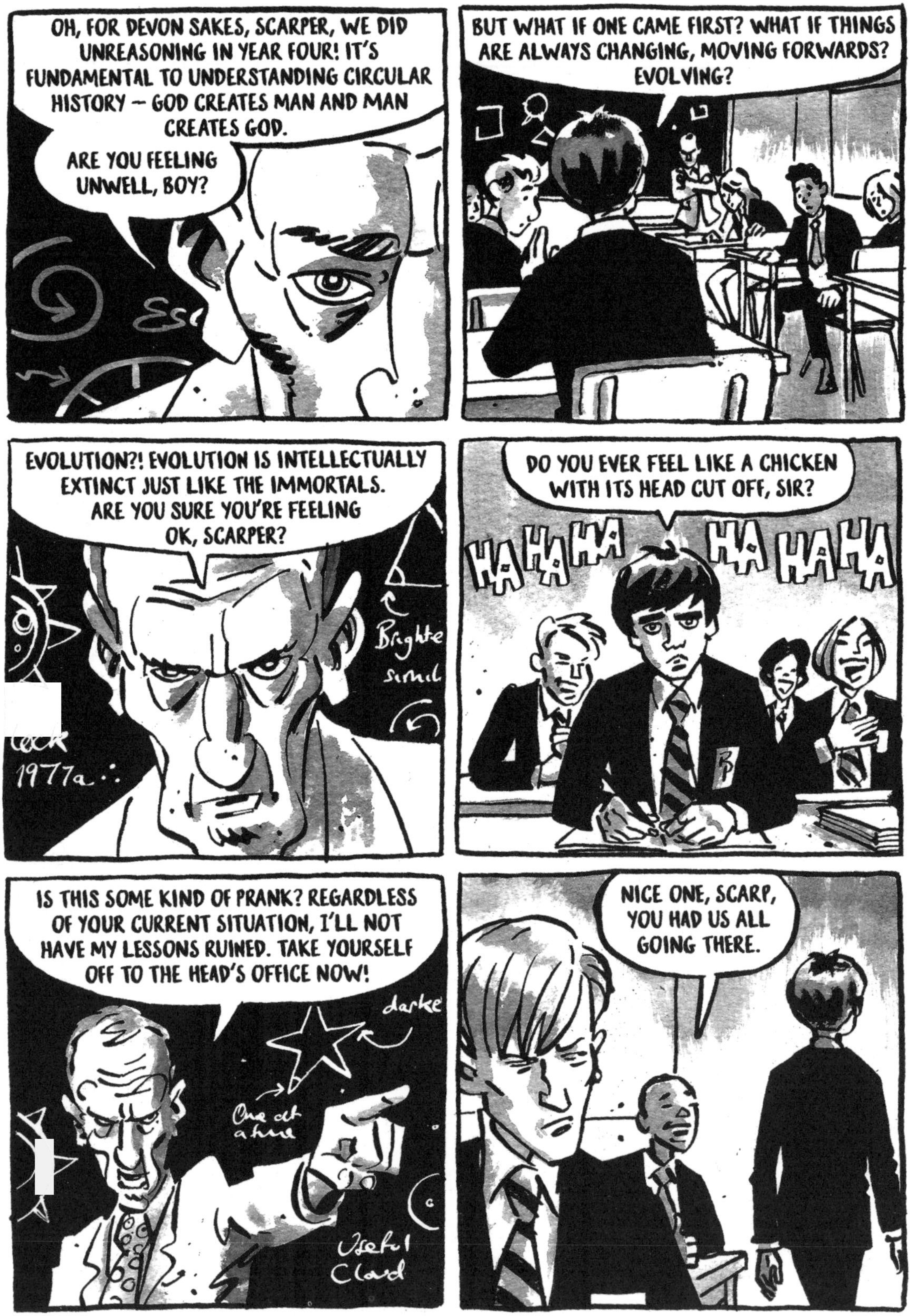
OH, FOR DEVON SAKES, SCARPER, WE DID UNREASONING IN YEAR FOUR! IT'S FUNDAMENTAL TO UNDERSTANDING CIRCULAR HISTORY – GOD CREATES MAN AND MAN CREATES GOD.
ARE YOU FEELING UNWELL, BOY?
BUT WHAT IF ONE CAME FIRST? WHAT IF THINGS ARE ALWAYS CHANGING, MOVING FORWARDS? EVOLVING?
EVOLUTION?! EVOLUTION IS INTELLECTUALLY EXTINCT JUST LIKE THE IMMORTALS. ARE YOU SURE YOU'RE FEELING OK, SCARPER?
DO YOU EVER FEEL LIKE A CHICKEN WITH ITS HEAD CUT OFF, SIR?
HAHAHA HA HAHA
IS THIS SOME KIND OF PRANK? REGARDLESS OF YOUR CURRENT SITUATION, I'LL NOT HAVE MY LESSONS RUINED. TAKE YOURSELF OFF TO THE HEAD'S OFFICE NOW!
NICE ONE, SCARP, YOU HAD US ALL GOING THERE.

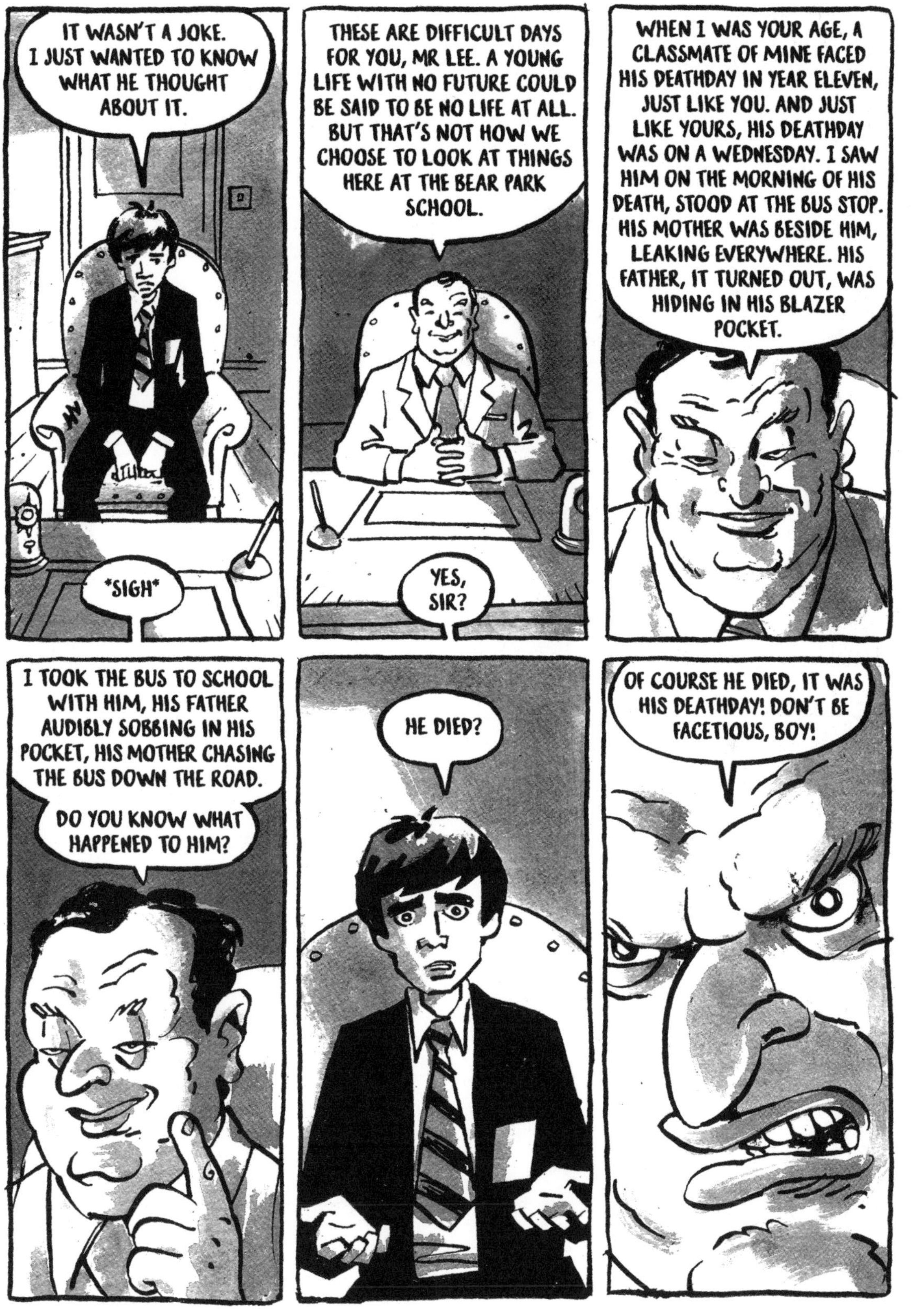
IT WASN'T A JOKE. I JUST WANTED TO KNOW WHAT HE THOUGHT ABOUT IT.
*SIGH*
THESE ARE DIFFICULT DAYS FOR YOU, MR LEE. A YOUNG LIFE WITH NO FUTURE COULD BE SAID TO BE NO LIFE AT ALL. BUT THAT'S NOT HOW WE CHOOSE TO LOOK AT THINGS HERE AT THE BEAR PARK SCHOOL.
YES, SIR?
WHEN I WAS YOUR AGE, A CLASSMATE OF MINE FACED HIS DEATHDAY IN YEAR ELEVEN, JUST LIKE YOU. AND JUST LIKE YOURS, HIS DEATHDAY WAS ON A WEDNESDAY. I SAW HIM ON THE MORNING OF HIS DEATH, STOOD AT THE BUS STOP. HIS MOTHER WAS BESIDE HIM, LEAKING EVERYWHERE. HIS FATHER, IT TURNED OUT, WAS HIDING IN HIS BLAZER POCKET.
I TOOK THE BUS TO SCHOOL WITH HIM, HIS FATHER AUDIBLY SOBBING IN HIS POCKET, HIS MOTHER CHASING THE BUS DOWN THE ROAD.
DO YOU KNOW WHAT HAPPENED TO HIM?
HE DIED?
OF COURSE HE DIED, IT WAS HIS DEATHDAY! DON'T BE FACETIOUS, BOY!

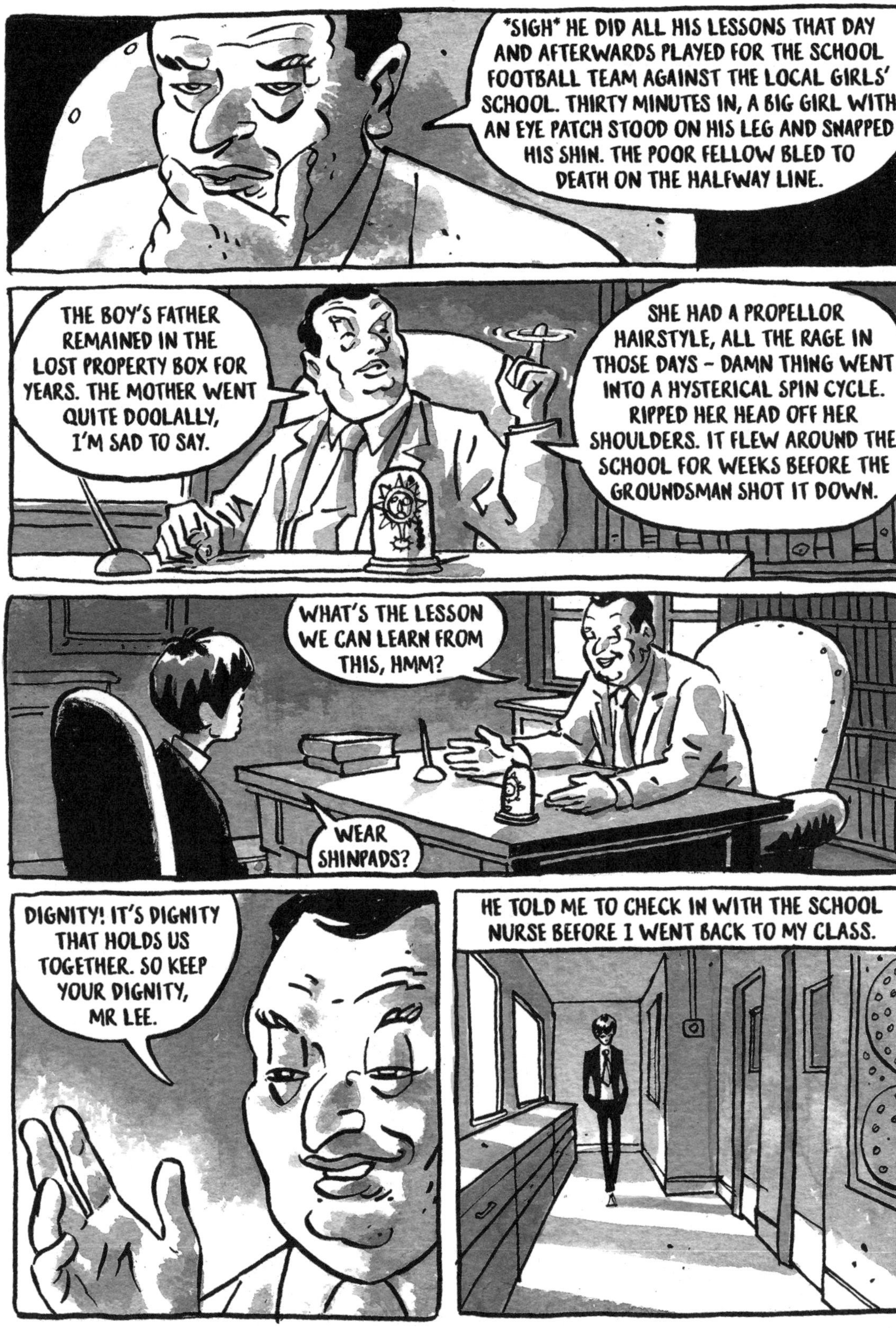
*SIGH* HE DID ALL HIS LESSONS THAT DAY AND AFTERWARDS PLAYED FOR THE SCHOOL FOOTBALL TEAM AGAINST THE LOCAL GIRLS' SCHOOL. THIRTY MINUTES IN, A BIG GIRL WITH AN EYE PATCH STOOD ON HIS LEG AND SNAPPED HIS SHIN. THE POOR FELLOW BLED TO DEATH ON THE HALFWAY LINE.
THE BOY'S FATHER REMAINED IN THE LOST PROPERTY BOX FOR YEARS. THE MOTHER WENT QUITE DOOLALLY, I'M SAD TO SAY.
SHE HAD A PROPELLOR HAIRSTYLE, ALL THE RAGE IN THOSE DAYS – DAMN THING WENT INTO A HYSTERICAL SPIN CYCLE. RIPPED HER HEAD OFF HER SHOULDERS. IT FLEW AROUND THE SCHOOL FOR WEEKS BEFORE THE GROUNDSMAN SHOT IT DOWN.
WHAT'S THE LESSON WE CAN LEARN FROM THIS, HMM?
WEAR SHINPADS?
DIGNITY! IT'S DIGNITY THAT HOLDS US TOGETHER. SO KEEP YOUR DIGNITY, MR LEE.
HE TOLD ME TO CHECK IN WITH THE SCHOOL NURSE BEFORE I WENT BACK TO MY CLASS.

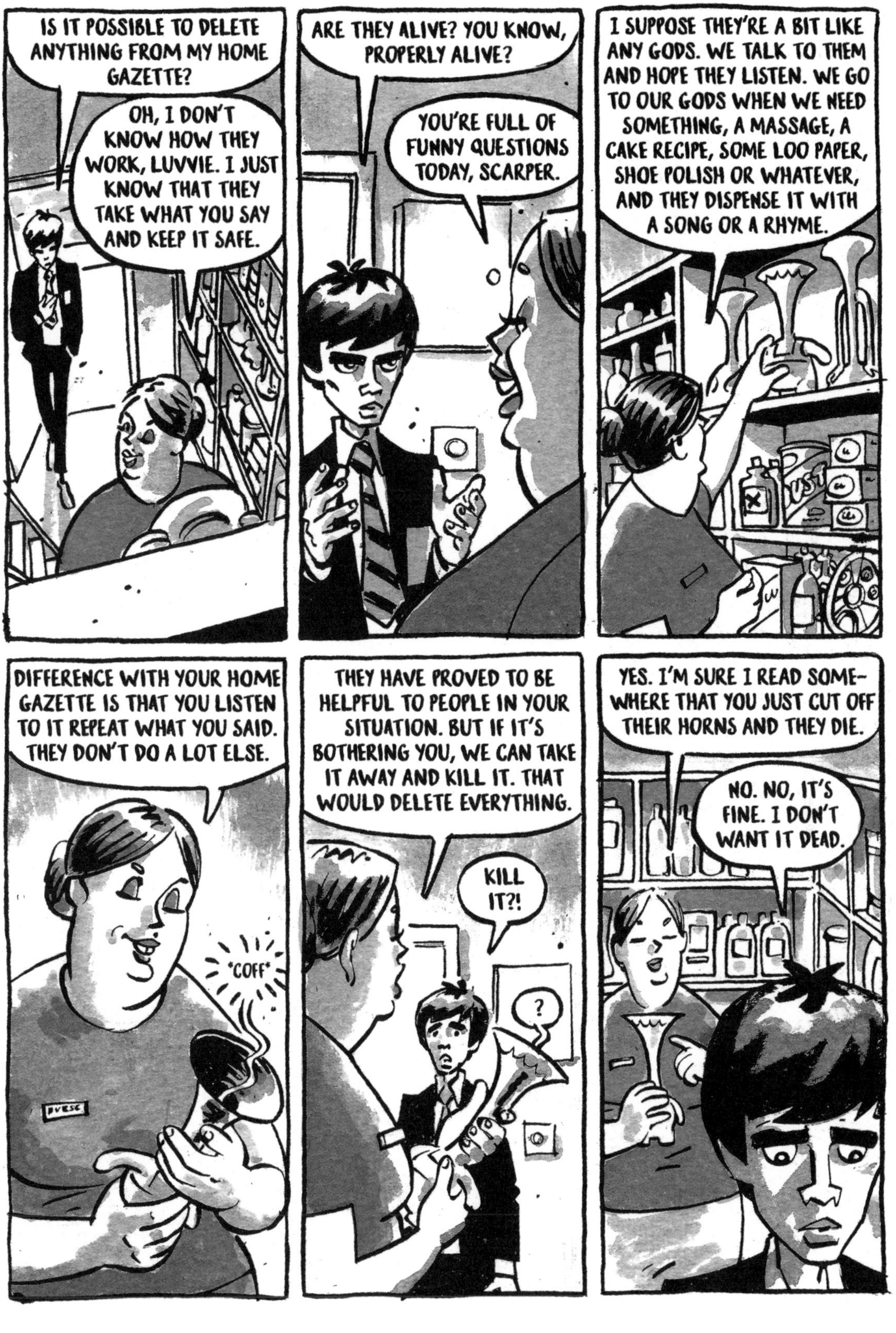
IS IT POSSIBLE TO DELETE ANYTHING FROM MY HOME GAZETTE?
OH, I DON'T KNOW HOW THEY WORK, LUVVIE. I JUST KNOW THAT THEY TAKE WHAT YOU SAY AND KEEP IT SAFE.
ARE THEY ALIVE? YOU KNOW, PROPERLY ALIVE?
YOU'RE FULL OF FUNNY QUESTIONS TODAY, SCARPER.
I SUPPOSE THEY'RE A BIT LIKE ANY GODS. WE TALK TO THEM AND HOPE THEY LISTEN. WE GO TO OUR GODS WHEN WE NEED SOMETHING, A MASSAGE, A CAKE RECIPE, SOME LOO PAPER, SHOE POLISH OR WHATEVER, AND THEY DISPENSE IT WITH A SONG OR A RHYME.
DIFFERENCE WITH YOUR HOME GAZETTE IS THAT YOU LISTEN TO IT REPEAT WHAT YOU SAID. THEY DON'T DO A LOT ELSE.
*COFF*
THEY HAVE PROVED TO BE HELPFUL TO PEOPLE IN YOUR SITUATION. BUT IF IT'S BOTHERING YOU, WE CAN TAKE IT AWAY AND KILL IT. THAT WOULD DELETE EVERYTHING.
KILL IT?!
?
YES. I'M SURE I READ SOMEWHERE THAT YOU JUST CUT OFF THEIR HORNS AND THEY DIE.
NO. NO, IT'S FINE. I DON'T WANT IT DEAD.

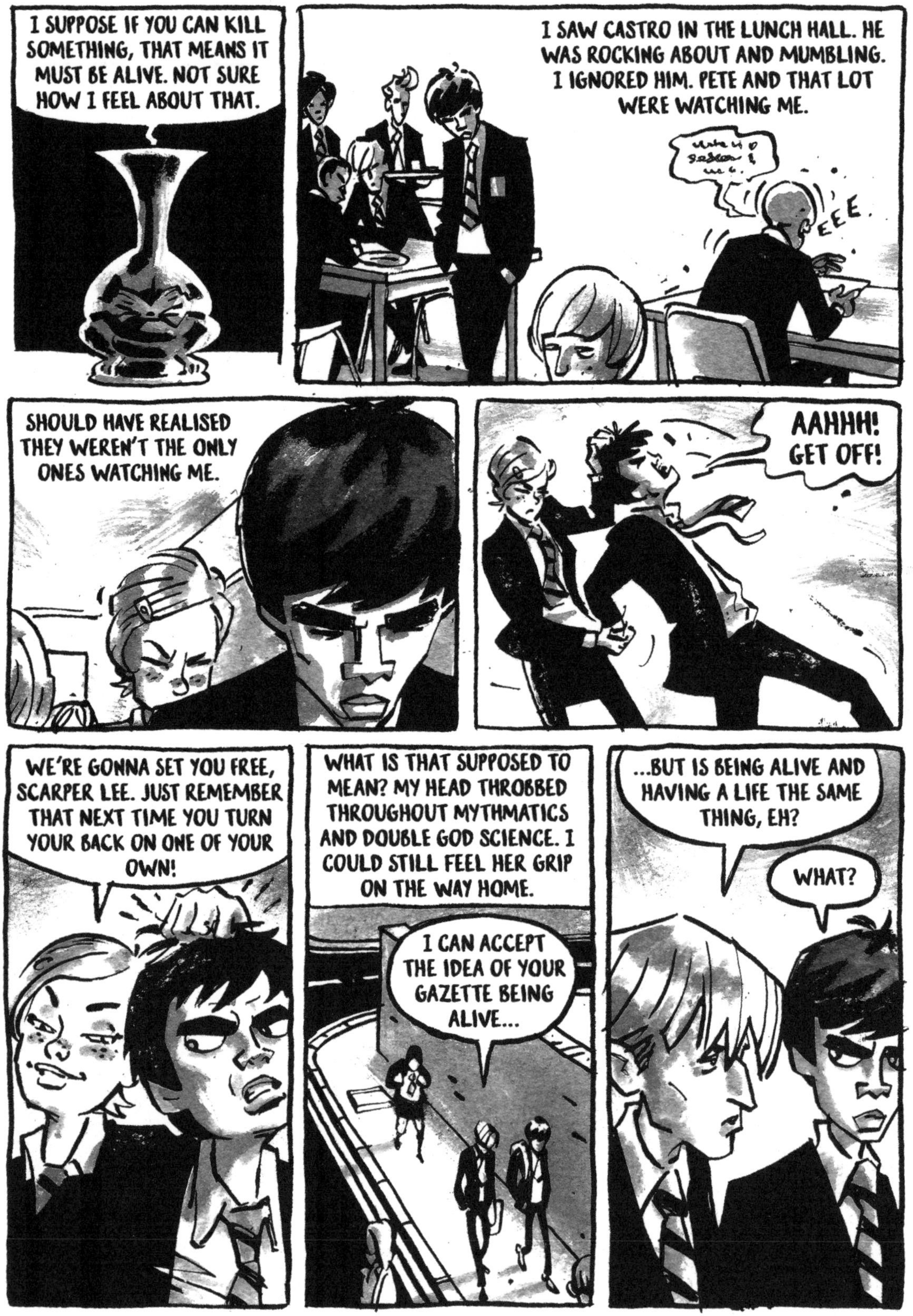
I SUPPOSE IF YOU CAN KILL SOMETHING, THAT MEANS IT MUST BE ALIVE. NOT SURE HOW I FEEL ABOUT THAT.
I SAW CASTRO IN THE LUNCH HALL. HE WAS ROCKING ABOUT AND MUMBLING. I IGNORED HIM. PETE AND THAT LOT WERE WATCHING ME.
EEE
SHOULD HAVE REALISED THEY WEREN'T THE ONLY ONES WATCHING ME.
AAHHH! GET OFF!
WE'RE GONNA SET YOU FREE, SCARPER LEE. JUST REMEMBER THAT NEXT TIME YOU TURN YOUR BACK ON ONE OF YOUR OWN!
WHAT IS THAT SUPPOSED TO MEAN? MY HEAD THROBBED THROUGHOUT MYTHMATICS AND DOUBLE GOD SCIENCE. I COULD STILL FEEL HER GRIP ON THE WAY HOME.
I CAN ACCEPT THE IDEA OF YOUR GAZETTE BEING ALIVE...
...BUT IS BEING ALIVE AND HAVING A LIFE THE SAME THING, EH?
WHAT?

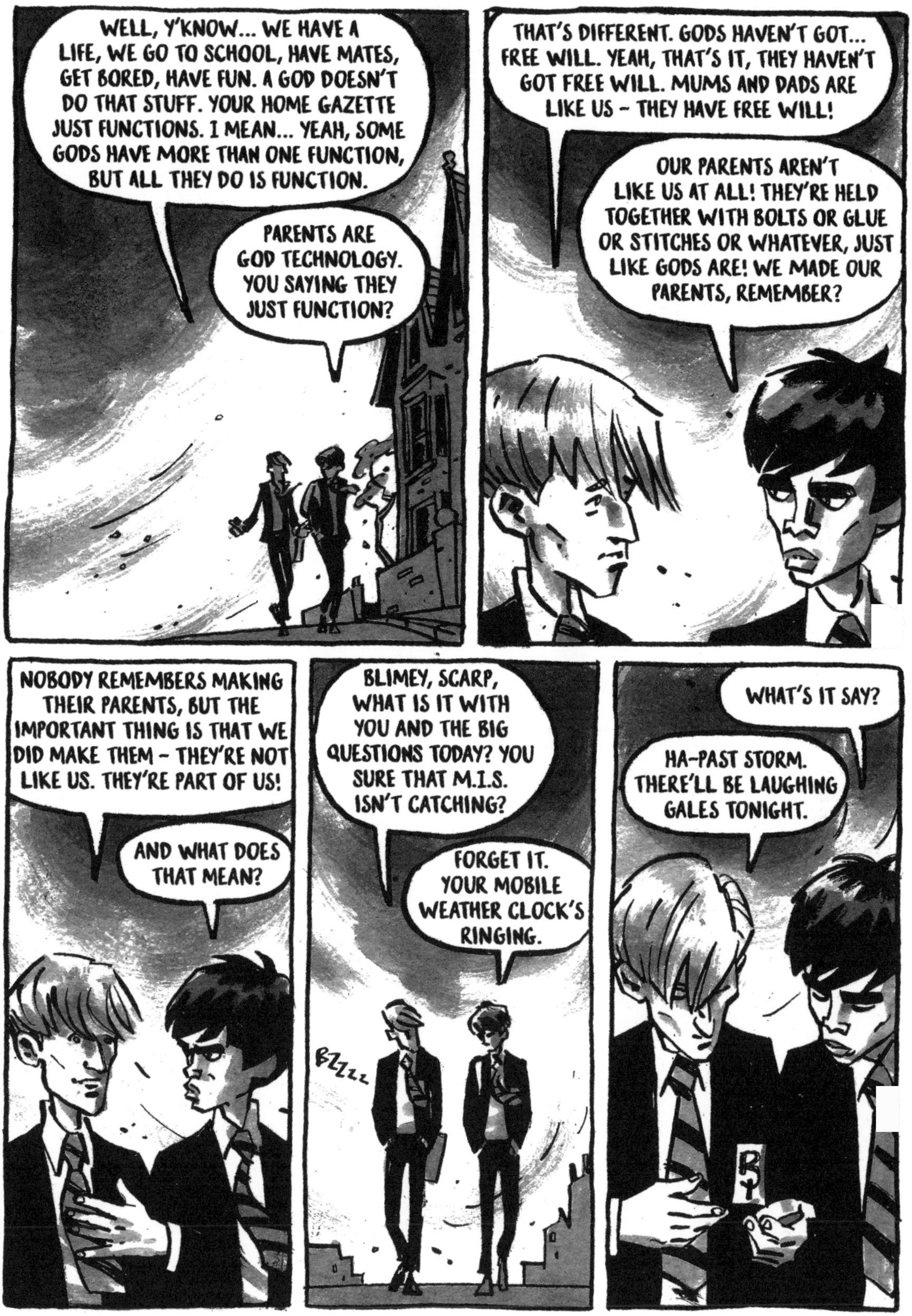
WELL, Y'KNOW... WE HAVE A LIFE, WE GO TO SCHOOL, HAVE MATES, GET BORED, HAVE FUN. A GOD DOESN'T DO THAT STUFF. YOUR HOME GAZETTE JUST FUNCTIONS. I MEAN... YEAH, SOME GODS HAVE MORE THAN ONE FUNCTION, BUT ALL THEY DO IS FUNCTION.
PARENTS ARE GOD TECHNOLOGY. YOU SAYING THEY JUST FUNCTION?
THAT'S DIFFERENT. GODS HAVEN'T GOT... FREE WILL. YEAH, THAT'S IT, THEY HAVEN'T GOT FREE WILL. MUMS AND DADS ARE LIKE US – THEY HAVE FREE WILL!
OUR PARENTS AREN'T LIKE US AT ALL! THEY'RE HELD TOGETHER WITH BOLTS OR GLUE OR STITCHES OR WHATEVER, JUST LIKE GODS ARE! WE MADE OUR PARENTS, REMEMBER?
NOBODY REMEMBERS MAKING THEIR PARENTS, BUT THE IMPORTANT THING IS THAT WE DID MAKE THEM – THEY'RE NOT LIKE US. THEY'RE PART OF US!
AND WHAT DOES THAT MEAN?
BLIMEY, SCARP, WHAT IS IT WITH YOU AND THE BIG QUESTIONS TODAY? YOU SURE THAT M.I.S. ISN'T CATCHING?
FORGET IT. YOUR MOBILE WEATHER CLOCK'S RINGING.
BZZzzz
WHAT'S IT SAY?
HA-PAST STORM. THERE'LL BE LAUGHING GALES TONIGHT.

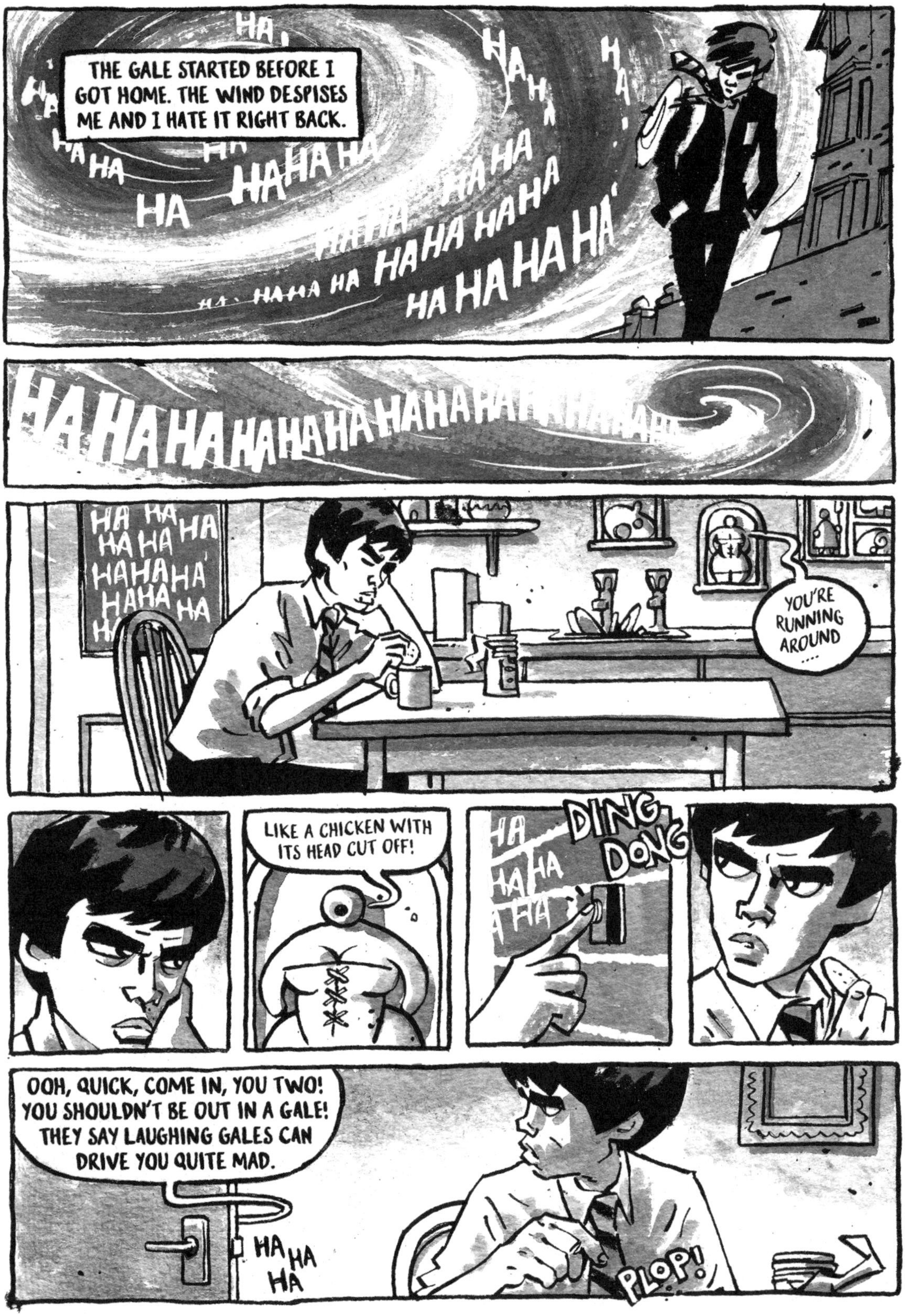
THE GALE STARTED BEFORE I GOT HOME. THE WIND DESPISES ME AND I HATE IT RIGHT BACK.
HA HA HA HAHAHA HA HAHA HA HAHA HAHAHA HAHA HA HAHAHAHA
HA HA HA HAHAHA HAHAHA
HA HA HA HA HA HA HAHA HA HAHA HA
YOU'RE RUNNING AROUND ....
LIKE A CHICKEN WITH ITS HEAD CUT OFF!
DING DONG
OOH, QUICK, COME IN, YOU TWO! YOU SHOULDN'T BE OUT IN A GALE! THEY SAY LAUGHING GALES CAN DRIVE YOU QUITE MAD.
HA HA HA
PLOP!

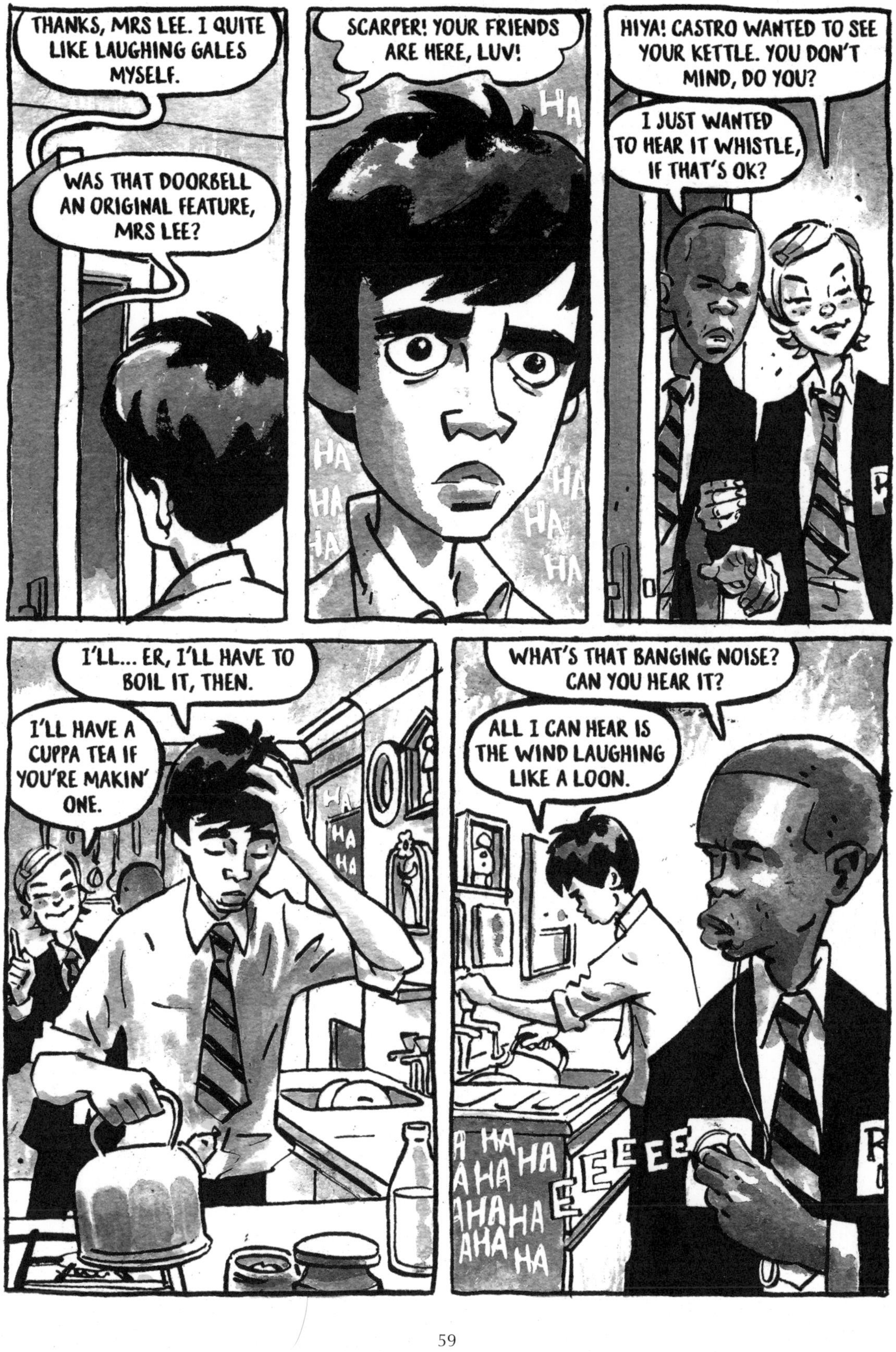
THANKS, MRS LEE. I QUITE LIKE LAUGHING GALES MYSELF.
WAS THAT DOORBELL AN ORIGINAL FEATURE, MRS LEE?
SCARPER! YOUR FRIENDS ARE HERE, LUV!
HA
HA HA HA
HA HA HA
HIYA! CASTRO WANTED TO SEE YOUR KETTLE. YOU DON'T MIND, DO YOU?
I JUST WANTED TO HEAR IT WHISTLE, IF THAT'S OK?
I'LL... ER, I'LL HAVE TO BOIL IT, THEN.
I'LL HAVE A CUPPA TEA IF YOU'RE MAKIN' ONE.
HA HA HA
WHAT'S THAT BANGING NOISE? CAN YOU HEAR IT?
ALL I CAN HEAR IS THE WIND LAUGHING LIKE A LOON.
EEEEEE

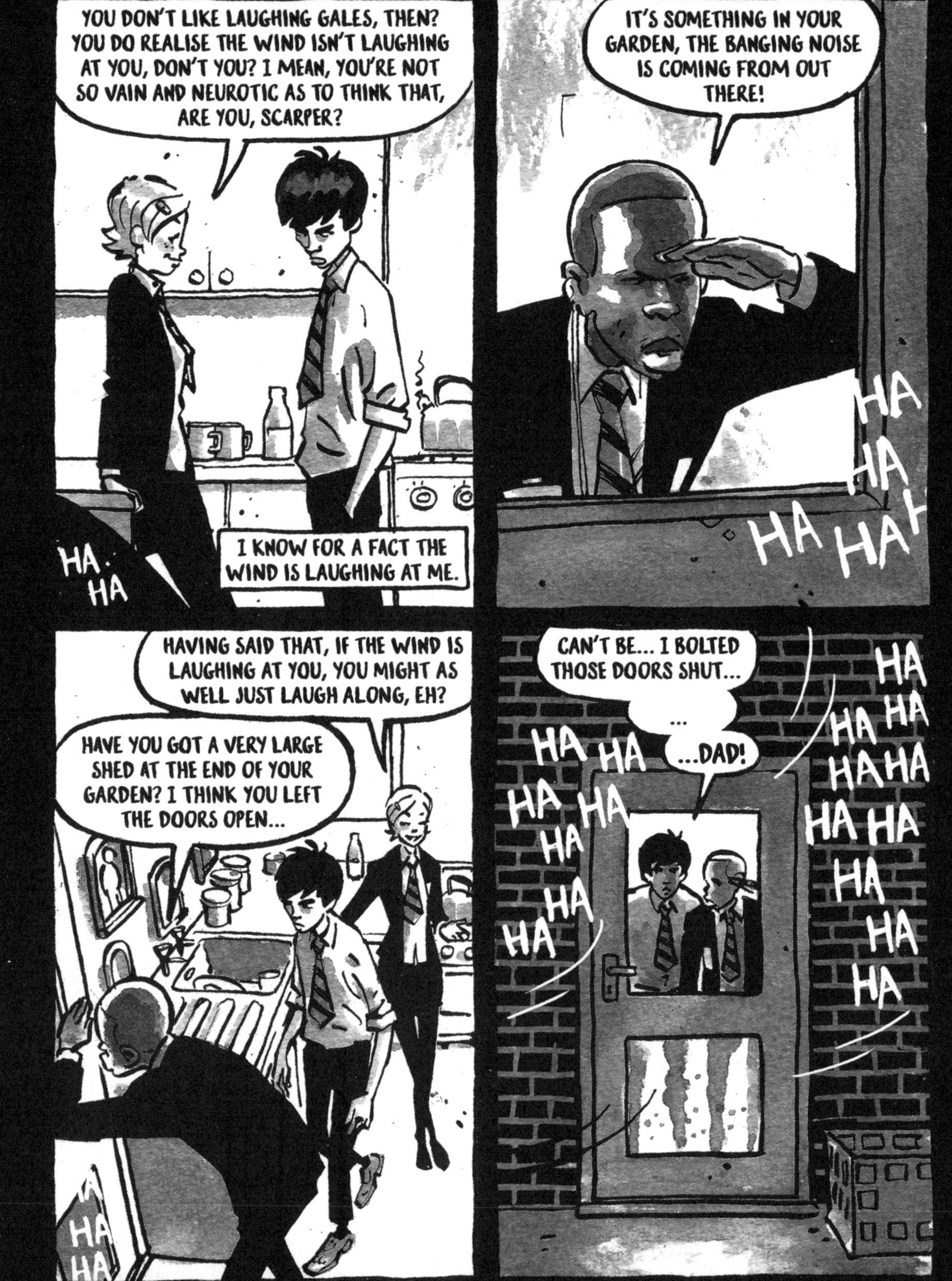

YOU DON'T LIKE LAUGHING GALES, THEN? YOU DO REALISE THE WIND ISN'T LAUGHING AT YOU, DON'T YOU? I MEAN, YOU'RE NOT SO VAIN AND NEUROTIC AS TO THINK THAT, ARE YOU, SCARPER?
I KNOW FOR A FACT THE WIND IS LAUGHING AT ME.
HA HA
IT'S SOMETHING IN YOUR GARDEN, THE BANGING NOISE IS COMING FROM OUT THERE!
HA HA HA HA HA
HAVING SAID THAT, IF THE WIND IS LAUGHING AT YOU, YOU MIGHT AS WELL JUST LAUGH ALONG, EH?
HAVE YOU GOT A VERY LARGE SHED AT THE END OF YOUR GARDEN? I THINK YOU LEFT THE DOORS OPEN...
HA HA
CAN'T BE... I BOLTED THOSE DOORS SHUT...
...
...DAD!
HA HA HA HA HA HA HA HA HA
HA HA HA HA HA HA HA HA HA HA HA HA

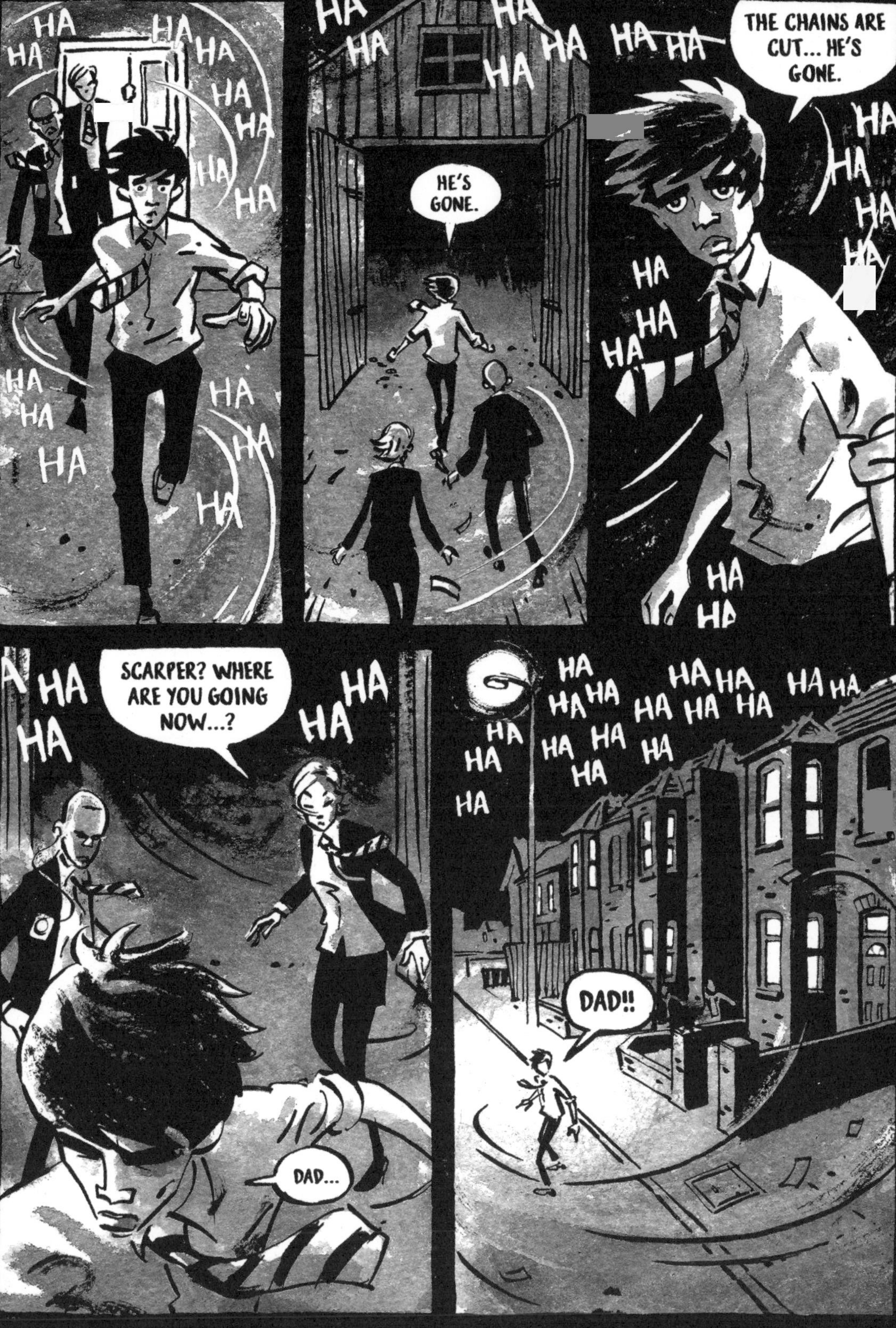
HA HA HA HA HA HA HA HA HA HA
HA HA HA HA HA HA
HA HA HA HA HA HA HA HA
HE'S GONE.
HA HA HA
THE CHAINS ARE CUT... HE'S GONE.
HA HA HA HA HA HA HA HA HA HA
HA HA HA HA HA
SCARPER? WHERE ARE YOU GOING NOW...?
DAD...
HA HA HA HA HA HA HA HA HA HA HA HA HA HA HA HA HA HA
DAD!!

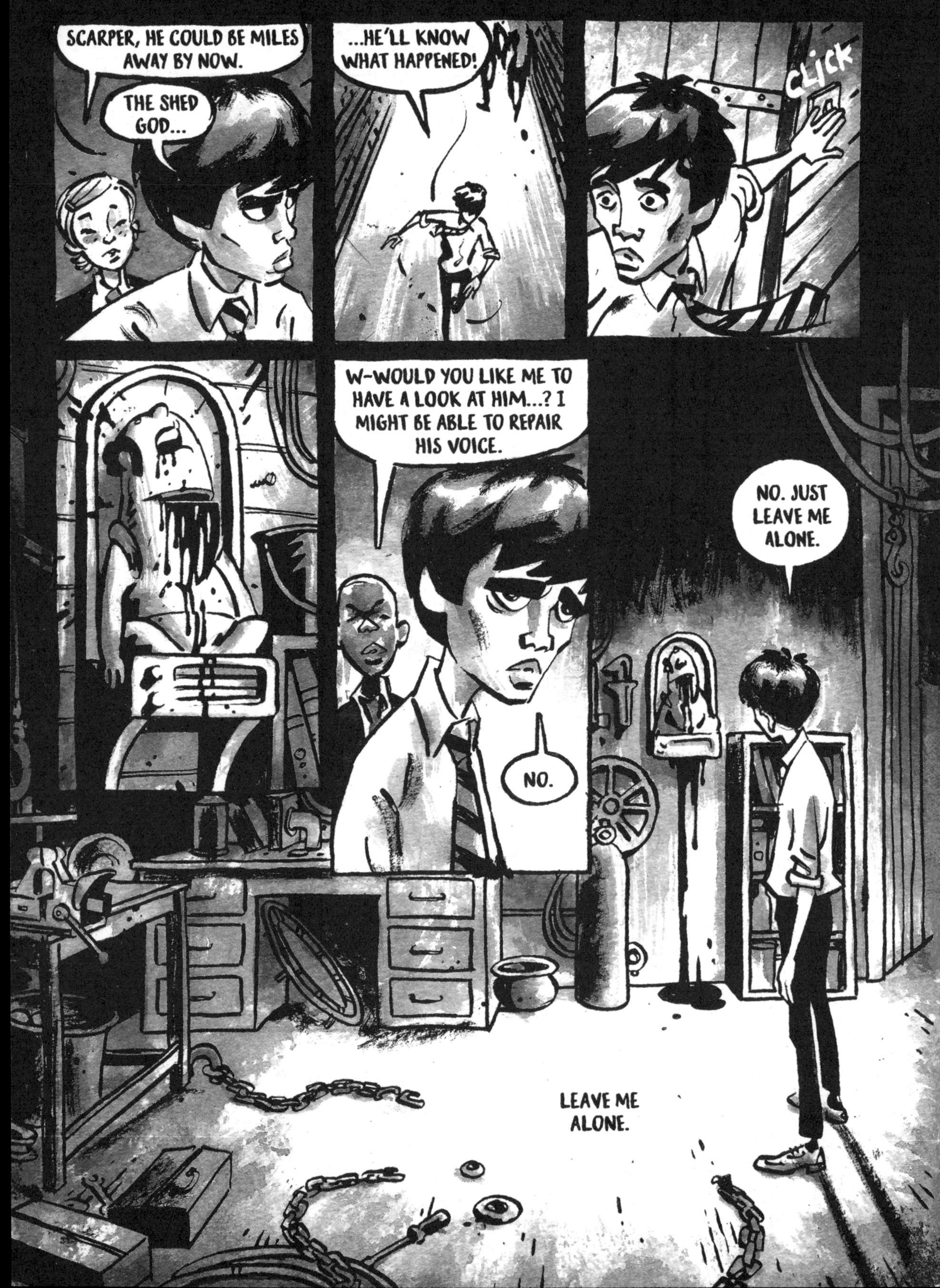
SCARPER, HE COULD BE MILES AWAY BY NOW.
THE SHED GOD...
...HE'LL KNOW WHAT HAPPENED!
CLICK
W-WOULD YOU LIKE ME TO HAVE A LOOK AT HIM...? I MIGHT BE ABLE TO REPAIR HIS VOICE.
NO.
NO. JUST LEAVE ME ALONE.
LEAVE ME ALONE.

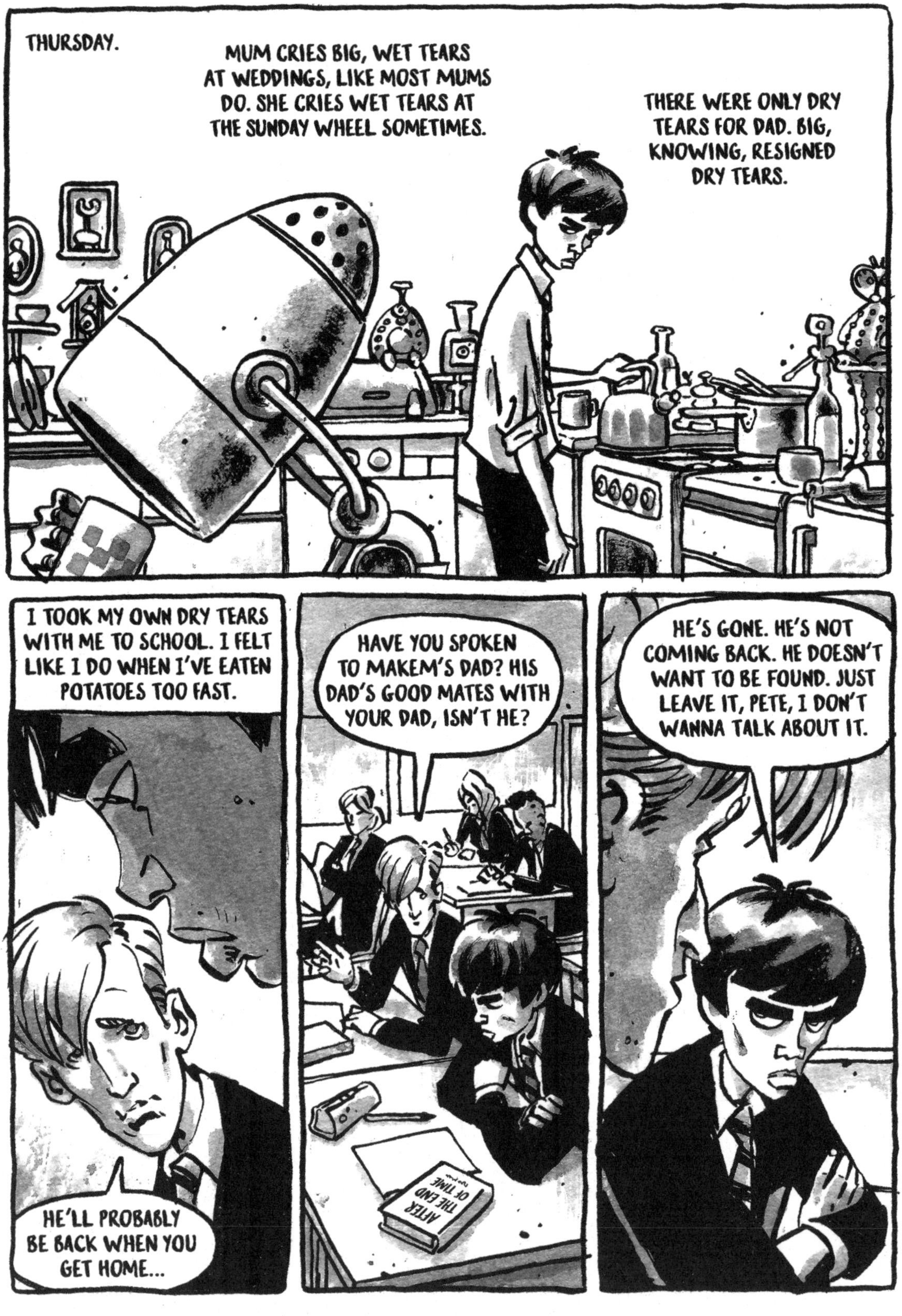
THURSDAY.
MUM CRIES BIG, WET TEARS AT WEDDINGS, LIKE MOST MUMS DO. SHE CRIES WET TEARS AT THE SUNDAY WHEEL SOMETIMES.
THERE WERE ONLY DRY TEARS FOR DAD. BIG, KNOWING, RESIGNED DRY TEARS.
I TOOK MY OWN DRY TEARS WITH ME TO SCHOOL. I FELT LIKE I DO WHEN I'VE EATEN POTATOES TOO FAST.
HE'LL PROBABLY BE BACK WHEN YOU GET HOME...
HAVE YOU SPOKEN TO MAKEM'S DAD? HIS DAD'S GOOD MATES WITH YOUR DAD, ISN'T HE?
AFTER THE END OF TIME
HE'S GONE. HE'S NOT COMING BACK. HE DOESN'T WANT TO BE FOUND. JUST LEAVE IT, PETE, I DON'T WANNA TALK ABOUT IT.

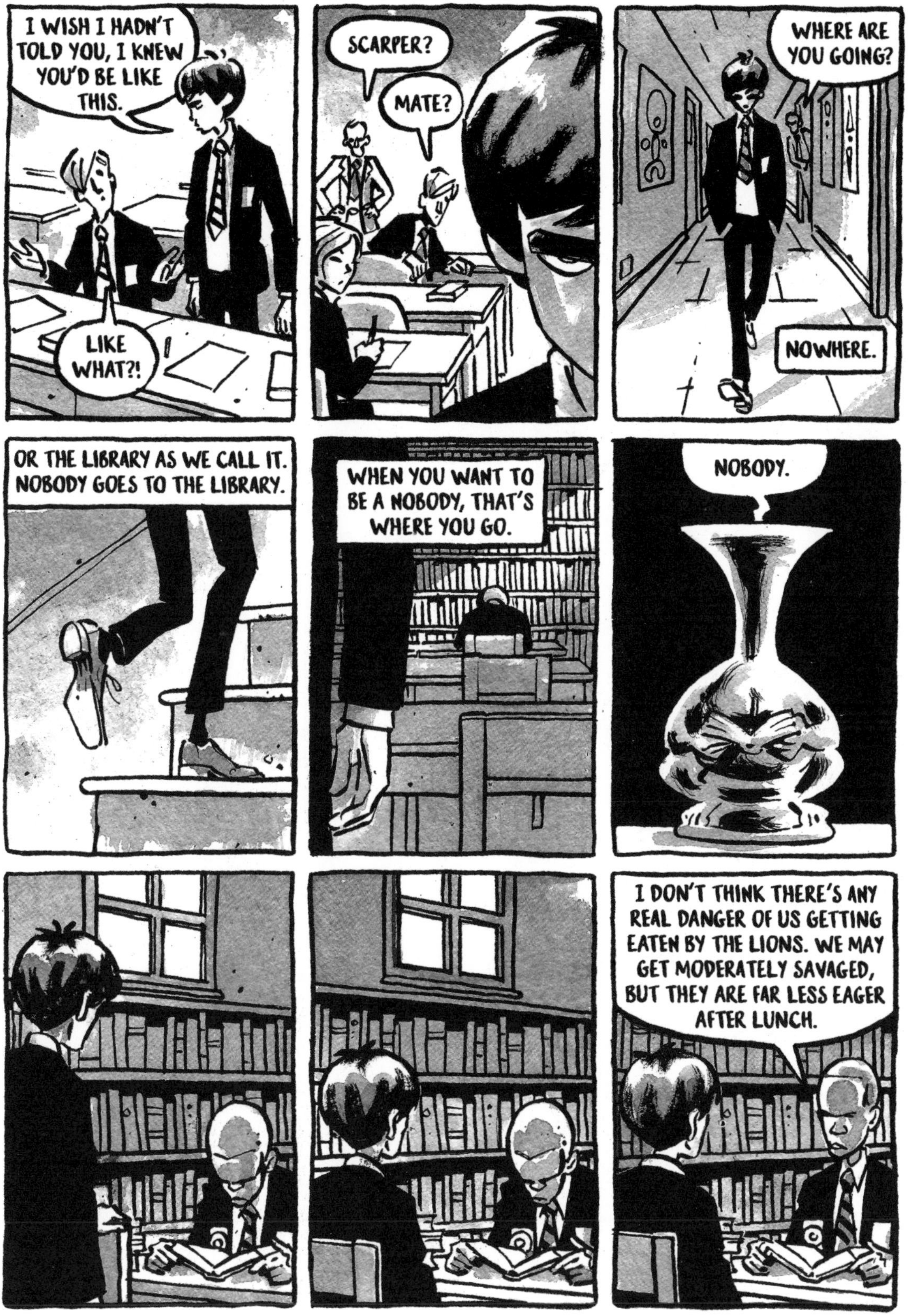
I WISH I HADN'T TOLD YOU, I KNEW YOU'D BE LIKE THIS.
LIKE WHAT?!
SCARPER?
MATE?
WHERE ARE YOU GOING?
NOWHERE.
OR THE LIBRARY AS WE CALL IT. NOBODY GOES TO THE LIBRARY.
WHEN YOU WANT TO BE A NOBODY, THAT'S WHERE YOU GO.
NOBODY.
I DON'T THINK THERE'S ANY REAL DANGER OF US GETTING EATEN BY THE LIONS. WE MAY GET MODERATELY SAVAGED, BUT THEY ARE FAR LESS EAGER AFTER LUNCH.

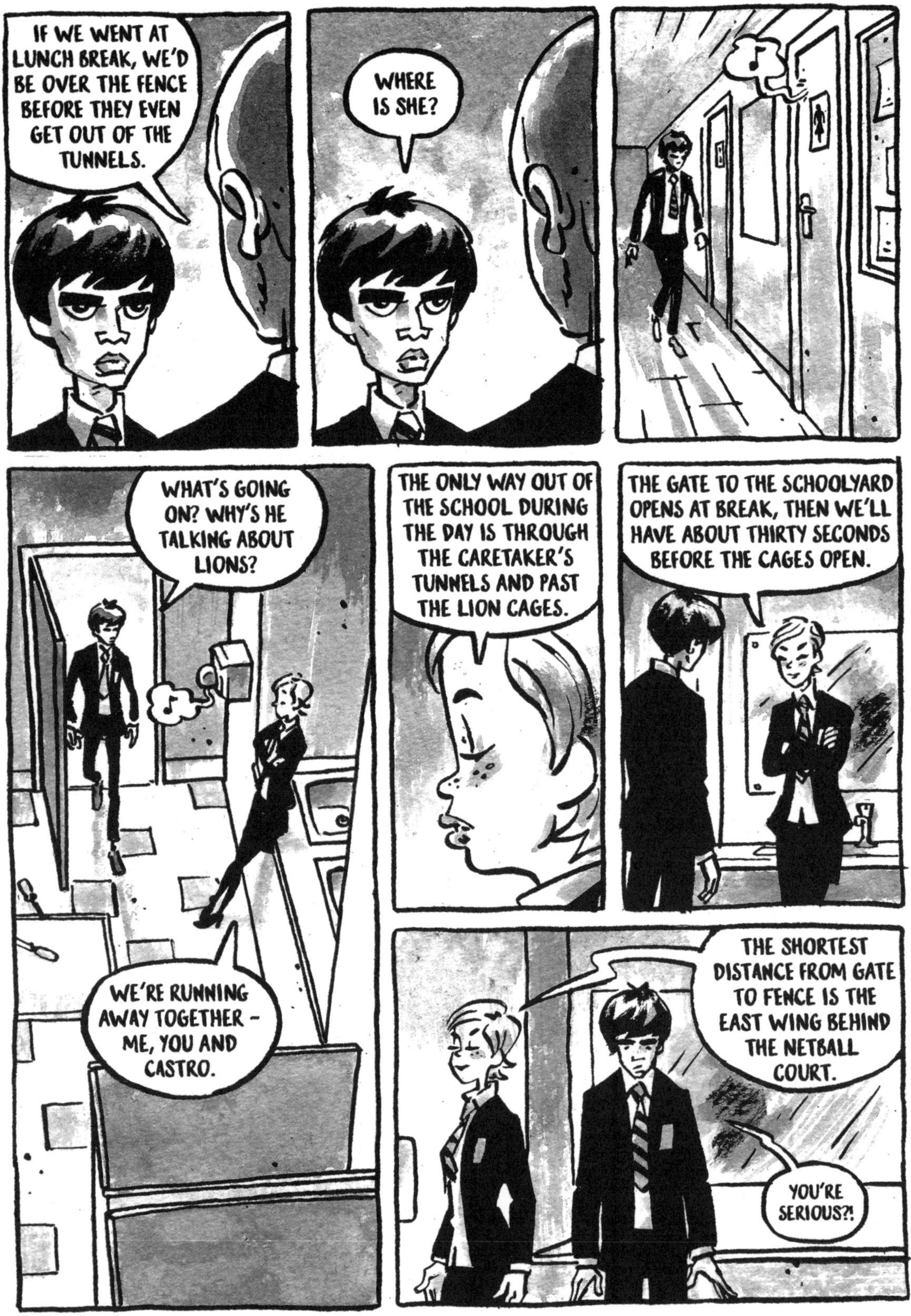
IF WE WENT AT LUNCH BREAK, WE'D BE OVER THE FENCE BEFORE THEY EVEN GET OUT OF THE TUNNELS.
WHERE IS SHE?
WHAT'S GOING ON? WHY'S HE TALKING ABOUT LIONS?
WE'RE RUNNING AWAY TOGETHER – ME, YOU AND CASTRO.
THE ONLY WAY OUT OF THE SCHOOL DURING THE DAY IS THROUGH THE CARETAKER'S TUNNELS AND PAST THE LION CAGES.
THE GATE TO THE SCHOOLYARD OPENS AT BREAK, THEN WE'LL HAVE ABOUT THIRTY SECONDS BEFORE THE CAGES OPEN.
THE SHORTEST DISTANCE FROM GATE TO FENCE IS THE EAST WING BEHIND THE NETBALL COURT.
YOU'RE SERIOUS?!

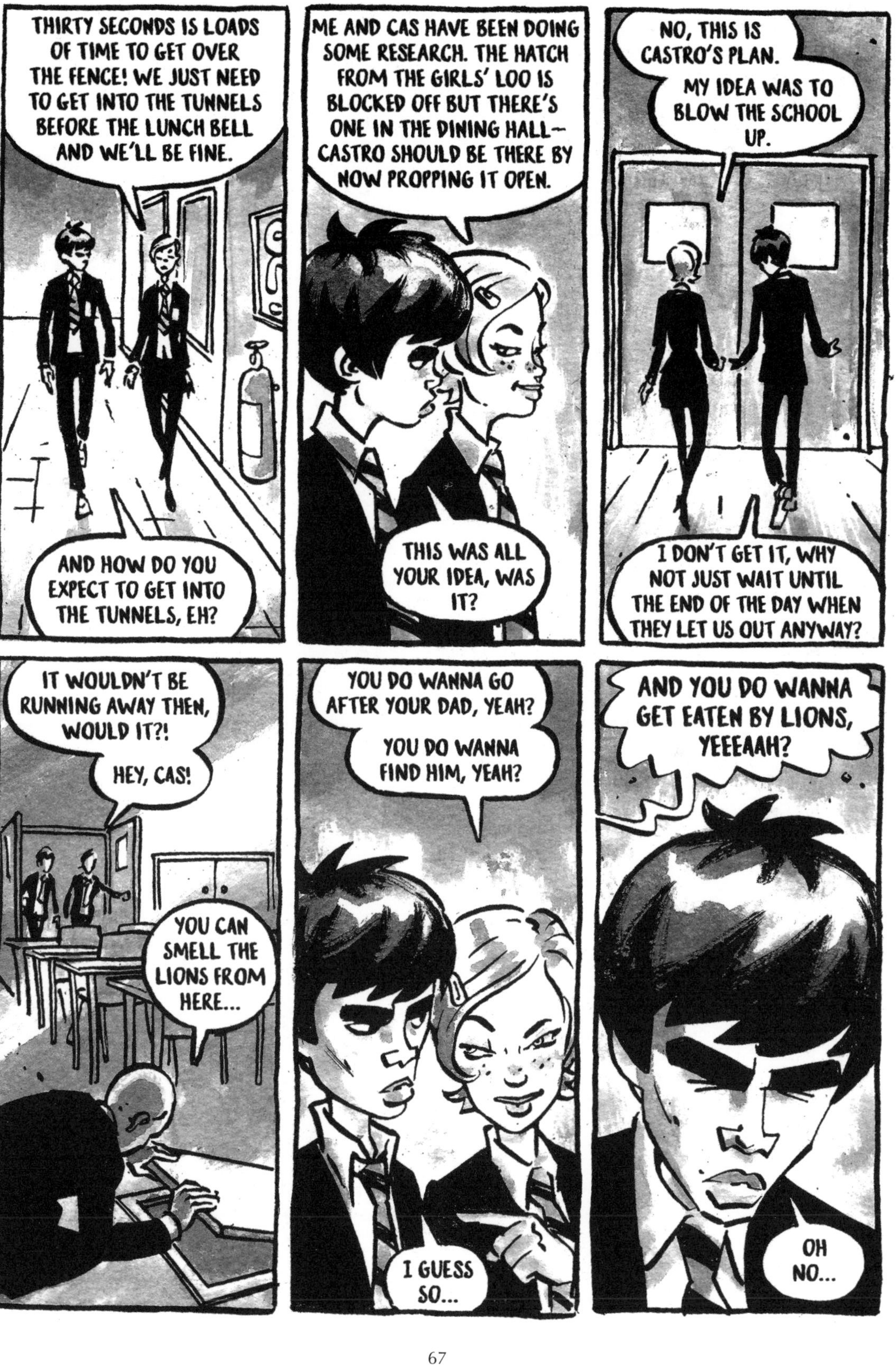
THIRTY SECONDS IS LOADS OF TIME TO GET OVER THE FENCE! WE JUST NEED TO GET INTO THE TUNNELS BEFORE THE LUNCH BELL AND WE'LL BE FINE.
AND HOW DO YOU EXPECT TO GET INTO THE TUNNELS, EH?
ME AND CAS HAVE BEEN DOING SOME RESEARCH. THE HATCH FROM THE GIRLS' LOO IS BLOCKED OFF BUT THERE'S ONE IN THE DINING HALL— CASTRO SHOULD BE THERE BY NOW PROPPING IT OPEN.
THIS WAS ALL YOUR IDEA, WAS IT?
NO, THIS IS CASTRO'S PLAN.
MY IDEA WAS TO BLOW THE SCHOOL UP.
I DON'T GET IT, WHY NOT JUST WAIT UNTIL THE END OF THE DAY WHEN THEY LET US OUT ANYWAY?
IT WOULDN'T BE RUNNING AWAY THEN, WOULD IT?!
HEY, CAS!
YOU CAN SMELL THE LIONS FROM HERE...
YOU DO WANNA GO AFTER YOUR DAD, YEAH?
YOU DO WANNA FIND HIM, YEAH?
I GUESS SO...
AND YOU DO WANNA GET EATEN BY LIONS, YEEEAAH?
OH NO...

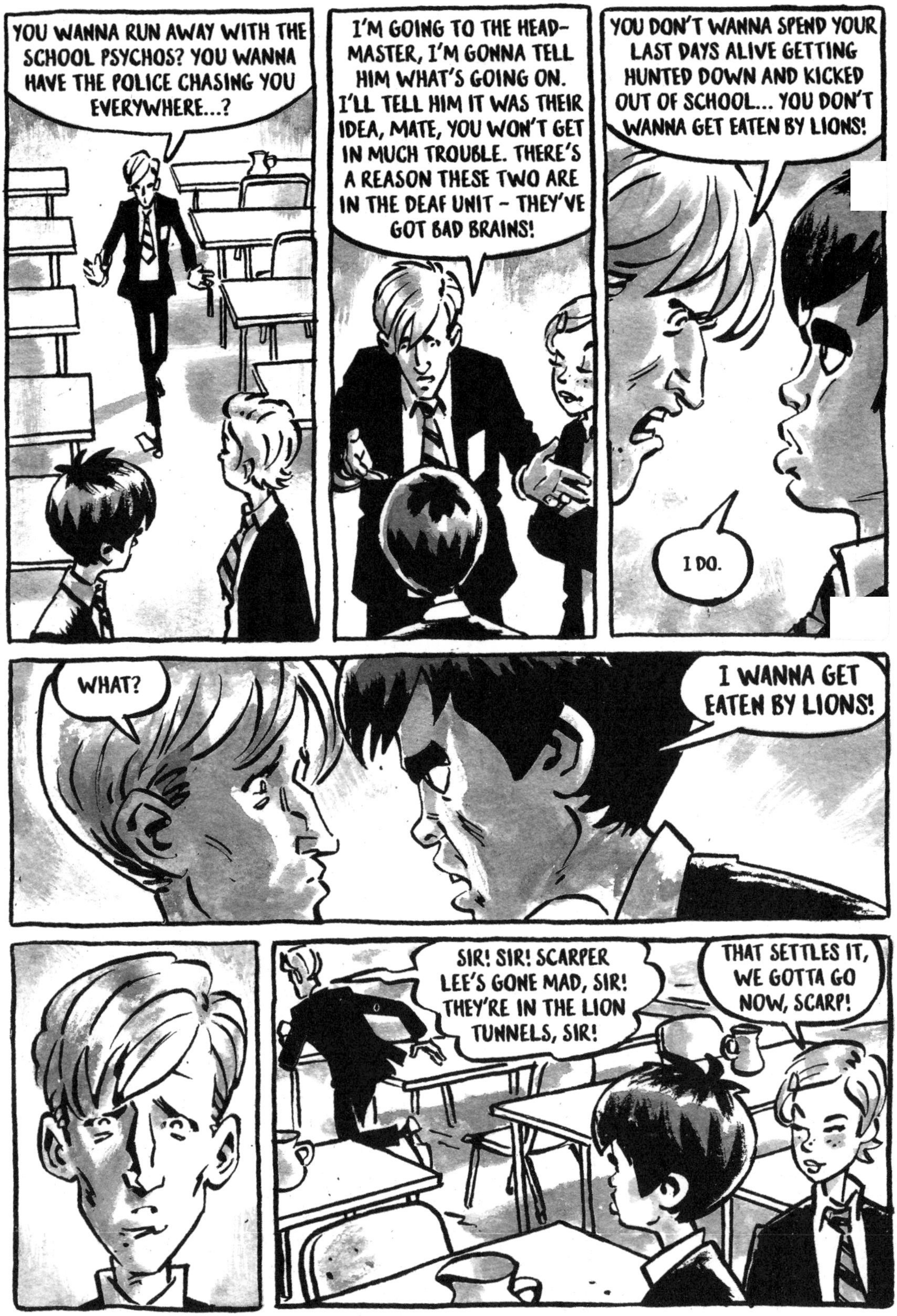
YOU WANNA RUN AWAY WITH THE SCHOOL PSYCHOS? YOU WANNA HAVE THE POLICE CHASING YOU EVERYWHERE...?
I'M GOING TO THE HEAD-MASTER, I'M GONNA TELL HIM WHAT'S GOING ON. I'LL TELL HIM IT WAS THEIR IDEA, MATE, YOU WON'T GET IN MUCH TROUBLE. THERE'S A REASON THESE TWO ARE IN THE DEAF UNIT – THEY'VE GOT BAD BRAINS!
YOU DON'T WANNA SPEND YOUR LAST DAYS ALIVE GETTING HUNTED DOWN AND KICKED OUT OF SCHOOL... YOU DON'T WANNA GET EATEN BY LIONS!
I DO.
WHAT?
I WANNA GET EATEN BY LIONS!
SIR! SIR! SCARPER LEE'S GONE MAD, SIR! THEY'RE IN THE LION TUNNELS, SIR!
THAT SETTLES IT, WE GOTTA GO NOW, SCARP!

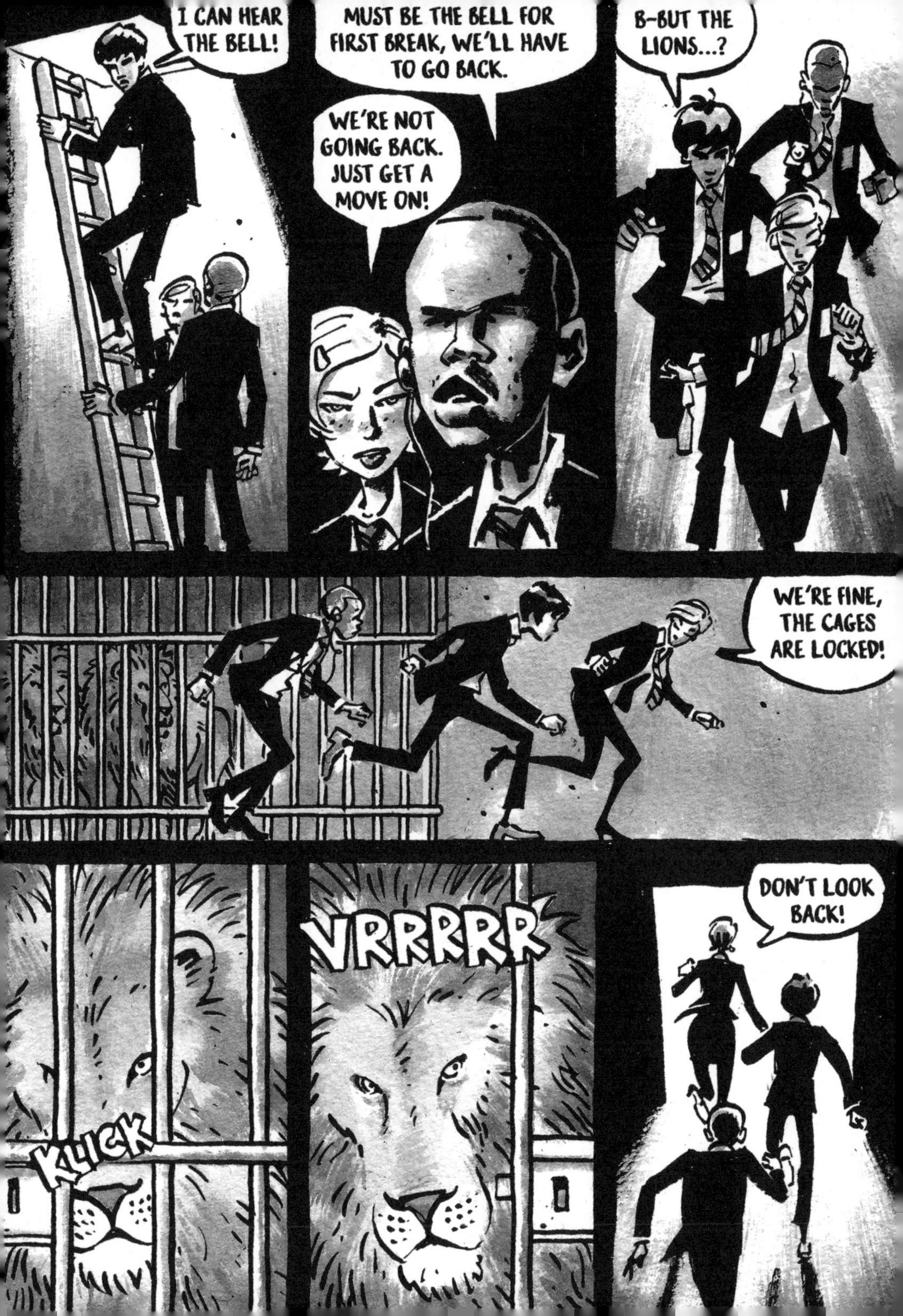
I CAN HEAR THE BELL!
MUST BE THE BELL FOR FIRST BREAK, WE'LL HAVE TO GO BACK.
WE'RE NOT GOING BACK. JUST GET A MOVE ON!
B-BUT THE LIONS...?
WE'RE FINE, THE CAGES ARE LOCKED!
KLICK
VRRRRR
DON'T LOOK BACK!

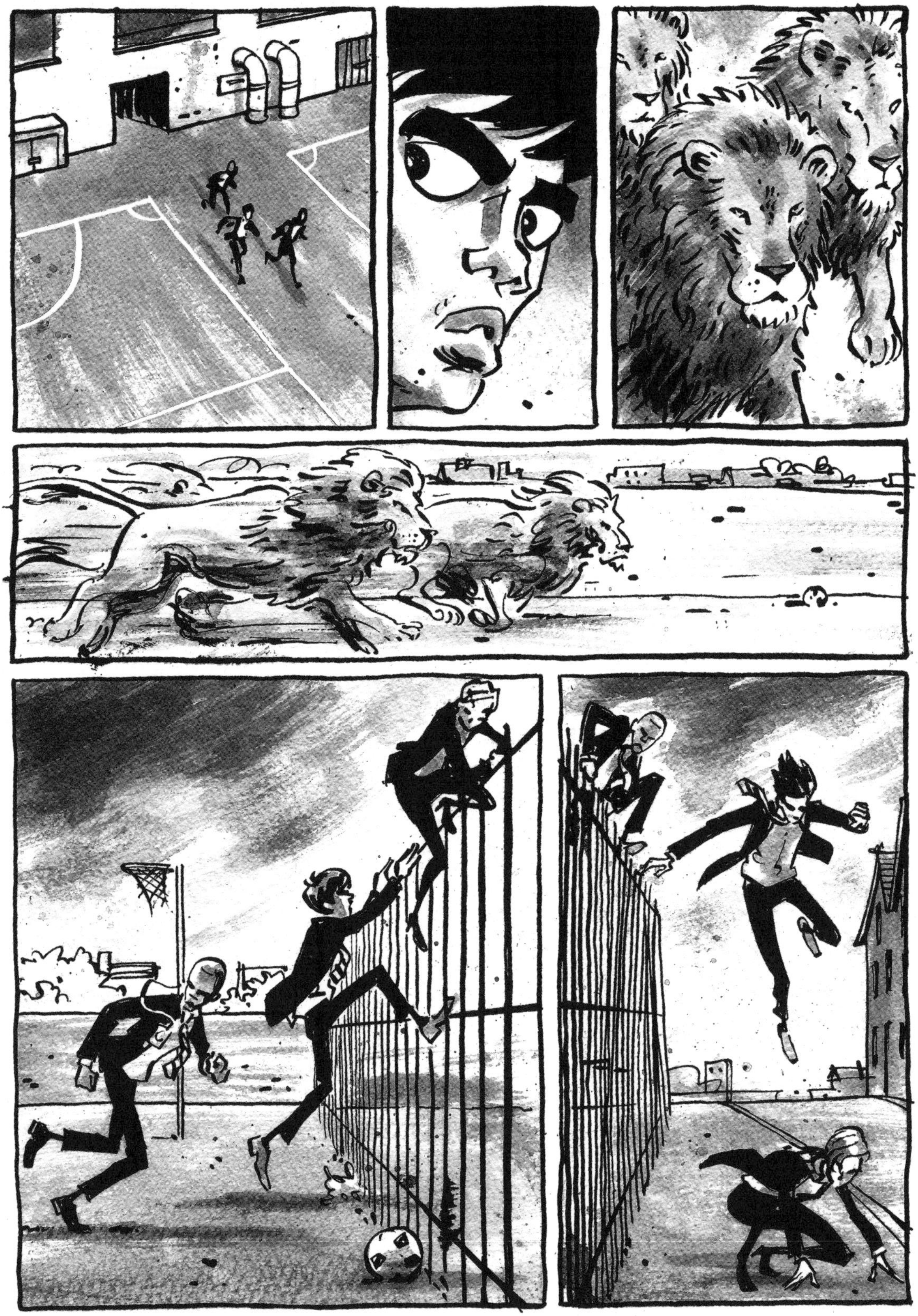

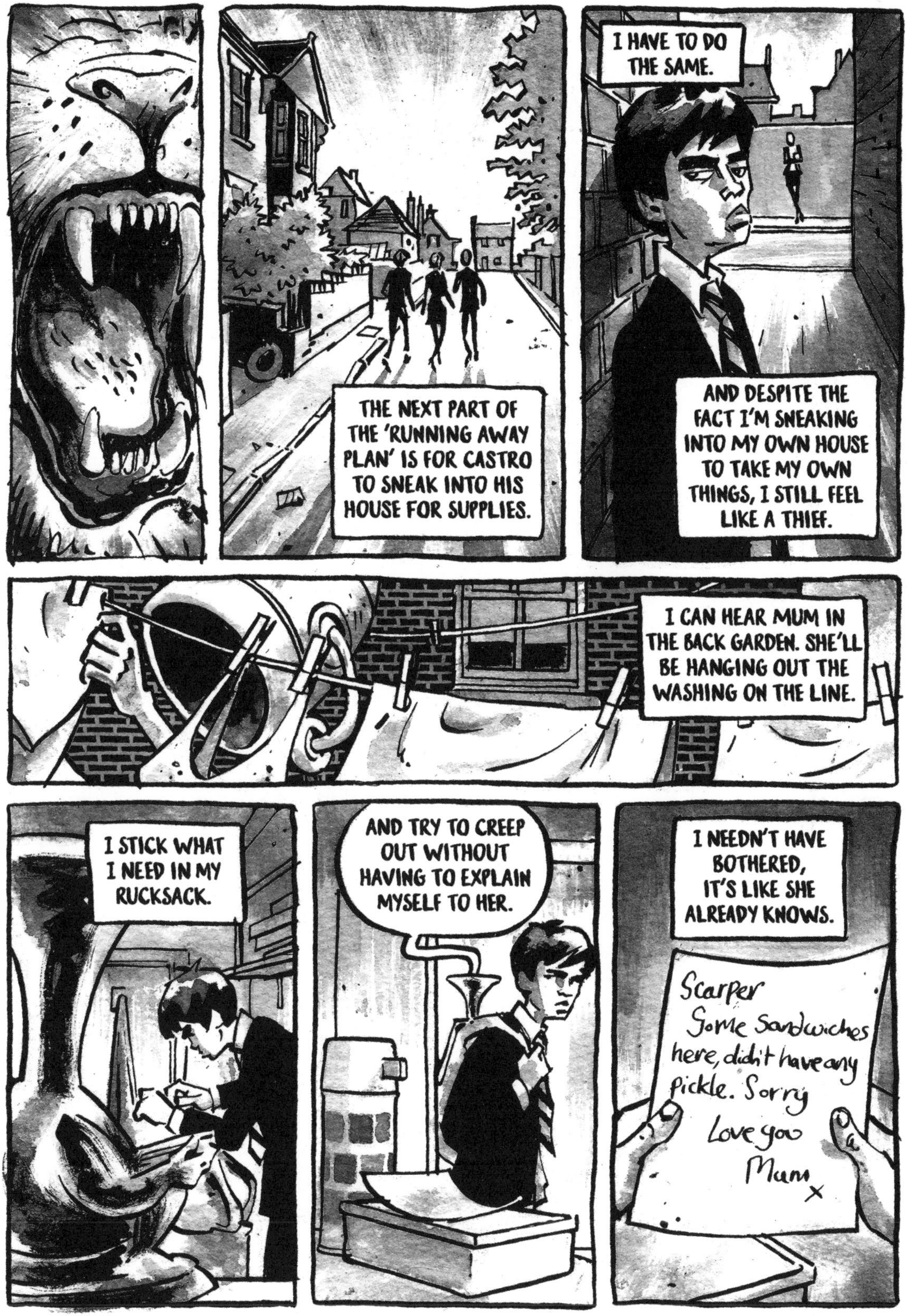
THE NEXT PART OF THE 'RUNNING AWAY PLAN' IS FOR CASTRO TO SNEAK INTO HIS HOUSE FOR SUPPLIES.
I HAVE TO DO THE SAME.
AND DESPITE THE FACT I'M SNEAKING INTO MY OWN HOUSE TO TAKE MY OWN THINGS, I STILL FEEL LIKE A THIEF.
I CAN HEAR MUM IN THE BACK GARDEN. SHE'LL BE HANGING OUT THE WASHING ON THE LINE.
I STICK WHAT I NEED IN MY RUCKSACK.
AND TRY TO CREEP OUT WITHOUT HAVING TO EXPLAIN MYSELF TO HER.
I NEEDN'T HAVE BOTHERED, IT'S LIKE SHE ALREADY KNOWS.
Scarper
Some sandwiches here, didn't have any pickle. Sorry
Love you
Mum x

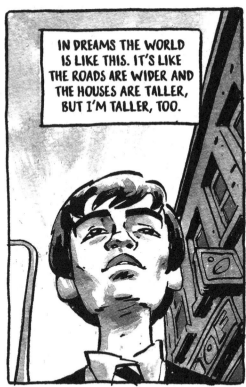

IN DREAMS THE WORLD IS LIKE THIS. IT'S LIKE THE ROADS ARE WIDER AND THE HOUSES ARE TALLER, BUT I'M TALLER, TOO.

CASTRO IS EXCITED.

THIS IS THE OUTSIDE — OUTSIDE OF SCHOOL — OUTSIDE OF SCHOOLING... UNSCHOOL... UNSIDE INSIDE MYSELF WITH GLEE I'M UNSIDE THE OUTSIDE WITH ME!

SHOULDN'T WE TURN HIM DOWN?

WE'RE GETTING A FEW FUNNY LOOKS.

SOD 'EM.

SOD YOU!

YOU TELL 'EM VERU! UNSCHOOL THEIR UNSIDES!

I WOULDN'T LET MY DAUGHTER SPEAK TO ME LIKE THAT!

SHOULD BE IN SCHOOL!

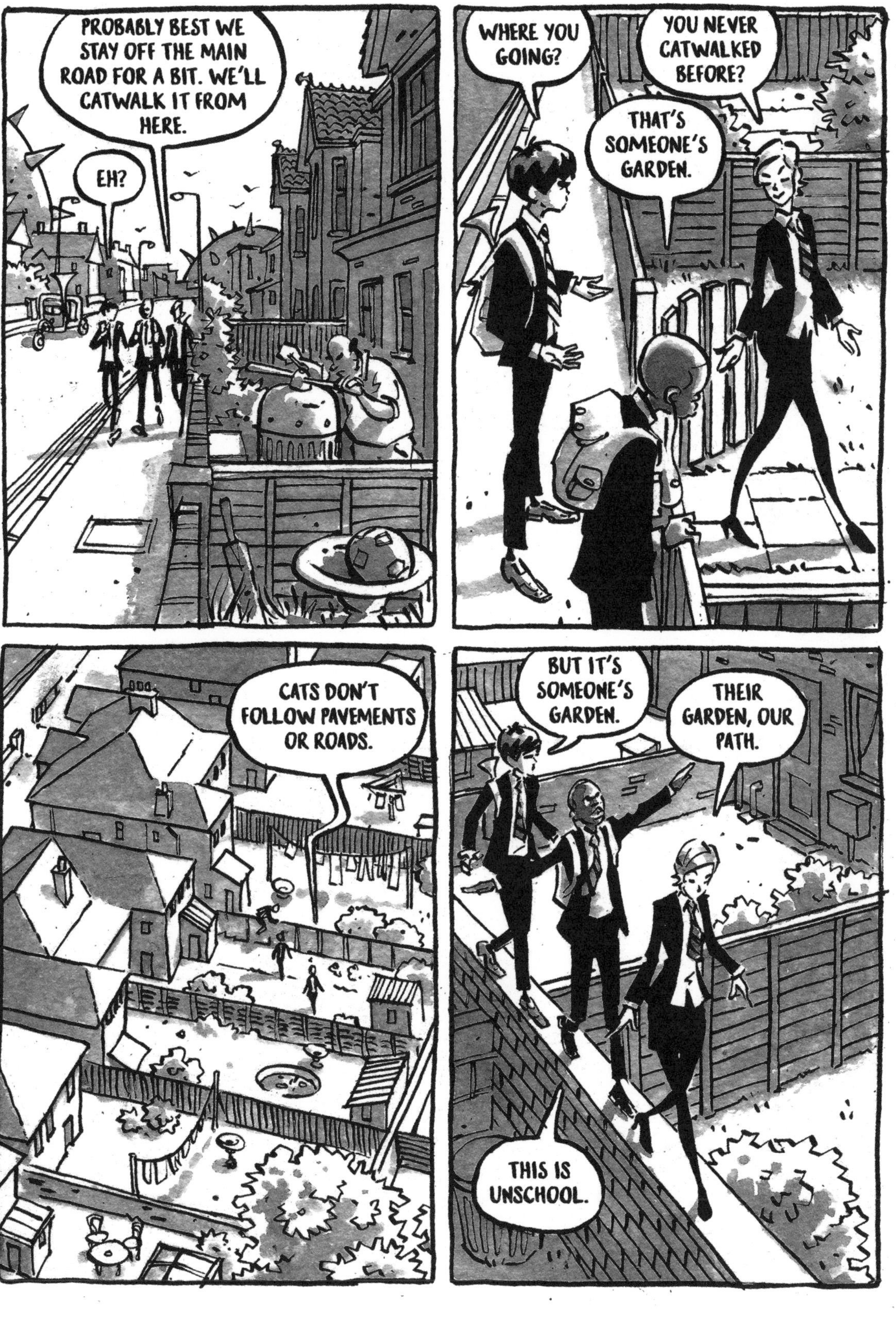
PROBABLY BEST WE STAY OFF THE MAIN ROAD FOR A BIT. WE'LL CATWALK IT FROM HERE.
EH?
WHERE YOU GOING?
YOU NEVER CATWALKED BEFORE?
THAT'S SOMEONE'S GARDEN.
CATS DON'T FOLLOW PAVEMENTS OR ROADS.
BUT IT'S SOMEONE'S GARDEN.
THEIR GARDEN, OUR PATH.
THIS IS UNSCHOOL.

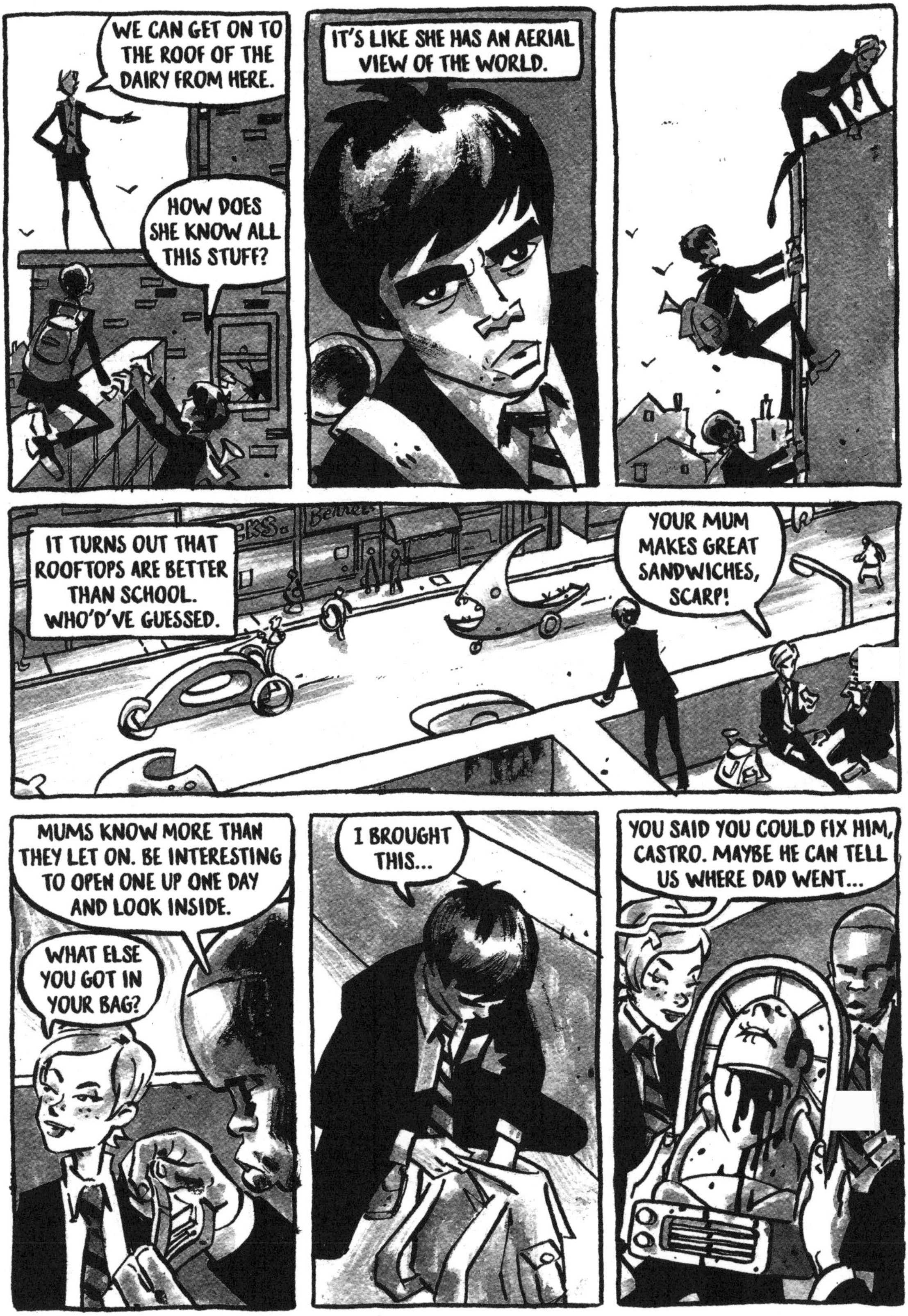
WE CAN GET ON TO THE ROOF OF THE DAIRY FROM HERE.
HOW DOES SHE KNOW ALL THIS STUFF?
IT'S LIKE SHE HAS AN AERIAL VIEW OF THE WORLD.
IT TURNS OUT THAT ROOFTOPS ARE BETTER THAN SCHOOL. WHO'D'VE GUESSED.
YOUR MUM MAKES GREAT SANDWICHES, SCARP!
MUMS KNOW MORE THAN THEY LET ON. BE INTERESTING TO OPEN ONE UP ONE DAY AND LOOK INSIDE.
WHAT ELSE YOU GOT IN YOUR BAG?
I BROUGHT THIS...
YOU SAID YOU COULD FIX HIM, CASTRO. MAYBE HE CAN TELL US WHERE DAD WENT...

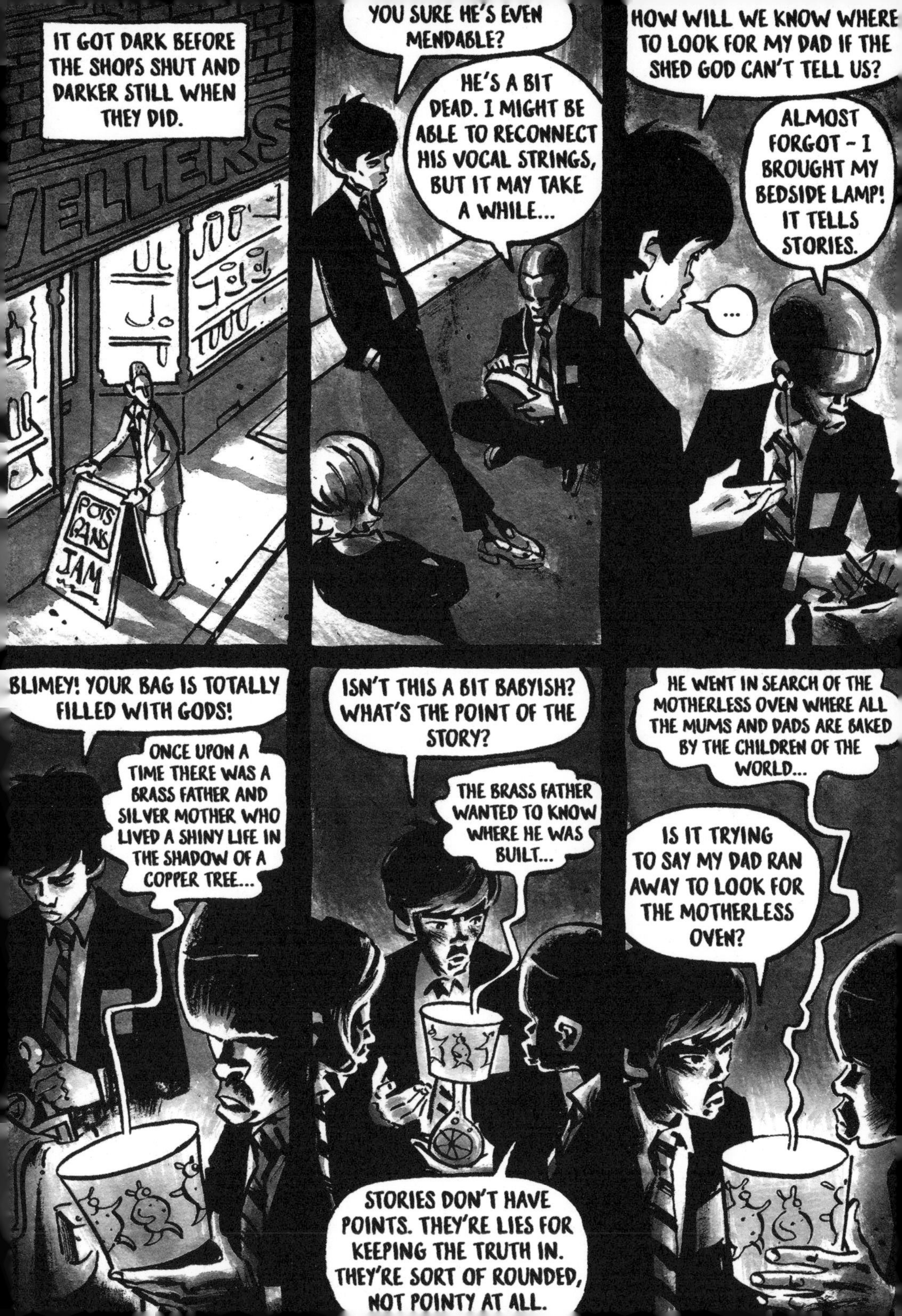
IT GOT DARK BEFORE THE SHOPS SHUT AND DARKER STILL WHEN THEY DID.
POTS PANS JAM
YOU SURE HE'S EVEN MENDABLE?
HE'S A BIT DEAD. I MIGHT BE ABLE TO RECONNECT HIS VOCAL STRINGS, BUT IT MAY TAKE A WHILE...
HOW WILL WE KNOW WHERE TO LOOK FOR MY DAD IF THE SHED GOD CAN'T TELL US?
ALMOST FORGOT – I BROUGHT MY BEDSIDE LAMP! IT TELLS STORIES.
...
BLIMEY! YOUR BAG IS TOTALLY FILLED WITH GODS!
ONCE UPON A TIME THERE WAS A BRASS FATHER AND SILVER MOTHER WHO LIVED A SHINY LIFE IN THE SHADOW OF A COPPER TREE...
ISN'T THIS A BIT BABYISH? WHAT'S THE POINT OF THE STORY?
THE BRASS FATHER WANTED TO KNOW WHERE HE WAS BUILT...
STORIES DON'T HAVE POINTS. THEY'RE LIES FOR KEEPING THE TRUTH IN. THEY'RE SORT OF ROUNDED, NOT POINTY AT ALL.
HE WENT IN SEARCH OF THE MOTHERLESS OVEN WHERE ALL THE MUMS AND DADS ARE BAKED BY THE CHILDREN OF THE WORLD...
IS IT TRYING TO SAY MY DAD RAN AWAY TO LOOK FOR THE MOTHERLESS OVEN?

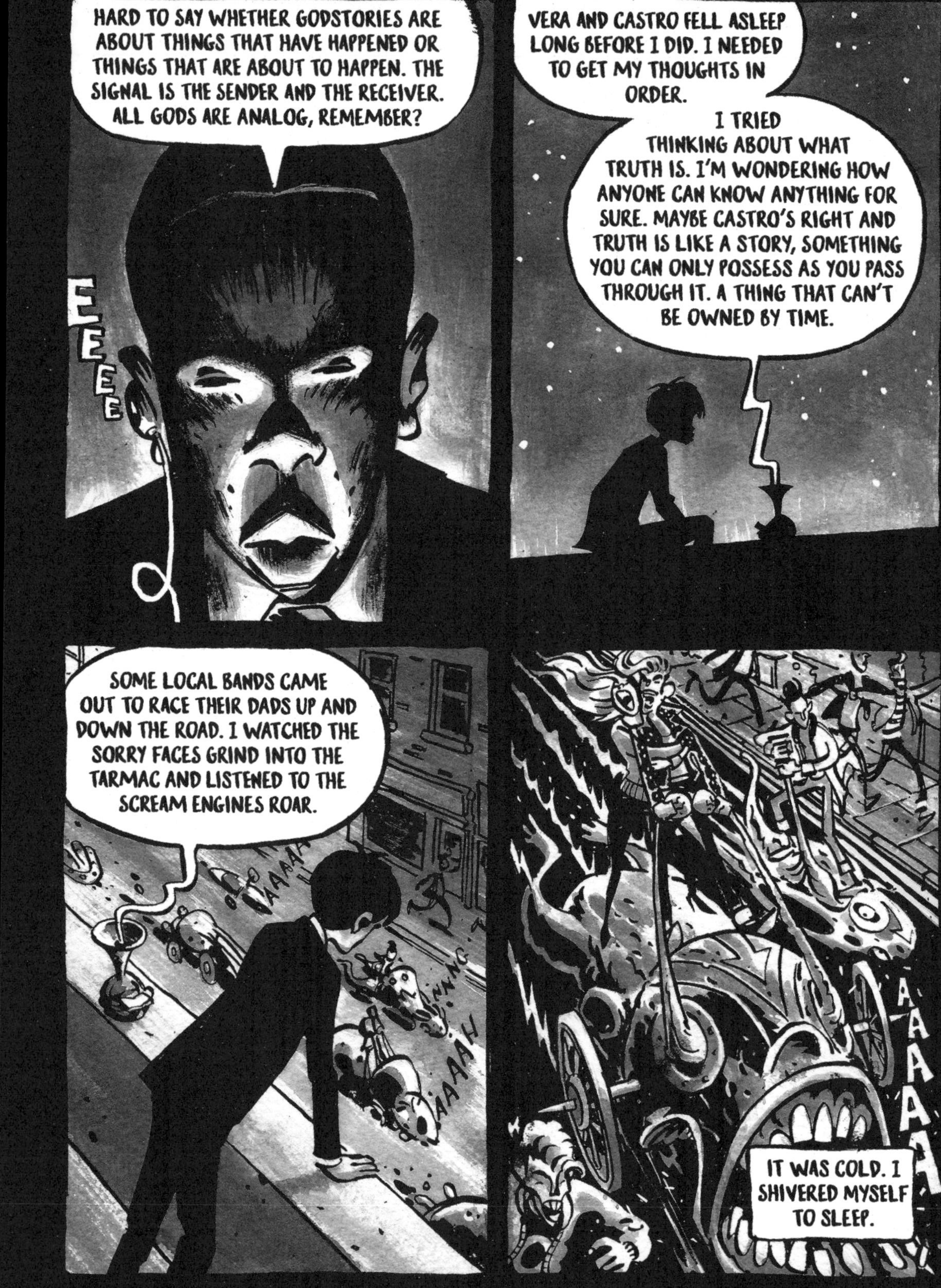
HARD TO SAY WHETHER GODSTORIES ARE ABOUT THINGS THAT HAVE HAPPENED OR THINGS THAT ARE ABOUT TO HAPPEN. THE SIGNAL IS THE SENDER AND THE RECEIVER. ALL GODS ARE ANALOG, REMEMBER?
EEEE
VERA AND CASTRO FELL ASLEEP LONG BEFORE I DID. I NEEDED TO GET MY THOUGHTS IN ORDER.
I TRIED THINKING ABOUT WHAT TRUTH IS. I'M WONDERING HOW ANYONE CAN KNOW ANYTHING FOR SURE. MAYBE CASTRO'S RIGHT AND TRUTH IS LIKE A STORY, SOMETHING YOU CAN ONLY POSSESS AS YOU PASS THROUGH IT. A THING THAT CAN'T BE OWNED BY TIME.
SOME LOCAL BANDS CAME OUT TO RACE THEIR DADS UP AND DOWN THE ROAD. I WATCHED THE SORRY FACES GRIND INTO THE TARMAC AND LISTENED TO THE SCREAM ENGINES ROAR.
IT WAS COLD. I SHIVERED MYSELF TO SLEEP.

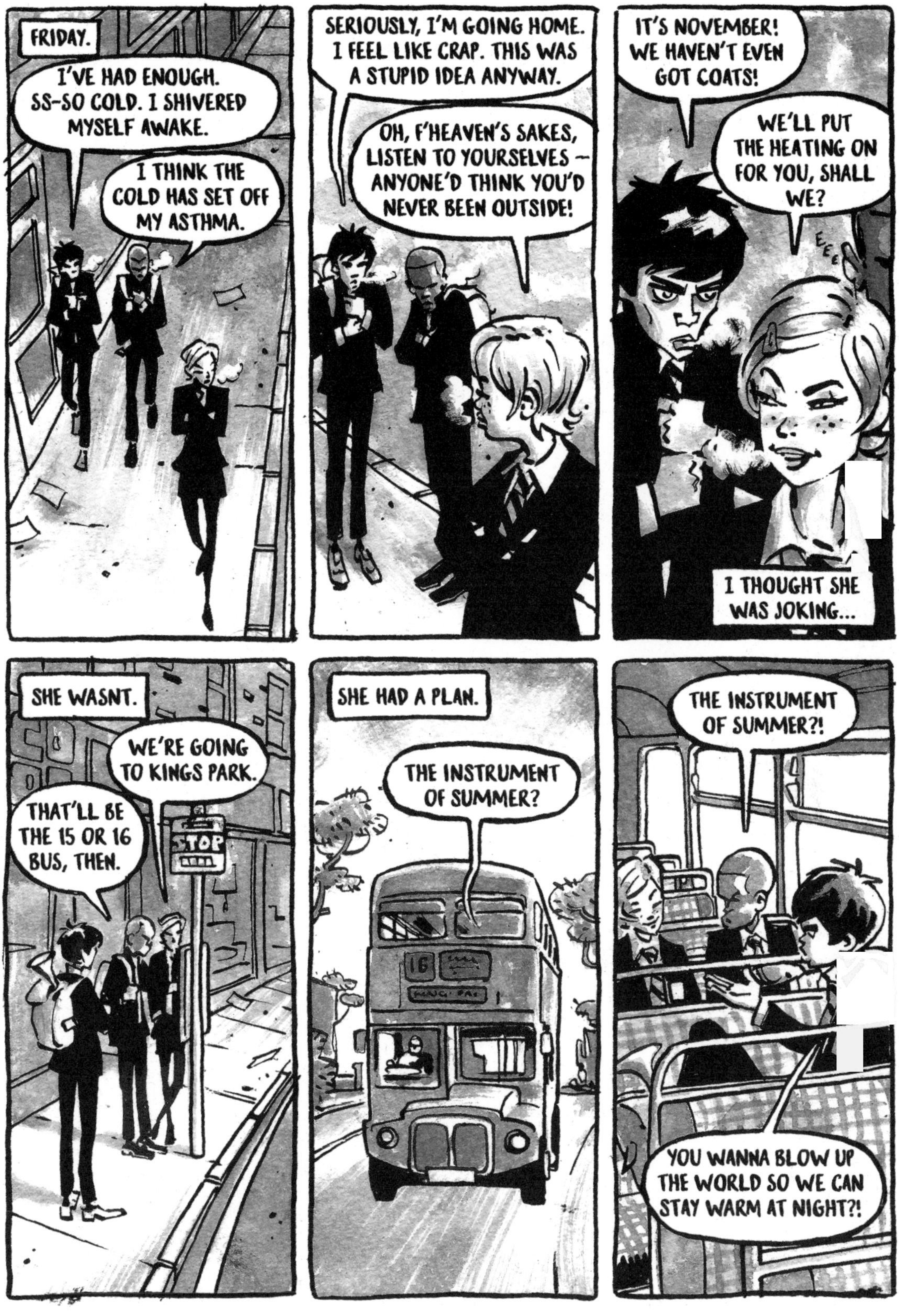
FRIDAY.
I'VE HAD ENOUGH. SS-SO COLD. I SHIVERED MYSELF AWAKE.
I THINK THE COLD HAS SET OFF MY ASTHMA.
SERIOUSLY, I'M GOING HOME. I FEEL LIKE CRAP. THIS WAS A STUPID IDEA ANYWAY.
OH, F'HEAVEN'S SAKES, LISTEN TO YOURSELVES — ANYONE'D THINK YOU'D NEVER BEEN OUTSIDE!
IT'S NOVEMBER! WE HAVEN'T EVEN GOT COATS!
WE'LL PUT THE HEATING ON FOR YOU, SHALL WE?
EEE
I THOUGHT SHE WAS JOKING...
SHE WASNT.
WE'RE GOING TO KINGS PARK.
THAT'LL BE THE 15 OR 16 BUS, THEN.
STOP
SHE HAD A PLAN.
THE INSTRUMENT OF SUMMER?
16
THE INSTRUMENT OF SUMMER?!
YOU WANNA BLOW UP THE WORLD SO WE CAN STAY WARM AT NIGHT?!

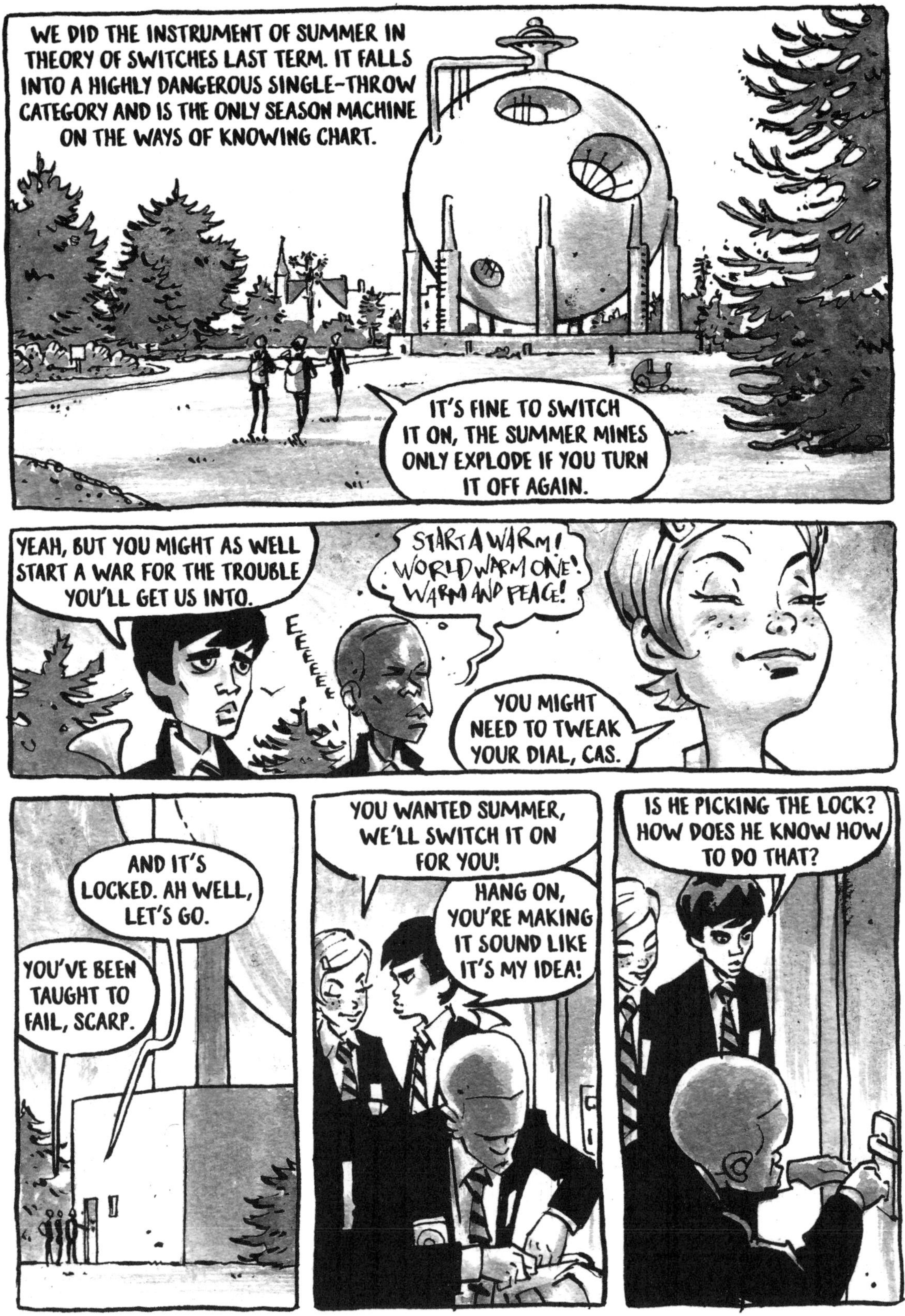
WE DID THE INSTRUMENT OF SUMMER IN THEORY OF SWITCHES LAST TERM. IT FALLS INTO A HIGHLY DANGEROUS SINGLE-THROW CATEGORY AND IS THE ONLY SEASON MACHINE ON THE WAYS OF KNOWING CHART.
IT'S FINE TO SWITCH IT ON, THE SUMMER MINES ONLY EXPLODE IF YOU TURN IT OFF AGAIN.
YEAH, BUT YOU MIGHT AS WELL START A WAR FOR THE TROUBLE YOU'LL GET US INTO.
START A WARM! WORLD WARM ONE! WARM AND PEACE!
EEEEEEE
YOU MIGHT NEED TO TWEAK YOUR DIAL, CAS.
AND IT'S LOCKED. AH WELL, LET'S GO.
YOU'VE BEEN TAUGHT TO FAIL, SCARP.
YOU WANTED SUMMER, WE'LL SWITCH IT ON FOR YOU!
HANG ON, YOU'RE MAKING IT SOUND LIKE IT'S MY IDEA!
IS HE PICKING THE LOCK? HOW DOES HE KNOW HOW TO DO THAT?

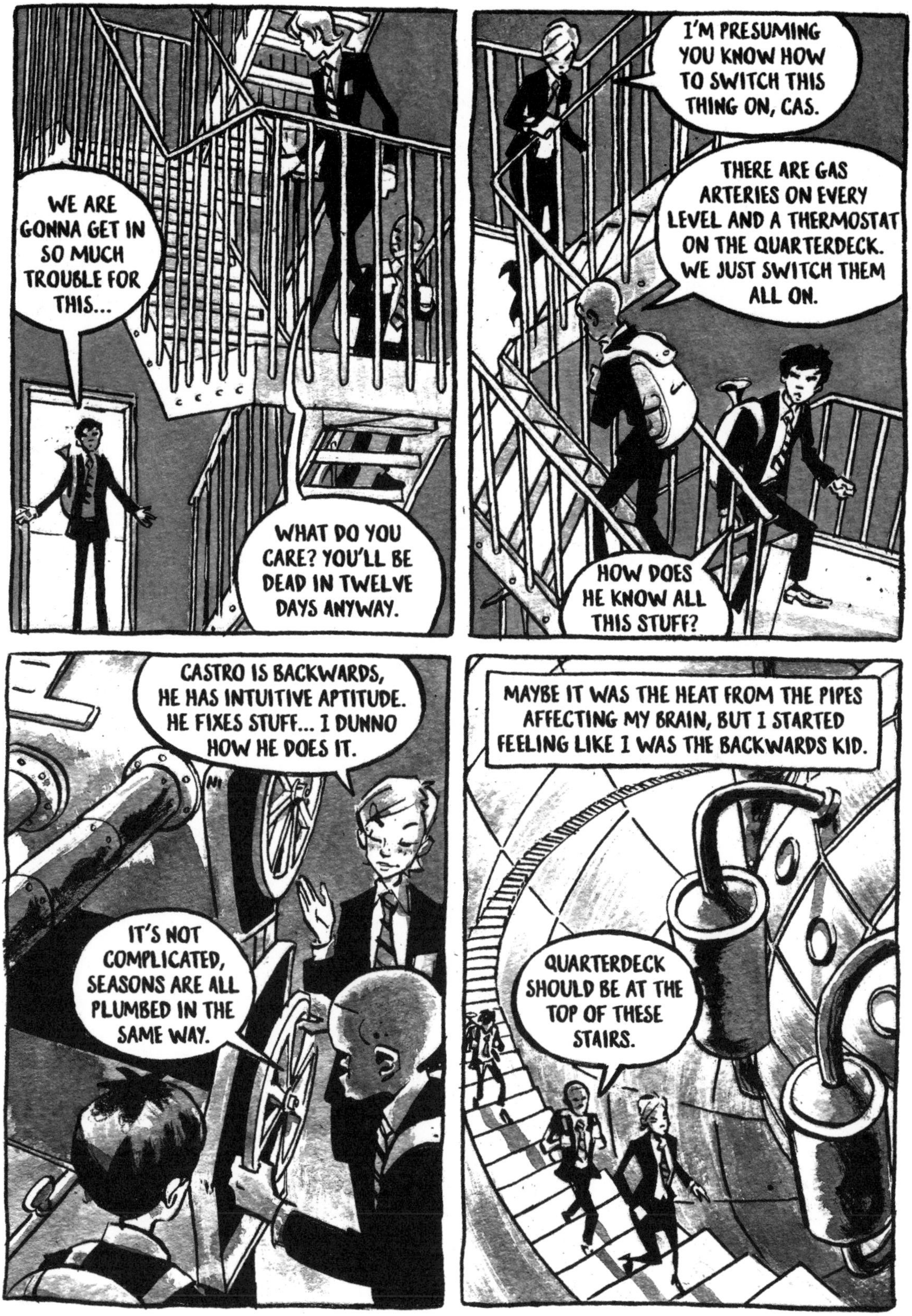
WE ARE GONNA GET IN SO MUCH TROUBLE FOR THIS...
WHAT DO YOU CARE? YOU'LL BE DEAD IN TWELVE DAYS ANYWAY.
I'M PRESUMING YOU KNOW HOW TO SWITCH THIS THING ON, CAS.
THERE ARE GAS ARTERIES ON EVERY LEVEL AND A THERMOSTAT ON THE QUARTERDECK. WE JUST SWITCH THEM ALL ON.
HOW DOES HE KNOW ALL THIS STUFF?
CASTRO IS BACKWARDS, HE HAS INTUITIVE APTITUDE. HE FIXES STUFF... I DUNNO HOW HE DOES IT.
IT'S NOT COMPLICATED, SEASONS ARE ALL PLUMBED IN THE SAME WAY.
MAYBE IT WAS THE HEAT FROM THE PIPES AFFECTING MY BRAIN, BUT I STARTED FEELING LIKE I WAS THE BACKWARDS KID.
QUARTERDECK SHOULD BE AT THE TOP OF THESE STAIRS.

FROM THE QUARTERDECK WE COULD SEE THE SUMMER MINES RISE AND FEEL THEM RADIATING.

WOW!

THE SOUND OF THE CHAINS ON THE MINES IS ALWAYS THE FIRST SIGN OF SUMMER.

KLANG. KLANG. KLANG.

KLA. KLANG. KLANG.

I USED TO DREAM THAT ONE DAY I'D GET TO CONDUCT THE SUMMER.

WARM UP THE BOMBS, RAISE THE BANDSTANDS. SWITCH ON THE BEES AND BURST THE TREES!

SO ONCE THE MINES GO UP, THE INSTRUMENT OF SUMMER CAN'T BE TURNED OFF OR THE MINES DROP AND

BOOM! MWAHAHA HA HA HA!

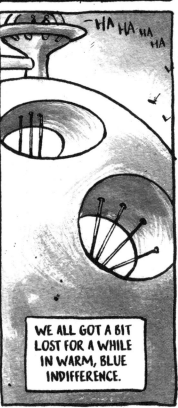

HA HA HA HA

WE ALL GOT A BIT LOST FOR A WHILE IN WARM, BLUE INDIFFERENCE.

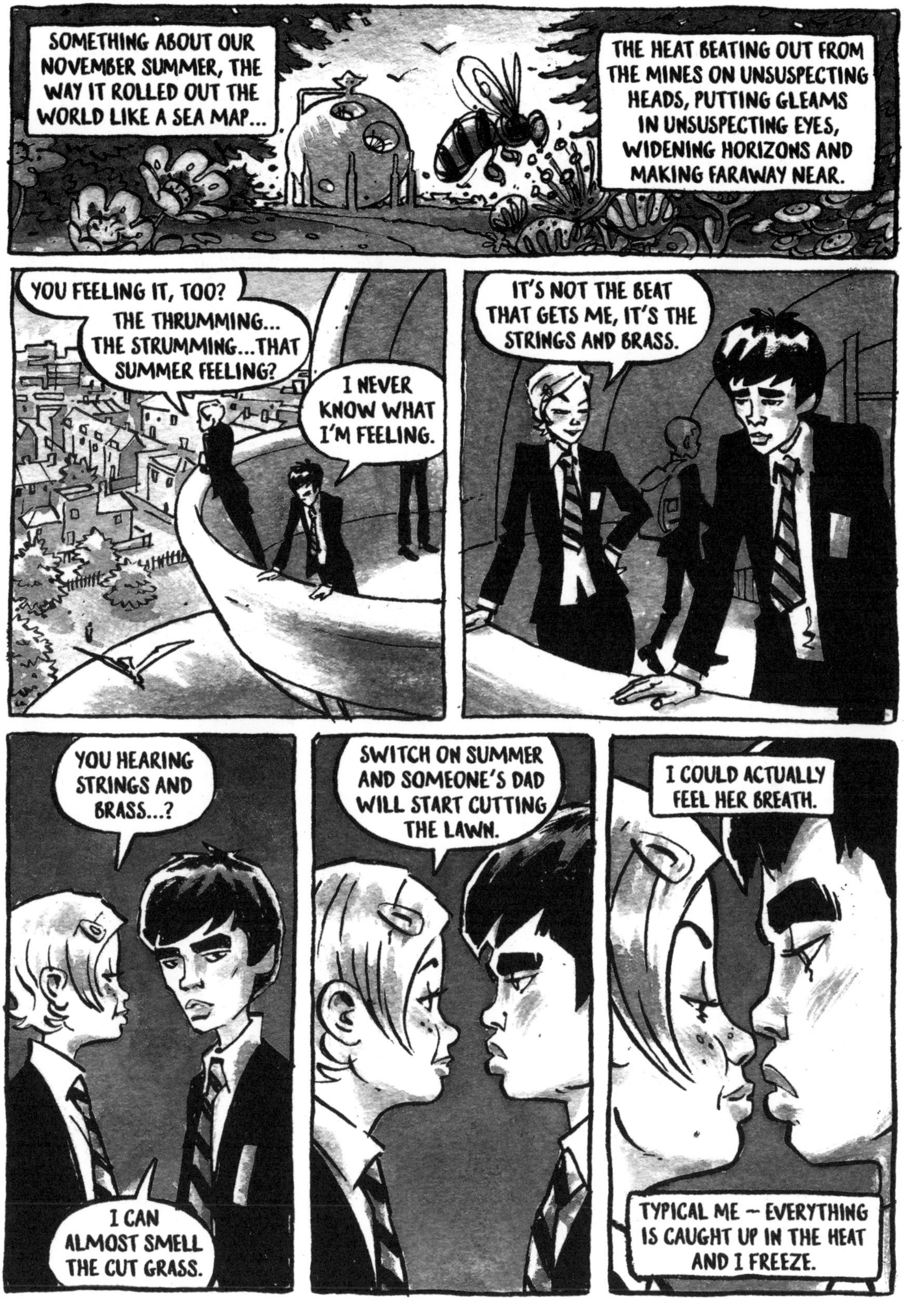
SOMETHING ABOUT OUR NOVEMBER SUMMER, THE WAY IT ROLLED OUT THE WORLD LIKE A SEA MAP...
THE HEAT BEATING OUT FROM THE MINES ON UNSUSPECTING HEADS, PUTTING GLEAMS IN UNSUSPECTING EYES, WIDENING HORIZONS AND MAKING FARAWAY NEAR.
YOU FEELING IT, TOO?
THE THRUMMING... THE STRUMMING...THAT SUMMER FEELING?
I NEVER KNOW WHAT I'M FEELING.
IT'S NOT THE BEAT THAT GETS ME, IT'S THE STRINGS AND BRASS.
YOU HEARING STRINGS AND BRASS...?
I CAN ALMOST SMELL THE CUT GRASS.
SWITCH ON SUMMER AND SOMEONE'S DAD WILL START CUTTING THE LAWN.
I COULD ACTUALLY FEEL HER BREATH.
TYPICAL ME — EVERYTHING IS CAUGHT UP IN THE HEAT AND I FREEZE.

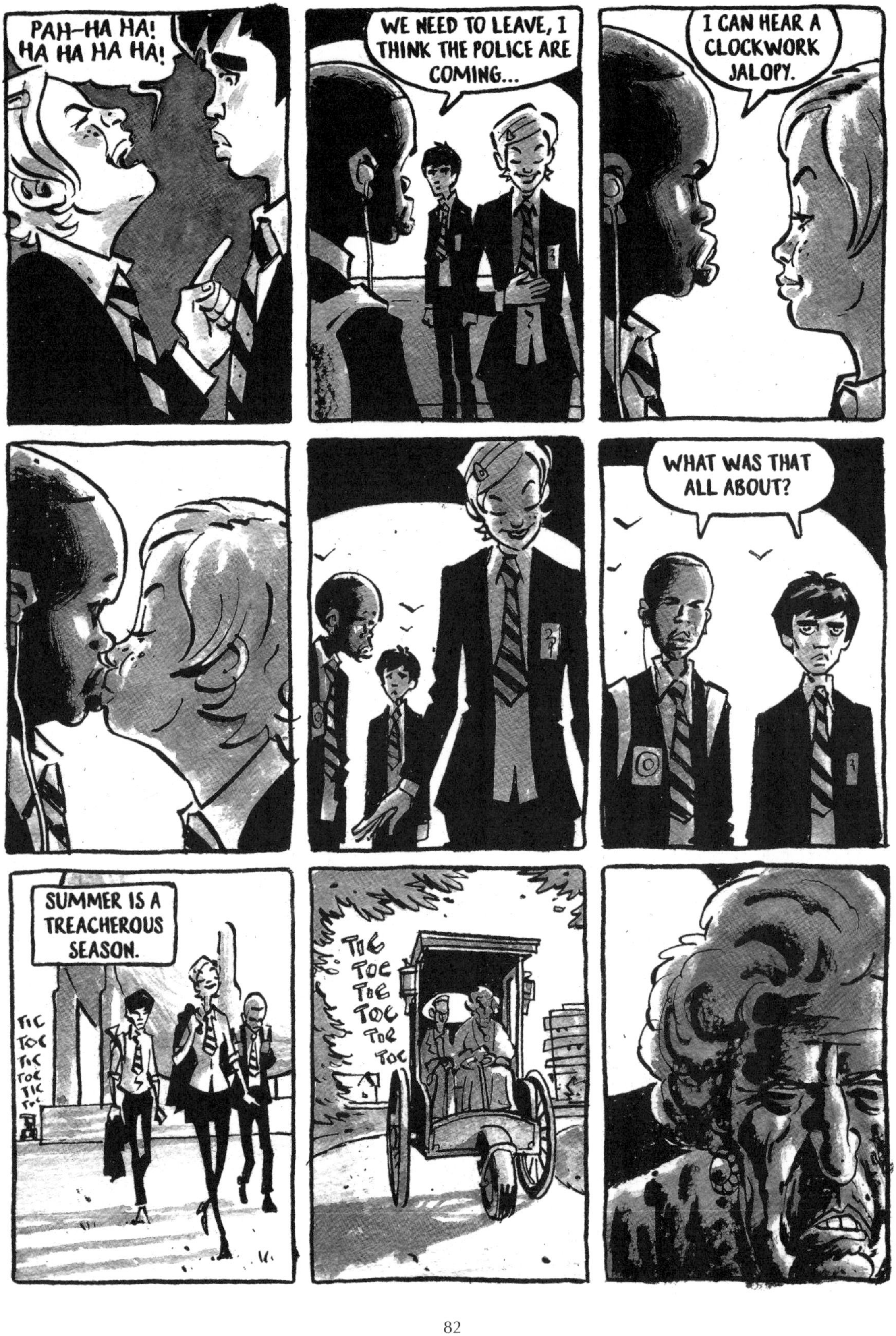
PAH-HA HA!
HA HA HA HA!
WE NEED TO LEAVE, I THINK THE POLICE ARE COMING...
I CAN HEAR A CLOCKWORK JALOPY.
WHAT WAS THAT ALL ABOUT?
SUMMER IS A TREACHEROUS SEASON.
TIC TOC TIC TOC TIC TOC
TIC TOC TIC TOC TIC TOC

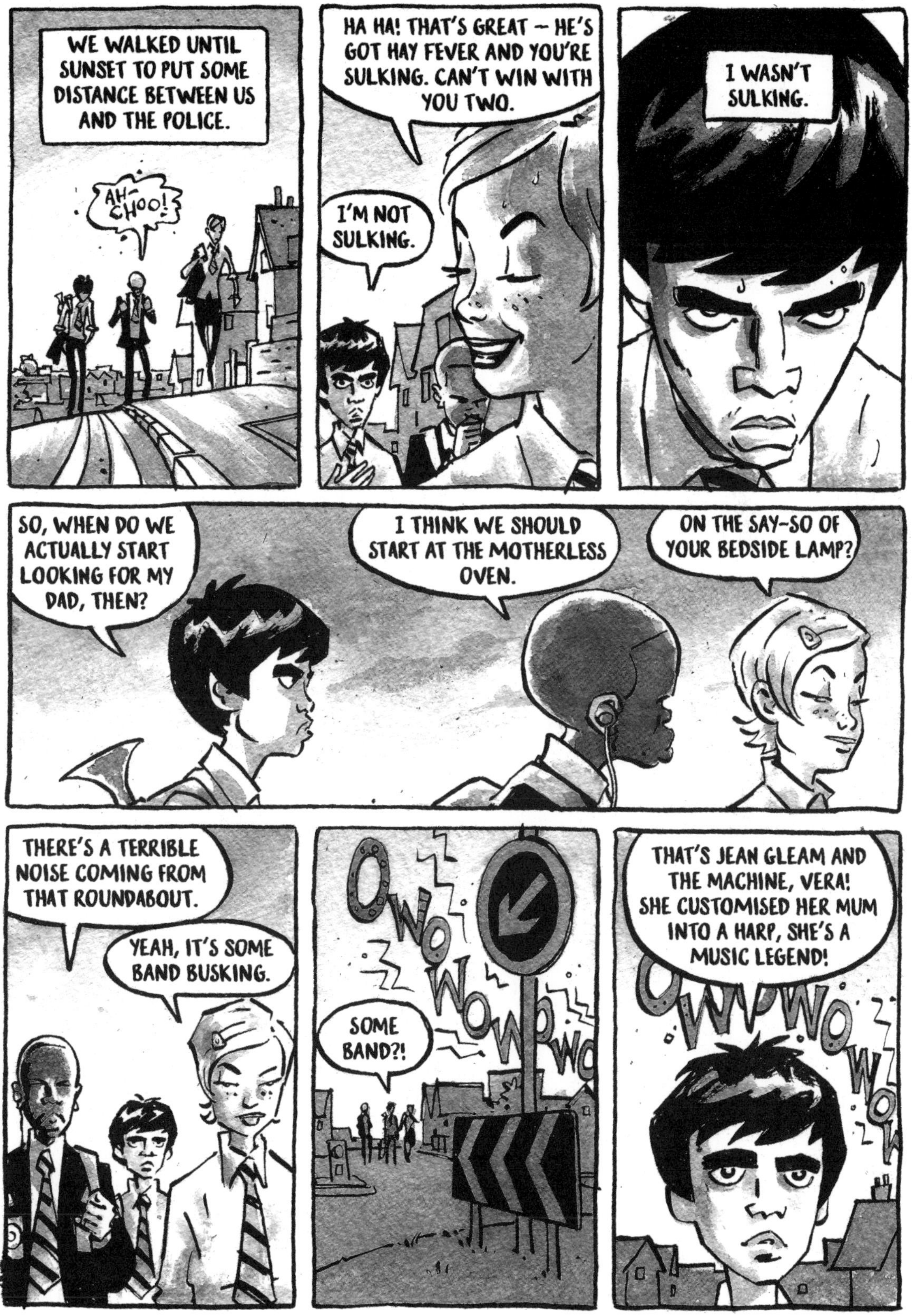
WE WALKED UNTIL SUNSET TO PUT SOME DISTANCE BETWEEN US AND THE POLICE.
AH-CHOO!
HA HA! THAT'S GREAT – HE'S GOT HAY FEVER AND YOU'RE SULKING. CAN'T WIN WITH YOU TWO.
I'M NOT SULKING.
I WASN'T SULKING.
SO, WHEN DO WE ACTUALLY START LOOKING FOR MY DAD, THEN?
I THINK WE SHOULD START AT THE MOTHERLESS OVEN.
ON THE SAY-SO OF YOUR BEDSIDE LAMP?
THERE'S A TERRIBLE NOISE COMING FROM THAT ROUNDABOUT.
YEAH, IT'S SOME BAND BUSKING.
OWOWOWOWOWO
SOME BAND?!
THAT'S JEAN GLEAM AND THE MACHINE, VERA! SHE CUSTOMISED HER MUM INTO A HARP, SHE'S A MUSIC LEGEND!
OWOWOWOWOW

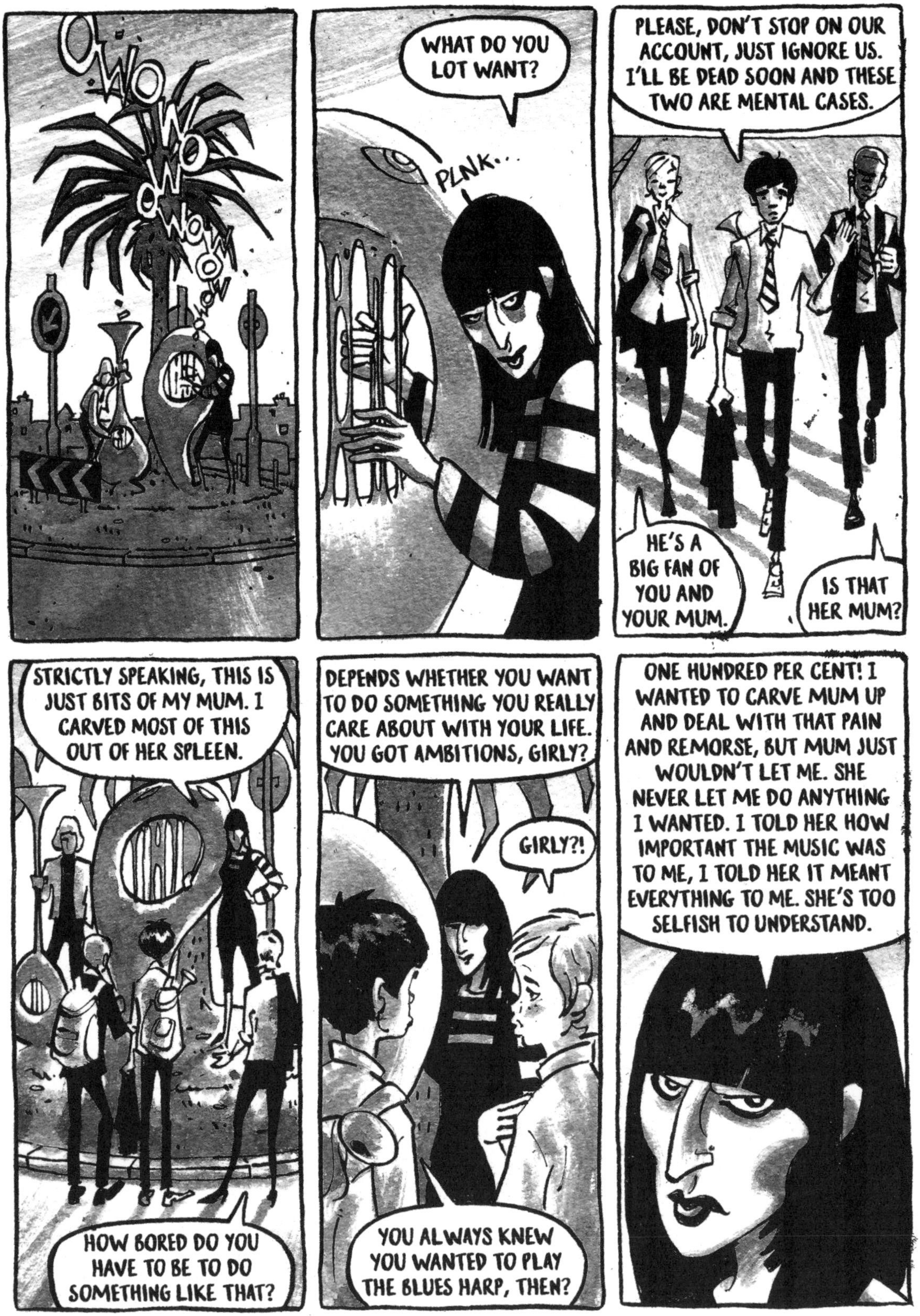
OWOWOWOWOWOW
WHAT DO YOU LOT WANT?
PLNK...
PLEASE, DON'T STOP ON OUR ACCOUNT, JUST IGNORE US. I'LL BE DEAD SOON AND THESE TWO ARE MENTAL CASES.
HE'S A BIG FAN OF YOU AND YOUR MUM.
IS THAT HER MUM?
STRICTLY SPEAKING, THIS IS JUST BITS OF MY MUM. I CARVED MOST OF THIS OUT OF HER SPLEEN.
HOW BORED DO YOU HAVE TO BE TO DO SOMETHING LIKE THAT?
DEPENDS WHETHER YOU WANT TO DO SOMETHING YOU REALLY CARE ABOUT WITH YOUR LIFE. YOU GOT AMBITIONS, GIRLY?
GIRLY?!
YOU ALWAYS KNEW YOU WANTED TO PLAY THE BLUES HARP, THEN?
ONE HUNDRED PER CENT! I WANTED TO CARVE MUM UP AND DEAL WITH THAT PAIN AND REMORSE, BUT MUM JUST WOULDN'T LET ME. SHE NEVER LET ME DO ANYTHING I WANTED. I TOLD HER HOW IMPORTANT THE MUSIC WAS TO ME, I TOLD HER IT MEANT EVERYTHING TO ME. SHE'S TOO SELFISH TO UNDERSTAND.

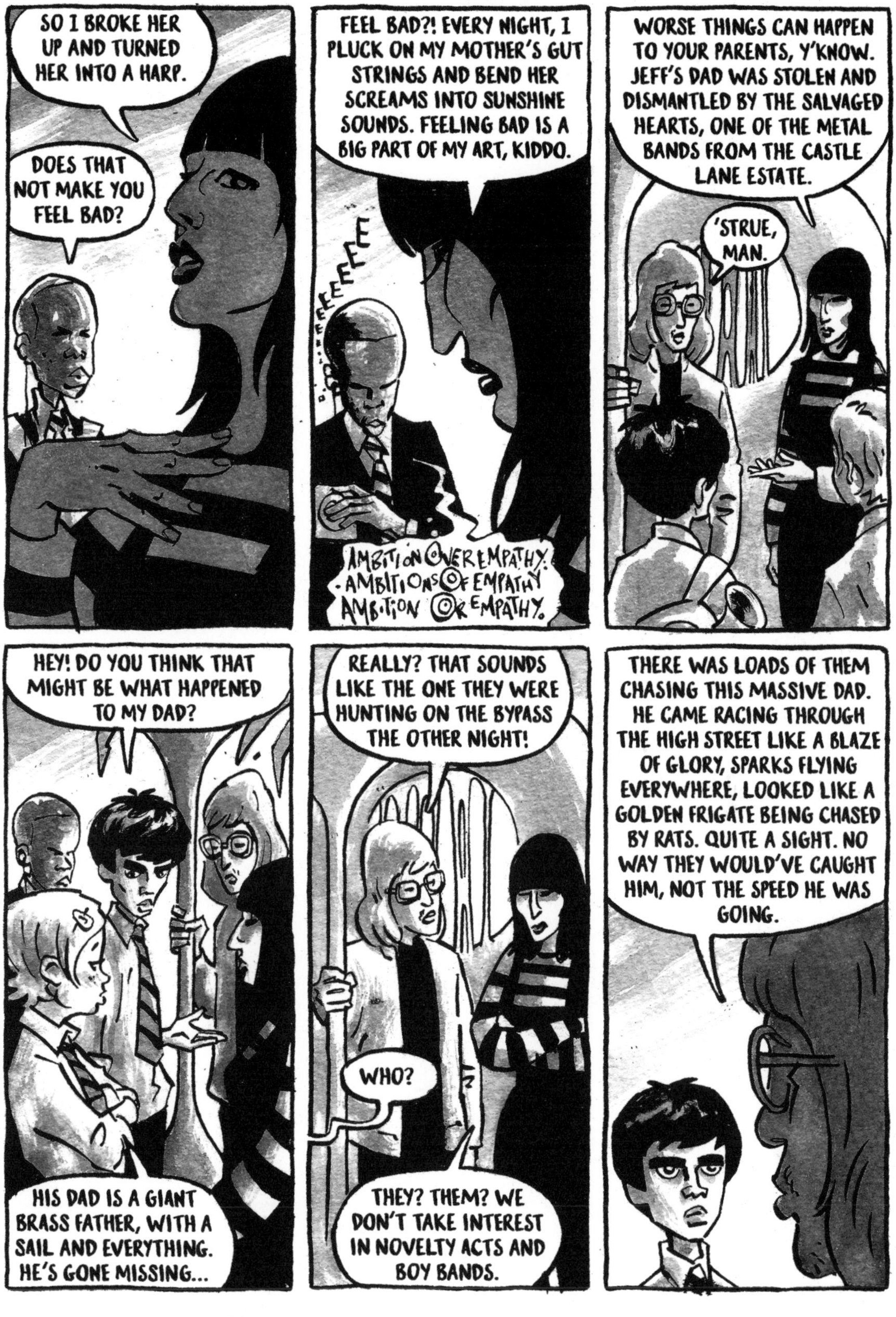
SO I BROKE HER UP AND TURNED HER INTO A HARP.
DOES THAT NOT MAKE YOU FEEL BAD?
FEEL BAD?! EVERY NIGHT, I PLUCK ON MY MOTHER'S GUT STRINGS AND BEND HER SCREAMS INTO SUNSHINE SOUNDS. FEELING BAD IS A BIG PART OF MY ART, KIDDO.
AMBITION OVER EMPATHY.
AMBITIONS OF EMPATHY
AMBITION OR EMPATHY.
WORSE THINGS CAN HAPPEN TO YOUR PARENTS, Y'KNOW. JEFF'S DAD WAS STOLEN AND DISMANTLED BY THE SALVAGED HEARTS, ONE OF THE METAL BANDS FROM THE CASTLE LANE ESTATE.
'STRUE, MAN.
HEY! DO YOU THINK THAT MIGHT BE WHAT HAPPENED TO MY DAD?
HIS DAD IS A GIANT BRASS FATHER, WITH A SAIL AND EVERYTHING. HE'S GONE MISSING...
REALLY? THAT SOUNDS LIKE THE ONE THEY WERE HUNTING ON THE BYPASS THE OTHER NIGHT!
WHO?
THEY? THEM? WE DON'T TAKE INTEREST IN NOVELTY ACTS AND BOY BANDS.
THERE WAS LOADS OF THEM CHASING THIS MASSIVE DAD. HE CAME RACING THROUGH THE HIGH STREET LIKE A BLAZE OF GLORY, SPARKS FLYING EVERYWHERE, LOOKED LIKE A GOLDEN FRIGATE BEING CHASED BY RATS. QUITE A SIGHT. NO WAY THEY WOULD'VE CAUGHT HIM, NOT THE SPEED HE WAS GOING.

CAN'T BELIEVE WE GOT TO SEE JEAN GLEAM. I COULD HEAR HER MUSIC WHEN I WAS GOING TO SLEEP AS A KID.

DO YOU THINK THAT COULD HAVE BEEN MY DAD THEY SAW BEING CHASED ON THE BYPASS?

NAH. PRETENTIOUS SODS LIKE THAT WILL SAY ANYTHING TO GET ATTENTION. I'D TAKE THE WORD OF CASTRO'S BEDSIDE LAMP OVER ANYTHING THOSE LEMONS SAY.

I THINK IT'S CRUEL TO TURN YOUR MOTHER INTO A MUSICAL INSTRUMENT. IF SOMEONE DOESN'T WANT TO SING, THEY SHOULDN'T BE MADE TO.

WHAT DO YOU THINK, CASTRO?

BY THE TIME WE GOT BACK ON TO THE MAIN ROAD IT WAS DARK, SO WE DECIDED TO SPEND ANOTHER NIGHT ON THE ROOF OF THE DAIRY AND BEGIN SEARCHING FOR DAD ON SATURDAY.

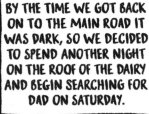

CASTRO HAD ONE OF HIS VERBAL FITS BEFORE HE WENT TO SLEEP. ME AND VERA STAYED AWAKE LAUGHING.

THEN SHE KISSED ME THEN SHE KISSED ME THEN SHE KISSED ME

THEN SHE KISSED ME THEN SHE KISSED ME THEN SHE KISSED ME

YEAH. IT WAS FUNNY.

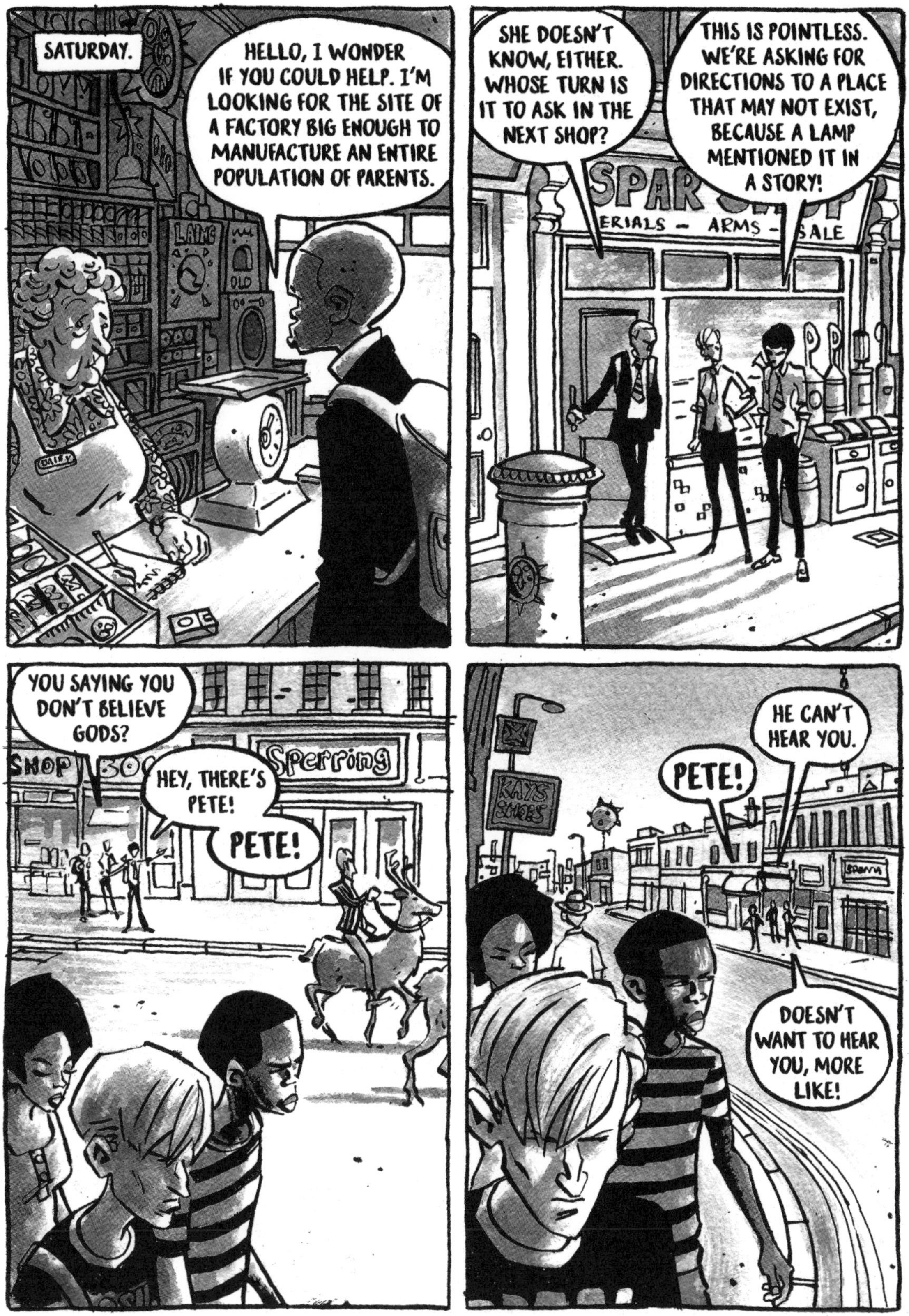
SATURDAY.
HELLO, I WONDER IF YOU COULD HELP. I'M LOOKING FOR THE SITE OF A FACTORY BIG ENOUGH TO MANUFACTURE AN ENTIRE POPULATION OF PARENTS.
LAMG
OLD
DAISY
SHE DOESN'T KNOW, EITHER. WHOSE TURN IS IT TO ASK IN THE NEXT SHOP?
THIS IS POINTLESS. WE'RE ASKING FOR DIRECTIONS TO A PLACE THAT MAY NOT EXIST, BECAUSE A LAMP MENTIONED IT IN A STORY!
SPAR
ERIALS - ARMS - SALE
YOU SAYING YOU DON'T BELIEVE GODS?
SHOP
Sperring
HEY, THERE'S PETE!
PETE!
KAYS SHOES
PETE!
HE CAN'T HEAR YOU.
DOESN'T WANT TO HEAR YOU, MORE LIKE!

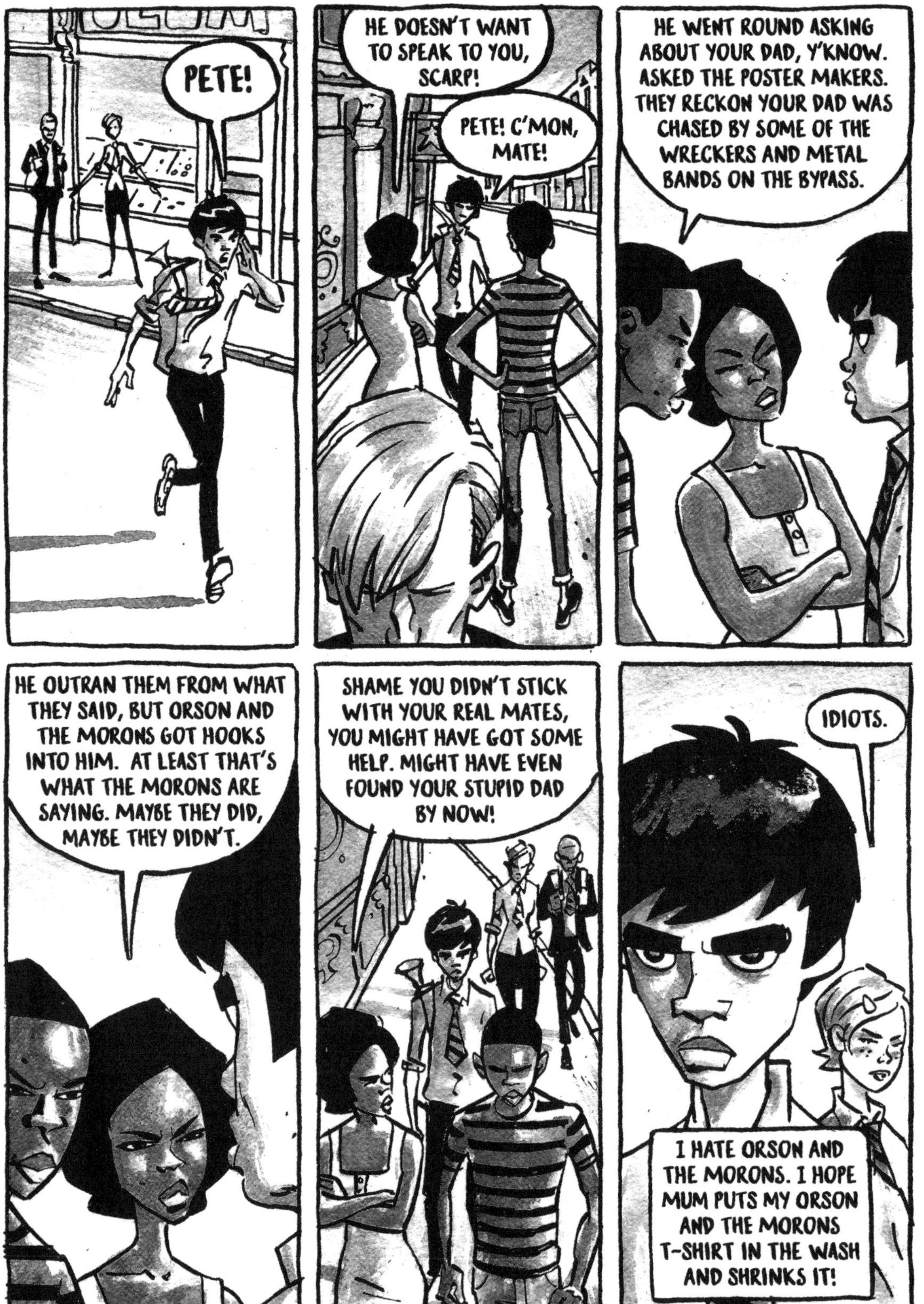
PETE!
HE DOESN'T WANT TO SPEAK TO YOU, SCARP!
PETE! C'MON, MATE!
HE WENT ROUND ASKING ABOUT YOUR DAD, Y'KNOW. ASKED THE POSTER MAKERS. THEY RECKON YOUR DAD WAS CHASED BY SOME OF THE WRECKERS AND METAL BANDS ON THE BYPASS.
HE OUTRAN THEM FROM WHAT THEY SAID, BUT ORSON AND THE MORONS GOT HOOKS INTO HIM. AT LEAST THAT'S WHAT THE MORONS ARE SAYING. MAYBE THEY DID, MAYBE THEY DIDN'T.
SHAME YOU DIDN'T STICK WITH YOUR REAL MATES, YOU MIGHT HAVE GOT SOME HELP. MIGHT HAVE EVEN FOUND YOUR STUPID DAD BY NOW!
IDIOTS.
I HATE ORSON AND THE MORONS. I HOPE MUM PUTS MY ORSON AND THE MORONS T-SHIRT IN THE WASH AND SHRINKS IT!

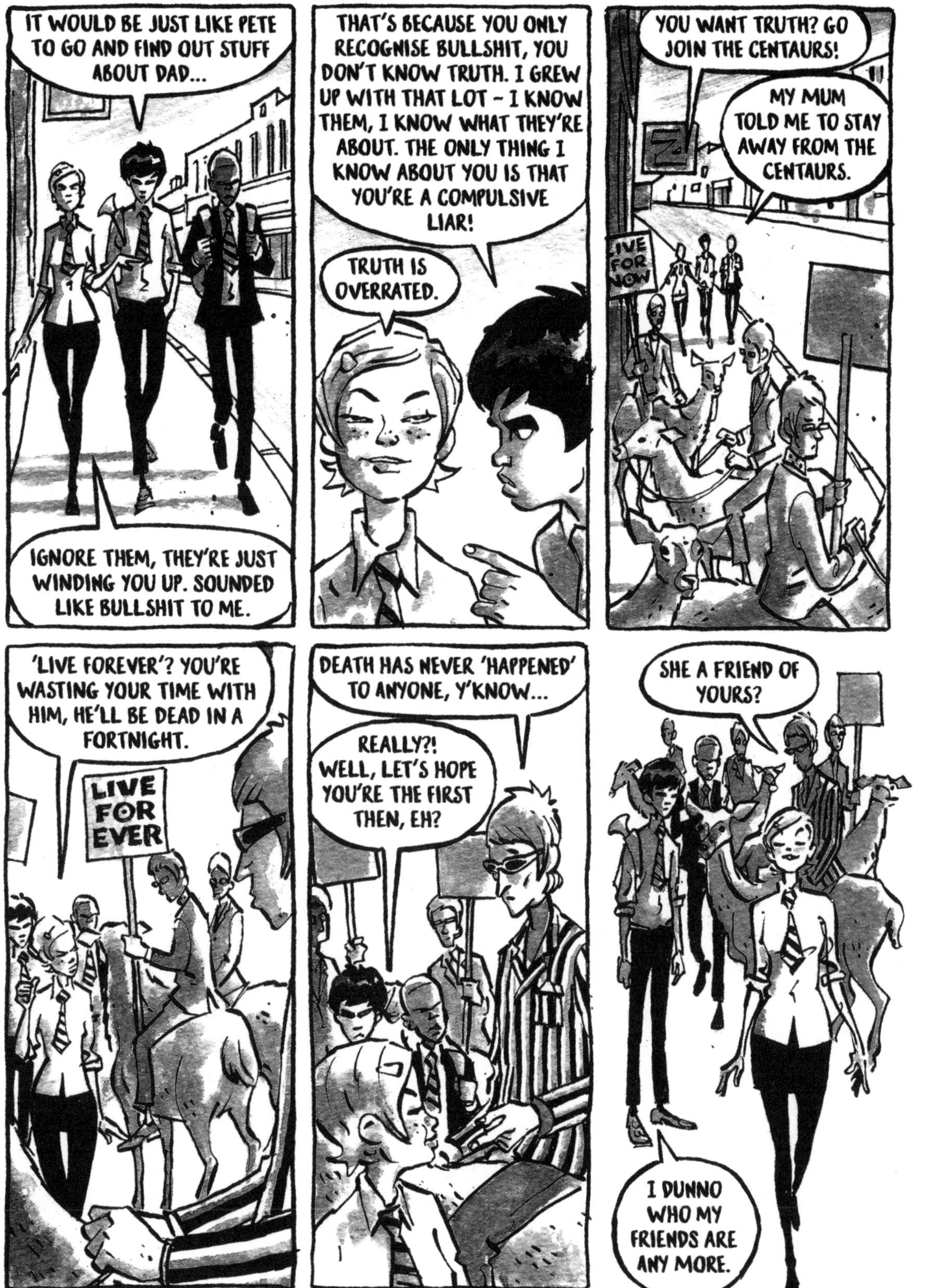
IT WOULD BE JUST LIKE PETE TO GO AND FIND OUT STUFF ABOUT DAD...
IGNORE THEM, THEY'RE JUST WINDING YOU UP. SOUNDED LIKE BULLSHIT TO ME.
THAT'S BECAUSE YOU ONLY RECOGNISE BULLSHIT, YOU DON'T KNOW TRUTH. I GREW UP WITH THAT LOT – I KNOW THEM, I KNOW WHAT THEY'RE ABOUT. THE ONLY THING I KNOW ABOUT YOU IS THAT YOU'RE A COMPULSIVE LIAR!
TRUTH IS OVERRATED.
YOU WANT TRUTH? GO JOIN THE CENTAURS!
MY MUM TOLD ME TO STAY AWAY FROM THE CENTAURS.
LIVE FOR NOW
'LIVE FOREVER'? YOU'RE WASTING YOUR TIME WITH HIM, HE'LL BE DEAD IN A FORTNIGHT.
LIVE FOR EVER
DEATH HAS NEVER 'HAPPENED' TO ANYONE, Y'KNOW...
REALLY?! WELL, LET'S HOPE YOU'RE THE FIRST THEN, EH?
SHE A FRIEND OF YOURS?
I DUNNO WHO MY FRIENDS ARE ANY MORE.

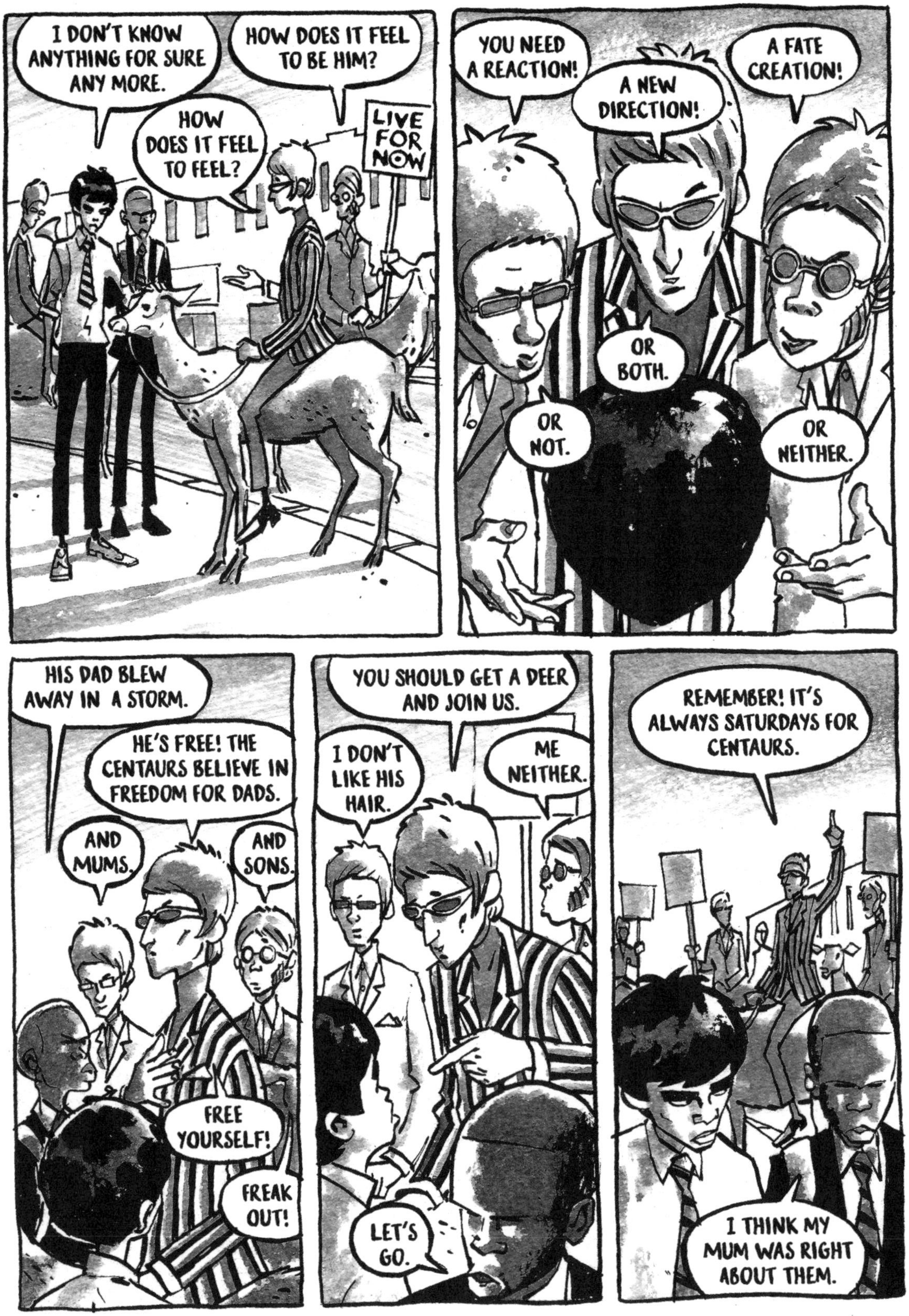
I DON'T KNOW ANYTHING FOR SURE ANY MORE.
HOW DOES IT FEEL TO BE HIM?
HOW DOES IT FEEL TO FEEL?
LIVE FOR NOW
YOU NEED A REACTION!
A NEW DIRECTION!
A FATE CREATION!
OR BOTH.
OR NOT.
OR NEITHER.
HIS DAD BLEW AWAY IN A STORM.
HE'S FREE! THE CENTAURS BELIEVE IN FREEDOM FOR DADS.
AND MUMS.
AND SONS.
FREE YOURSELF!
FREAK OUT!
YOU SHOULD GET A DEER AND JOIN US.
I DON'T LIKE HIS HAIR.
ME NEITHER.
LET'S GO.
REMEMBER! IT'S ALWAYS SATURDAYS FOR CENTAURS.
I THINK MY MUM WAS RIGHT ABOUT THEM.

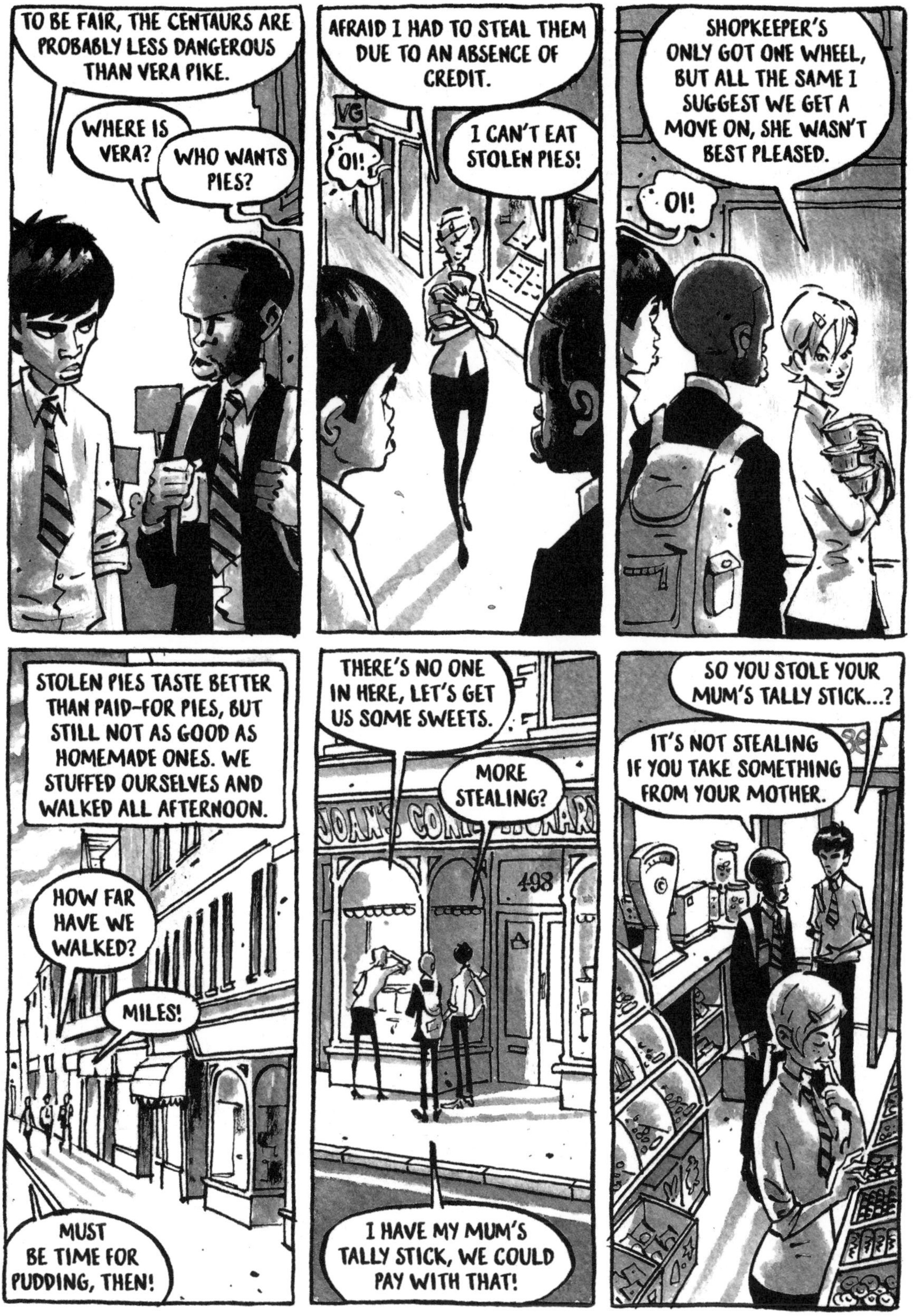
TO BE FAIR, THE CENTAURS ARE PROBABLY LESS DANGEROUS THAN VERA PIKE.
WHERE IS VERA?
WHO WANTS PIES?
AFRAID I HAD TO STEAL THEM DUE TO AN ABSENCE OF CREDIT.
VG
OI!
I CAN'T EAT STOLEN PIES!
SHOPKEEPER'S ONLY GOT ONE WHEEL, BUT ALL THE SAME I SUGGEST WE GET A MOVE ON, SHE WASN'T BEST PLEASED.
OI!
STOLEN PIES TASTE BETTER THAN PAID-FOR PIES, BUT STILL NOT AS GOOD AS HOMEMADE ONES. WE STUFFED OURSELVES AND WALKED ALL AFTERNOON.
HOW FAR HAVE WE WALKED?
MILES!
MUST BE TIME FOR PUDDING, THEN!
THERE'S NO ONE IN HERE, LET'S GET US SOME SWEETS.
MORE STEALING?
498
I HAVE MY MUM'S TALLY STICK, WE COULD PAY WITH THAT!
SO YOU STOLE YOUR MUM'S TALLY STICK...?
IT'S NOT STEALING IF YOU TAKE SOMETHING FROM YOUR MOTHER.

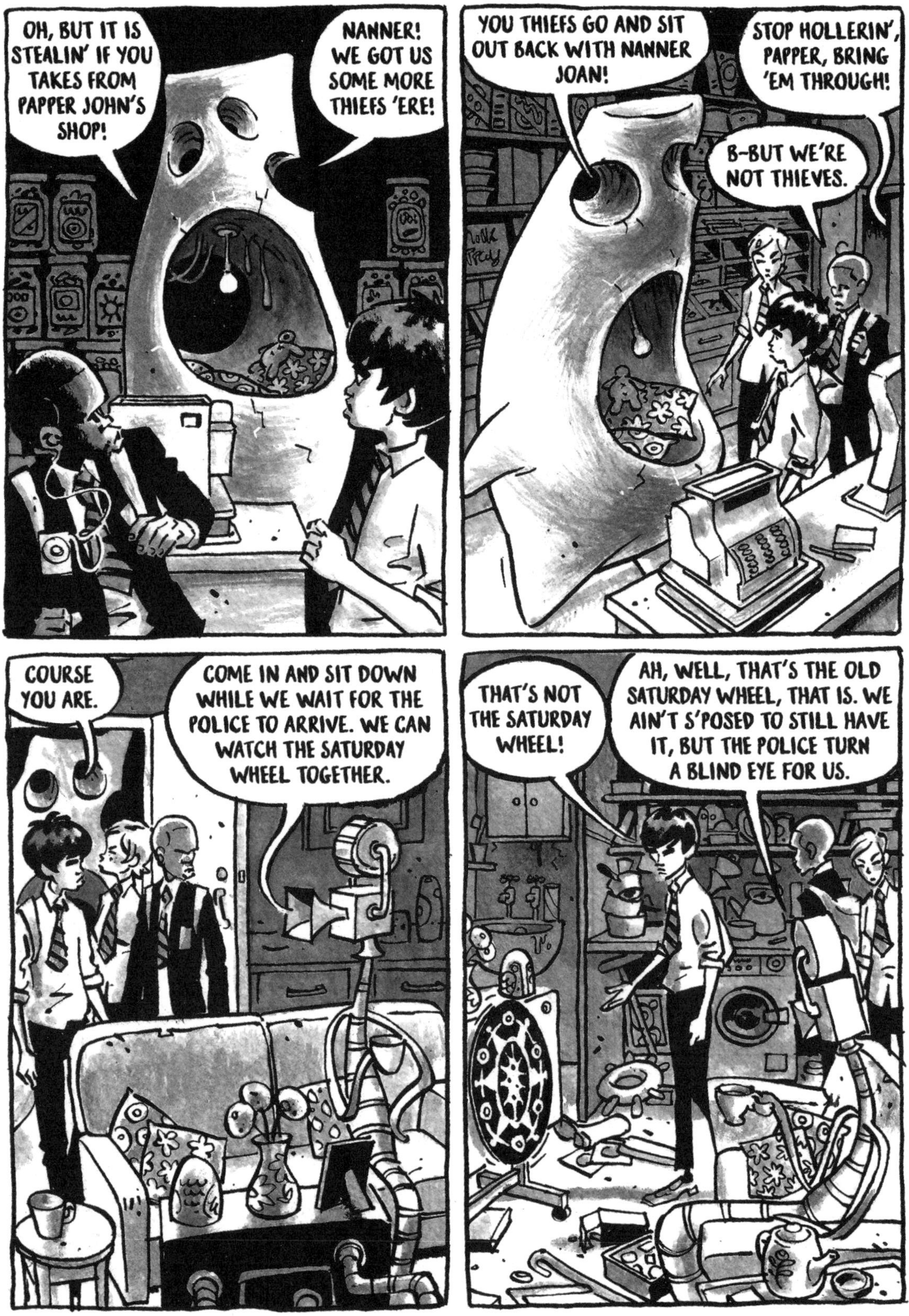
OH, BUT IT IS STEALIN' IF YOU TAKES FROM PAPPER JOHN'S SHOP!
NANNER! WE GOT US SOME MORE THIEFS 'ERE!
YOU THIEFS GO AND SIT OUT BACK WITH NANNER JOAN!
STOP HOLLERIN', PAPPER, BRING 'EM THROUGH!
B-BUT WE'RE NOT THIEVES.
COURSE YOU ARE.
COME IN AND SIT DOWN WHILE WE WAIT FOR THE POLICE TO ARRIVE. WE CAN WATCH THE SATURDAY WHEEL TOGETHER.
THAT'S NOT THE SATURDAY WHEEL!
AH, WELL, THAT'S THE OLD SATURDAY WHEEL, THAT IS. WE AIN'T S'POSED TO STILL HAVE IT, BUT THE POLICE TURN A BLIND EYE FOR US.

THE NEW SATURDAY WHEEL WAS INTRODUCED FOR THE CORONATION OF THE WEATHER CLOCK. WHEN DID SHE TAKE THE THRONE...? DOZEN OR MORE YEARS BACK. ANY RATE, ME AND NANNER DIDN'T LIKE IT, SO WE KEPT THE OLD ONE. WE CATCH SO MANY THIEFS THE POLICE DON'T MIND.

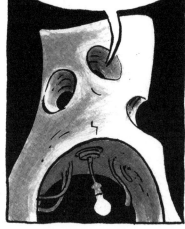

EXCUSE ME, PAPPER JOHN, BUT WHAT IS THIS OBJECT FOR?

THAT? OOOH... THAT'S AN OLD LOOKY SEE, A BIRD'S EYE. I GOT IT OFF A FLAPPER IN THE OLD DAYS.

IT'S LIKE A MAP OF THE BEAR PARK ESTATE.

AUDREY HER NAME WAS. THAT'S HOW THE WORLD WOULD HAVE LOOKED TO HER FIFTY-ODD YEARS AGO.

NANNER DON'T LIKE ME MENTIONING AUDREY...

I CAN'T VOUCH FOR THE ACCURACY OF THE THING, HAVIN' NEVER FLYED AND NOT HAVING BEEN ALIVE FIFTY YEARS AGO WHEN THAT WAS MADE.

HOW OLD ARE YOU, THEN? YOU LOOK ANCIENT!

YOU NIPPERS ASK SOME WEIRD QUESTIONS. LET ME SEE... IF OUR GARY LEFT HOME TWENTY YEARS AGO AND HE WOULD HAVE BAKED ME IN PRIMARY... OH, I DUNNO.

DO YOU KNOW WHERE YOU WERE BAKED? DO YOU KNOW WHERE THE MOTHERLESS OVEN IS?

HE'S A FUNNY ONE, THIS BOY WITH THE BRAIN AID. CAN'T YOU TURN HIS DIAL DOWN OR SUMMAT? HE'S UPSETTING NANNER JOAN, LOOK!

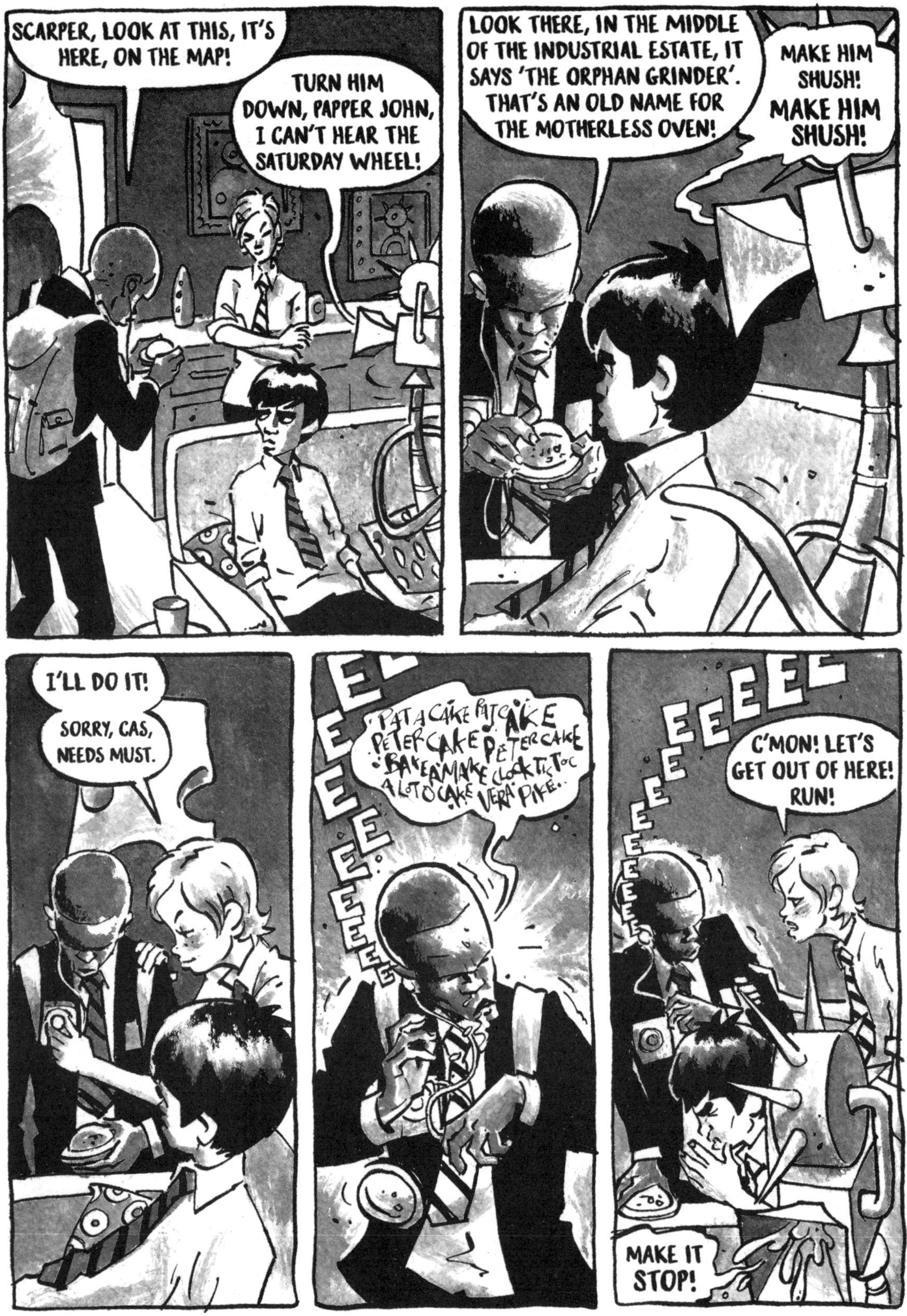
SCARPER, LOOK AT THIS, IT'S HERE, ON THE MAP!
TURN HIM DOWN, PAPPER JOHN, I CAN'T HEAR THE SATURDAY WHEEL!
LOOK THERE, IN THE MIDDLE OF THE INDUSTRIAL ESTATE, IT SAYS 'THE ORPHAN GRINDER'. THAT'S AN OLD NAME FOR THE MOTHERLESS OVEN!
MAKE HIM SHUSH! MAKE HIM SHUSH!
I'LL DO IT!
SORRY, CAS, NEEDS MUST.
EEEEEEEEE
PAT A CAKE PAT CAKE PETER CAKE PETER CAKE BAKE A MAKE CLOCK TIC TOC A LOT O CAKE VERA PIKE.
EEEEEEEEEEEEE
C'MON! LET'S GET OUT OF HERE! RUN!
MAKE IT STOP!

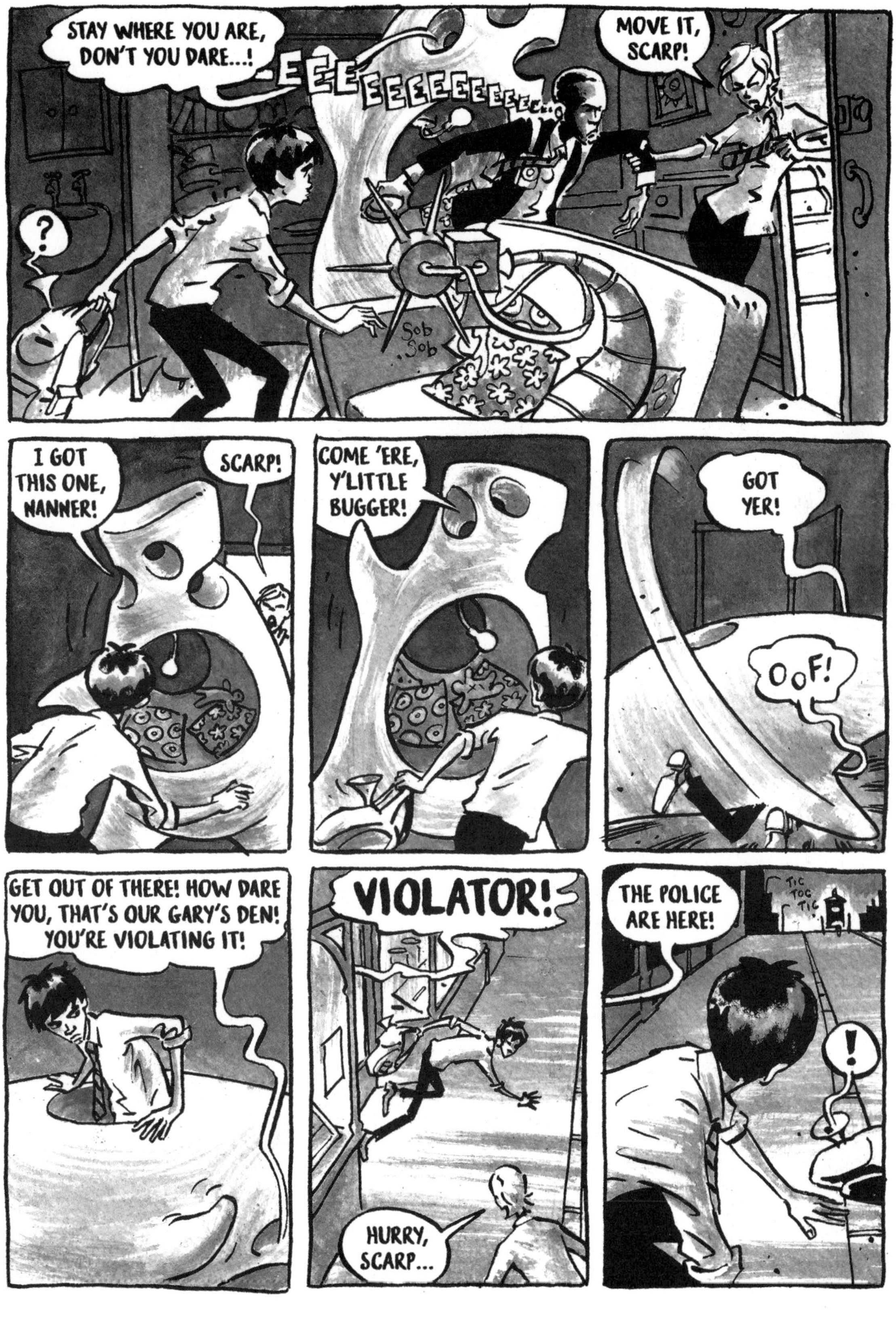
STAY WHERE YOU ARE, DON'T YOU DARE...!
EEEEEEEEEEEEEEEE...
MOVE IT, SCARP!
?
Sob Sob
I GOT THIS ONE, NANNER!
SCARP!
COME 'ERE, Y'LITTLE BUGGER!
GOT YER!
OOF!
GET OUT OF THERE! HOW DARE YOU, THAT'S OUR GARY'S DEN! YOU'RE VIOLATING IT!
VIOLATOR!
HURRY, SCARP...
THE POLICE ARE HERE!
TIC TOC TIC
!

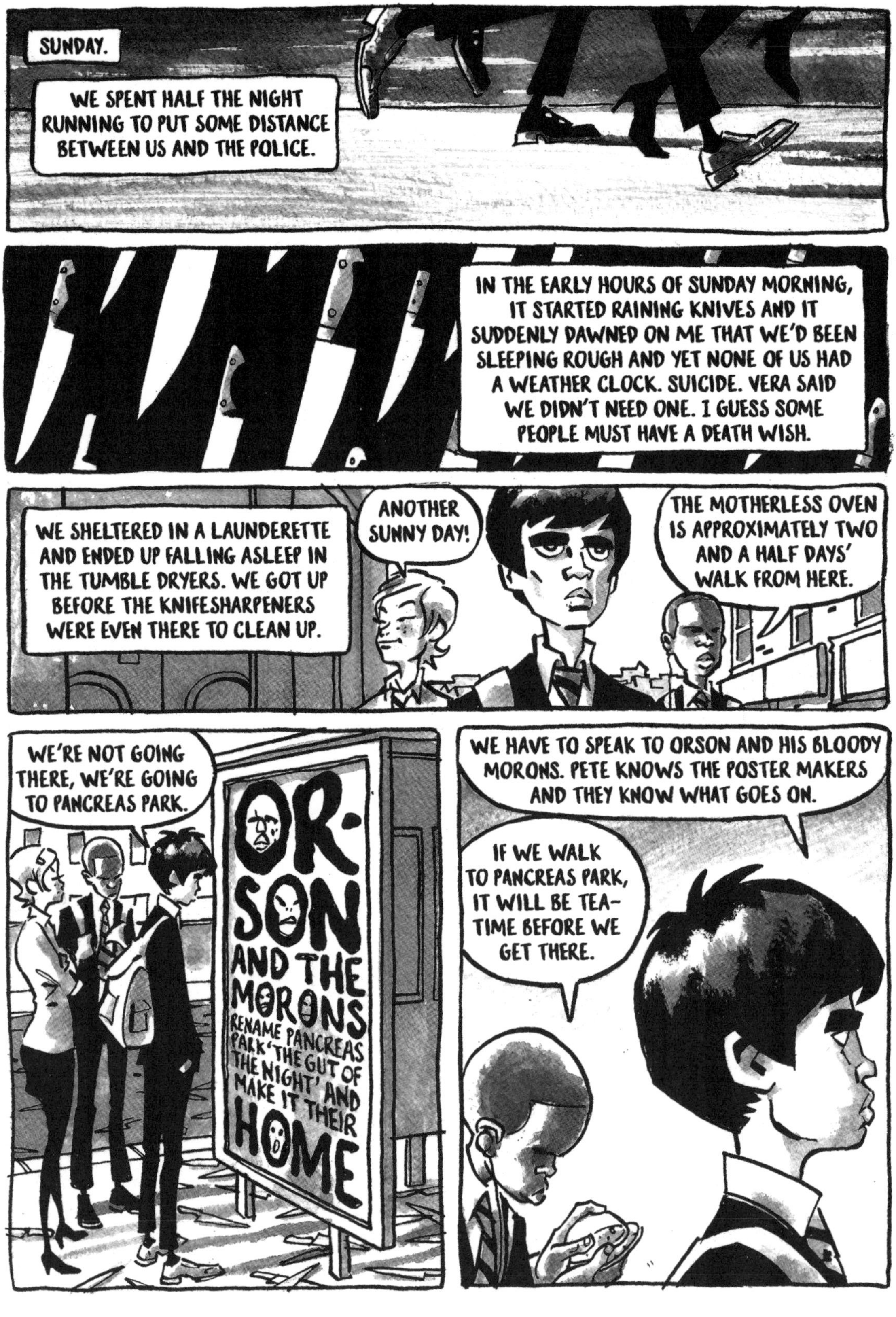
SUNDAY.
WE SPENT HALF THE NIGHT RUNNING TO PUT SOME DISTANCE BETWEEN US AND THE POLICE.
IN THE EARLY HOURS OF SUNDAY MORNING, IT STARTED RAINING KNIVES AND IT SUDDENLY DAWNED ON ME THAT WE'D BEEN SLEEPING ROUGH AND YET NONE OF US HAD A WEATHER CLOCK. SUICIDE. VERA SAID WE DIDN'T NEED ONE. I GUESS SOME PEOPLE MUST HAVE A DEATH WISH.
WE SHELTERED IN A LAUNDERETTE AND ENDED UP FALLING ASLEEP IN THE TUMBLE DRYERS. WE GOT UP BEFORE THE KNIFESHARPENERS WERE EVEN THERE TO CLEAN UP.
ANOTHER SUNNY DAY!
THE MOTHERLESS OVEN IS APPROXIMATELY TWO AND A HALF DAYS' WALK FROM HERE.
WE'RE NOT GOING THERE, WE'RE GOING TO PANCREAS PARK.
OR-SON AND THE MORONS RENAME PANCREAS PARK 'THE GUT OF THE NIGHT' AND MAKE IT THEIR HOME
WE HAVE TO SPEAK TO ORSON AND HIS BLOODY MORONS. PETE KNOWS THE POSTER MAKERS AND THEY KNOW WHAT GOES ON.
IF WE WALK TO PANCREAS PARK, IT WILL BE TEA-TIME BEFORE WE GET THERE.

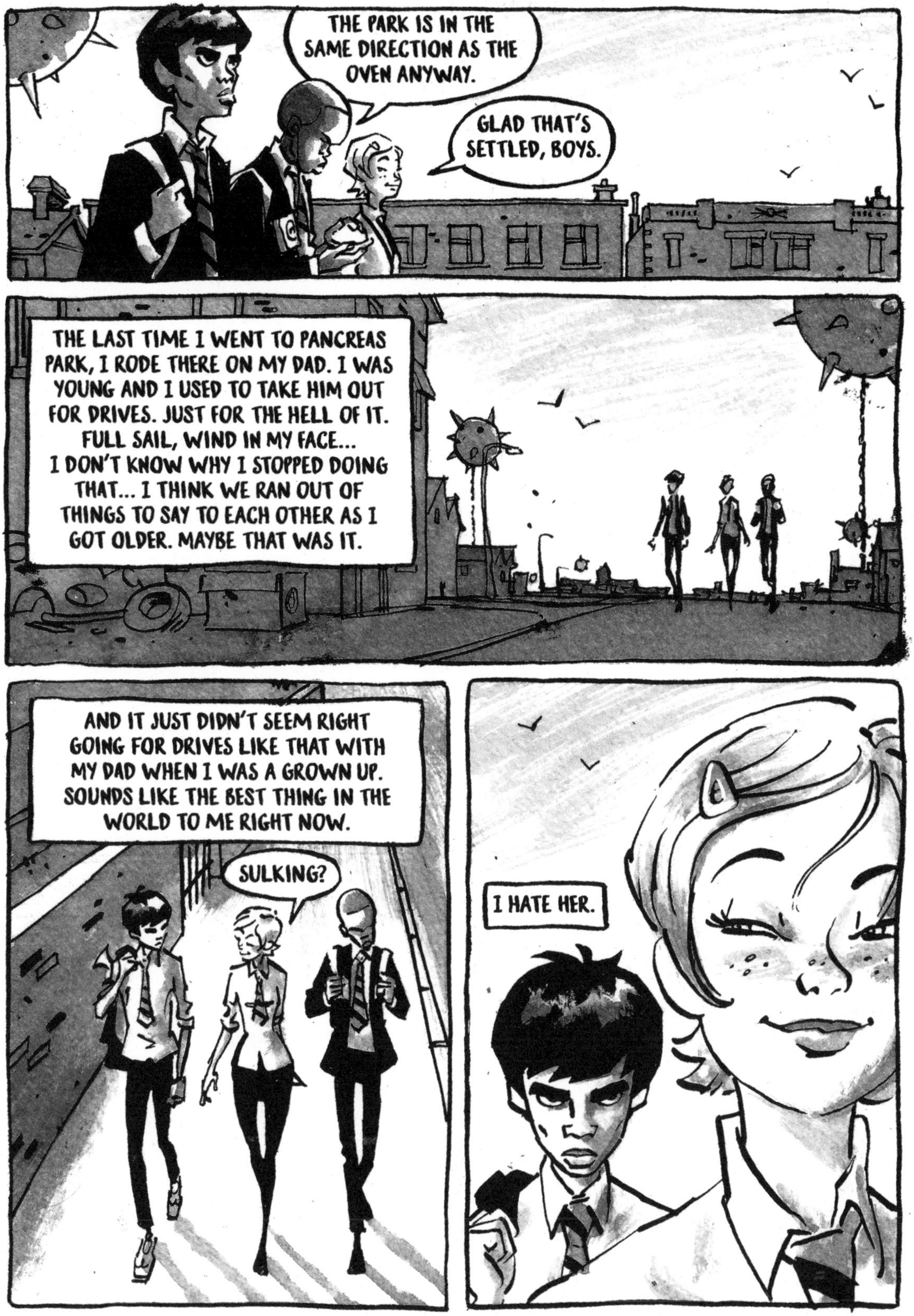
THE PARK IS IN THE SAME DIRECTION AS THE OVEN ANYWAY.
GLAD THAT'S SETTLED, BOYS.
THE LAST TIME I WENT TO PANCREAS PARK, I RODE THERE ON MY DAD. I WAS YOUNG AND I USED TO TAKE HIM OUT FOR DRIVES. JUST FOR THE HELL OF IT. FULL SAIL, WIND IN MY FACE... I DON'T KNOW WHY I STOPPED DOING THAT... I THINK WE RAN OUT OF THINGS TO SAY TO EACH OTHER AS I GOT OLDER. MAYBE THAT WAS IT.
AND IT JUST DIDN'T SEEM RIGHT GOING FOR DRIVES LIKE THAT WITH MY DAD WHEN I WAS A GROWN UP. SOUNDS LIKE THE BEST THING IN THE WORLD TO ME RIGHT NOW.
SULKING?
I HATE HER.

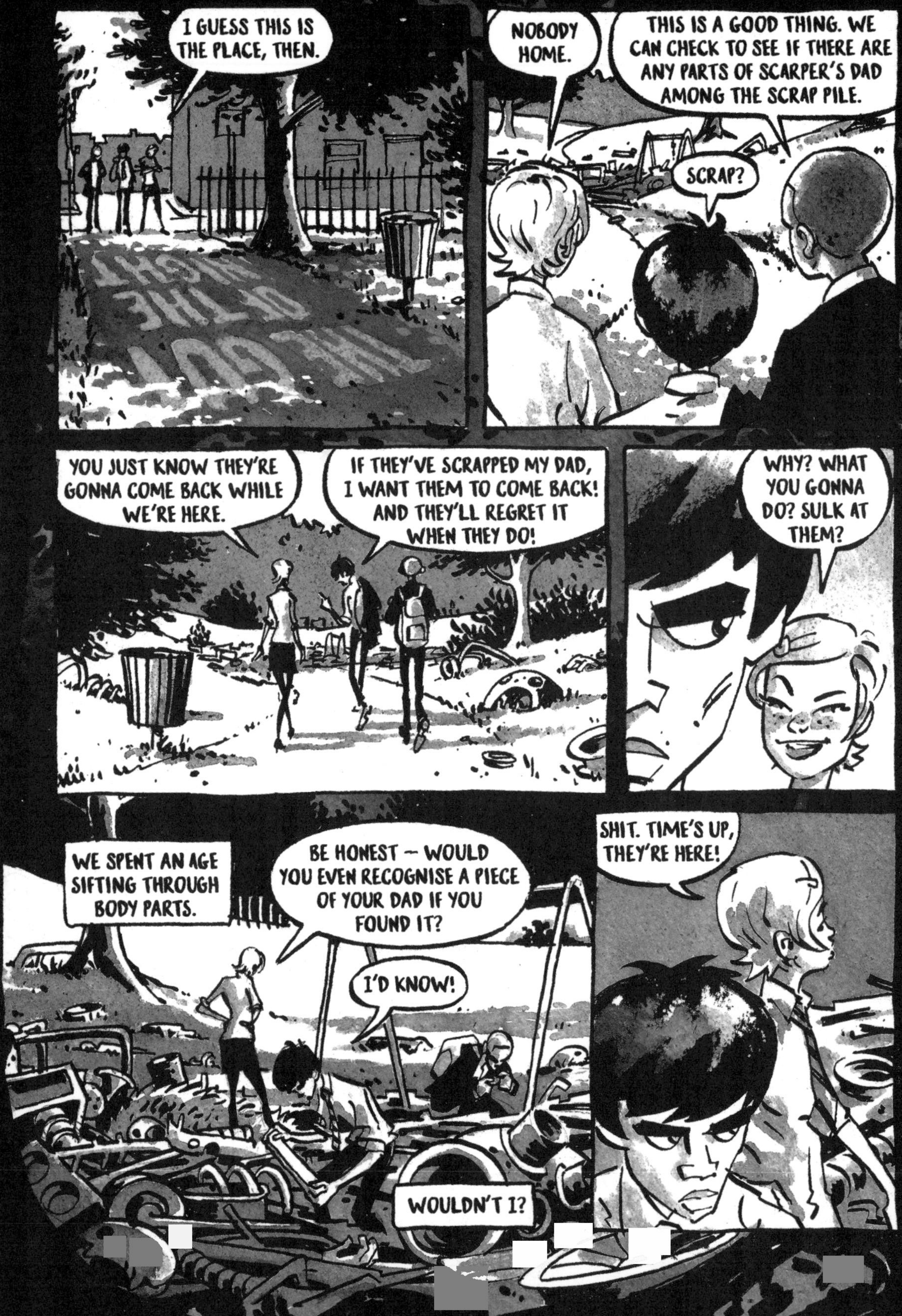

I GUESS THIS IS THE PLACE, THEN.
NOBODY HOME.
THIS IS A GOOD THING. WE CAN CHECK TO SEE IF THERE ARE ANY PARTS OF SCARPER'S DAD AMONG THE SCRAP PILE.
SCRAP?
YOU JUST KNOW THEY'RE GONNA COME BACK WHILE WE'RE HERE.
IF THEY'VE SCRAPPED MY DAD, I WANT THEM TO COME BACK! AND THEY'LL REGRET IT WHEN THEY DO!
WHY? WHAT YOU GONNA DO? SULK AT THEM?
WE SPENT AN AGE SIFTING THROUGH BODY PARTS.
BE HONEST — WOULD YOU EVEN RECOGNISE A PIECE OF YOUR DAD IF YOU FOUND IT?
I'D KNOW!
WOULDN'T I?
SHIT. TIME'S UP, THEY'RE HERE!

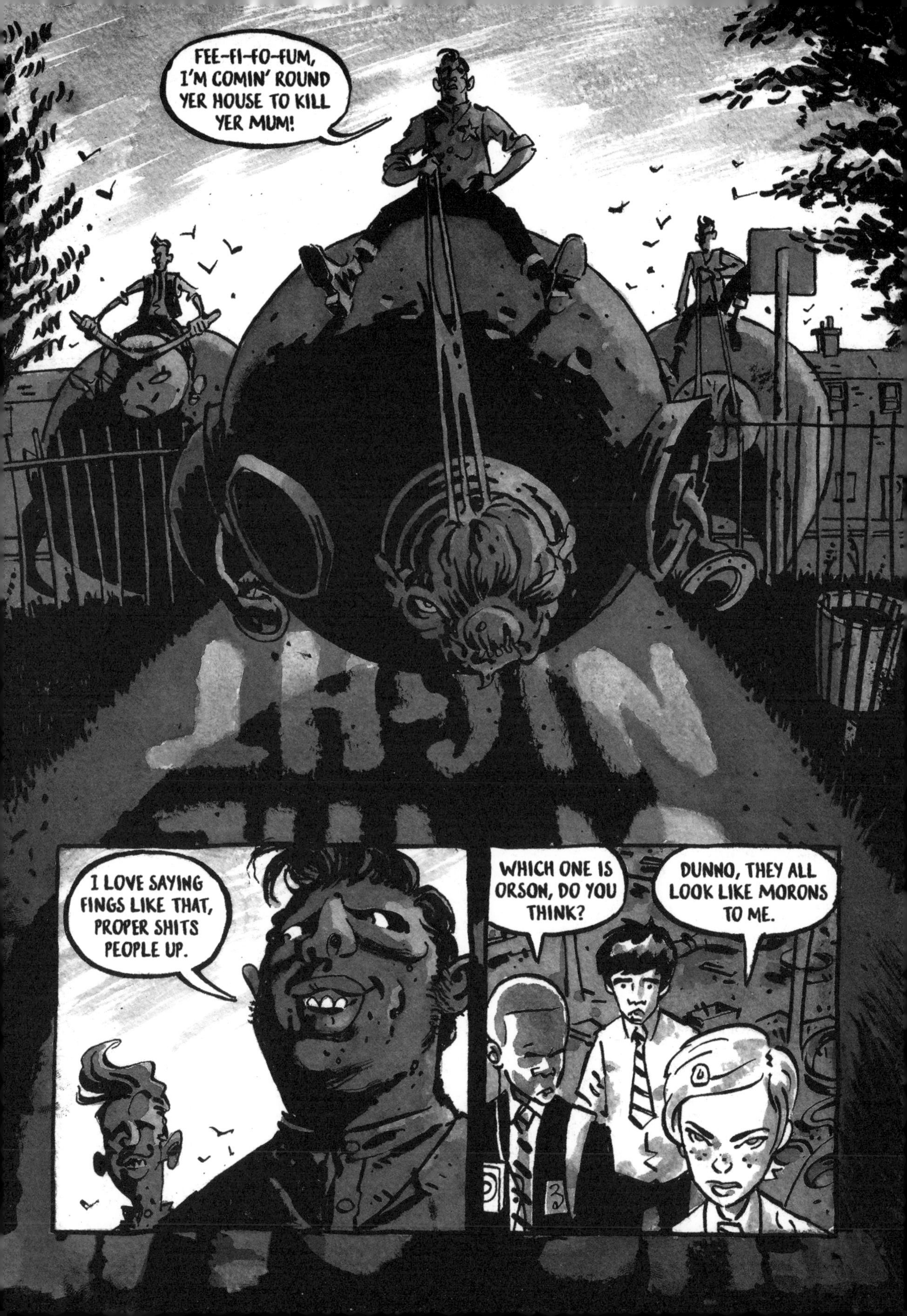
FEE-FI-FO-FUM, I'M COMIN' ROUND YER HOUSE TO KILL YER MUM!
I LOVE SAYING FINGS LIKE THAT, PROPER SHITS PEOPLE UP.
WHICH ONE IS ORSON, DO YOU THINK?
DUNNO, THEY ALL LOOK LIKE MORONS TO ME.

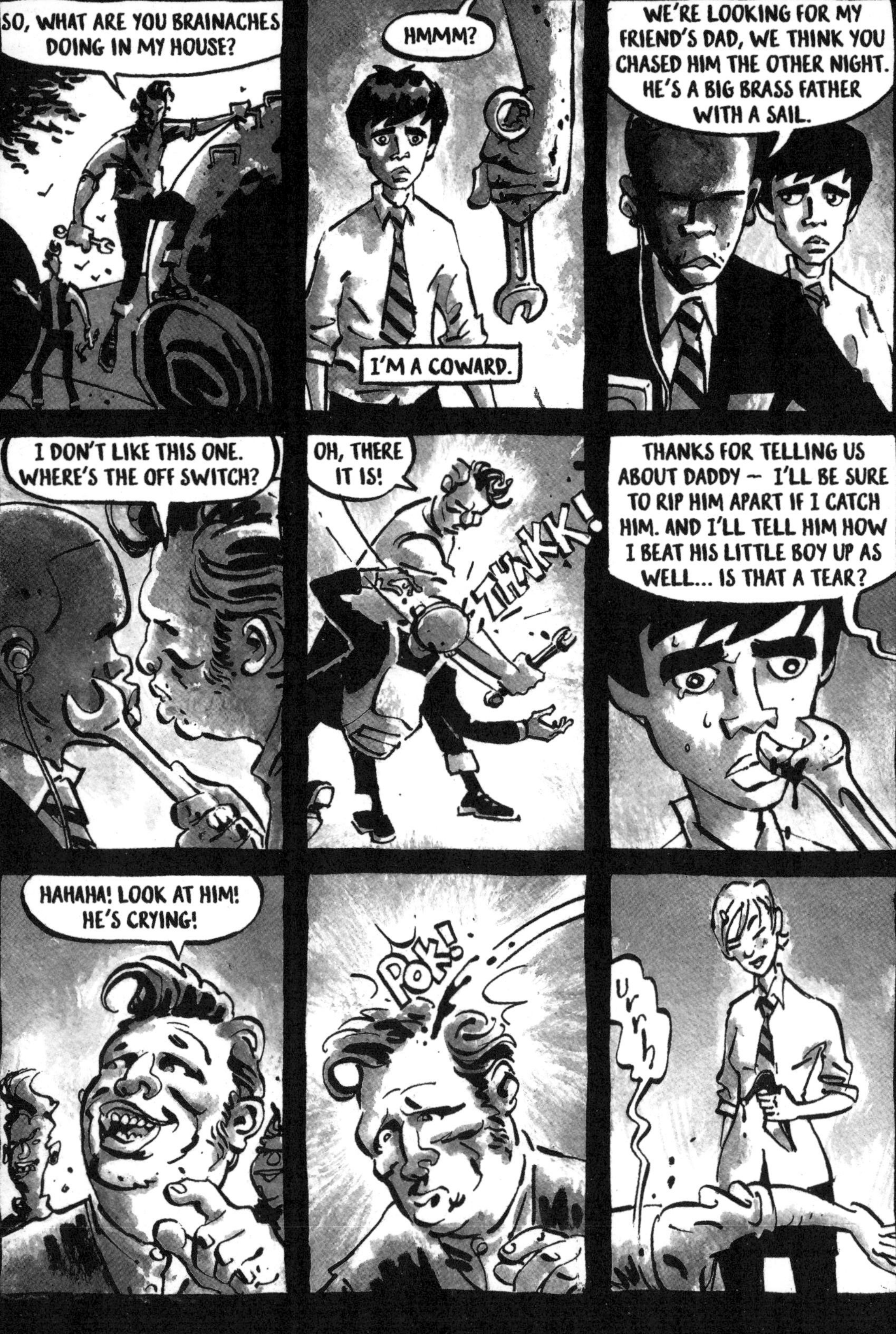
SO, WHAT ARE YOU BRAINACHES DOING IN MY HOUSE?
HMMM?
I'M A COWARD.
WE'RE LOOKING FOR MY FRIEND'S DAD, WE THINK YOU CHASED HIM THE OTHER NIGHT. HE'S A BIG BRASS FATHER WITH A SAIL.
I DON'T LIKE THIS ONE. WHERE'S THE OFF SWITCH?
OH, THERE IT IS!
THWKK!
THANKS FOR TELLING US ABOUT DADDY -- I'LL BE SURE TO RIP HIM APART IF I CATCH HIM. AND I'LL TELL HIM HOW I BEAT HIS LITTLE BOY UP AS WELL... IS THAT A TEAR?
HAHAHA! LOOK AT HIM! HE'S CRYING!
POK!
Urrh

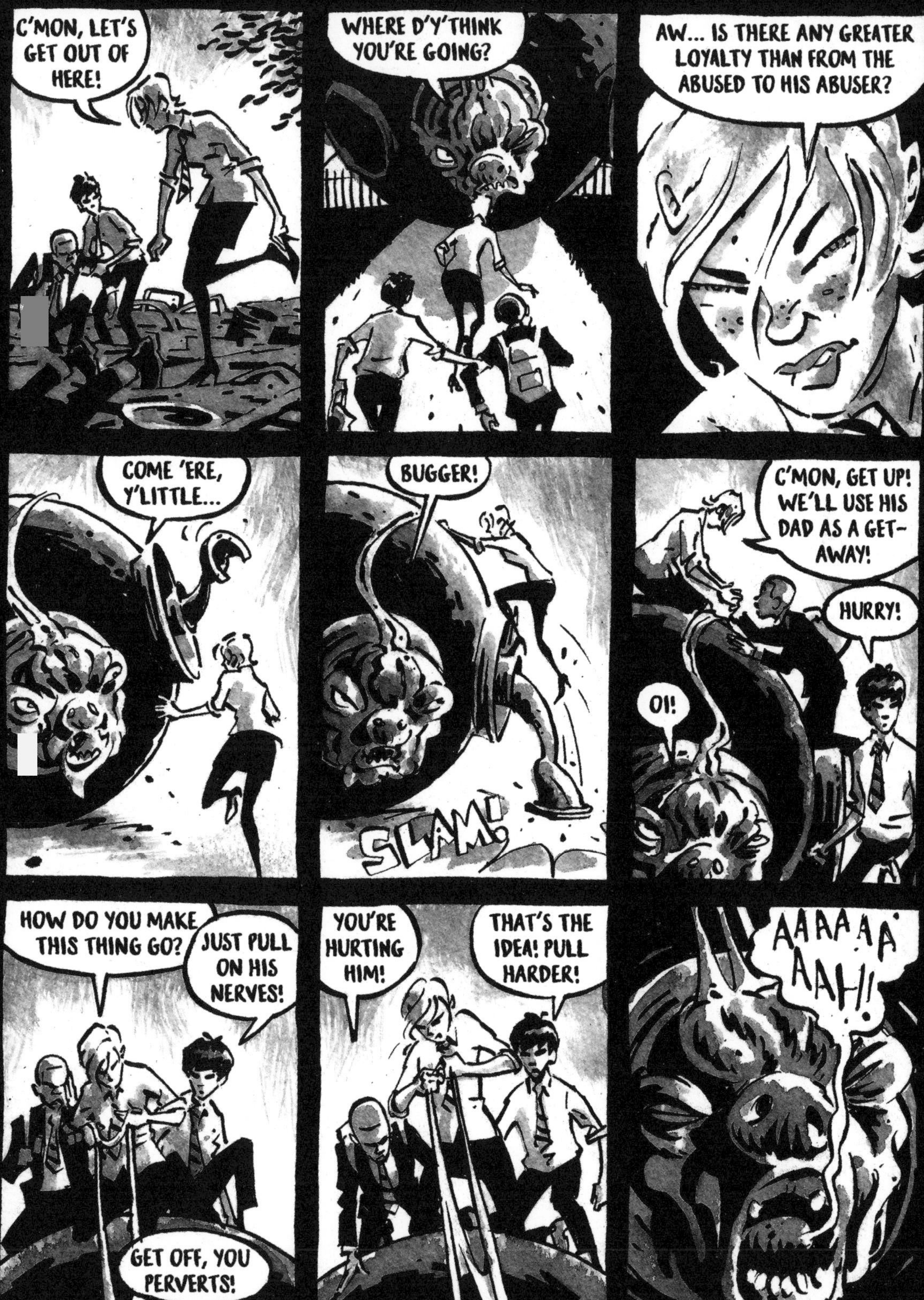
C'MON, LET'S GET OUT OF HERE!
WHERE D'Y'THINK YOU'RE GOING?
AW... IS THERE ANY GREATER LOYALTY THAN FROM THE ABUSED TO HIS ABUSER?
COME 'ERE, Y'LITTLE...
BUGGER!
SLAM!
C'MON, GET UP! WE'LL USE HIS DAD AS A GET-AWAY!
HURRY!
OI!
HOW DO YOU MAKE THIS THING GO?
JUST PULL ON HIS NERVES!
GET OFF, YOU PERVERTS!
YOU'RE HURTING HIM!
THAT'S THE IDEA! PULL HARDER!
AAAAAAAAH!

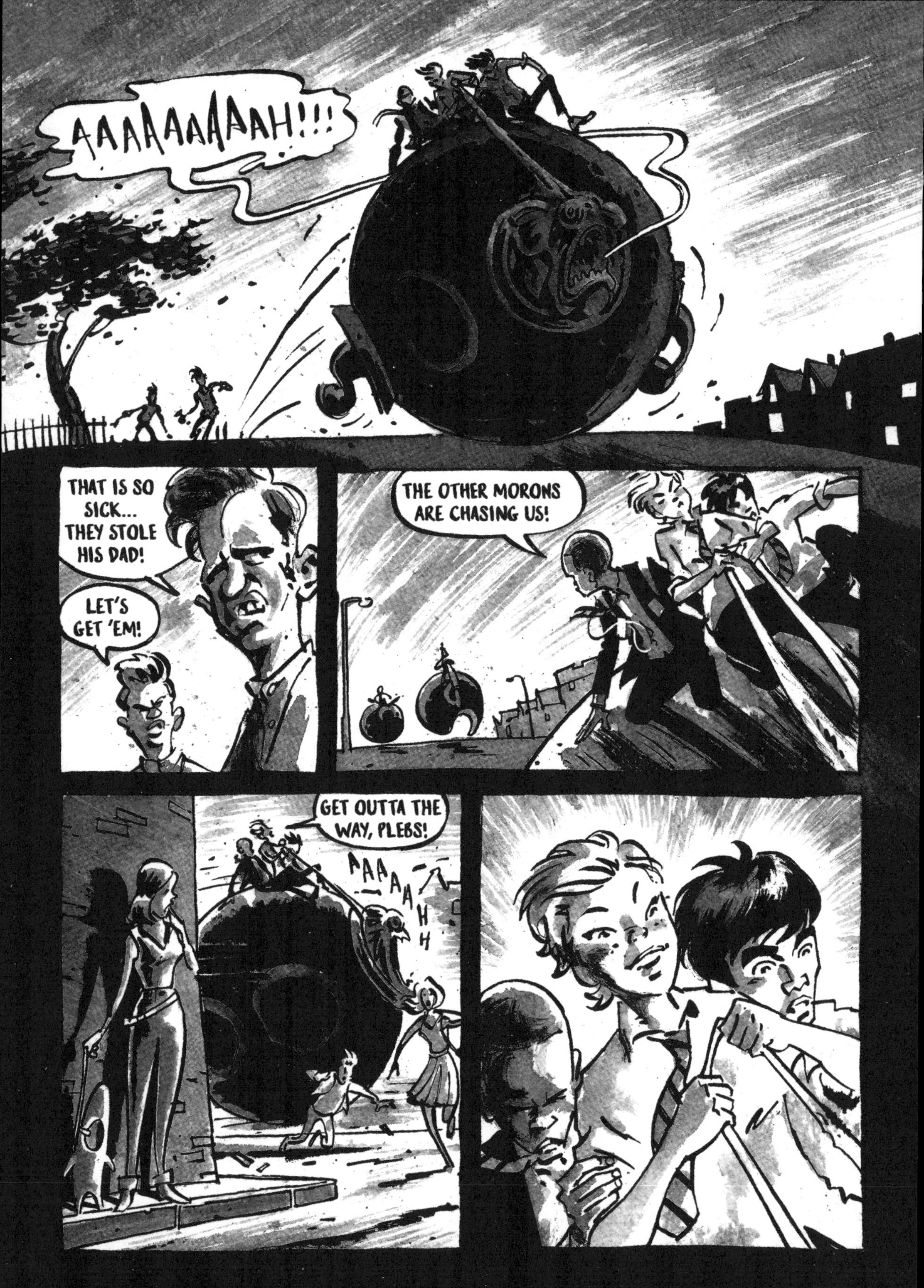
AAAAAAAAAH!!!
THAT IS SO SICK... THEY STOLE HIS DAD!
LET'S GET 'EM!
THE OTHER MORONS ARE CHASING US!
GET OUTTA THE WAY, PLEBS!
AAAAAHH

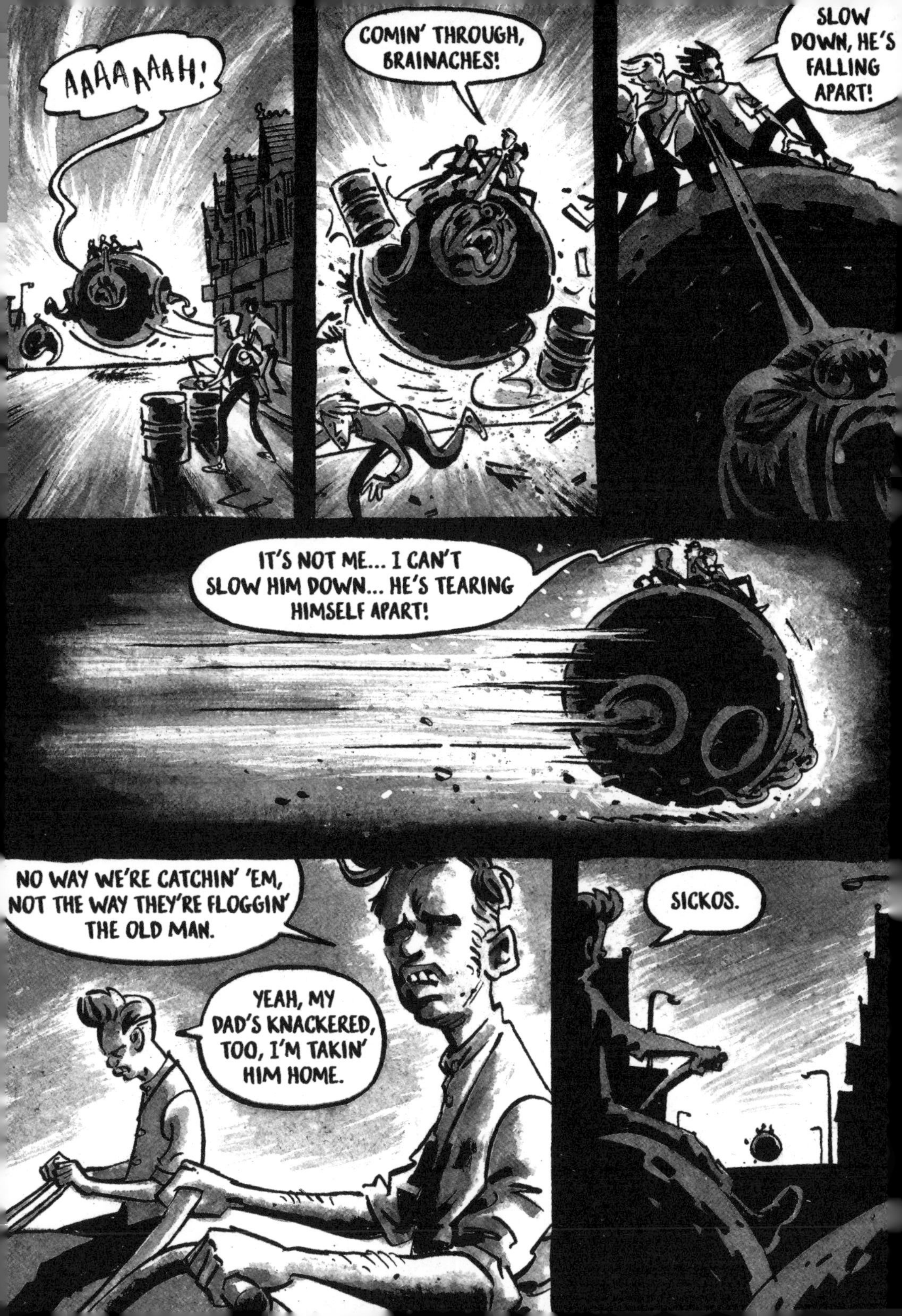
AAAAAAAH!
COMIN' THROUGH, BRAINACHES!
SLOW DOWN, HE'S FALLING APART!
IT'S NOT ME... I CAN'T SLOW HIM DOWN... HE'S TEARING HIMSELF APART!
NO WAY WE'RE CATCHIN' 'EM, NOT THE WAY THEY'RE FLOGGIN' THE OLD MAN.
YEAH, MY DAD'S KNACKERED, TOO, I'M TAKIN' HIM HOME.
SICKOS.

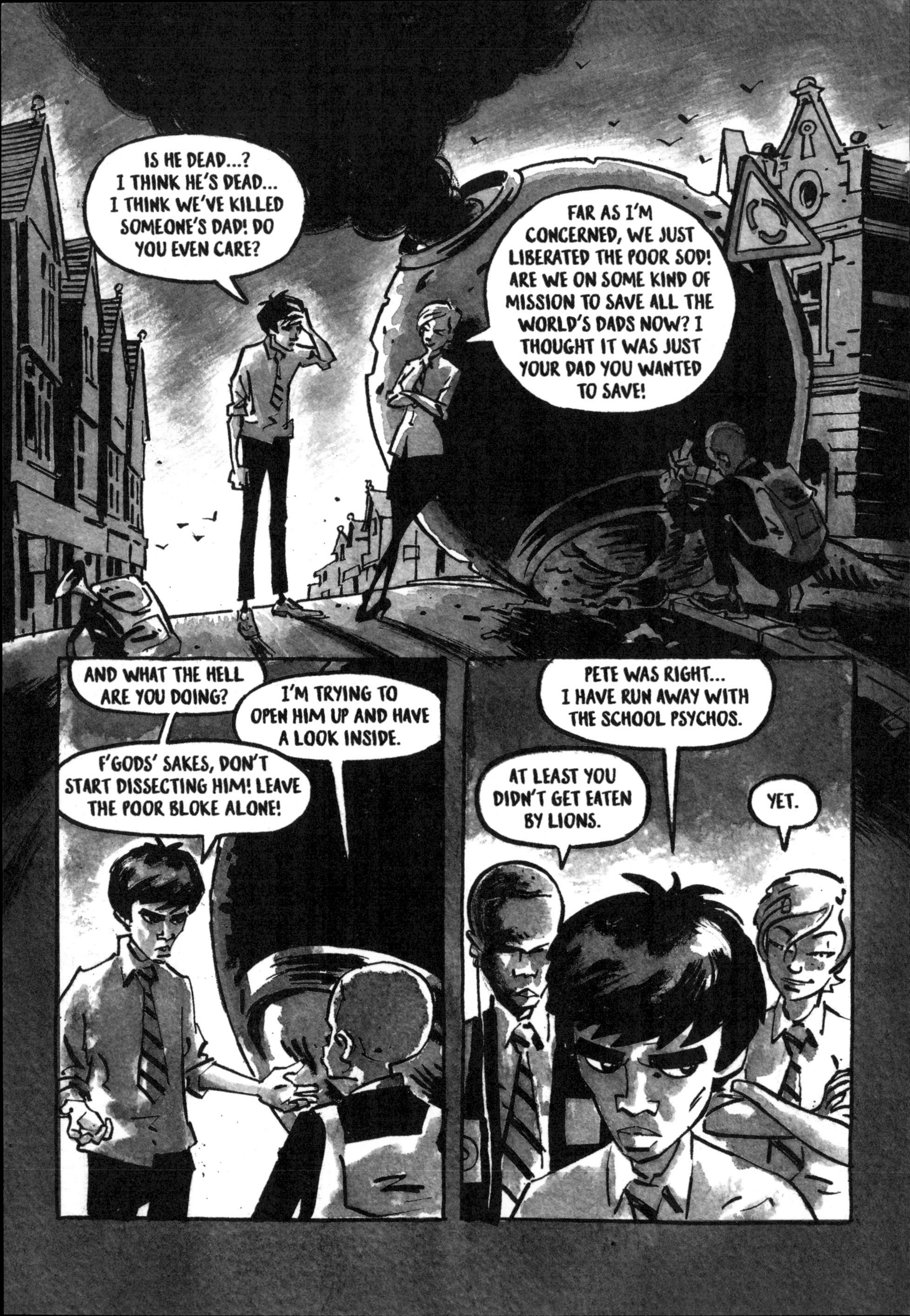
IS HE DEAD...? I THINK HE'S DEAD... I THINK WE'VE KILLED SOMEONE'S DAD! DO YOU EVEN CARE?
FAR AS I'M CONCERNED, WE JUST LIBERATED THE POOR SOD! ARE WE ON SOME KIND OF MISSION TO SAVE ALL THE WORLD'S DADS NOW? I THOUGHT IT WAS JUST YOUR DAD YOU WANTED TO SAVE!
AND WHAT THE HELL ARE YOU DOING?
I'M TRYING TO OPEN HIM UP AND HAVE A LOOK INSIDE.
F'GODS' SAKES, DON'T START DISSECTING HIM! LEAVE THE POOR BLOKE ALONE!
PETE WAS RIGHT... I HAVE RUN AWAY WITH THE SCHOOL PSYCHOS.
AT LEAST YOU DIDN'T GET EATEN BY LIONS.
YET.

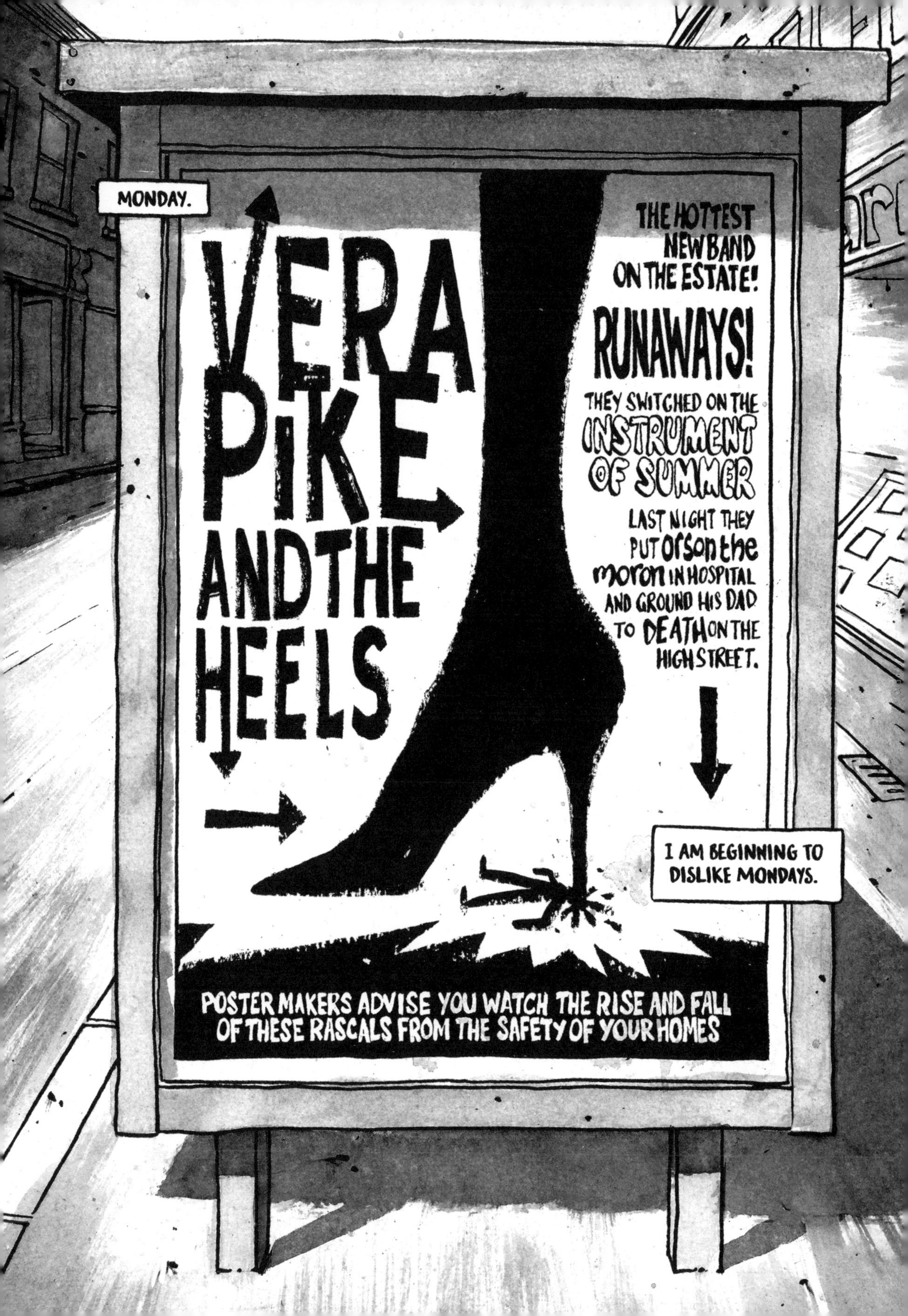
MONDAY.
VERA PIKE AND THE HEELS
THE HOTTEST NEW BAND ON THE ESTATE!
RUNAWAYS!
THEY SWITCHED ON THE INSTRUMENT OF SUMMER
LAST NIGHT THEY PUT ORSON THE MORON IN HOSPITAL AND GROUND HIS DAD TO DEATH ON THE HIGH STREET.
POSTER MAKERS ADVISE YOU WATCH THE RISE AND FALL OF THESE RASCALS FROM THE SAFETY OF YOUR HOMES
I AM BEGINNING TO DISLIKE MONDAYS.

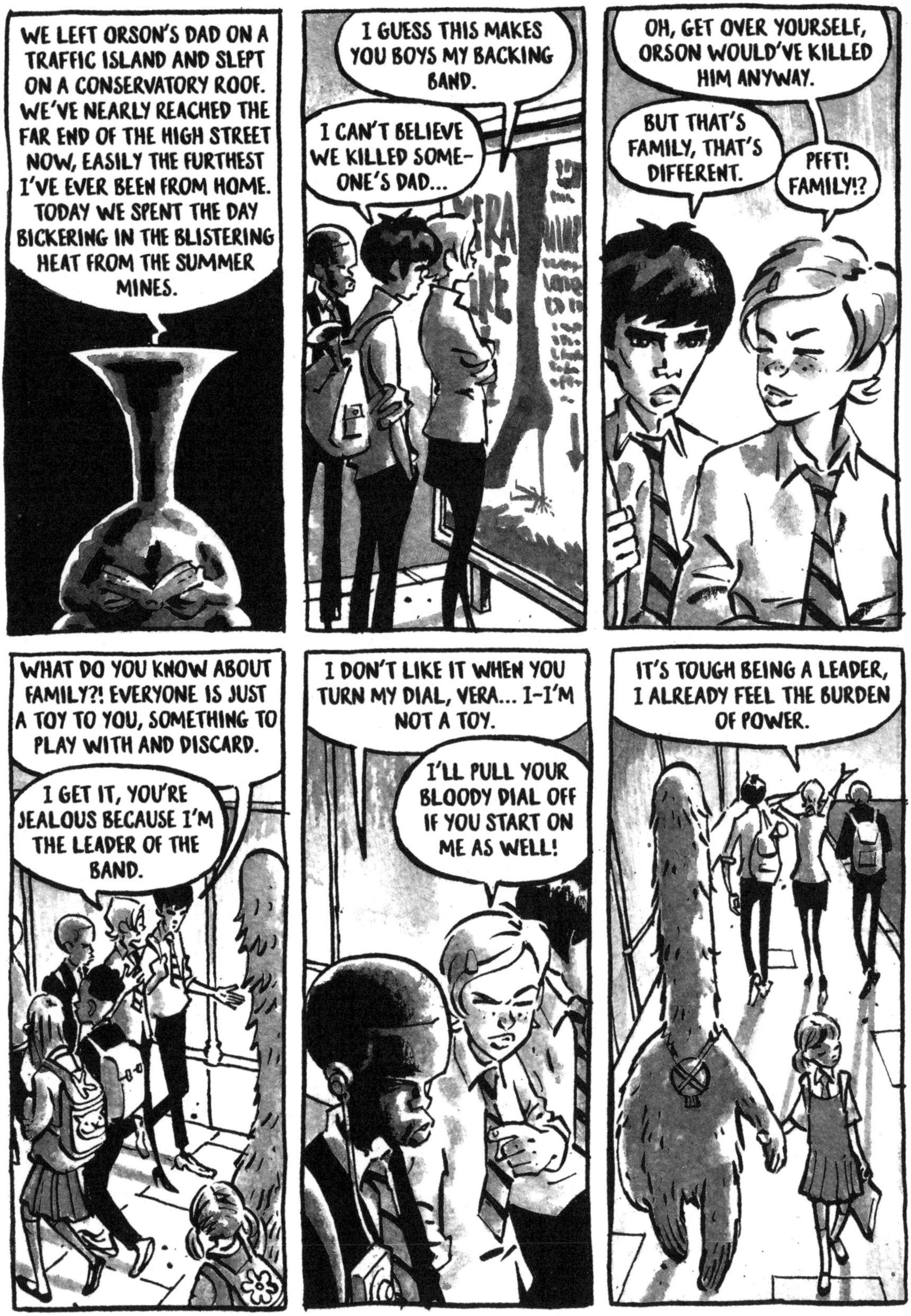
WE LEFT ORSON'S DAD ON A TRAFFIC ISLAND AND SLEPT ON A CONSERVATORY ROOF. WE'VE NEARLY REACHED THE FAR END OF THE HIGH STREET NOW, EASILY THE FURTHEST I'VE EVER BEEN FROM HOME. TODAY WE SPENT THE DAY BICKERING IN THE BLISTERING HEAT FROM THE SUMMER MINES.
I GUESS THIS MAKES YOU BOYS MY BACKING BAND.
I CAN'T BELIEVE WE KILLED SOME-ONE'S DAD...
OH, GET OVER YOURSELF, ORSON WOULD'VE KILLED HIM ANYWAY.
BUT THAT'S FAMILY, THAT'S DIFFERENT.
PFFT! FAMILY!?
WHAT DO YOU KNOW ABOUT FAMILY?! EVERYONE IS JUST A TOY TO YOU, SOMETHING TO PLAY WITH AND DISCARD.
I GET IT, YOU'RE JEALOUS BECAUSE I'M THE LEADER OF THE BAND.
I DON'T LIKE IT WHEN YOU TURN MY DIAL, VERA... I-I'M NOT A TOY.
I'LL PULL YOUR BLOODY DIAL OFF IF YOU START ON ME AS WELL!
IT'S TOUGH BEING A LEADER, I ALREADY FEEL THE BURDEN OF POWER.

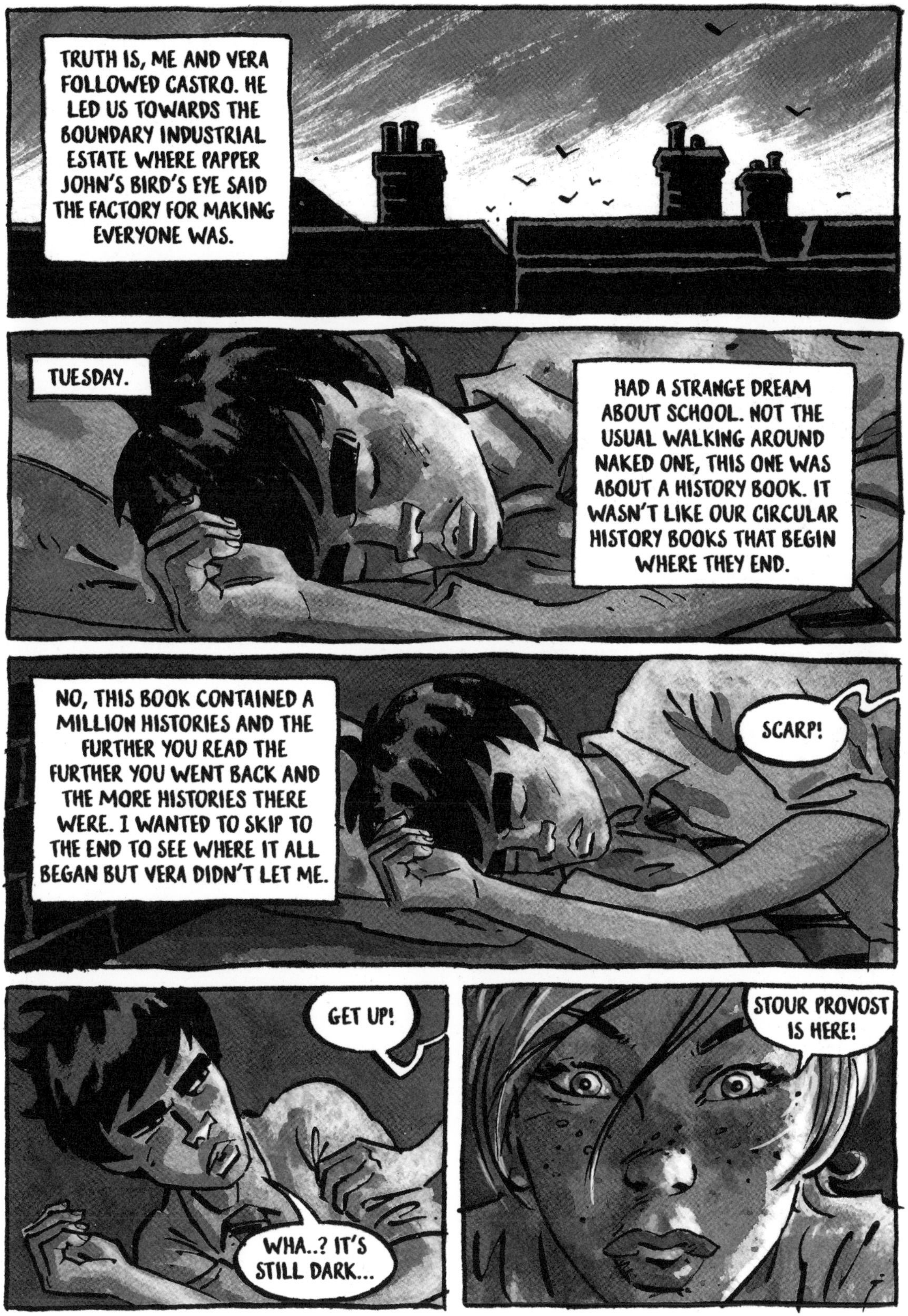
TRUTH IS, ME AND VERA FOLLOWED CASTRO. HE LED US TOWARDS THE BOUNDARY INDUSTRIAL ESTATE WHERE PAPPER JOHN'S BIRD'S EYE SAID THE FACTORY FOR MAKING EVERYONE WAS.
TUESDAY.
HAD A STRANGE DREAM ABOUT SCHOOL. NOT THE USUAL WALKING AROUND NAKED ONE, THIS ONE WAS ABOUT A HISTORY BOOK. IT WASN'T LIKE OUR CIRCULAR HISTORY BOOKS THAT BEGIN WHERE THEY END.
NO, THIS BOOK CONTAINED A MILLION HISTORIES AND THE FURTHER YOU READ THE FURTHER YOU WENT BACK AND THE MORE HISTORIES THERE WERE. I WANTED TO SKIP TO THE END TO SEE WHERE IT ALL BEGAN BUT VERA DIDN'T LET ME.
SCARP!
GET UP!
WHA..? IT'S STILL DARK...
STOUR PROVOST IS HERE!

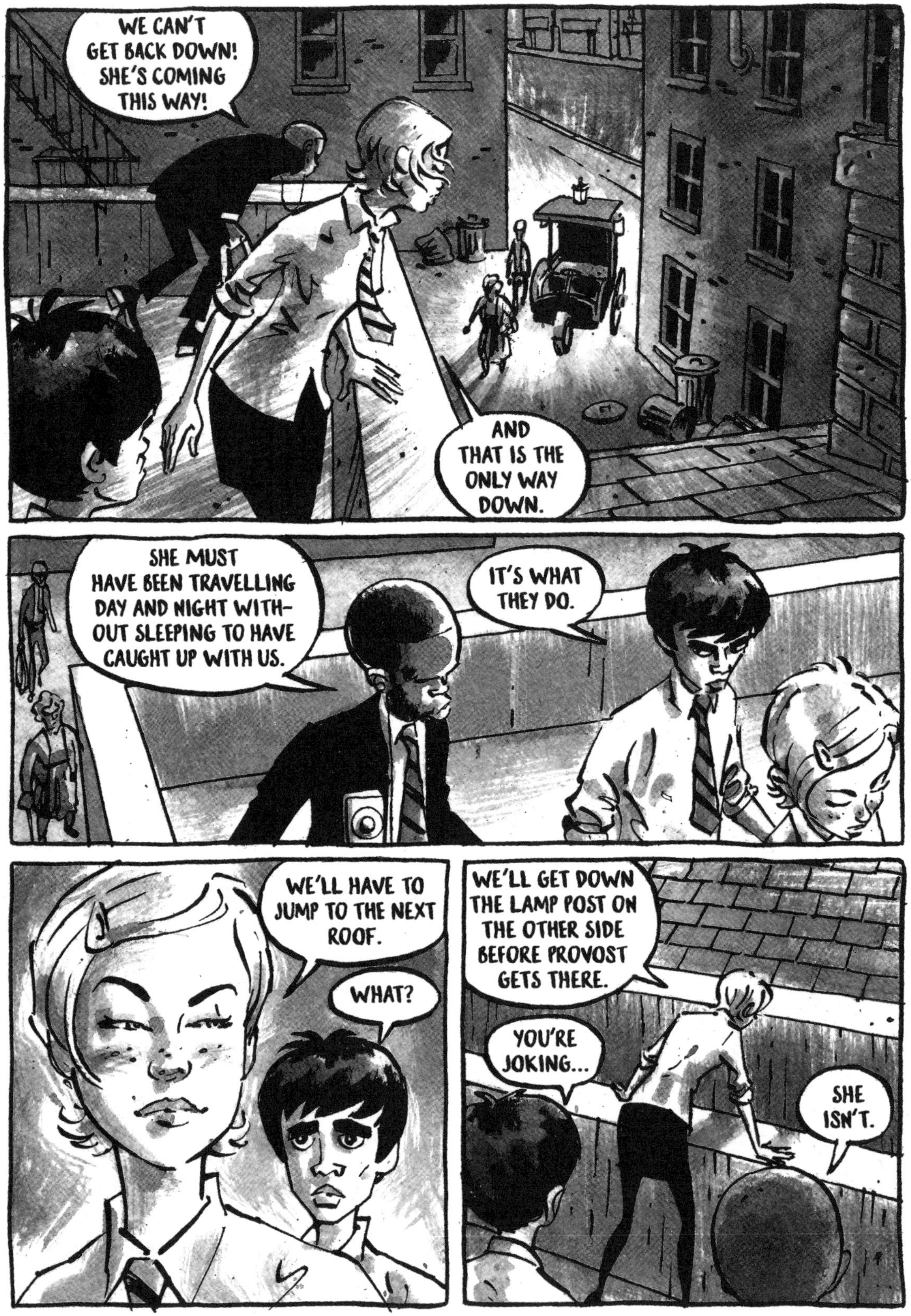

WE CAN'T GET BACK DOWN! SHE'S COMING THIS WAY!
AND THAT IS THE ONLY WAY DOWN.
SHE MUST HAVE BEEN TRAVELLING DAY AND NIGHT WITHOUT SLEEPING TO HAVE CAUGHT UP WITH US.
IT'S WHAT THEY DO.
WE'LL HAVE TO JUMP TO THE NEXT ROOF.
WHAT?
WE'LL GET DOWN THE LAMP POST ON THE OTHER SIDE BEFORE PROVOST GETS THERE.
YOU'RE JOKING...
SHE ISN'T.

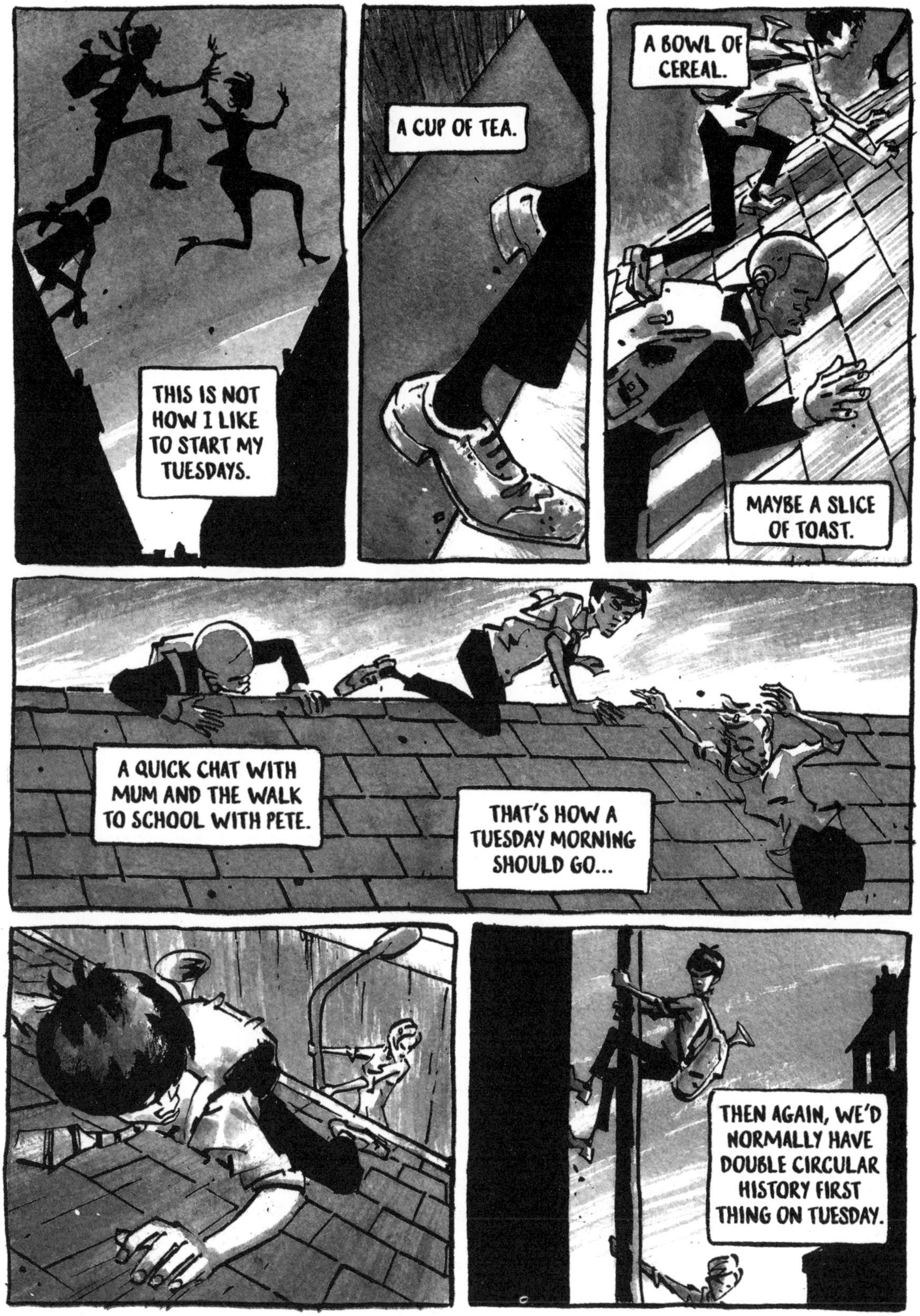
THIS IS NOT HOW I LIKE TO START MY TUESDAYS.
A CUP OF TEA.
A BOWL OF CEREAL.
MAYBE A SLICE OF TOAST.
A QUICK CHAT WITH MUM AND THE WALK TO SCHOOL WITH PETE.
THAT'S HOW A TUESDAY MORNING SHOULD GO...
THEN AGAIN, WE'D NORMALLY HAVE DOUBLE CIRCULAR HISTORY FIRST THING ON TUESDAY.

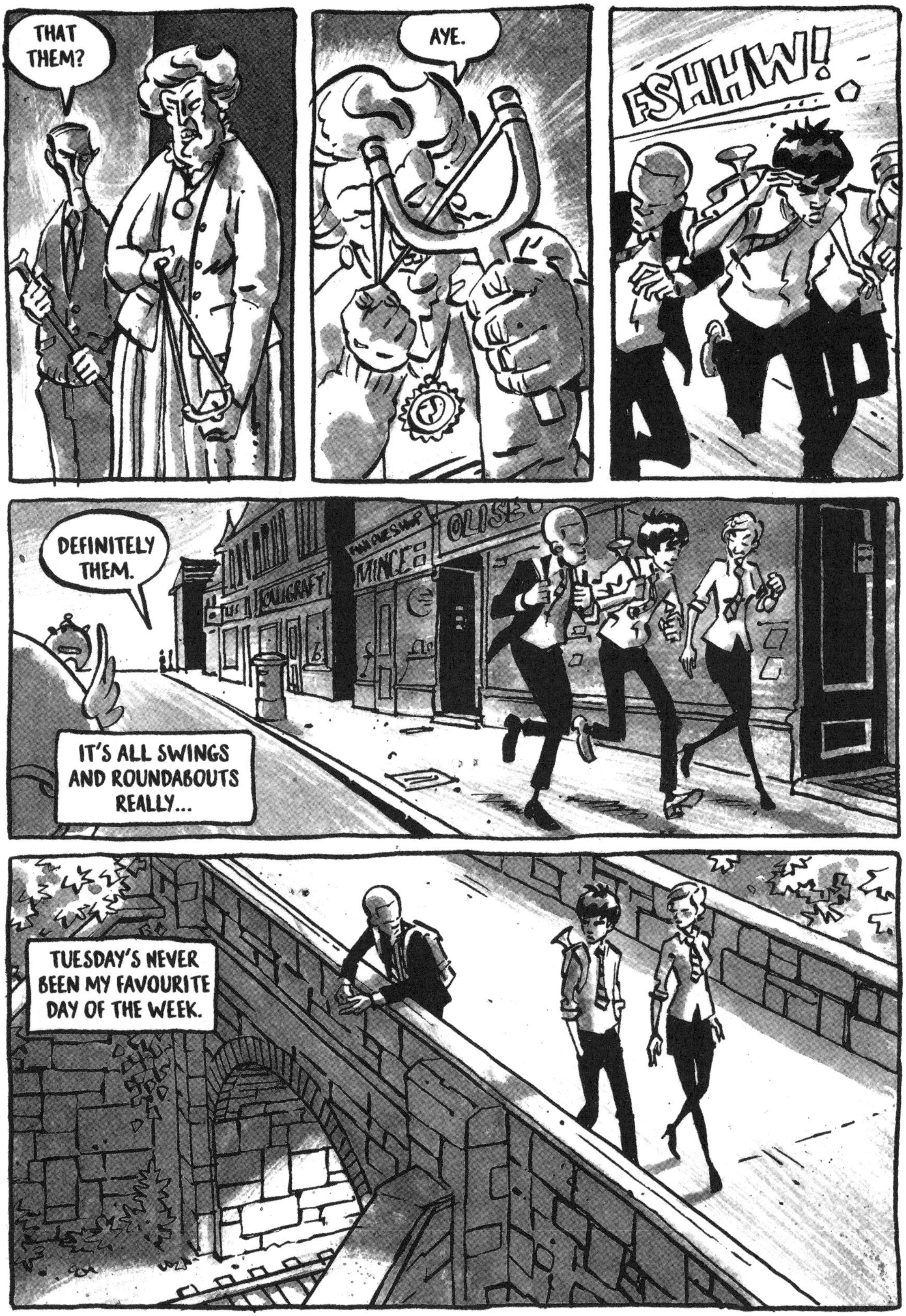
THAT THEM?
AYE.
FSHHW!
DEFINITELY THEM.
IT'S ALL SWINGS AND ROUNDABOUTS REALLY...
TUESDAY'S NEVER BEEN MY FAVOURITE DAY OF THE WEEK.

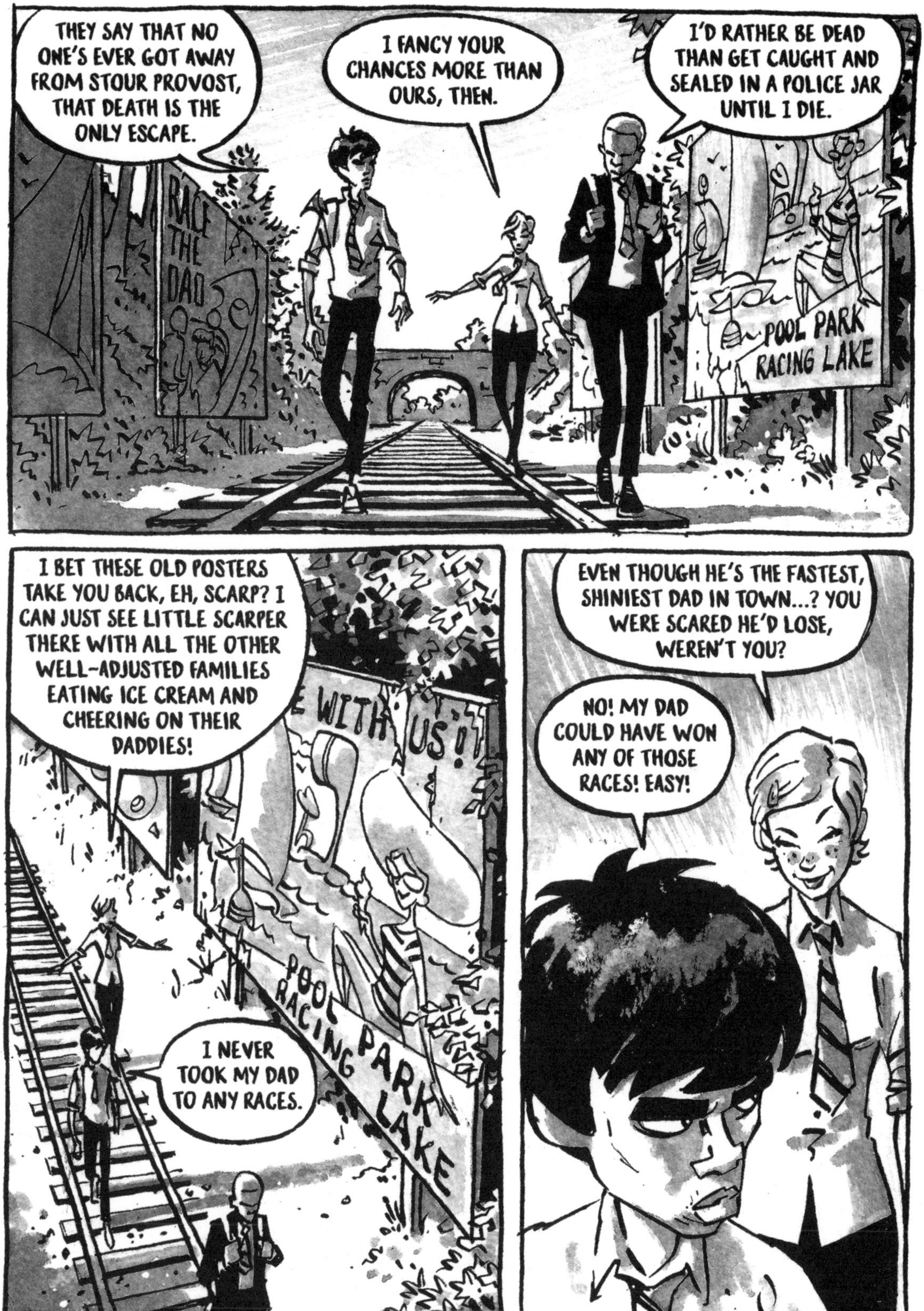
THEY SAY THAT NO ONE'S EVER GOT AWAY FROM STOUR PROVOST, THAT DEATH IS THE ONLY ESCAPE.
I FANCY YOUR CHANCES MORE THAN OURS, THEN.
I'D RATHER BE DEAD THAN GET CAUGHT AND SEALED IN A POLICE JAR UNTIL I DIE.
RACE THE DAD
POOL PARK RACING LAKE
I BET THESE OLD POSTERS TAKE YOU BACK, EH, SCARP? I CAN JUST SEE LITTLE SCARPER THERE WITH ALL THE OTHER WELL-ADJUSTED FAMILIES EATING ICE CREAM AND CHEERING ON THEIR DADDIES!
E WITH US!
POOL PARK RACING LAKE
I NEVER TOOK MY DAD TO ANY RACES.
EVEN THOUGH HE'S THE FASTEST, SHINIEST DAD IN TOWN...? YOU WERE SCARED HE'D LOSE, WEREN'T YOU?
NO! MY DAD COULD HAVE WON ANY OF THOSE RACES! EASY!

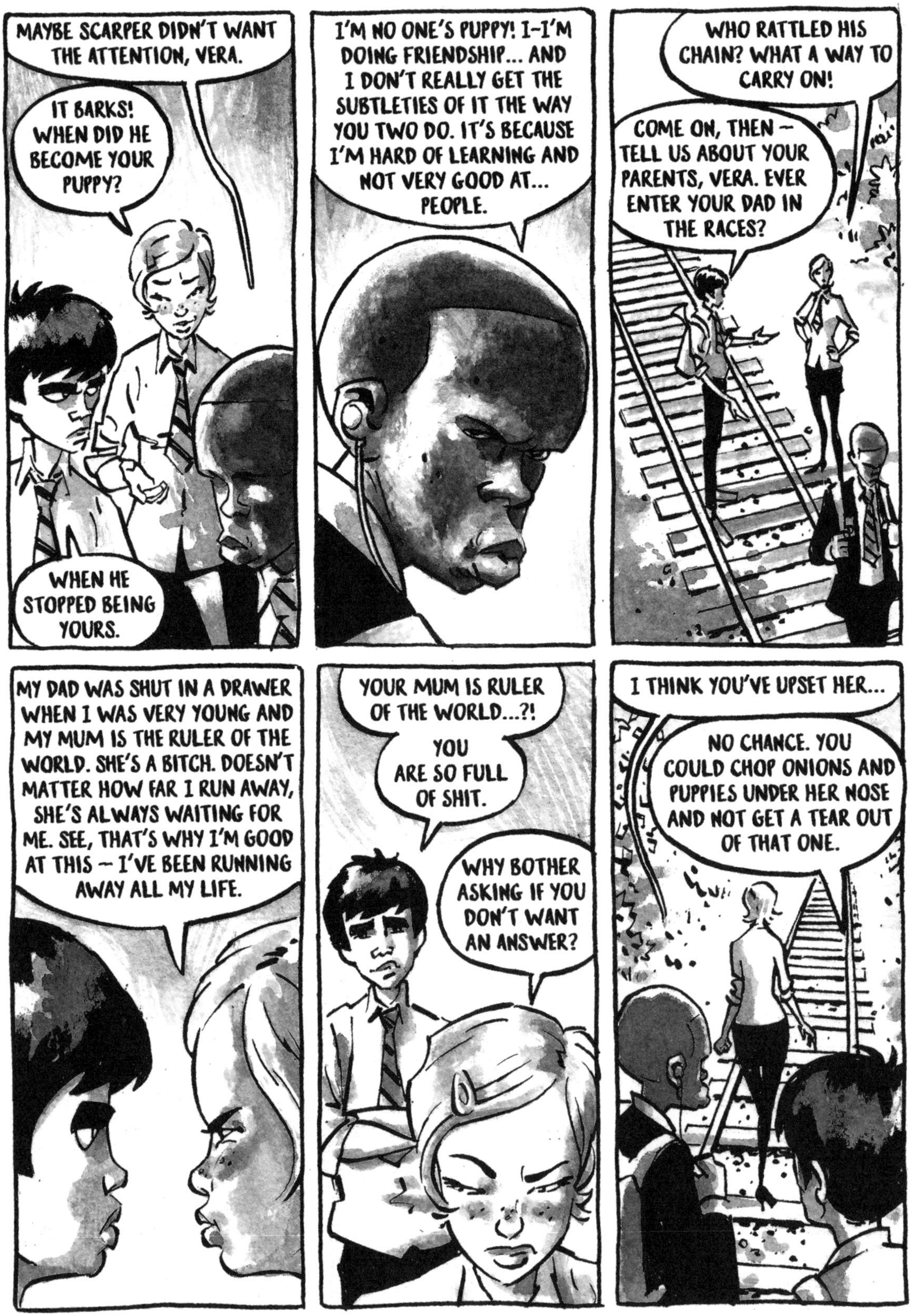
MAYBE SCARPER DIDN'T WANT THE ATTENTION, VERA.
IT BARKS! WHEN DID HE BECOME YOUR PUPPY?
WHEN HE STOPPED BEING YOURS.
I'M NO ONE'S PUPPY! I-I'M DOING FRIENDSHIP... AND I DON'T REALLY GET THE SUBTLETIES OF IT THE WAY YOU TWO DO. IT'S BECAUSE I'M HARD OF LEARNING AND NOT VERY GOOD AT... PEOPLE.
WHO RATTLED HIS CHAIN? WHAT A WAY TO CARRY ON!
COME ON, THEN – TELL US ABOUT YOUR PARENTS, VERA. EVER ENTER YOUR DAD IN THE RACES?
MY DAD WAS SHUT IN A DRAWER WHEN I WAS VERY YOUNG AND MY MUM IS THE RULER OF THE WORLD. SHE'S A BITCH. DOESN'T MATTER HOW FAR I RUN AWAY, SHE'S ALWAYS WAITING FOR ME. SEE, THAT'S WHY I'M GOOD AT THIS – I'VE BEEN RUNNING AWAY ALL MY LIFE.
YOUR MUM IS RULER OF THE WORLD...?!
YOU ARE SO FULL OF SHIT.
WHY BOTHER ASKING IF YOU DON'T WANT AN ANSWER?
I THINK YOU'VE UPSET HER...
NO CHANCE. YOU COULD CHOP ONIONS AND PUPPIES UNDER HER NOSE AND NOT GET A TEAR OUT OF THAT ONE.

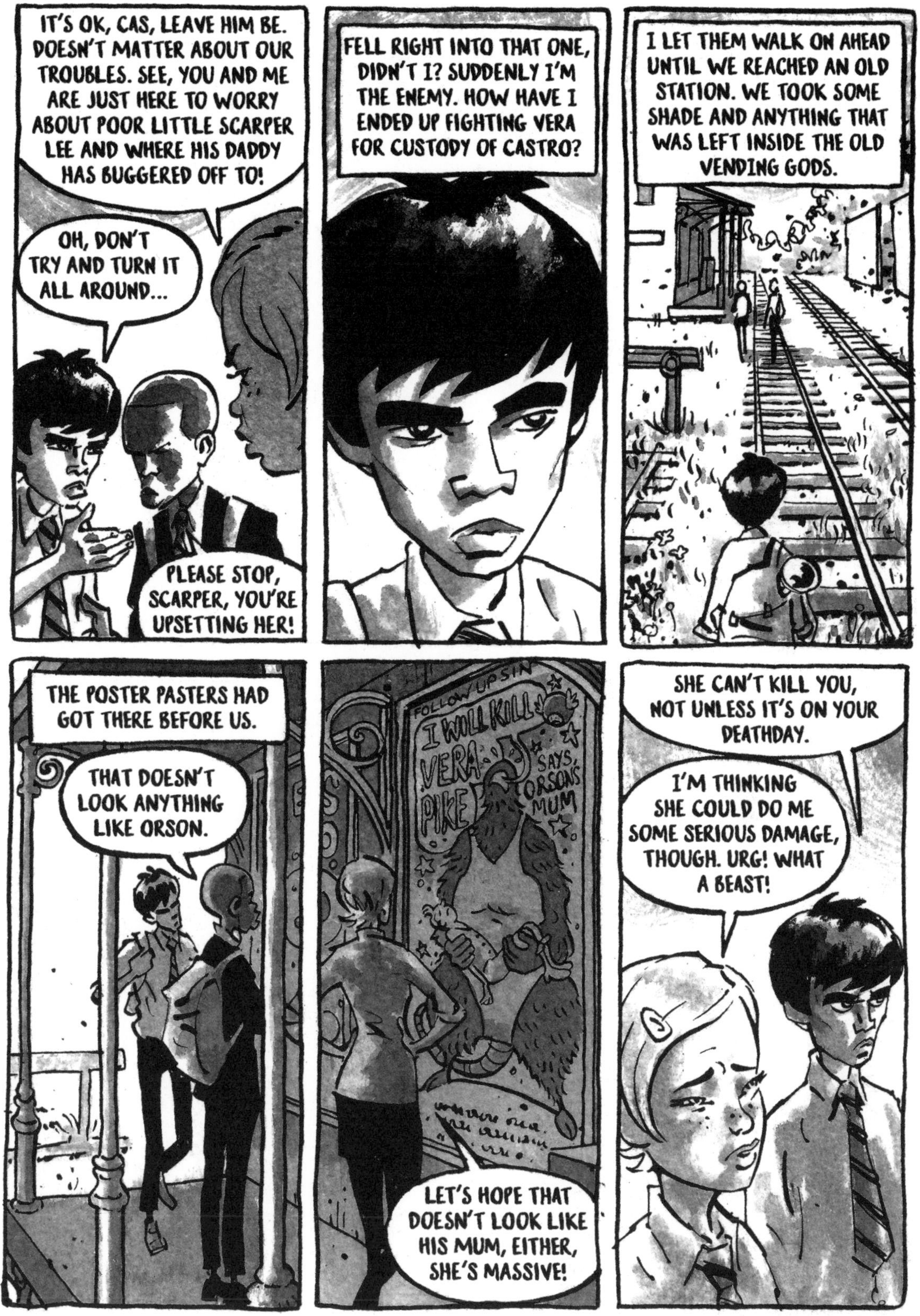
IT'S OK, CAS, LEAVE HIM BE. DOESN'T MATTER ABOUT OUR TROUBLES. SEE, YOU AND ME ARE JUST HERE TO WORRY ABOUT POOR LITTLE SCARPER LEE AND WHERE HIS DADDY HAS BUGGERED OFF TO!
OH, DON'T TRY AND TURN IT ALL AROUND...
PLEASE STOP, SCARPER, YOU'RE UPSETTING HER!
FELL RIGHT INTO THAT ONE, DIDN'T I? SUDDENLY I'M THE ENEMY. HOW HAVE I ENDED UP FIGHTING VERA FOR CUSTODY OF CASTRO?
I LET THEM WALK ON AHEAD UNTIL WE REACHED AN OLD STATION. WE TOOK SOME SHADE AND ANYTHING THAT WAS LEFT INSIDE THE OLD VENDING GODS.
THE POSTER PASTERS HAD GOT THERE BEFORE US.
THAT DOESN'T LOOK ANYTHING LIKE ORSON.
FOLLOW UP SIN
I WOLL KILL VERA PIKE
SAYS, ORSON'S MUM
LET'S HOPE THAT DOESN'T LOOK LIKE HIS MUM, EITHER, SHE'S MASSIVE!
SHE CAN'T KILL YOU, NOT UNLESS IT'S ON YOUR DEATHDAY.
I'M THINKING SHE COULD DO ME SOME SERIOUS DAMAGE, THOUGH. URG! WHAT A BEAST!

THEY SAY IT'S NATURAL FOR MOTHERS TO BE PROTECTIVE OF THEIR KIDS. I DON'T SEE WHY. THEY NEED PROTECTING AS MUCH AS WE DO. AND YET NEARLY ALL MUMS ARE MADE THAT WAY.

WHAT DOES NATURAL MEAN?

MEANS NON-ARTIFICIAL.

IT MEANS MADE BY NATURE.

BUT NATURE CAN'T MAKE THINGS, IT'S NOT A PERSON.

NATURE IS THE THINGS THAT AREN'T MADE BY PEOPLE.

BUT WE'RE MADE BY PEOPLE, SO WHAT DOES THAT MAKE US? ARE WE ARTIFICIAL?

THIS IS WHY WE'RE GOING TO FIND THE MOTHERLESS OVEN — TO SEE WHERE PEOPLE ARE MADE AND WHERE PEOPLE MAKE THEIR PARENTS. WE'RE GOING THERE FOR ANSWERS.

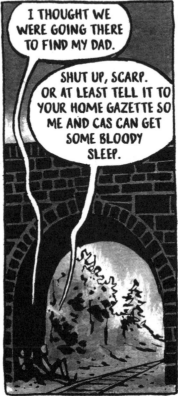

I THOUGHT WE WERE GOING THERE TO FIND MY DAD.

SHUT UP, SCARP. OR AT LEAST TELL IT TO YOUR HOME GAZETTE SO ME AND CAS CAN GET SOME BLOODY SLEEP.

EVERYTHING IS MADE, BUT ONLY PEOPLE MAKE THINGS. I MEAN, HOW CAN A THING EXIST IF IT ISN'T MADE? HOW CAN A SHAPE BE A SHAPE IF IT ISN'T SHAPED?

PFFT. TUESDAYS, EH?

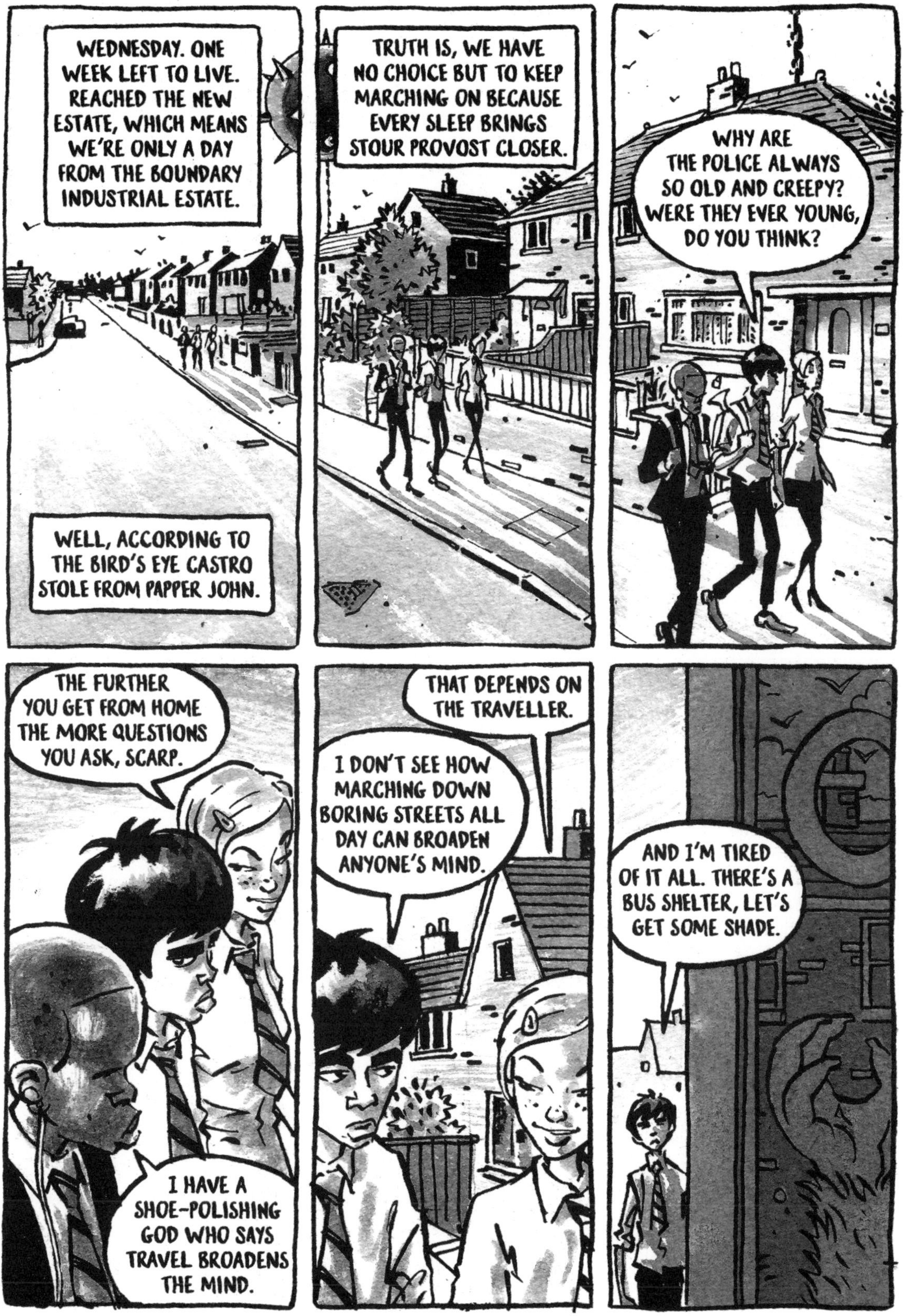
WEDNESDAY. ONE WEEK LEFT TO LIVE. REACHED THE NEW ESTATE, WHICH MEANS WE'RE ONLY A DAY FROM THE BOUNDARY INDUSTRIAL ESTATE.
WELL, ACCORDING TO THE BIRD'S EYE CASTRO STOLE FROM PAPPER JOHN.
TRUTH IS, WE HAVE NO CHOICE BUT TO KEEP MARCHING ON BECAUSE EVERY SLEEP BRINGS STOUR PROVOST CLOSER.
WHY ARE THE POLICE ALWAYS SO OLD AND CREEPY? WERE THEY EVER YOUNG, DO YOU THINK?
THE FURTHER YOU GET FROM HOME THE MORE QUESTIONS YOU ASK, SCARP.
I HAVE A SHOE-POLISHING GOD WHO SAYS TRAVEL BROADENS THE MIND.
THAT DEPENDS ON THE TRAVELLER.
I DON'T SEE HOW MARCHING DOWN BORING STREETS ALL DAY CAN BROADEN ANYONE'S MIND.
AND I'M TIRED OF IT ALL. THERE'S A BUS SHELTER, LET'S GET SOME SHADE.

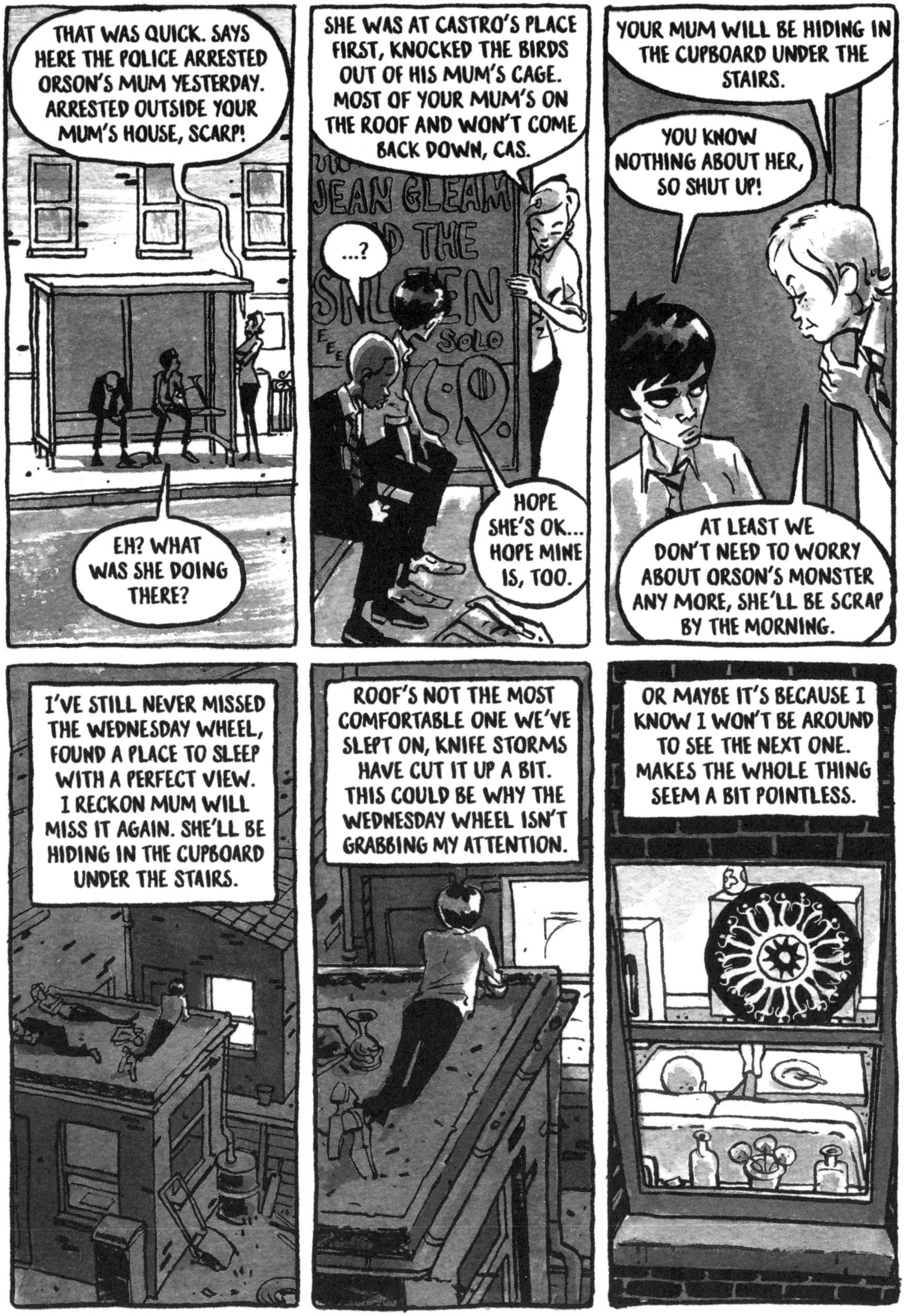
THAT WAS QUICK. SAYS HERE THE POLICE ARRESTED ORSON'S MUM YESTERDAY. ARRESTED OUTSIDE YOUR MUM'S HOUSE, SCARP!
EH? WHAT WAS SHE DOING THERE?
SHE WAS AT CASTRO'S PLACE FIRST, KNOCKED THE BIRDS OUT OF HIS MUM'S CAGE. MOST OF YOUR MUM'S ON THE ROOF AND WON'T COME BACK DOWN, CAS.
JEAN GLEAM
...?
HOPE SHE'S OK... HOPE MINE IS, TOO.
YOUR MUM WILL BE HIDING IN THE CUPBOARD UNDER THE STAIRS.
YOU KNOW NOTHING ABOUT HER, SO SHUT UP!
AT LEAST WE DON'T NEED TO WORRY ABOUT ORSON'S MONSTER ANY MORE, SHE'LL BE SCRAP BY THE MORNING.
I'VE STILL NEVER MISSED THE WEDNESDAY WHEEL, FOUND A PLACE TO SLEEP WITH A PERFECT VIEW. I RECKON MUM WILL MISS IT AGAIN. SHE'LL BE HIDING IN THE CUPBOARD UNDER THE STAIRS.
ROOF'S NOT THE MOST COMFORTABLE ONE WE'VE SLEPT ON, KNIFE STORMS HAVE CUT IT UP A BIT. THIS COULD BE WHY THE WEDNESDAY WHEEL ISN'T GRABBING MY ATTENTION.
OR MAYBE IT'S BECAUSE I KNOW I WON'T BE AROUND TO SEE THE NEXT ONE. MAKES THE WHOLE THING SEEM A BIT POINTLESS.

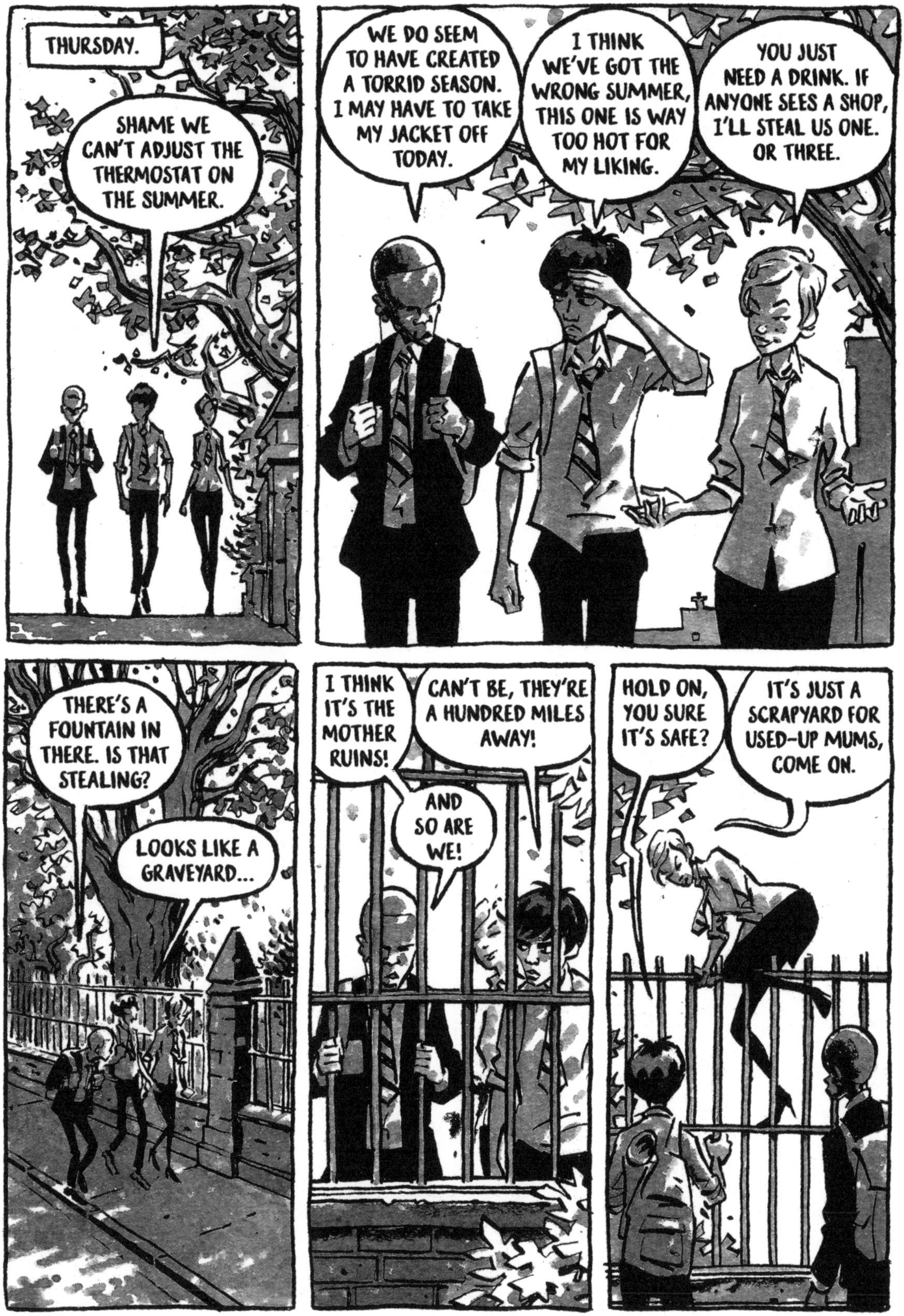
THURSDAY.
SHAME WE CAN'T ADJUST THE THERMOSTAT ON THE SUMMER.
WE DO SEEM TO HAVE CREATED A TORRID SEASON. I MAY HAVE TO TAKE MY JACKET OFF TODAY.
I THINK WE'VE GOT THE WRONG SUMMER, THIS ONE IS WAY TOO HOT FOR MY LIKING.
YOU JUST NEED A DRINK. IF ANYONE SEES A SHOP, I'LL STEAL US ONE. OR THREE.
THERE'S A FOUNTAIN IN THERE. IS THAT STEALING?
LOOKS LIKE A GRAVEYARD...
I THINK IT'S THE MOTHER RUINS!
CAN'T BE, THEY'RE A HUNDRED MILES AWAY!
AND SO ARE WE!
HOLD ON, YOU SURE IT'S SAFE?
IT'S JUST A SCRAPYARD FOR USED-UP MUMS, COME ON.

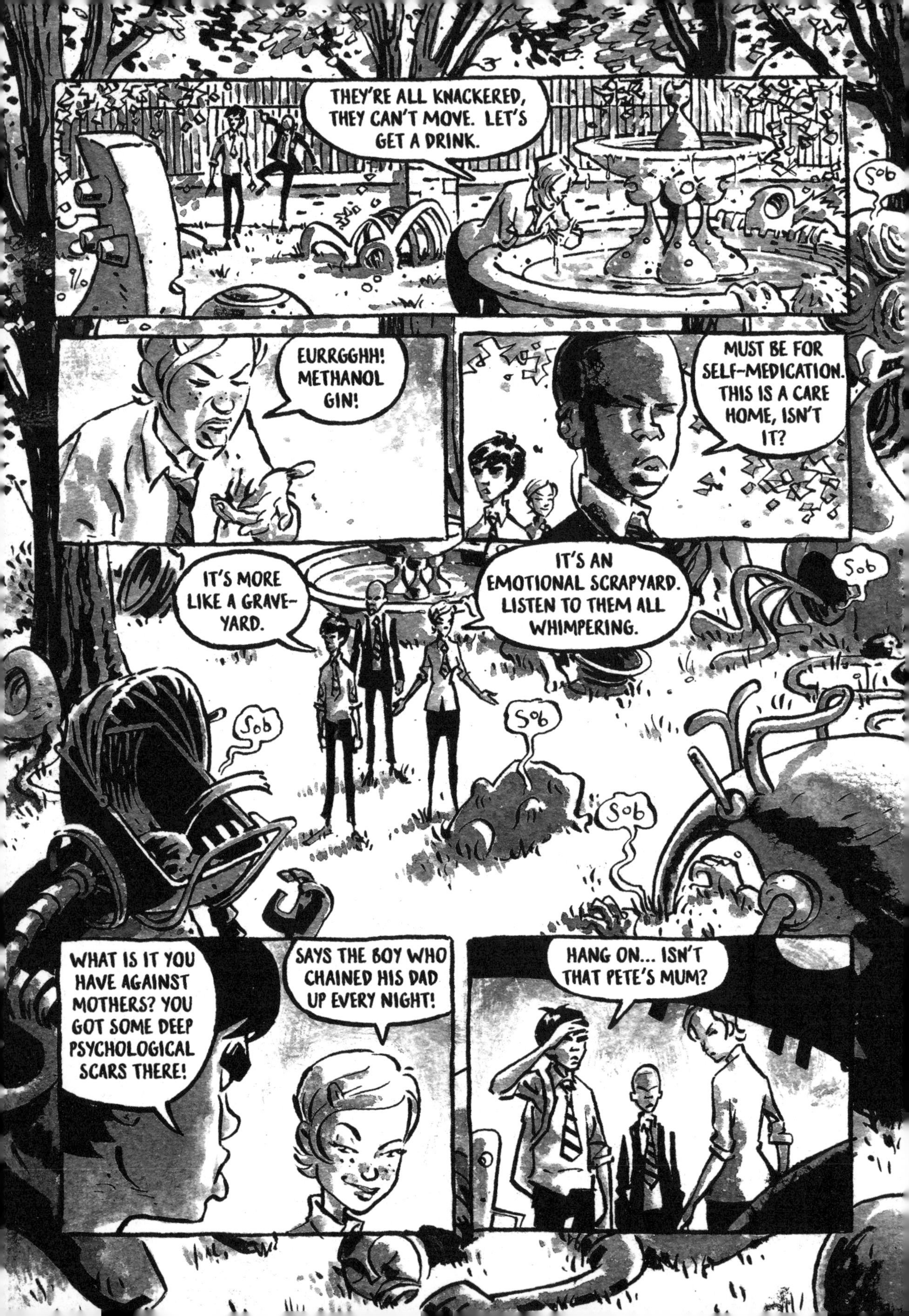
THEY'RE ALL KNACKERED, THEY CAN'T MOVE. LET'S GET A DRINK.
Sob
EURRGGHH! METHANOL GIN!
MUST BE FOR SELF-MEDICATION. THIS IS A CARE HOME, ISN'T IT?
IT'S MORE LIKE A GRAVEYARD.
IT'S AN EMOTIONAL SCRAPYARD. LISTEN TO THEM ALL WHIMPERING.
Sob
Sob
Sob
Sob
WHAT IS IT YOU HAVE AGAINST MOTHERS? YOU GOT SOME DEEP PSYCHOLOGICAL SCARS THERE!
SAYS THE BOY WHO CHAINED HIS DAD UP EVERY NIGHT!
HANG ON... ISN'T THAT PETE'S MUM?

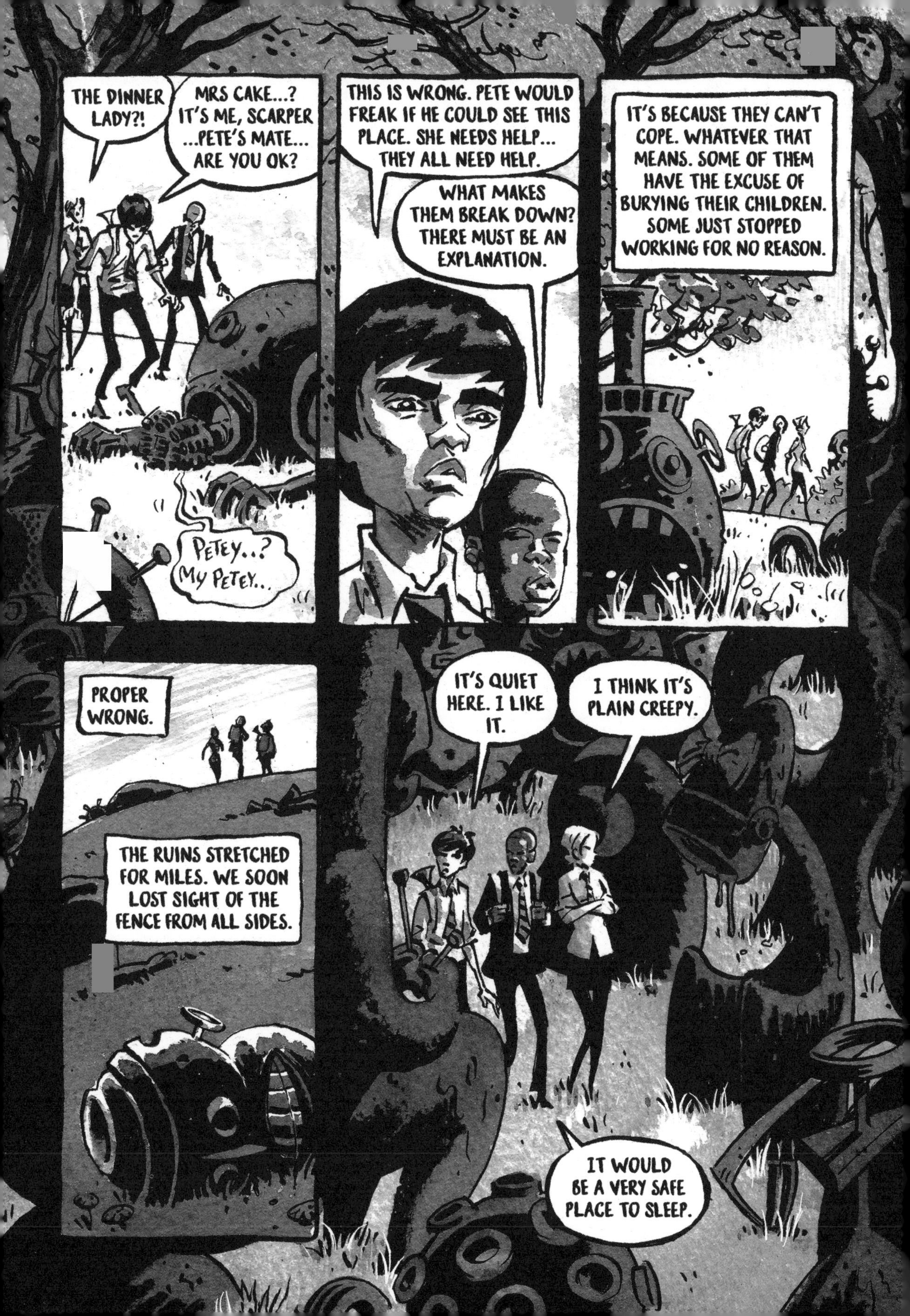
THE DINNER LADY?!
MRS CAKE...? IT'S ME, SCARPER ...PETE'S MATE... ARE YOU OK?
PETEY..? MY PETEY...
THIS IS WRONG. PETE WOULD FREAK IF HE COULD SEE THIS PLACE. SHE NEEDS HELP... THEY ALL NEED HELP.
WHAT MAKES THEM BREAK DOWN? THERE MUST BE AN EXPLANATION.
IT'S BECAUSE THEY CAN'T COPE. WHATEVER THAT MEANS. SOME OF THEM HAVE THE EXCUSE OF BURYING THEIR CHILDREN. SOME JUST STOPPED WORKING FOR NO REASON.
PROPER WRONG.
THE RUINS STRETCHED FOR MILES. WE SOON LOST SIGHT OF THE FENCE FROM ALL SIDES.
IT'S QUIET HERE. I LIKE IT.
I THINK IT'S PLAIN CREEPY.
IT WOULD BE A VERY SAFE PLACE TO SLEEP.

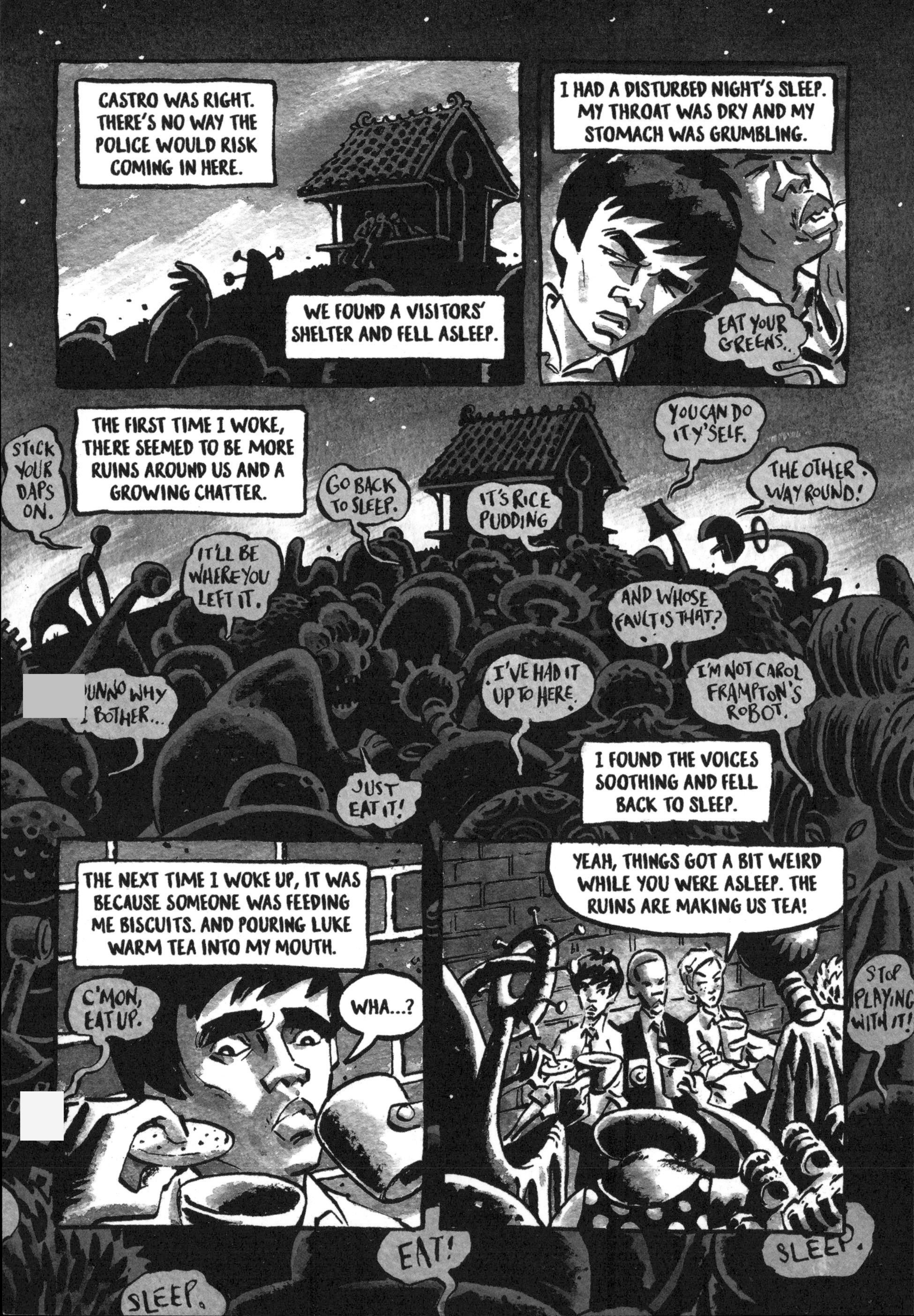
CASTRO WAS RIGHT. THERE'S NO WAY THE POLICE WOULD RISK COMING IN HERE.
WE FOUND A VISITORS' SHELTER AND FELL ASLEEP.
I HAD A DISTURBED NIGHT'S SLEEP. MY THROAT WAS DRY AND MY STOMACH WAS GRUMBLING.
EAT YOUR GREENS...
THE FIRST TIME I WOKE, THERE SEEMED TO BE MORE RUINS AROUND US AND A GROWING CHATTER.
STICK YOUR DAPS ON.
GO BACK TO SLEEP.
IT'S RICE PUDDING
YOU CAN DO IT Y'SELF.
THE OTHER WAY ROUND!
IT'LL BE WHERE YOU LEFT IT.
AND WHOSE FAULT IS THAT?
UNNO WHY BOTHER...
I'VE HAD IT UP TO HERE.
I'M NOT CAROL FRAMPTON'S ROBOT.
JUST EAT IT!
I FOUND THE VOICES SOOTHING AND FELL BACK TO SLEEP.
THE NEXT TIME I WOKE UP, IT WAS BECAUSE SOMEONE WAS FEEDING ME BISCUITS. AND POURING LUKE WARM TEA INTO MY MOUTH.
C'MON, EAT UP.
WHA...?
YEAH, THINGS GOT A BIT WEIRD WHILE YOU WERE ASLEEP. THE RUINS ARE MAKING US TEA!
STOP PLAYING WITH IT!
EAT!
SLEEP.
SLEEP.

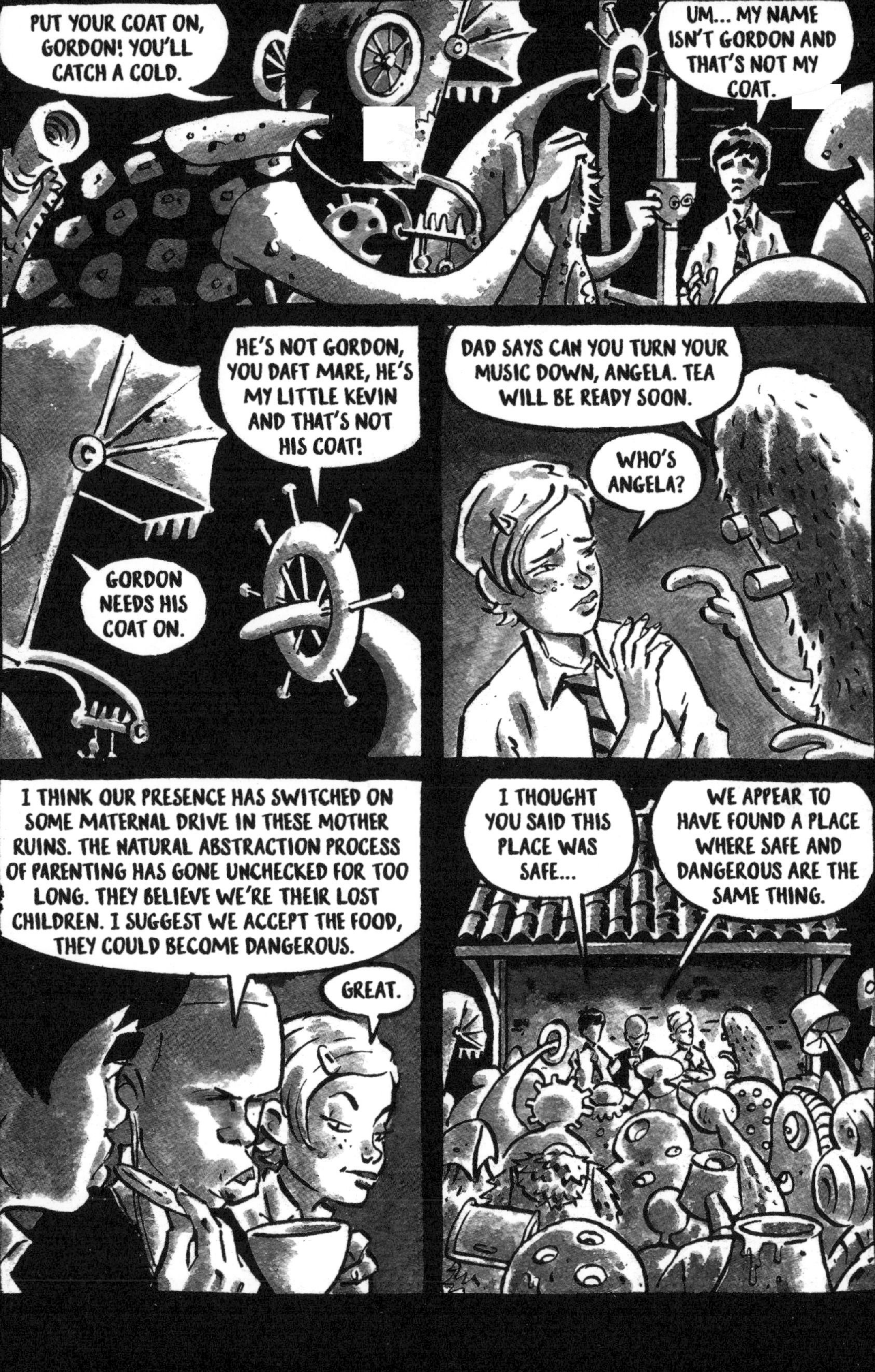
PUT YOUR COAT ON, GORDON! YOU'LL CATCH A COLD.
UM... MY NAME ISN'T GORDON AND THAT'S NOT MY COAT.
HE'S NOT GORDON, YOU DAFT MARE, HE'S MY LITTLE KEVIN AND THAT'S NOT HIS COAT!
GORDON NEEDS HIS COAT ON.
DAD SAYS CAN YOU TURN YOUR MUSIC DOWN, ANGELA. TEA WILL BE READY SOON.
WHO'S ANGELA?
I THINK OUR PRESENCE HAS SWITCHED ON SOME MATERNAL DRIVE IN THESE MOTHER RUINS. THE NATURAL ABSTRACTION PROCESS OF PARENTING HAS GONE UNCHECKED FOR TOO LONG. THEY BELIEVE WE'RE THEIR LOST CHILDREN. I SUGGEST WE ACCEPT THE FOOD, THEY COULD BECOME DANGEROUS.
GREAT.
I THOUGHT YOU SAID THIS PLACE WAS SAFE...
WE APPEAR TO HAVE FOUND A PLACE WHERE SAFE AND DANGEROUS ARE THE SAME THING.

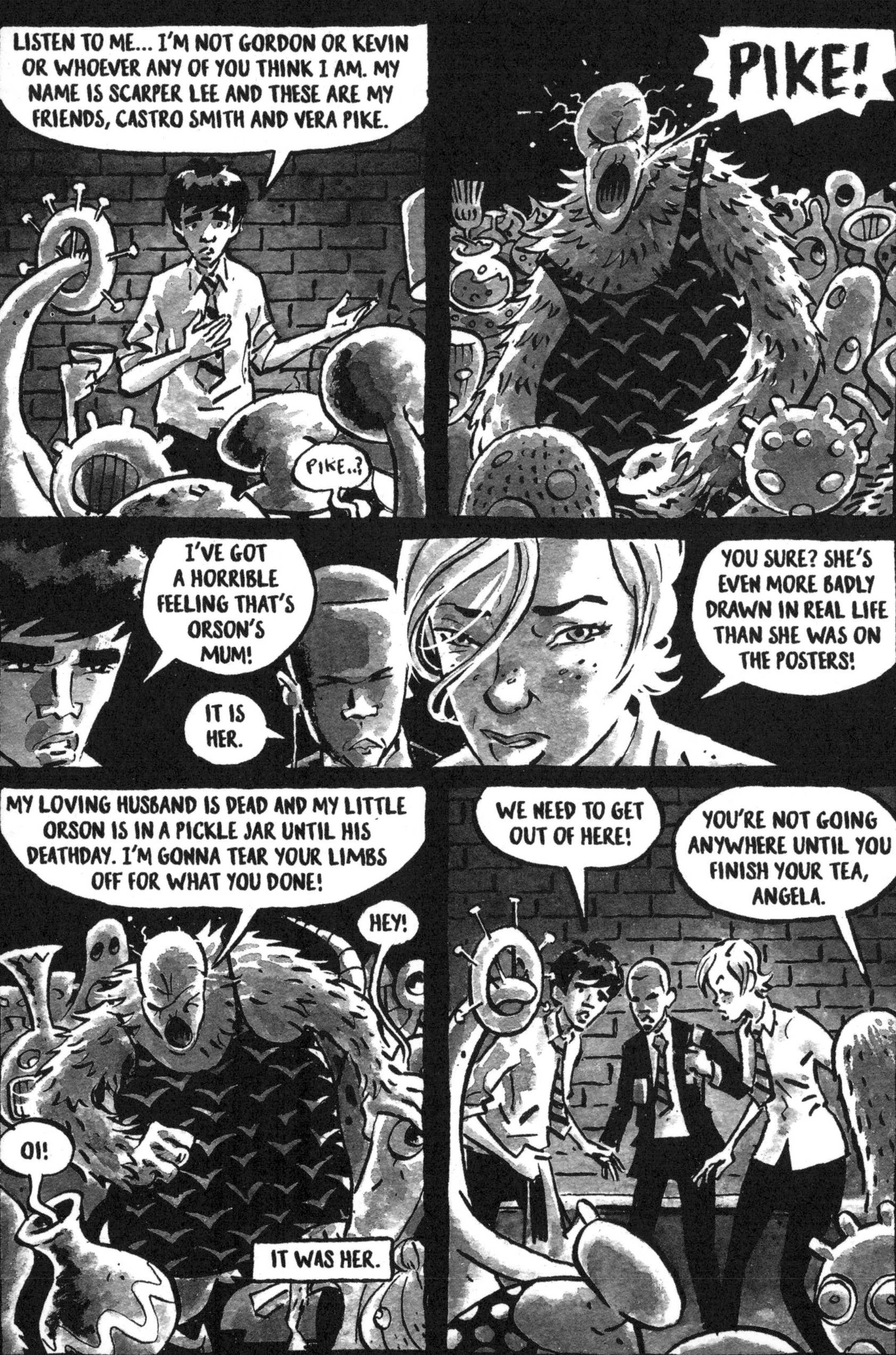
LISTEN TO ME... I'M NOT GORDON OR KEVIN OR WHOEVER ANY OF YOU THINK I AM. MY NAME IS SCARPER LEE AND THESE ARE MY FRIENDS, CASTRO SMITH AND VERA PIKE.
PIKE..?
PIKE!
I'VE GOT A HORRIBLE FEELING THAT'S ORSON'S MUM!
IT IS HER.
YOU SURE? SHE'S EVEN MORE BADLY DRAWN IN REAL LIFE THAN SHE WAS ON THE POSTERS!
MY LOVING HUSBAND IS DEAD AND MY LITTLE ORSON IS IN A PICKLE JAR UNTIL HIS DEATHDAY. I'M GONNA TEAR YOUR LIMBS OFF FOR WHAT YOU DONE!
HEY!
OI!
IT WAS HER.
WE NEED TO GET OUT OF HERE!
YOU'RE NOT GOING ANYWHERE UNTIL YOU FINISH YOUR TEA, ANGELA.

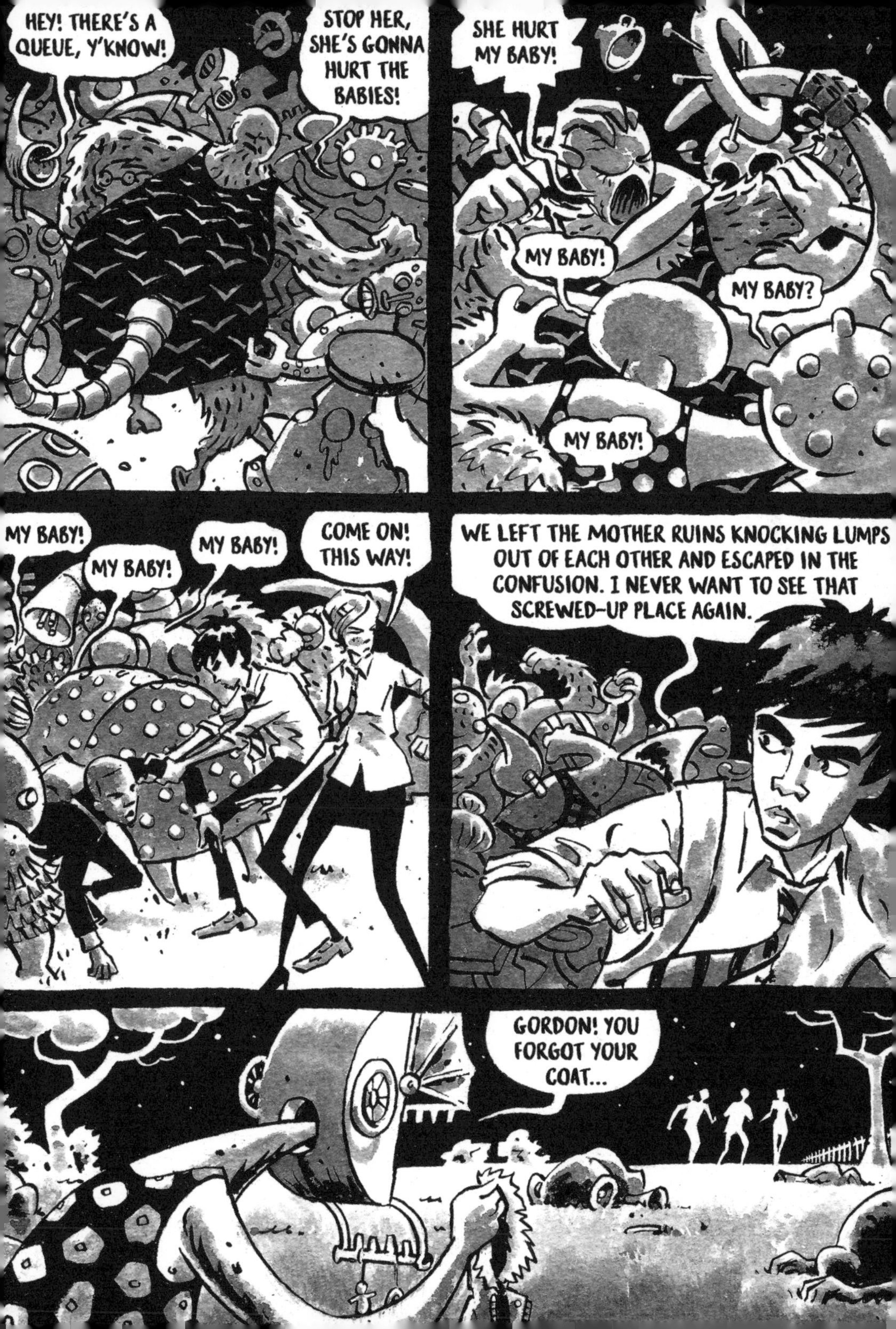
HEY! THERE'S A QUEUE, Y'KNOW!
STOP HER, SHE'S GONNA HURT THE BABIES!
SHE HURT MY BABY!
MY BABY!
MY BABY?
MY BABY!
MY BABY!
MY BABY!
MY BABY!
COME ON! THIS WAY!
WE LEFT THE MOTHER RUINS KNOCKING LUMPS OUT OF EACH OTHER AND ESCAPED IN THE CONFUSION. I NEVER WANT TO SEE THAT SCREWED-UP PLACE AGAIN.
GORDON! YOU FORGOT YOUR COAT...

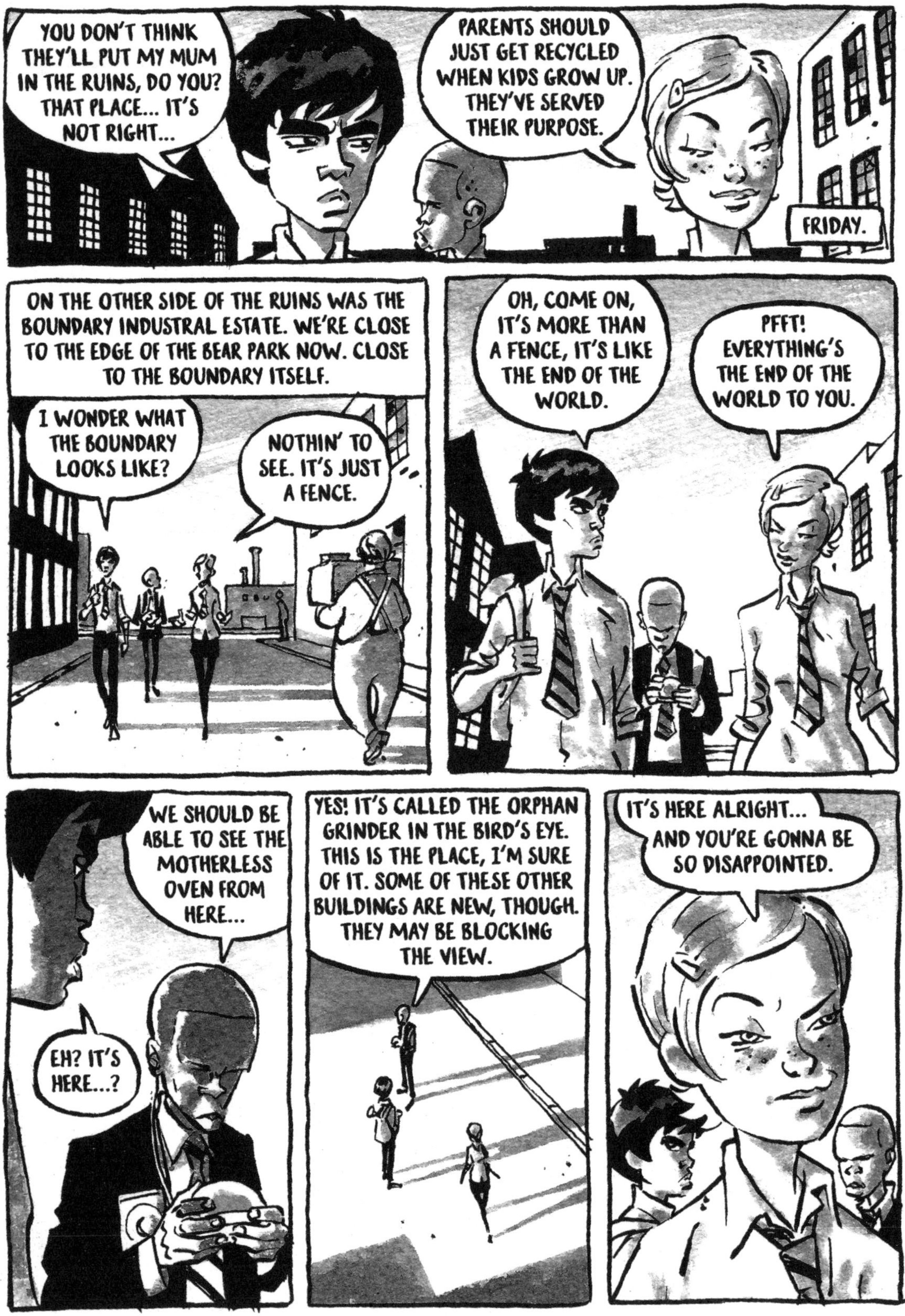
YOU DON'T THINK THEY'LL PUT MY MUM IN THE RUINS, DO YOU? THAT PLACE... IT'S NOT RIGHT...
PARENTS SHOULD JUST GET RECYCLED WHEN KIDS GROW UP. THEY'VE SERVED THEIR PURPOSE.
FRIDAY.
ON THE OTHER SIDE OF THE RUINS WAS THE BOUNDARY INDUSTRIAL ESTATE. WE'RE CLOSE TO THE EDGE OF THE BEAR PARK NOW. CLOSE TO THE BOUNDARY ITSELF.
I WONDER WHAT THE BOUNDARY LOOKS LIKE?
NOTHIN' TO SEE. IT'S JUST A FENCE.
OH, COME ON, IT'S MORE THAN A FENCE, IT'S LIKE THE END OF THE WORLD.
PFFT! EVERYTHING'S THE END OF THE WORLD TO YOU.
WE SHOULD BE ABLE TO SEE THE MOTHERLESS OVEN FROM HERE...
EH? IT'S HERE...?
YES! IT'S CALLED THE ORPHAN GRINDER IN THE BIRD'S EYE. THIS IS THE PLACE, I'M SURE OF IT. SOME OF THESE OTHER BUILDINGS ARE NEW, THOUGH. THEY MAY BE BLOCKING THE VIEW.
IT'S HERE ALRIGHT...
AND YOU'RE GONNA BE SO DISAPPOINTED.

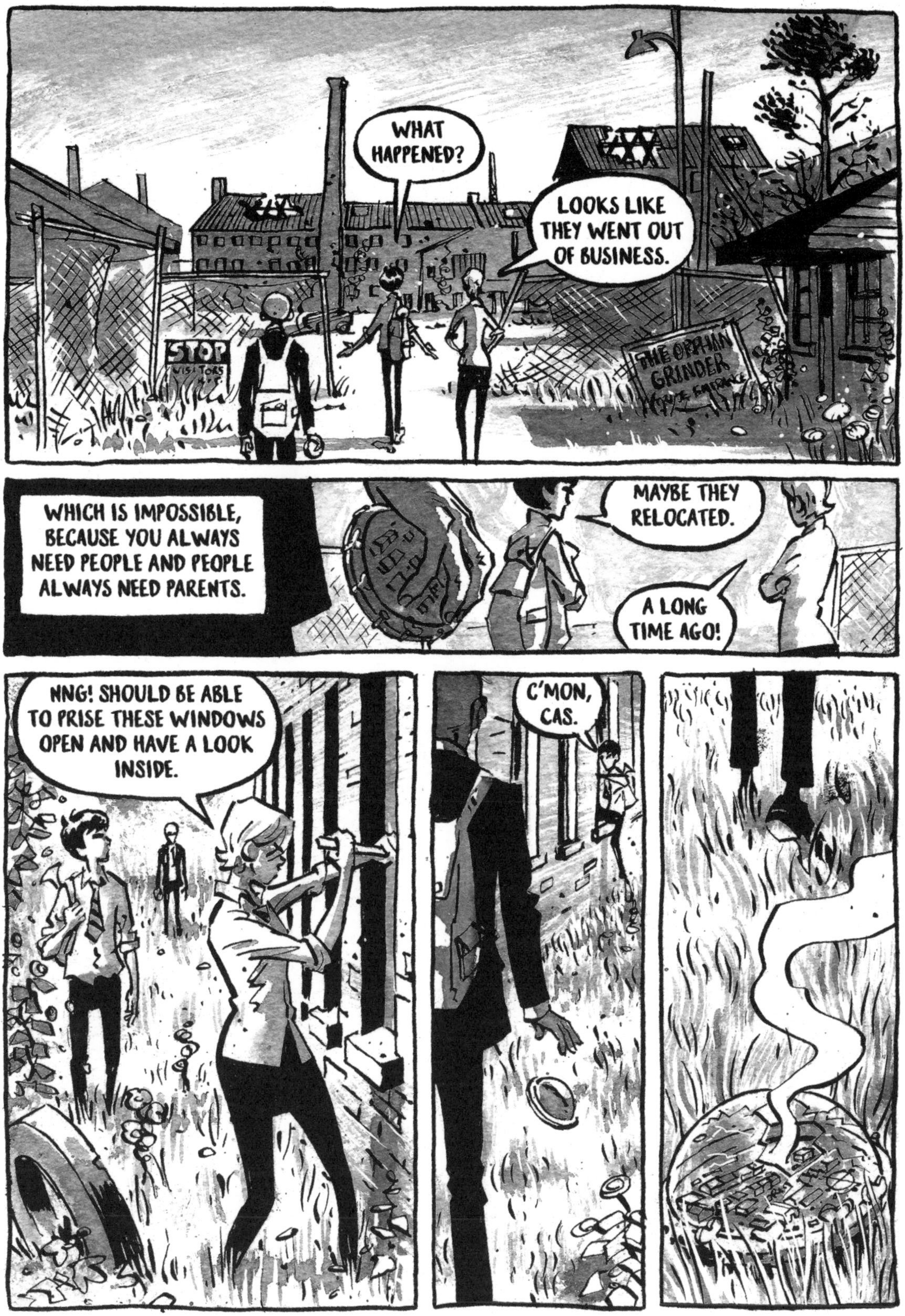
WHAT HAPPENED?
LOOKS LIKE THEY WENT OUT OF BUSINESS.
STOP
VISITORS
THE ORPHAN GRINDER
WHICH IS IMPOSSIBLE, BECAUSE YOU ALWAYS NEED PEOPLE AND PEOPLE ALWAYS NEED PARENTS.
MAYBE THEY RELOCATED.
A LONG TIME AGO!
NNG! SHOULD BE ABLE TO PRISE THESE WINDOWS OPEN AND HAVE A LOOK INSIDE.
C'MON, CAS.

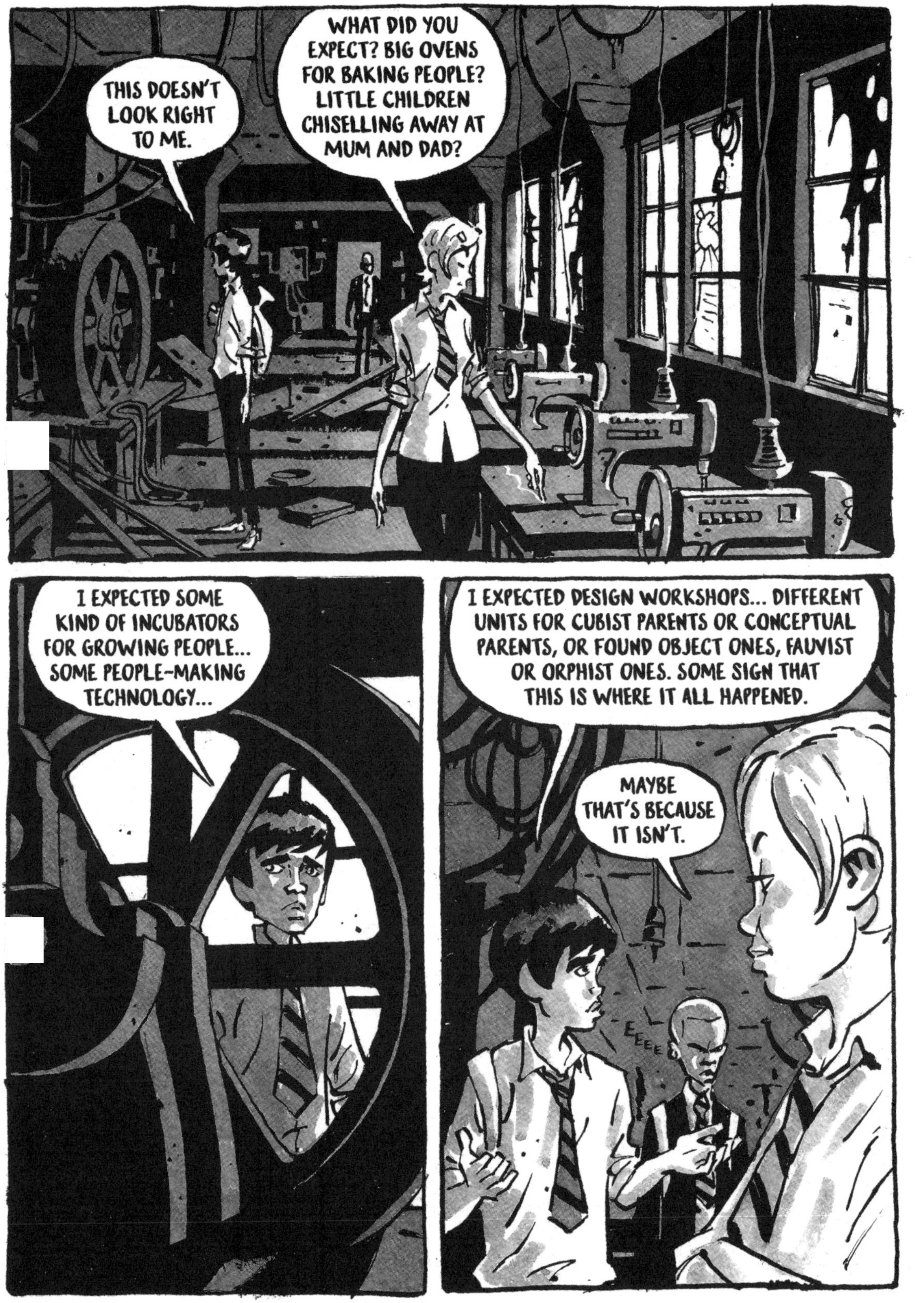
THIS DOESN'T LOOK RIGHT TO ME.
WHAT DID YOU EXPECT? BIG OVENS FOR BAKING PEOPLE? LITTLE CHILDREN CHISELLING AWAY AT MUM AND DAD?
I EXPECTED SOME KIND OF INCUBATORS FOR GROWING PEOPLE... SOME PEOPLE-MAKING TECHNOLOGY...
I EXPECTED DESIGN WORKSHOPS... DIFFERENT UNITS FOR CUBIST PARENTS OR CONCEPTUAL PARENTS, OR FOUND OBJECT ONES, FAUVIST OR ORPHIST ONES. SOME SIGN THAT THIS IS WHERE IT ALL HAPPENED.
MAYBE THAT'S BECAUSE IT ISN'T.
EEEE

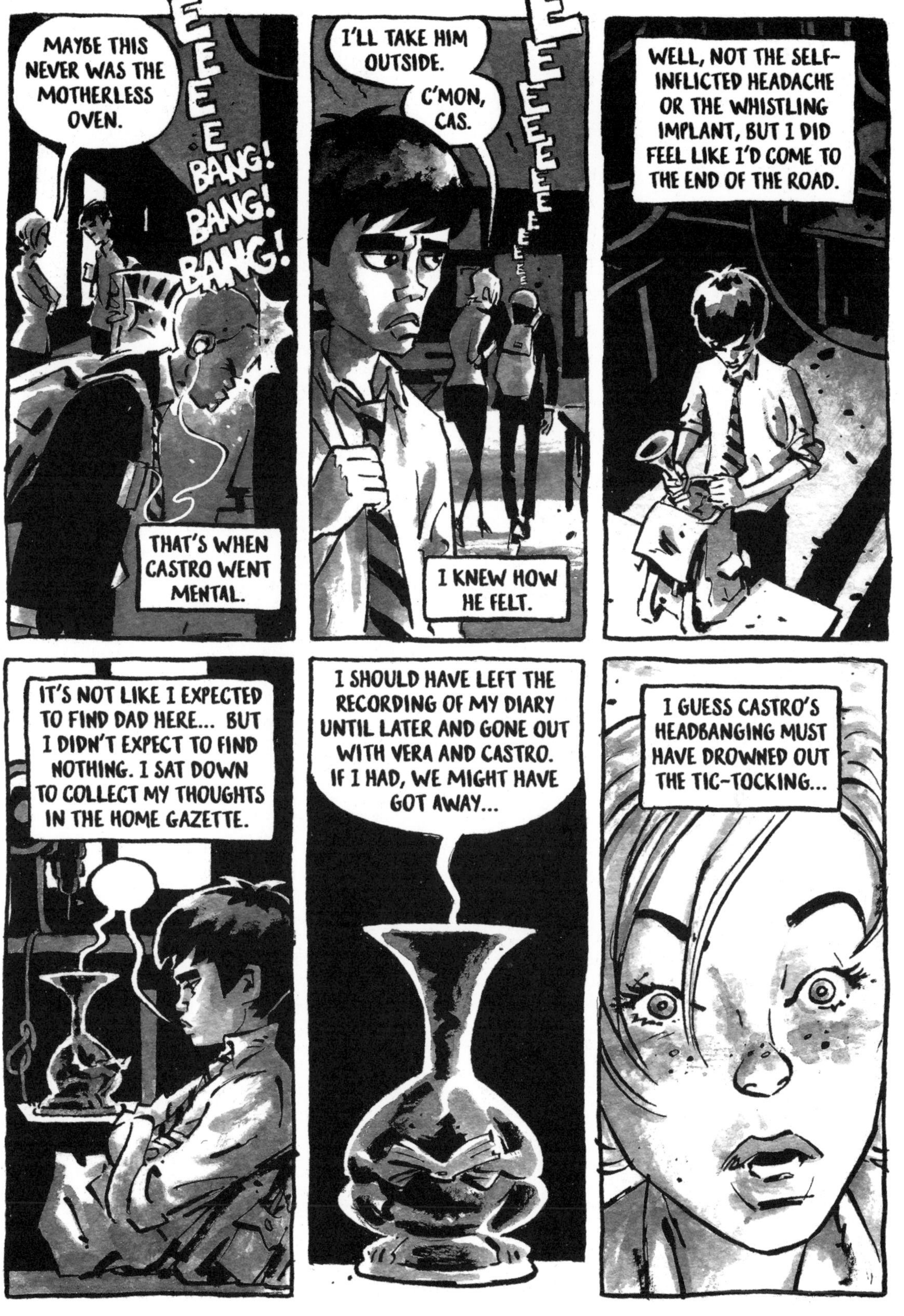

MAYBE THIS NEVER WAS THE MOTHERLESS OVEN.
EEEEE
BANG! BANG! BANG!
THAT'S WHEN CASTRO WENT MENTAL.
I'LL TAKE HIM OUTSIDE.
C'MON, CAS.
EEEEEEEE
I KNEW HOW HE FELT.
WELL, NOT THE SELF-INFLICTED HEADACHE OR THE WHISTLING IMPLANT, BUT I DID FEEL LIKE I'D COME TO THE END OF THE ROAD.
IT'S NOT LIKE I EXPECTED TO FIND DAD HERE... BUT I DIDN'T EXPECT TO FIND NOTHING. I SAT DOWN TO COLLECT MY THOUGHTS IN THE HOME GAZETTE.
I SHOULD HAVE LEFT THE RECORDING OF MY DIARY UNTIL LATER AND GONE OUT WITH VERA AND CASTRO. IF I HAD, WE MIGHT HAVE GOT AWAY...
I GUESS CASTRO'S HEADBANGING MUST HAVE DROWNED OUT THE TIC-TOCKING...

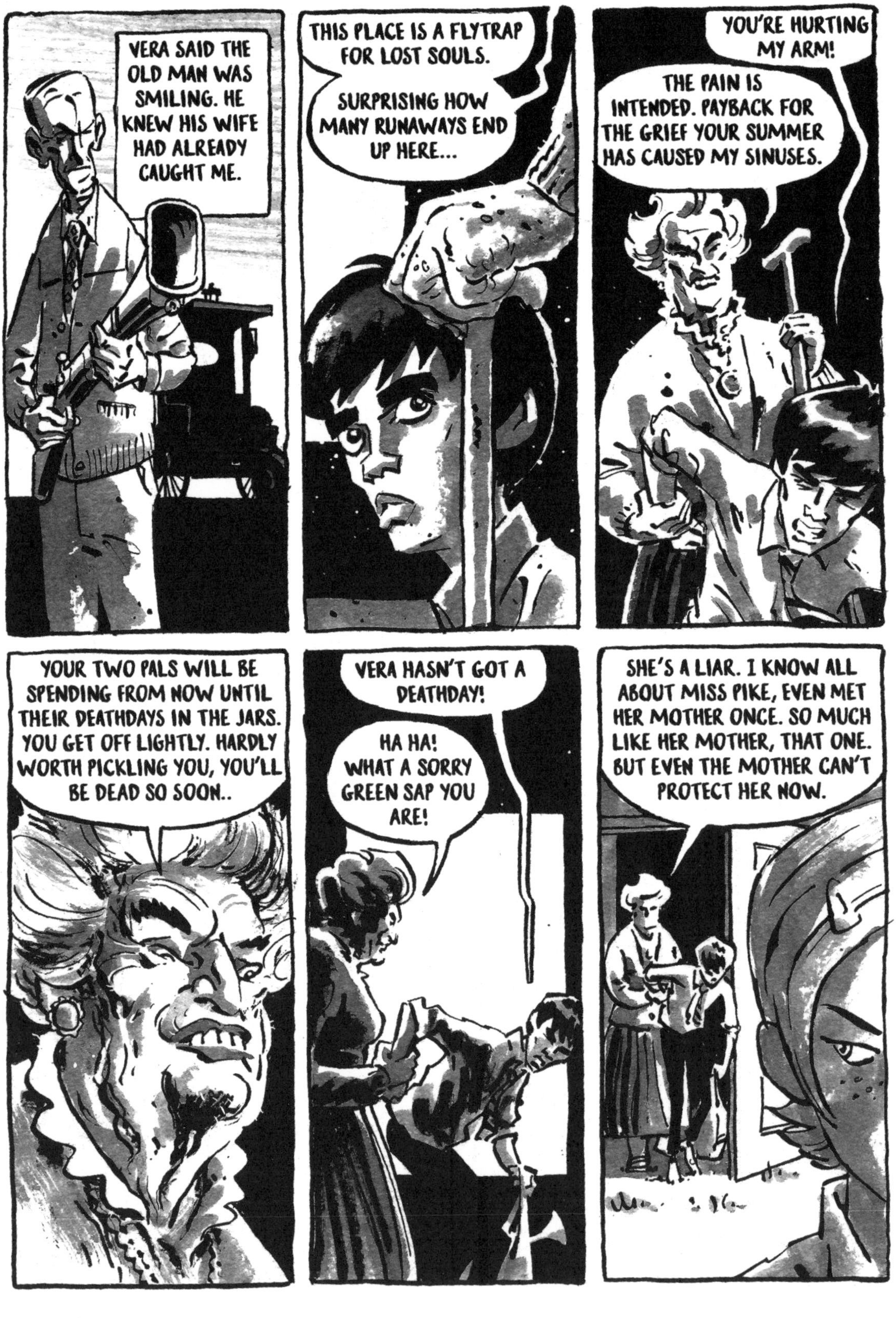
VERA SAID THE OLD MAN WAS SMILING. HE KNEW HIS WIFE HAD ALREADY CAUGHT ME.
THIS PLACE IS A FLYTRAP FOR LOST SOULS.
SURPRISING HOW MANY RUNAWAYS END UP HERE...
YOU'RE HURTING MY ARM!
THE PAIN IS INTENDED. PAYBACK FOR THE GRIEF YOUR SUMMER HAS CAUSED MY SINUSES.
YOUR TWO PALS WILL BE SPENDING FROM NOW UNTIL THEIR DEATHDAYS IN THE JARS. YOU GET OFF LIGHTLY. HARDLY WORTH PICKLING YOU, YOU'LL BE DEAD SO SOON..
VERA HASN'T GOT A DEATHDAY!
HA HA! WHAT A SORRY GREEN SAP YOU ARE!
SHE'S A LIAR. I KNOW ALL ABOUT MISS PIKE, EVEN MET HER MOTHER ONCE. SO MUCH LIKE HER MOTHER, THAT ONE. BUT EVEN THE MOTHER CAN'T PROTECT HER NOW.

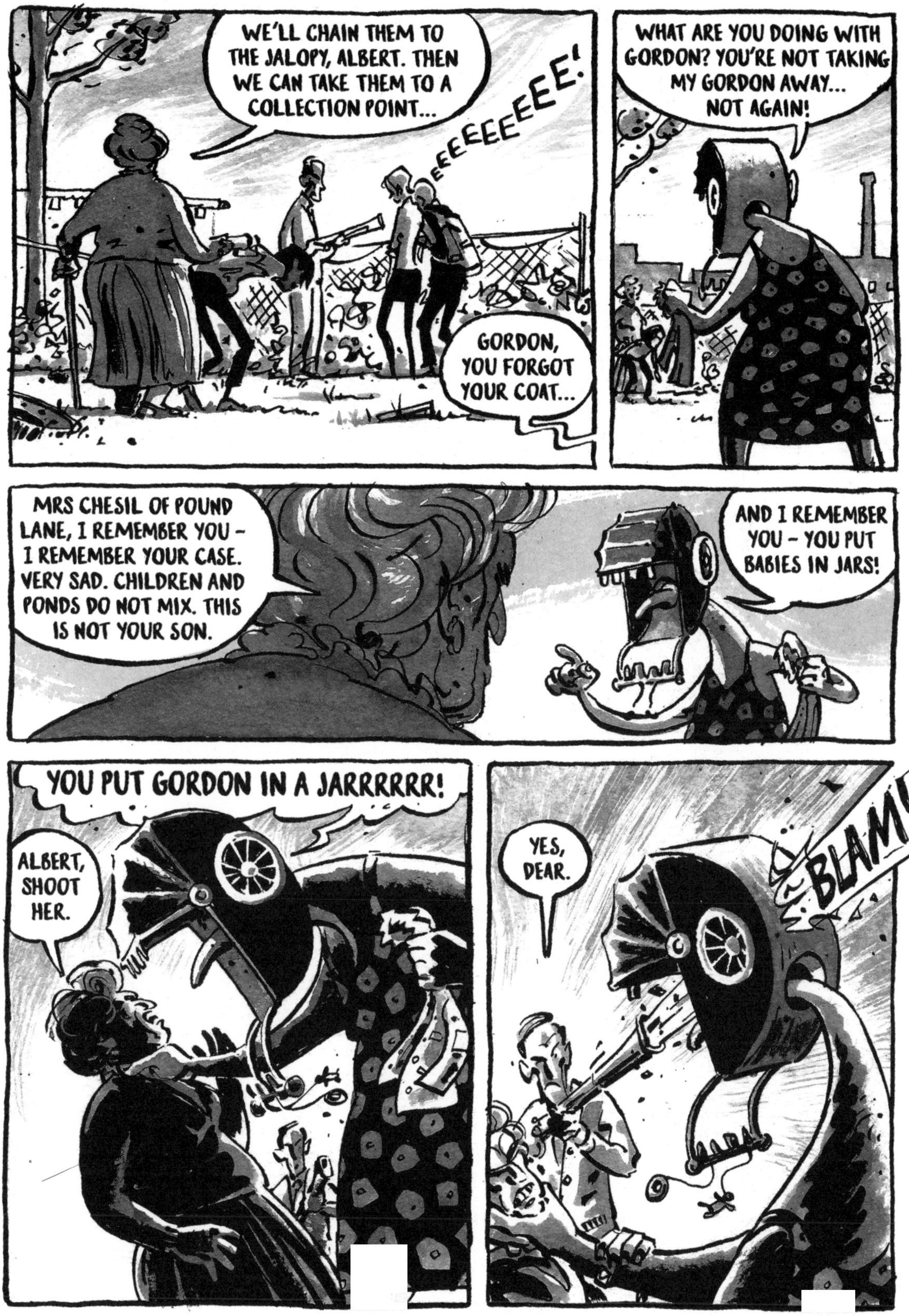

WE'LL CHAIN THEM TO THE JALOPY, ALBERT. THEN WE CAN TAKE THEM TO A COLLECTION POINT...
EEEEEEEEEEE!
GORDON, YOU FORGOT YOUR COAT...
WHAT ARE YOU DOING WITH GORDON? YOU'RE NOT TAKING MY GORDON AWAY... NOT AGAIN!
MRS CHESIL OF POUND LANE, I REMEMBER YOU - I REMEMBER YOUR CASE. VERY SAD. CHILDREN AND PONDS DO NOT MIX. THIS IS NOT YOUR SON.
AND I REMEMBER YOU - YOU PUT BABIES IN JARS!
YOU PUT GORDON IN A JARRRRRR!
ALBERT, SHOOT HER.
YES, DEAR.
BLAM!

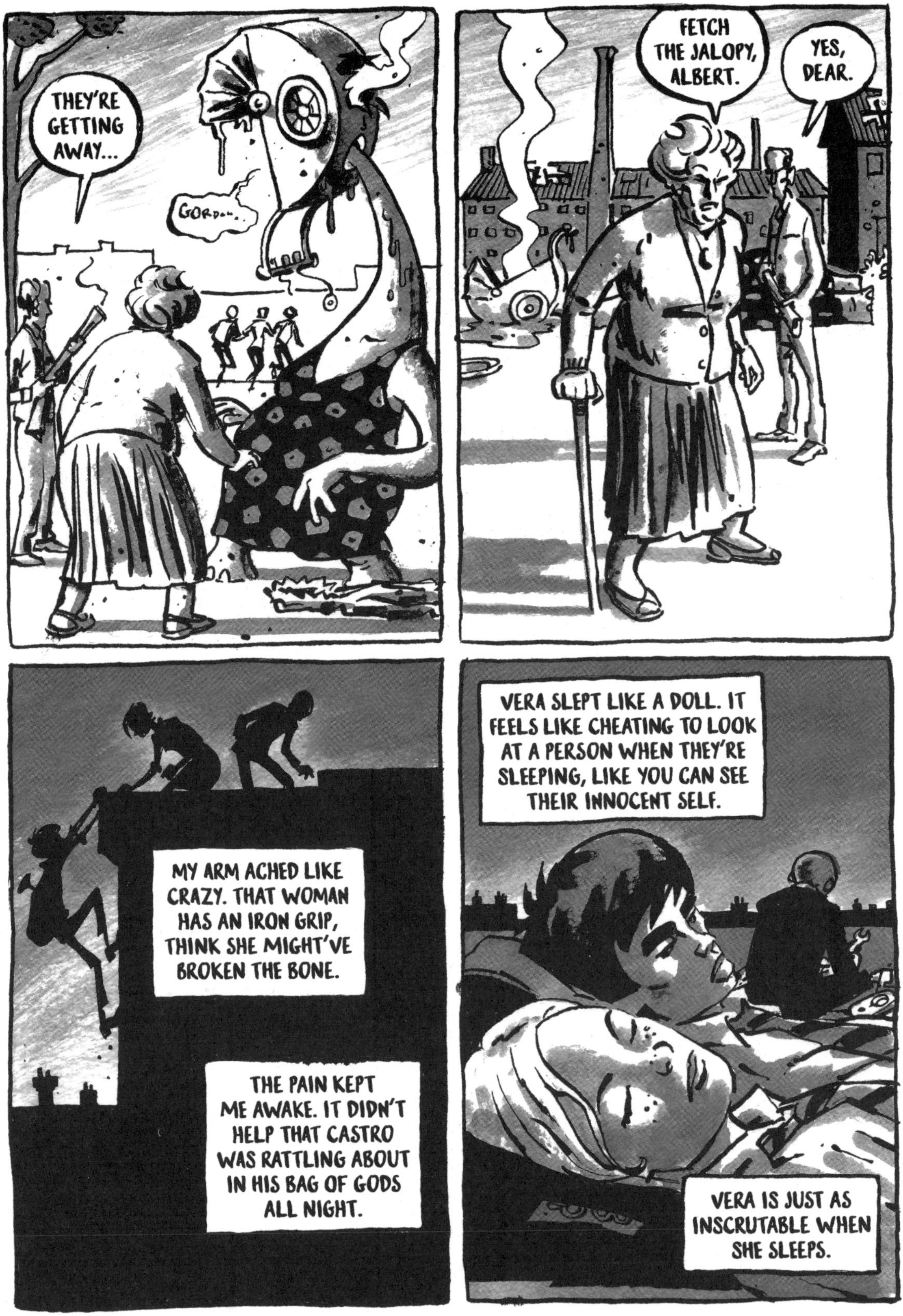
THEY'RE GETTING AWAY...
GORD...
FETCH THE JALOPY, ALBERT.
YES, DEAR.
MY ARM ACHED LIKE CRAZY. THAT WOMAN HAS AN IRON GRIP, THINK SHE MIGHT'VE BROKEN THE BONE.
THE PAIN KEPT ME AWAKE. IT DIDN'T HELP THAT CASTRO WAS RATTLING ABOUT IN HIS BAG OF GODS ALL NIGHT.
VERA SLEPT LIKE A DOLL. IT FEELS LIKE CHEATING TO LOOK AT A PERSON WHEN THEY'RE SLEEPING, LIKE YOU CAN SEE THEIR INNOCENT SELF.
VERA IS JUST AS INSCRUTABLE WHEN SHE SLEEPS.

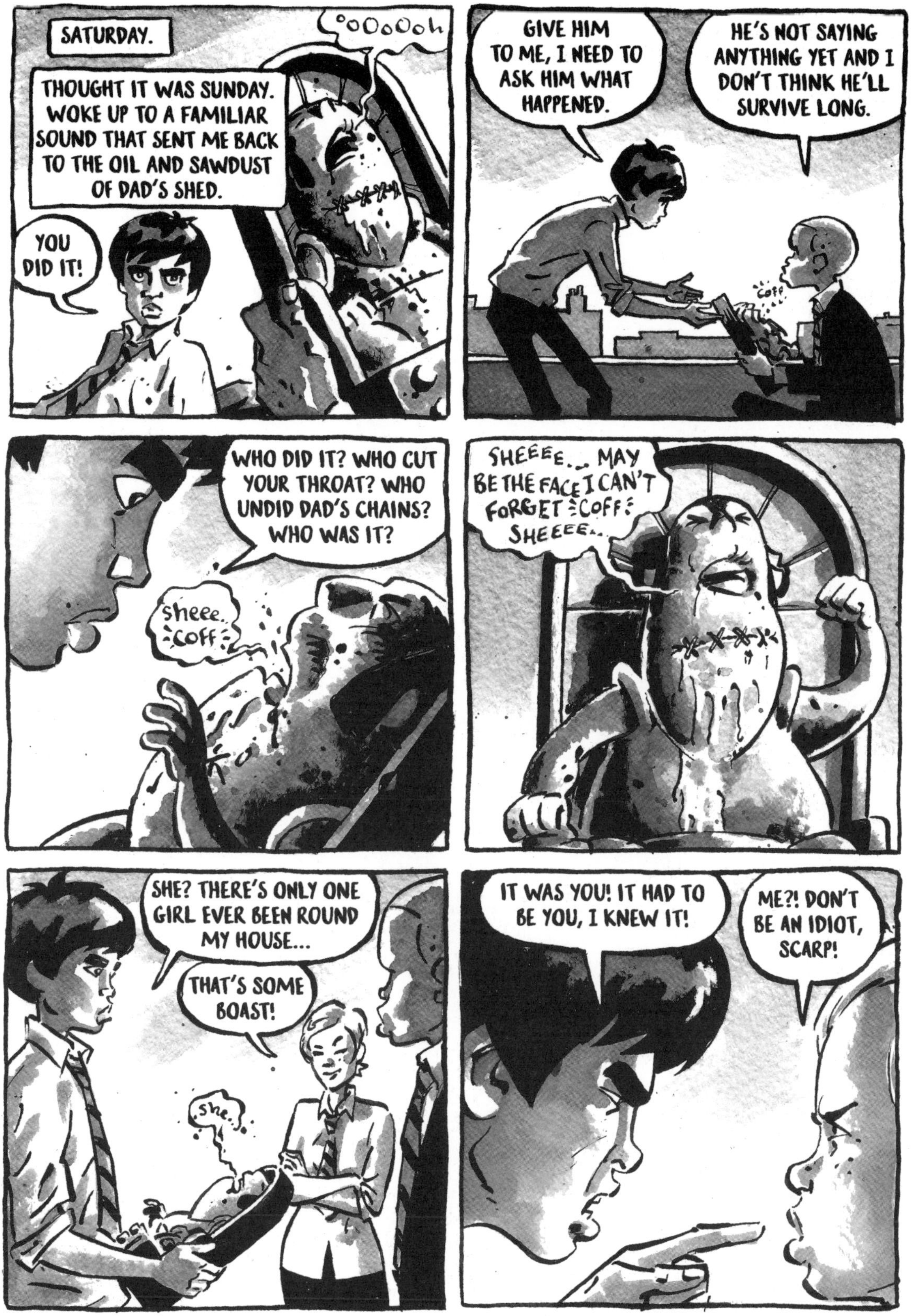

SATURDAY.
°oOoOoh
THOUGHT IT WAS SUNDAY. WOKE UP TO A FAMILIAR SOUND THAT SENT ME BACK TO THE OIL AND SAWDUST OF DAD'S SHED.
YOU DID IT!
GIVE HIM TO ME, I NEED TO ASK HIM WHAT HAPPENED.
HE'S NOT SAYING ANYTHING YET AND I DON'T THINK HE'LL SURVIVE LONG.
COFF
WHO DID IT? WHO CUT YOUR THROAT? WHO UNDID DAD'S CHAINS? WHO WAS IT?
sheee.. COFF
SHEEEE... MAY BE THE FACE I CAN'T FORGET COFF SHEEEE..
SHE? THERE'S ONLY ONE GIRL EVER BEEN ROUND MY HOUSE...
THAT'S SOME BOAST!
she..
IT WAS YOU! IT HAD TO BE YOU, I KNEW IT!
ME?! DON'T BE AN IDIOT, SCARP!

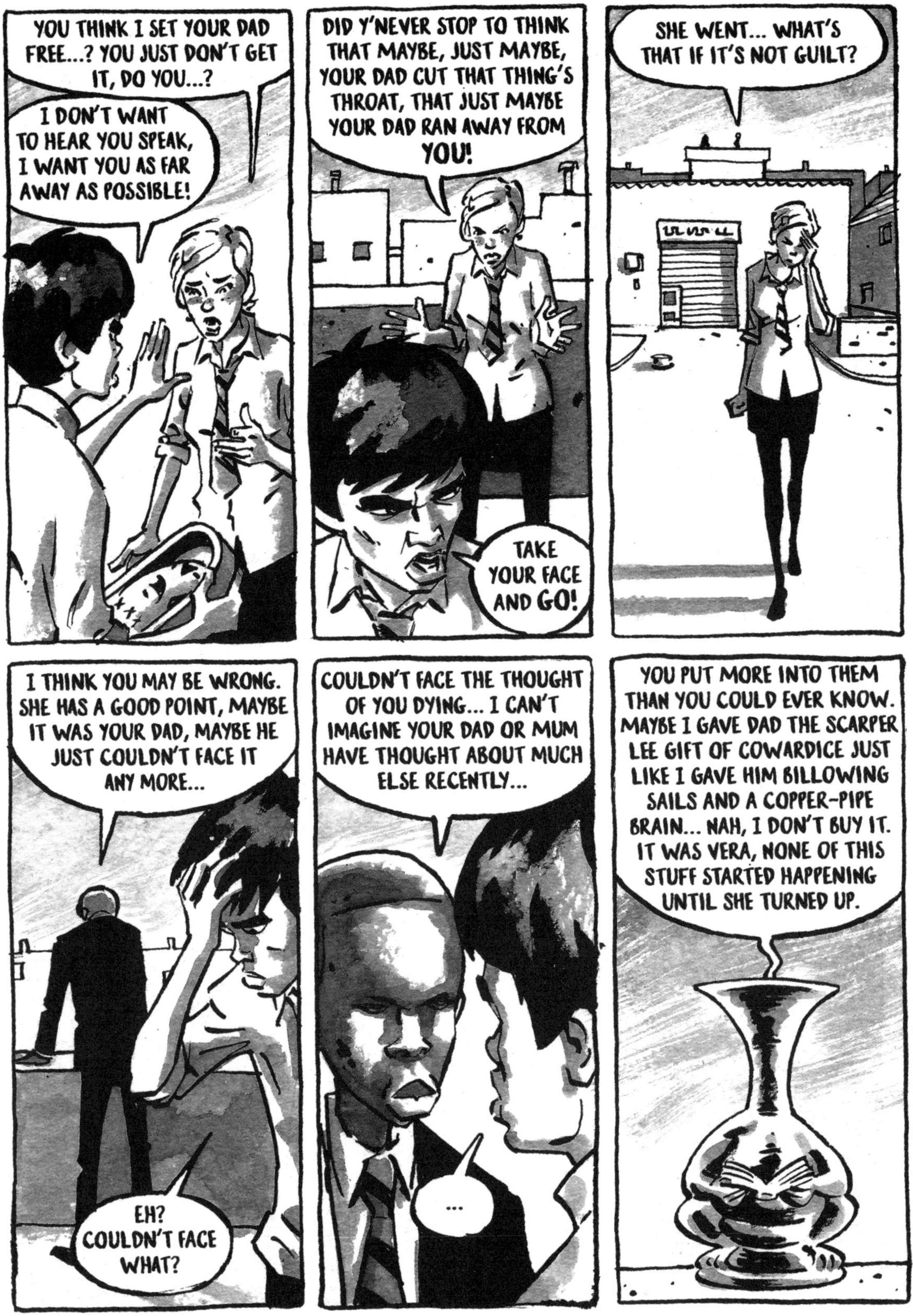
YOU THINK I SET YOUR DAD FREE...? YOU JUST DON'T GET IT, DO YOU...?
I DON'T WANT TO HEAR YOU SPEAK, I WANT YOU AS FAR AWAY AS POSSIBLE!
DID Y'NEVER STOP TO THINK THAT MAYBE, JUST MAYBE, YOUR DAD CUT THAT THING'S THROAT, THAT JUST MAYBE YOUR DAD RAN AWAY FROM YOU!
TAKE YOUR FACE AND GO!
SHE WENT... WHAT'S THAT IF IT'S NOT GUILT?
I THINK YOU MAY BE WRONG. SHE HAS A GOOD POINT, MAYBE IT WAS YOUR DAD, MAYBE HE JUST COULDN'T FACE IT ANY MORE...
EH? COULDN'T FACE WHAT?
COULDN'T FACE THE THOUGHT OF YOU DYING... I CAN'T IMAGINE YOUR DAD OR MUM HAVE THOUGHT ABOUT MUCH ELSE RECENTLY...
...
YOU PUT MORE INTO THEM THAN YOU COULD EVER KNOW. MAYBE I GAVE DAD THE SCARPER LEE GIFT OF COWARDICE JUST LIKE I GAVE HIM BILLOWING SAILS AND A COPPER-PIPE BRAIN... NAH, I DON'T BUY IT. IT WAS VERA, NONE OF THIS STUFF STARTED HAPPENING UNTIL SHE TURNED UP.

THE SHED GOD DIED. WE LEFT HIM ON THE ROOF. SEEMED A BIT HEARTLESS, BUT IT'S ONE LESS THING TO CARRY.

ME AND CASTRO HARDLY SPOKE ALL DAY. I RECKON HE WAS THINKING HE SHOULD HAVE GONE WITH VERA. OR MAYBE, LIKE ME, HE WAS WONDERING IF WE'RE JUST GONNA KEEP WALKING 'TIL WE REACH THE BOUNDARY FENCE.

WHEEL. MAKERS AND TURNERS

THE LONGER YOU GO WITHOUT TALKING, THE HARDER IT GETS TO BREAK THE SILENCE...

THANK HEAVEN'S FOR THE GOD REPAIR SHOP, EH?

IS THAT WHAT I THINK IT IS?

LOOKS LIKE THE WEATHER CLOCK FROM THE TOWN HALL.

NOT FAR WRONG, BOY.

LEAVE GODS SWITCHED OFF

THAT'S THE OLD ONE. PACKED UP, SHE DID, SO WE HAD TO REPLACE HER WITH ANOTHER.

TURNED UP HER TOES AND DIED ON US, SHE DID.

LEAVE GODS

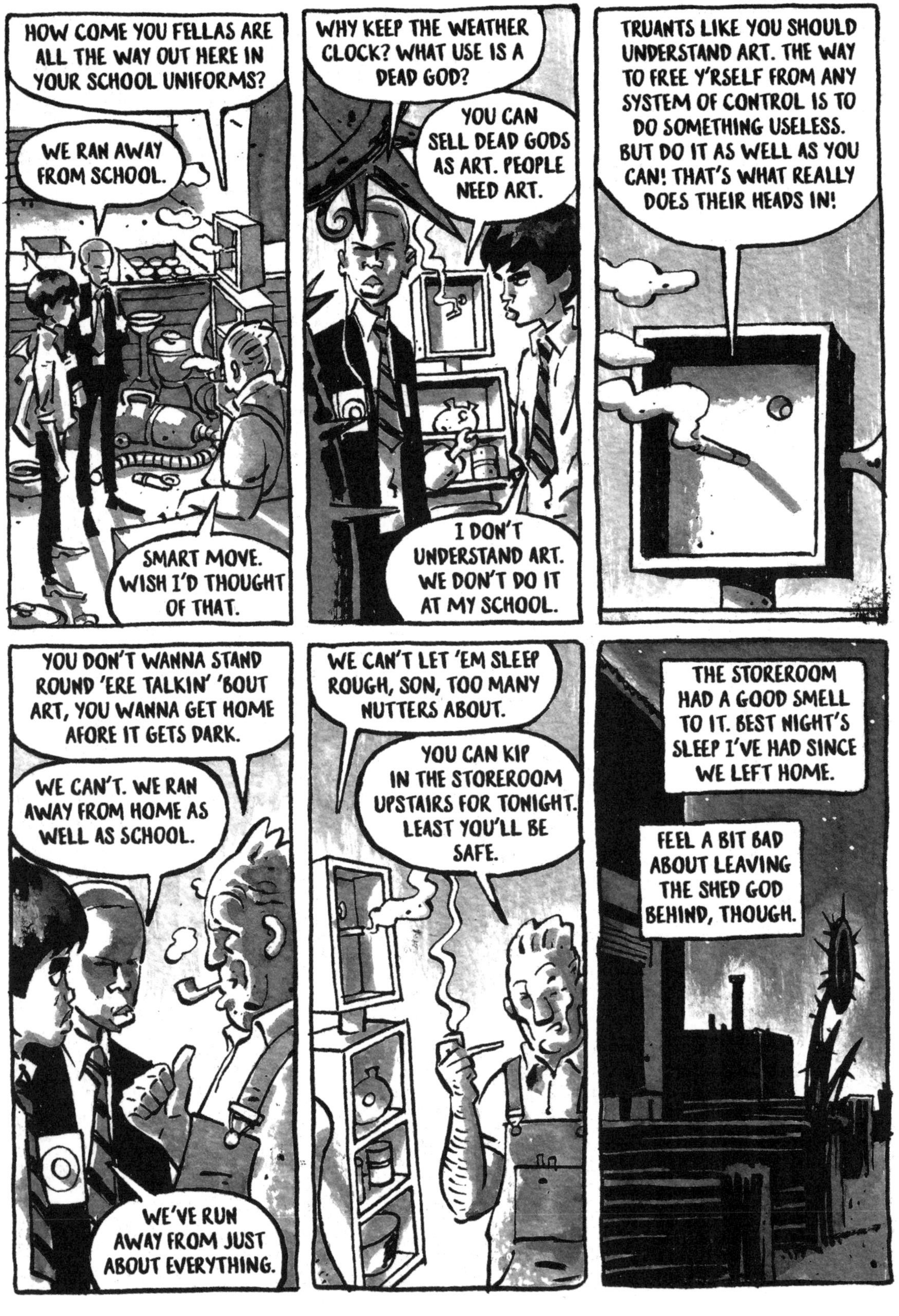
HOW COME YOU FELLAS ARE ALL THE WAY OUT HERE IN YOUR SCHOOL UNIFORMS?
WE RAN AWAY FROM SCHOOL.
SMART MOVE. WISH I'D THOUGHT OF THAT.
WHY KEEP THE WEATHER CLOCK? WHAT USE IS A DEAD GOD?
YOU CAN SELL DEAD GODS AS ART. PEOPLE NEED ART.
I DON'T UNDERSTAND ART. WE DON'T DO IT AT MY SCHOOL.
TRUANTS LIKE YOU SHOULD UNDERSTAND ART. THE WAY TO FREE Y'RSELF FROM ANY SYSTEM OF CONTROL IS TO DO SOMETHING USELESS. BUT DO IT AS WELL AS YOU CAN! THAT'S WHAT REALLY DOES THEIR HEADS IN!
YOU DON'T WANNA STAND ROUND 'ERE TALKIN' 'BOUT ART, YOU WANNA GET HOME AFORE IT GETS DARK.
WE CAN'T. WE RAN AWAY FROM HOME AS WELL AS SCHOOL.
WE'VE RUN AWAY FROM JUST ABOUT EVERYTHING.
WE CAN'T LET 'EM SLEEP ROUGH, SON, TOO MANY NUTTERS ABOUT.
YOU CAN KIP IN THE STOREROOM UPSTAIRS FOR TONIGHT. LEAST YOU'LL BE SAFE.
THE STOREROOM HAD A GOOD SMELL TO IT. BEST NIGHT'S SLEEP I'VE HAD SINCE WE LEFT HOME.
FEEL A BIT BAD ABOUT LEAVING THE SHED GOD BEHIND, THOUGH.

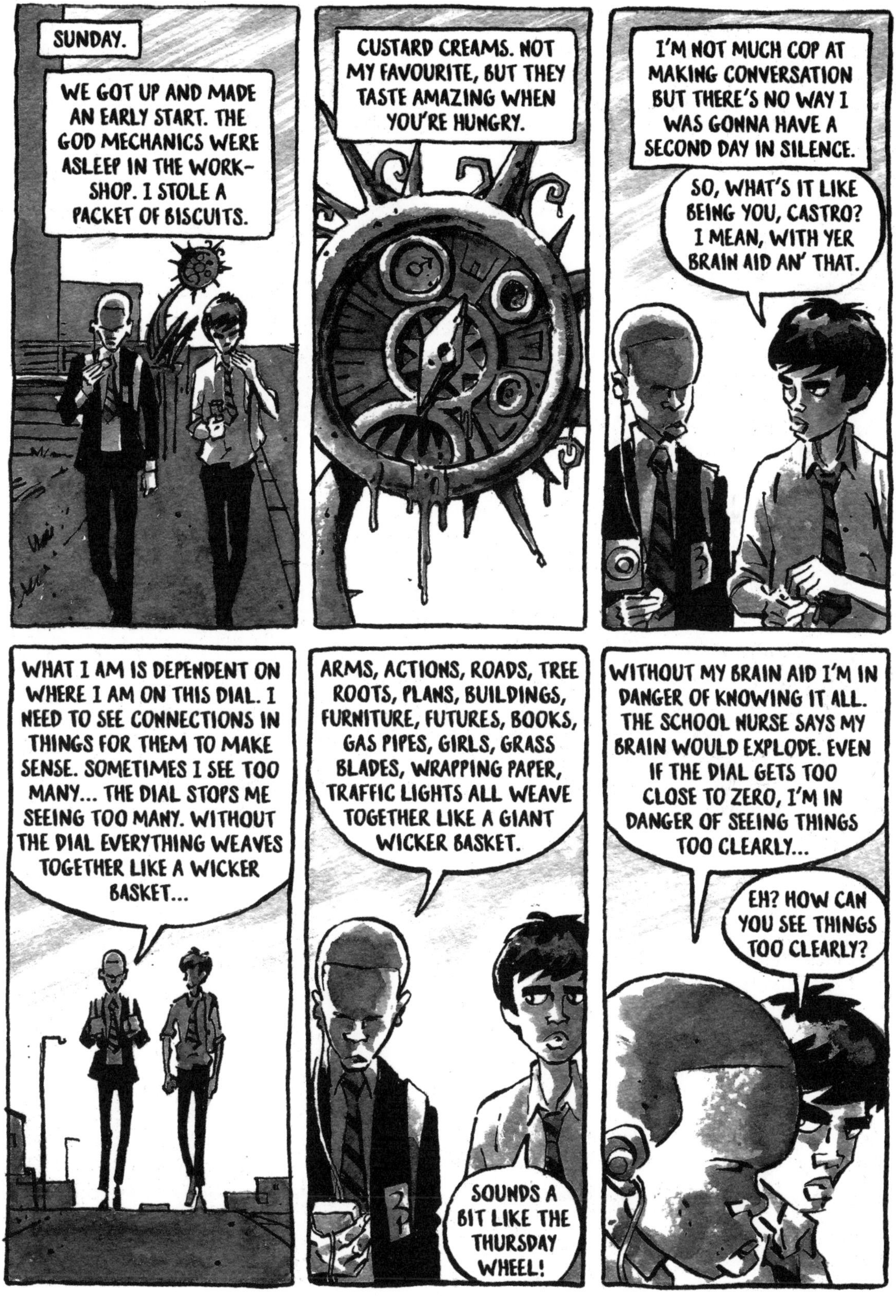
SUNDAY.
WE GOT UP AND MADE AN EARLY START. THE GOD MECHANICS WERE ASLEEP IN THE WORK-SHOP. I STOLE A PACKET OF BISCUITS.
CUSTARD CREAMS. NOT MY FAVOURITE, BUT THEY TASTE AMAZING WHEN YOU'RE HUNGRY.
I'M NOT MUCH COP AT MAKING CONVERSATION BUT THERE'S NO WAY I WAS GONNA HAVE A SECOND DAY IN SILENCE.
SO, WHAT'S IT LIKE BEING YOU, CASTRO? I MEAN, WITH YER BRAIN AID AN' THAT.
WHAT I AM IS DEPENDENT ON WHERE I AM ON THIS DIAL. I NEED TO SEE CONNECTIONS IN THINGS FOR THEM TO MAKE SENSE. SOMETIMES I SEE TOO MANY... THE DIAL STOPS ME SEEING TOO MANY. WITHOUT THE DIAL EVERYTHING WEAVES TOGETHER LIKE A WICKER BASKET...
ARMS, ACTIONS, ROADS, TREE ROOTS, PLANS, BUILDINGS, FURNITURE, FUTURES, BOOKS, GAS PIPES, GIRLS, GRASS BLADES, WRAPPING PAPER, TRAFFIC LIGHTS ALL WEAVE TOGETHER LIKE A GIANT WICKER BASKET.
SOUNDS A BIT LIKE THE THURSDAY WHEEL!
WITHOUT MY BRAIN AID I'M IN DANGER OF KNOWING IT ALL. THE SCHOOL NURSE SAYS MY BRAIN WOULD EXPLODE. EVEN IF THE DIAL GETS TOO CLOSE TO ZERO, I'M IN DANGER OF SEEING THINGS TOO CLEARLY...
EH? HOW CAN YOU SEE THINGS TOO CLEARLY?

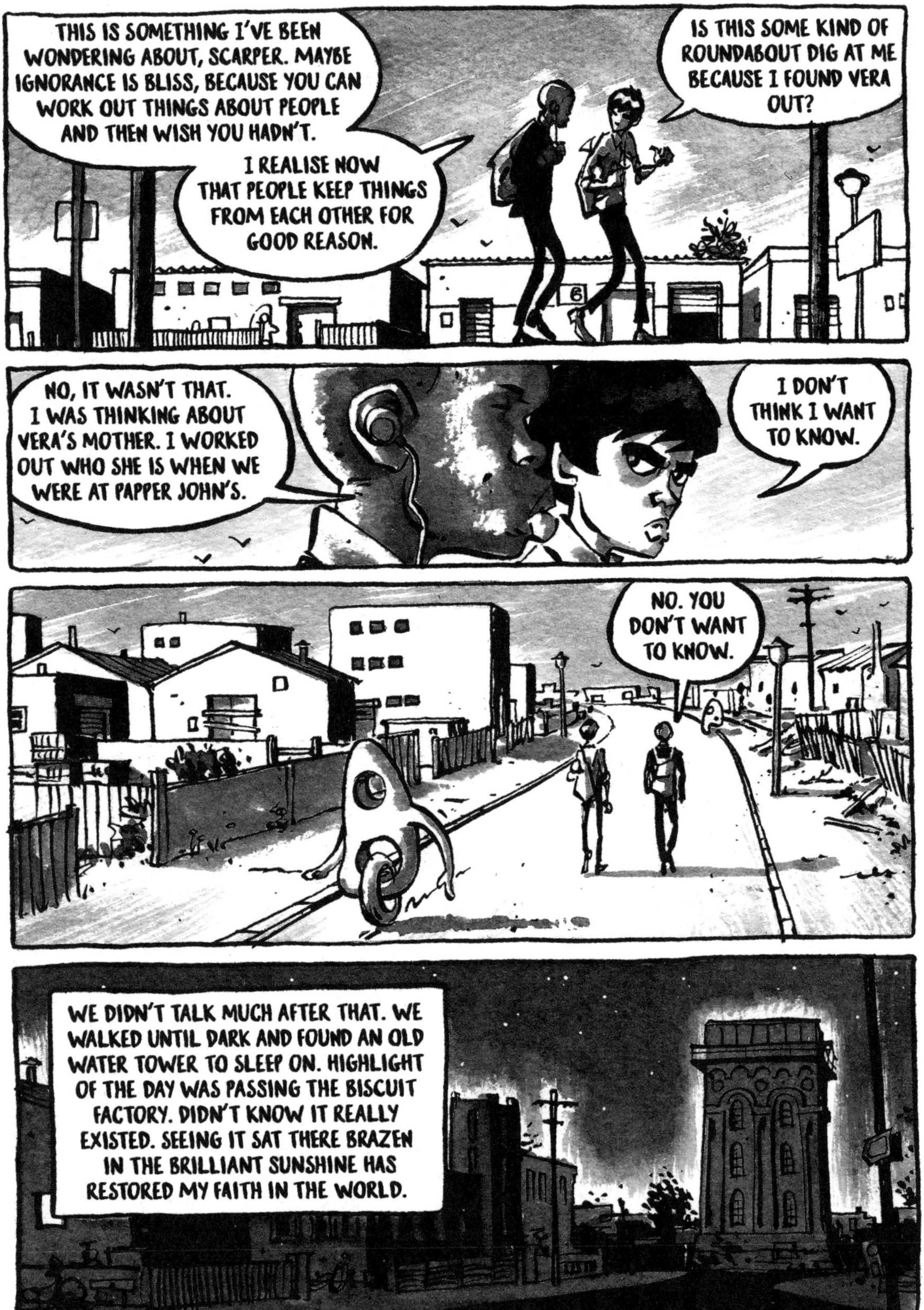
THIS IS SOMETHING I'VE BEEN WONDERING ABOUT, SCARPER. MAYBE IGNORANCE IS BLISS, BECAUSE YOU CAN WORK OUT THINGS ABOUT PEOPLE AND THEN WISH YOU HADN'T.
I REALISE NOW THAT PEOPLE KEEP THINGS FROM EACH OTHER FOR GOOD REASON.
IS THIS SOME KIND OF ROUNDABOUT DIG AT ME BECAUSE I FOUND VERA OUT?
NO, IT WASN'T THAT. I WAS THINKING ABOUT VERA'S MOTHER. I WORKED OUT WHO SHE IS WHEN WE WERE AT PAPPER JOHN'S.
I DON'T THINK I WANT TO KNOW.
NO. YOU DON'T WANT TO KNOW.
WE DIDN'T TALK MUCH AFTER THAT. WE WALKED UNTIL DARK AND FOUND AN OLD WATER TOWER TO SLEEP ON. HIGHLIGHT OF THE DAY WAS PASSING THE BISCUIT FACTORY. DIDN'T KNOW IT REALLY EXISTED. SEEING IT SAT THERE BRAZEN IN THE BRILLIANT SUNSHINE HAS RESTORED MY FAITH IN THE WORLD.

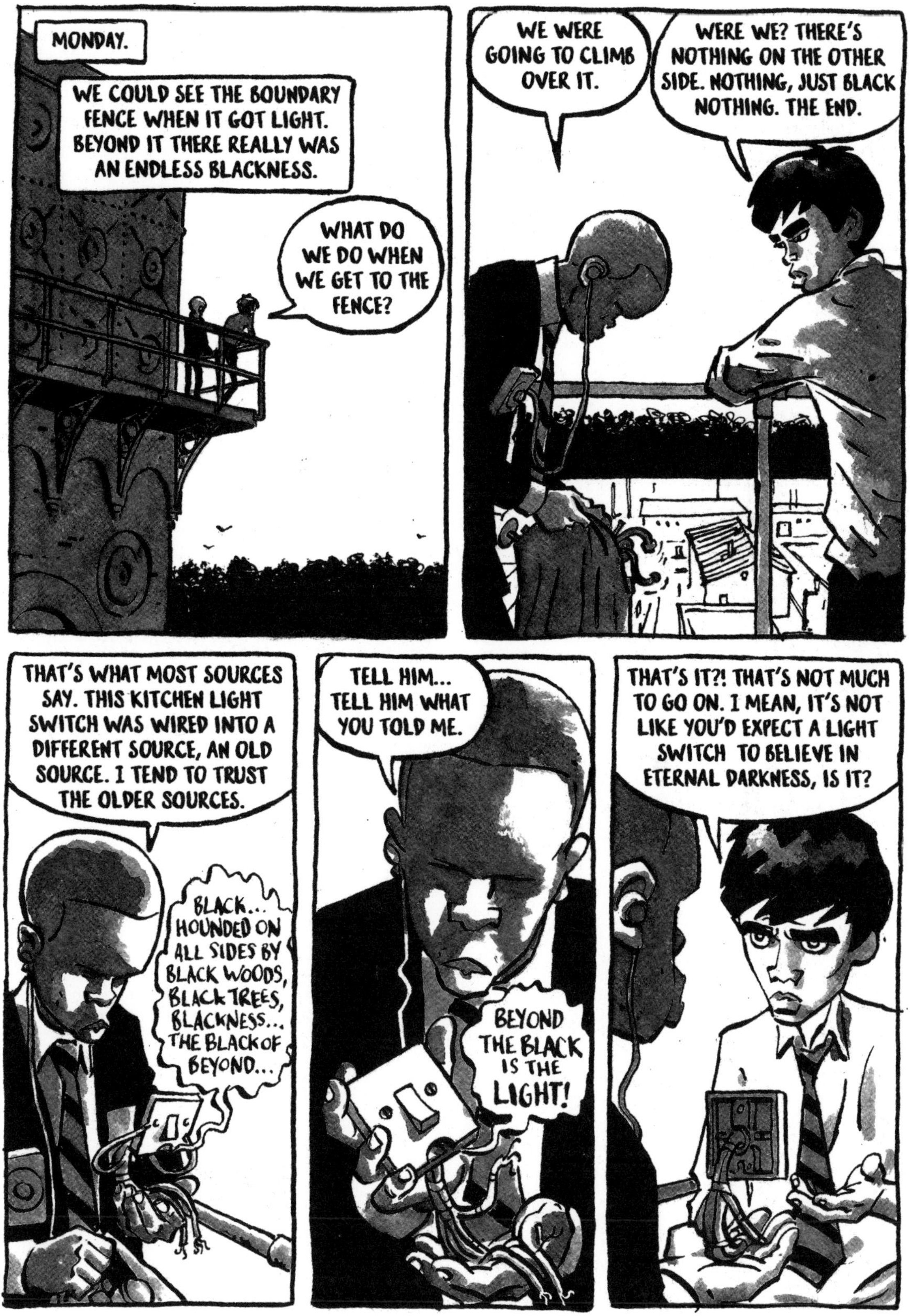

MONDAY.
WE COULD SEE THE BOUNDARY FENCE WHEN IT GOT LIGHT. BEYOND IT THERE REALLY WAS AN ENDLESS BLACKNESS.
WHAT DO WE DO WHEN WE GET TO THE FENCE?
WE WERE GOING TO CLIMB OVER IT.
WERE WE? THERE'S NOTHING ON THE OTHER SIDE. NOTHING, JUST BLACK NOTHING. THE END.
THAT'S WHAT MOST SOURCES SAY. THIS KITCHEN LIGHT SWITCH WAS WIRED INTO A DIFFERENT SOURCE, AN OLD SOURCE. I TEND TO TRUST THE OLDER SOURCES.
BLACK... HOUNDED ON ALL SIDES BY BLACK WOODS, BLACK TREES, BLACKNESS... THE BLACK OF BEYOND...
TELL HIM... TELL HIM WHAT YOU TOLD ME.
BEYOND THE BLACK IS THE LIGHT!
THAT'S IT?! THAT'S NOT MUCH TO GO ON. I MEAN, IT'S NOT LIKE YOU'D EXPECT A LIGHT SWITCH TO BELIEVE IN ETERNAL DARKNESS, IS IT?

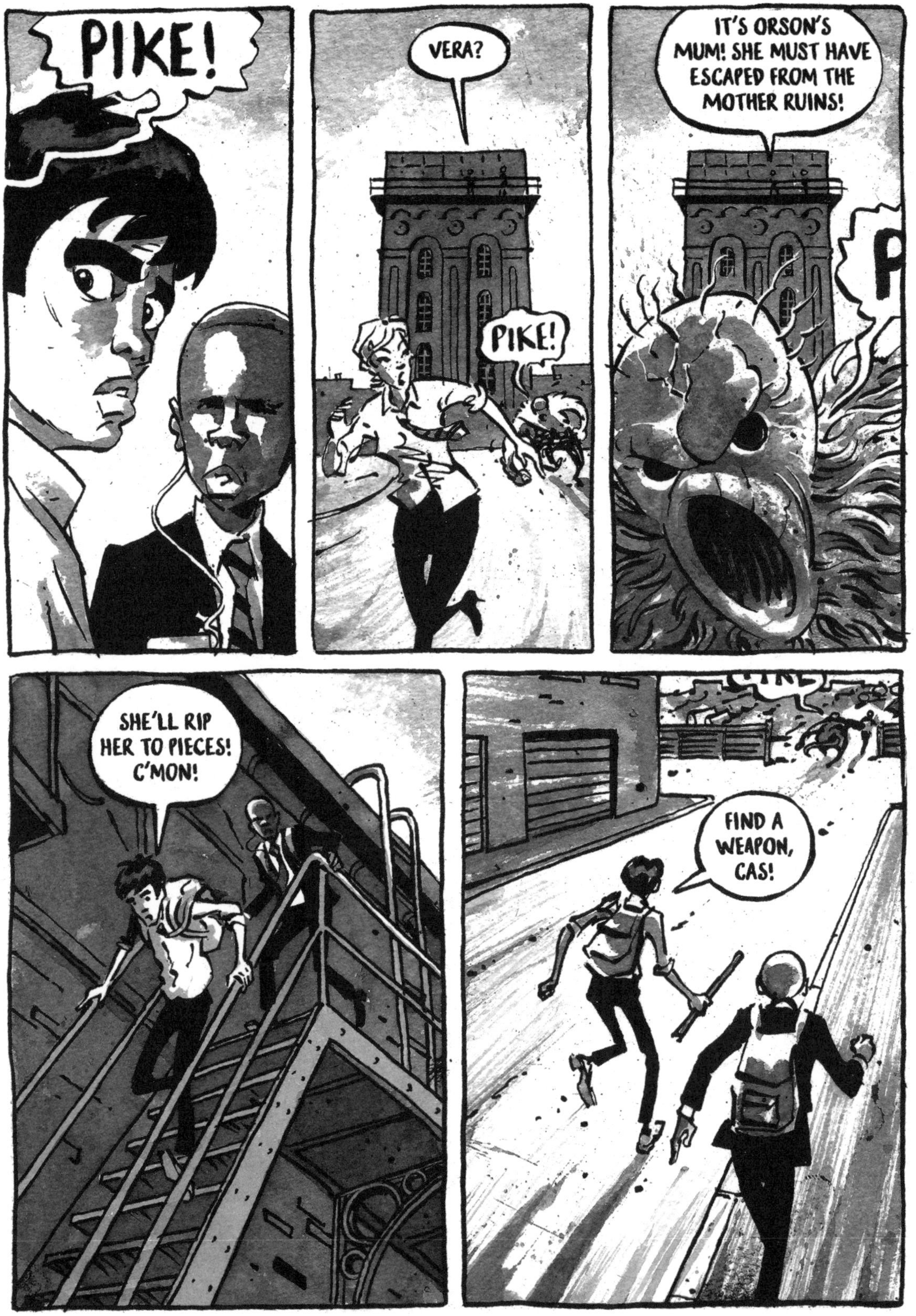
PIKE!
VERA?
PIKE!
IT'S ORSON'S MUM! SHE MUST HAVE ESCAPED FROM THE MOTHER RUINS!
SHE'LL RIP HER TO PIECES! C'MON!
FIND A WEAPON, CAS!

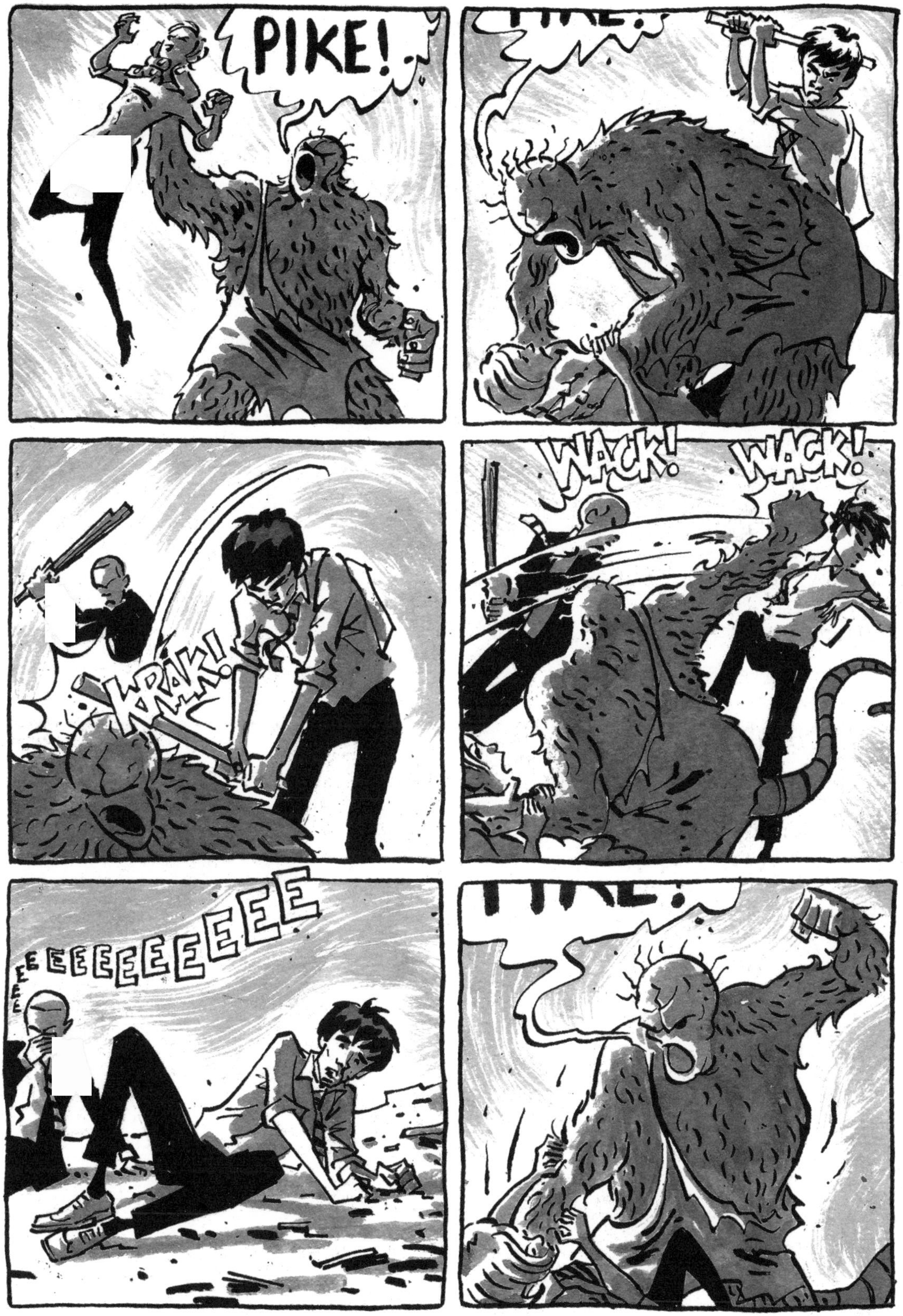
PIKE!
KRAK!
WACK!
WACK!
EEEEEEEEEEEEEEE

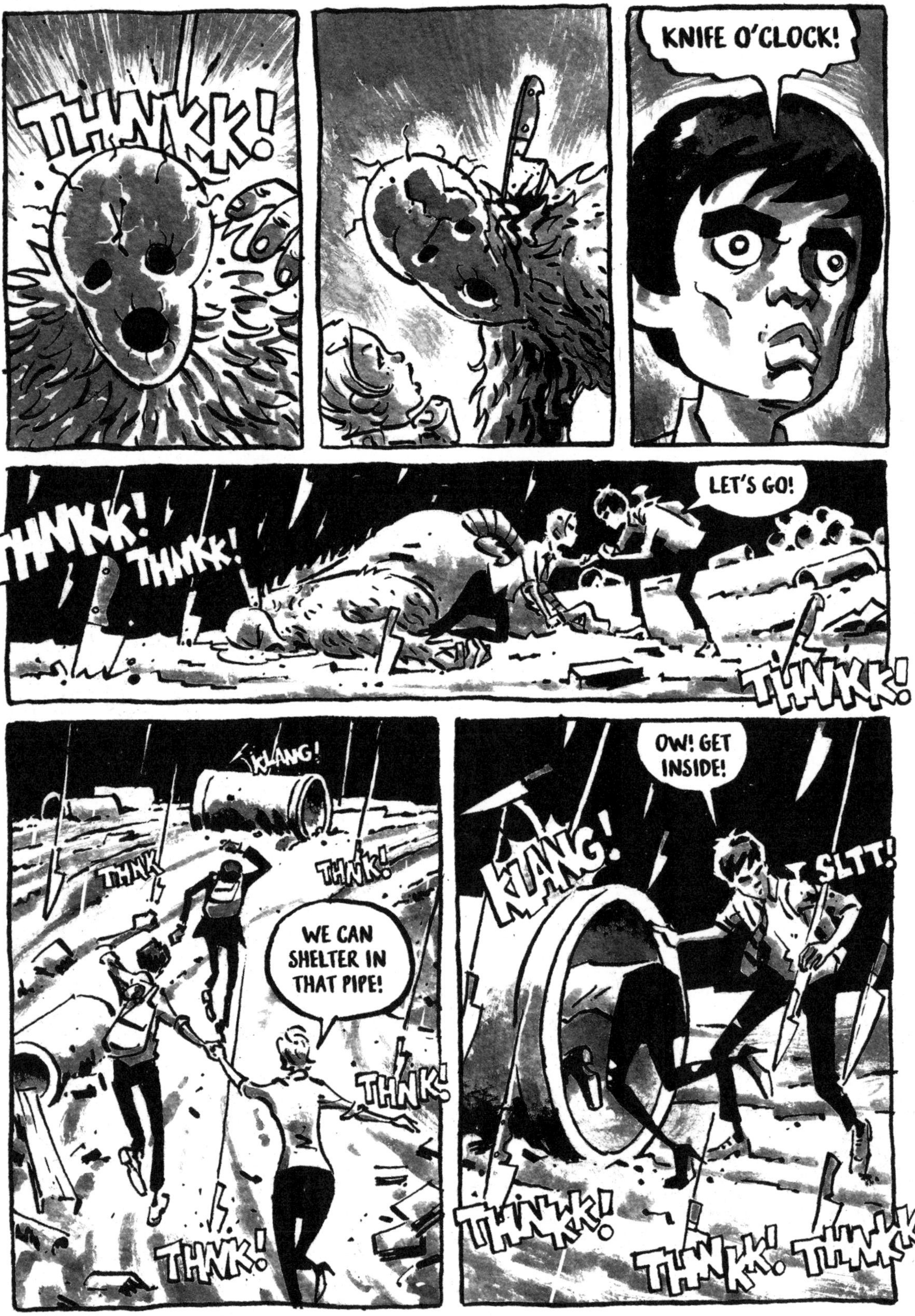
THNKK!
KNIFE O'CLOCK!
THNKK!
THNKK!
LET'S GO!
THNKK!
KLANG!
THNK
THNK!
WE CAN SHELTER IN THAT PIPE!
THNK!
THNK!
OW! GET INSIDE!
KLANG!
SLTT!
THNKK!
THNKK!
THNKK!

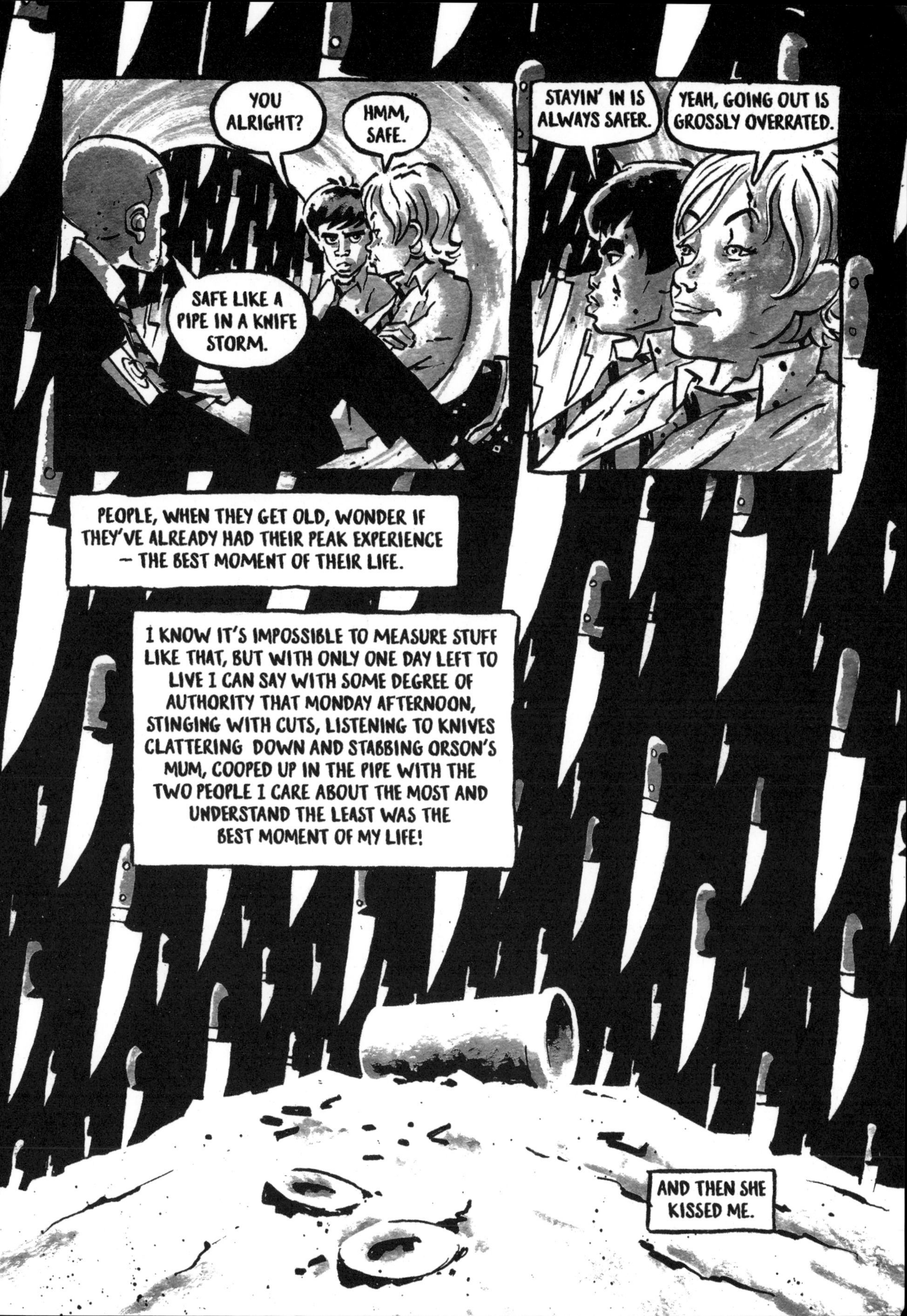
YOU ALRIGHT?
HMM, SAFE.
SAFE LIKE A PIPE IN A KNIFE STORM.
STAYIN' IN IS ALWAYS SAFER.
YEAH, GOING OUT IS GROSSLY OVERRATED.
PEOPLE, WHEN THEY GET OLD, WONDER IF THEY'VE ALREADY HAD THEIR PEAK EXPERIENCE – THE BEST MOMENT OF THEIR LIFE.
I KNOW IT'S IMPOSSIBLE TO MEASURE STUFF LIKE THAT, BUT WITH ONLY ONE DAY LEFT TO LIVE I CAN SAY WITH SOME DEGREE OF AUTHORITY THAT MONDAY AFTERNOON, STINGING WITH CUTS, LISTENING TO KNIVES CLATTERING DOWN AND STABBING ORSON'S MUM, COOPED UP IN THE PIPE WITH THE TWO PEOPLE I CARE ABOUT THE MOST AND UNDERSTAND THE LEAST WAS THE BEST MOMENT OF MY LIFE!
AND THEN SHE KISSED ME.

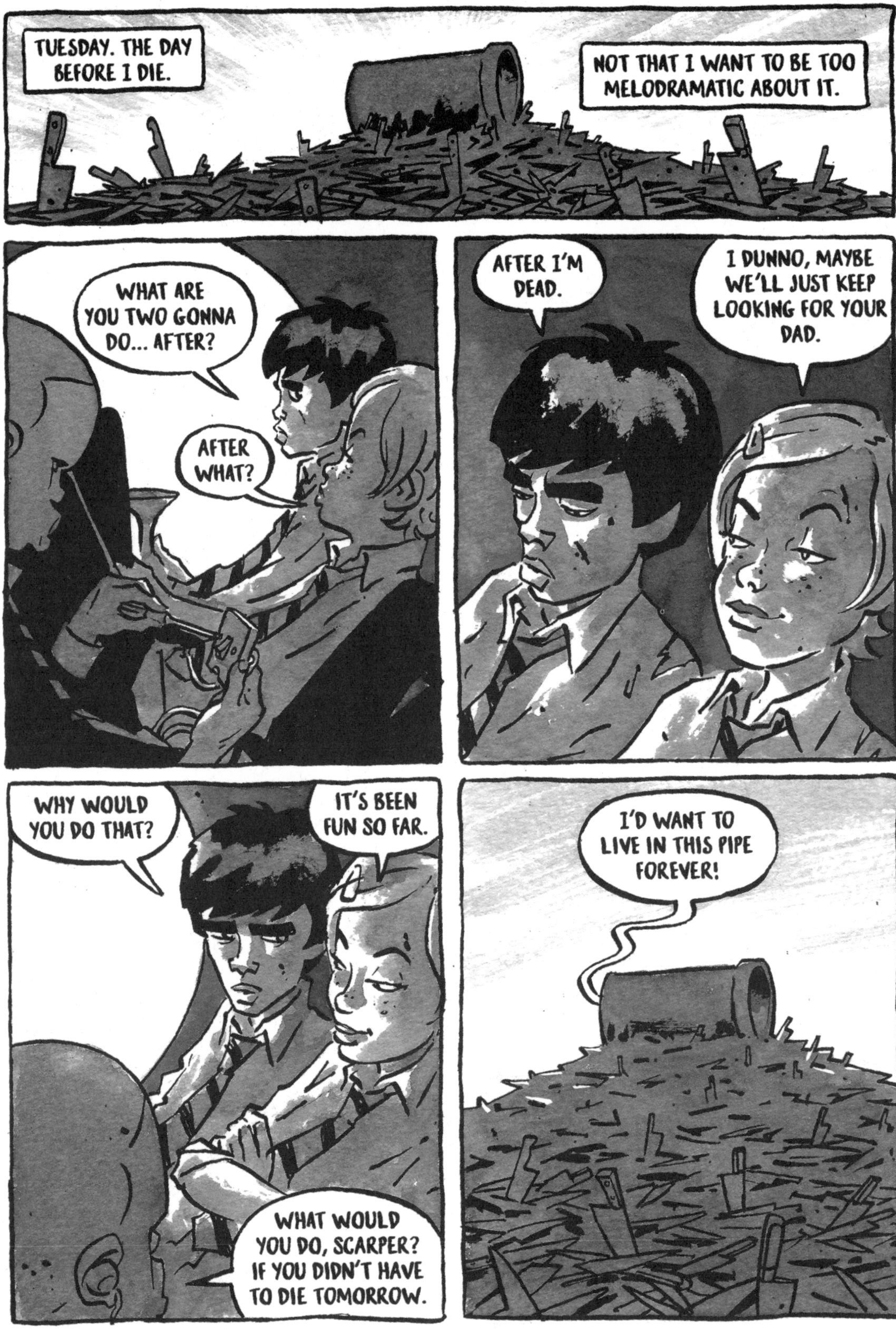
TUESDAY. THE DAY BEFORE I DIE.
NOT THAT I WANT TO BE TOO MELODRAMATIC ABOUT IT.
WHAT ARE YOU TWO GONNA DO... AFTER?
AFTER WHAT?
AFTER I'M DEAD.
I DUNNO, MAYBE WE'LL JUST KEEP LOOKING FOR YOUR DAD.
WHY WOULD YOU DO THAT?
IT'S BEEN FUN SO FAR.
WHAT WOULD YOU DO, SCARPER? IF YOU DIDN'T HAVE TO DIE TOMORROW.
I'D WANT TO LIVE IN THIS PIPE FOREVER!

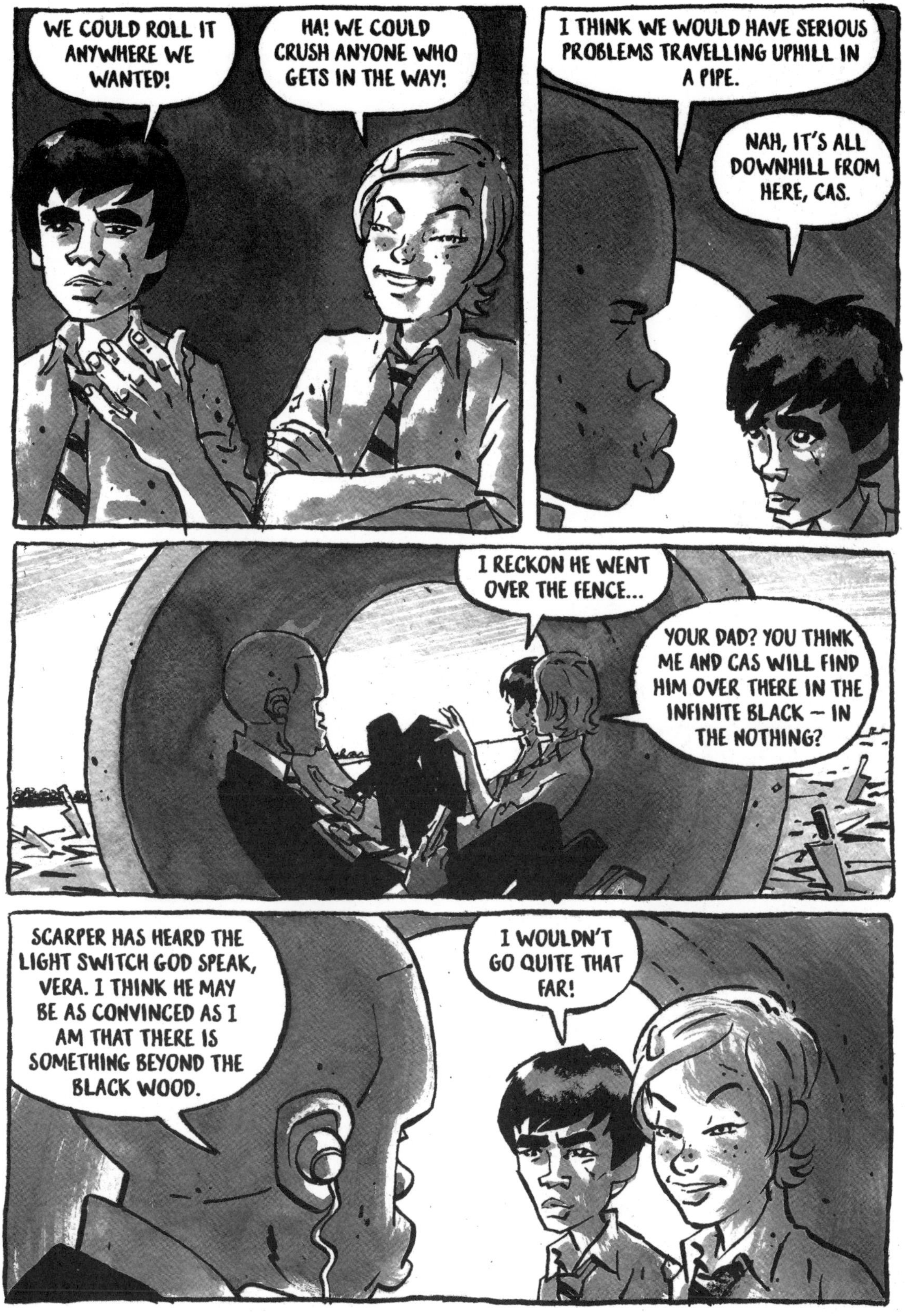
WE COULD ROLL IT ANYWHERE WE WANTED!
HA! WE COULD CRUSH ANYONE WHO GETS IN THE WAY!
I THINK WE WOULD HAVE SERIOUS PROBLEMS TRAVELLING UPHILL IN A PIPE.
NAH, IT'S ALL DOWNHILL FROM HERE, CAS.
I RECKON HE WENT OVER THE FENCE...
YOUR DAD? YOU THINK ME AND CAS WILL FIND HIM OVER THERE IN THE INFINITE BLACK – IN THE NOTHING?
SCARPER HAS HEARD THE LIGHT SWITCH GOD SPEAK, VERA. I THINK HE MAY BE AS CONVINCED AS I AM THAT THERE IS SOMETHING BEYOND THE BLACK WOOD.
I WOULDN'T GO QUITE THAT FAR!

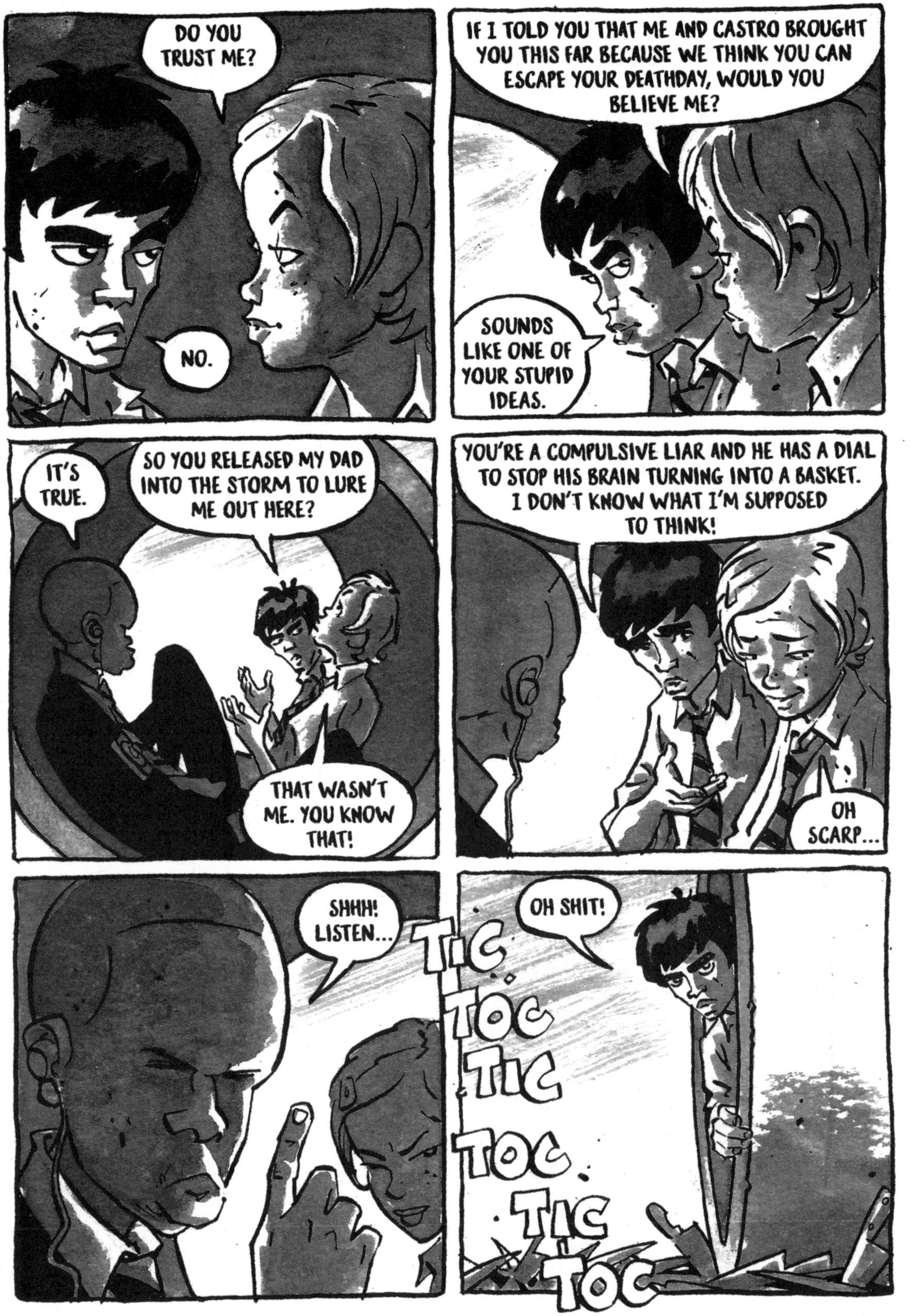
DO YOU TRUST ME?
NO.
IF I TOLD YOU THAT ME AND CASTRO BROUGHT YOU THIS FAR BECAUSE WE THINK YOU CAN ESCAPE YOUR DEATHDAY, WOULD YOU BELIEVE ME?
SOUNDS LIKE ONE OF YOUR STUPID IDEAS.
IT'S TRUE.
SO YOU RELEASED MY DAD INTO THE STORM TO LURE ME OUT HERE?
THAT WASN'T ME. YOU KNOW THAT!
YOU'RE A COMPULSIVE LIAR AND HE HAS A DIAL TO STOP HIS BRAIN TURNING INTO A BASKET. I DON'T KNOW WHAT I'M SUPPOSED TO THINK!
OH SCARP...
SHHH! LISTEN...
OH SHIT!
TIC
TOC
TIC
TOC
TIC
TOC

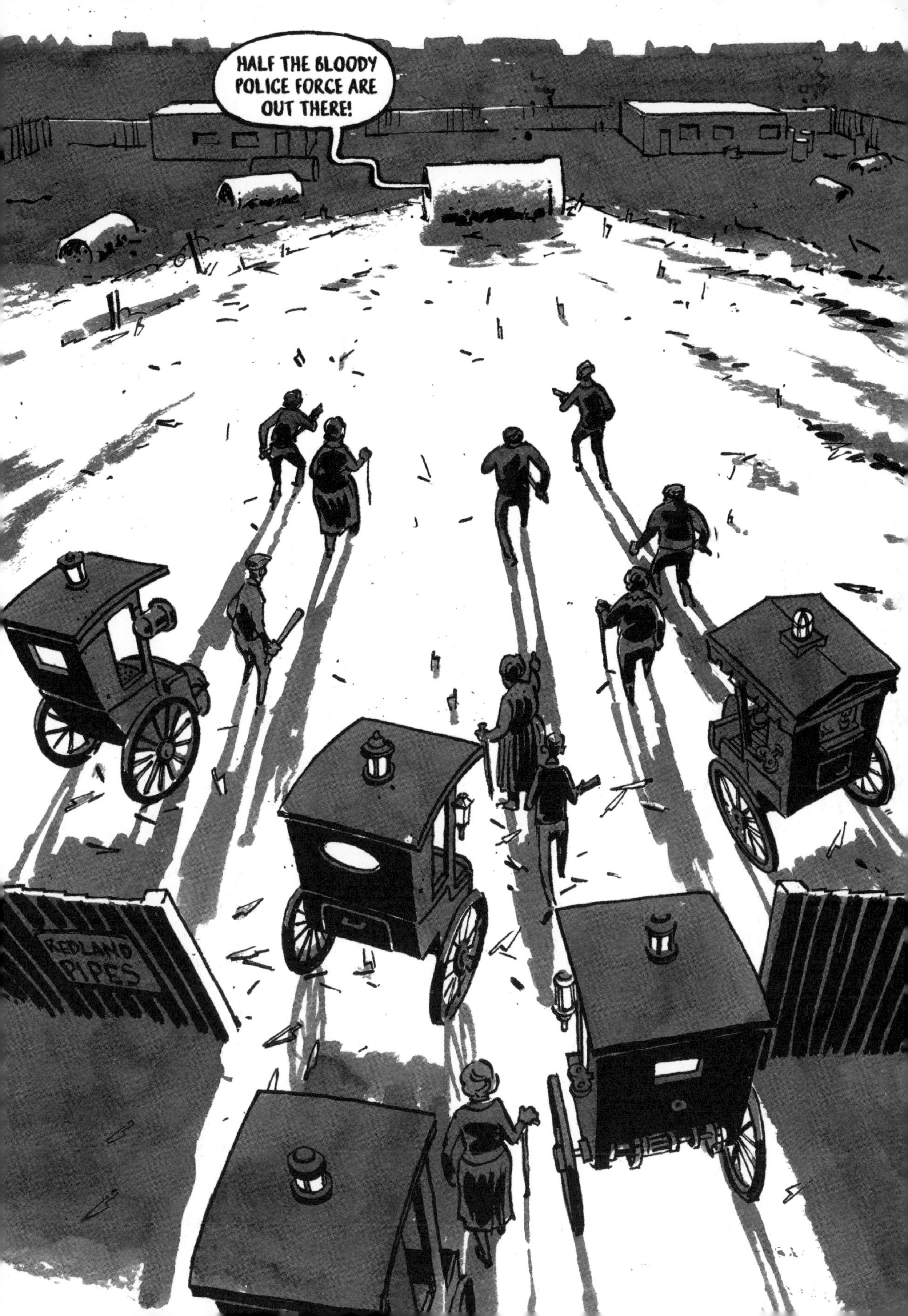
HALF THE BLOODY POLICE FORCE ARE OUT THERE!
REDLAND PIPES

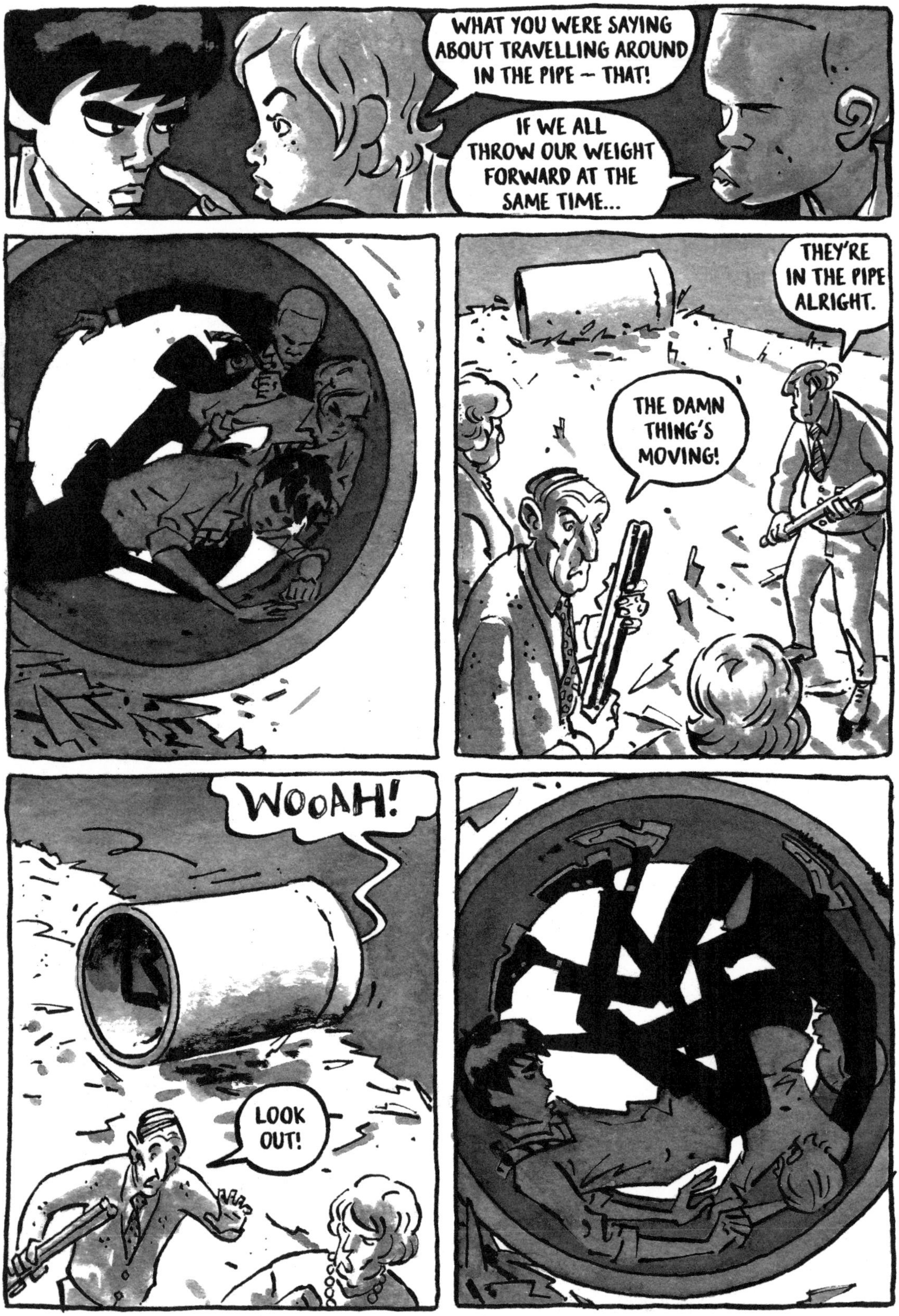
WHAT YOU WERE SAYING ABOUT TRAVELLING AROUND IN THE PIPE – THAT!
IF WE ALL THROW OUR WEIGHT FORWARD AT THE SAME TIME...
THEY'RE IN THE PIPE ALRIGHT.
THE DAMN THING'S MOVING!
WOOAH!
LOOK OUT!

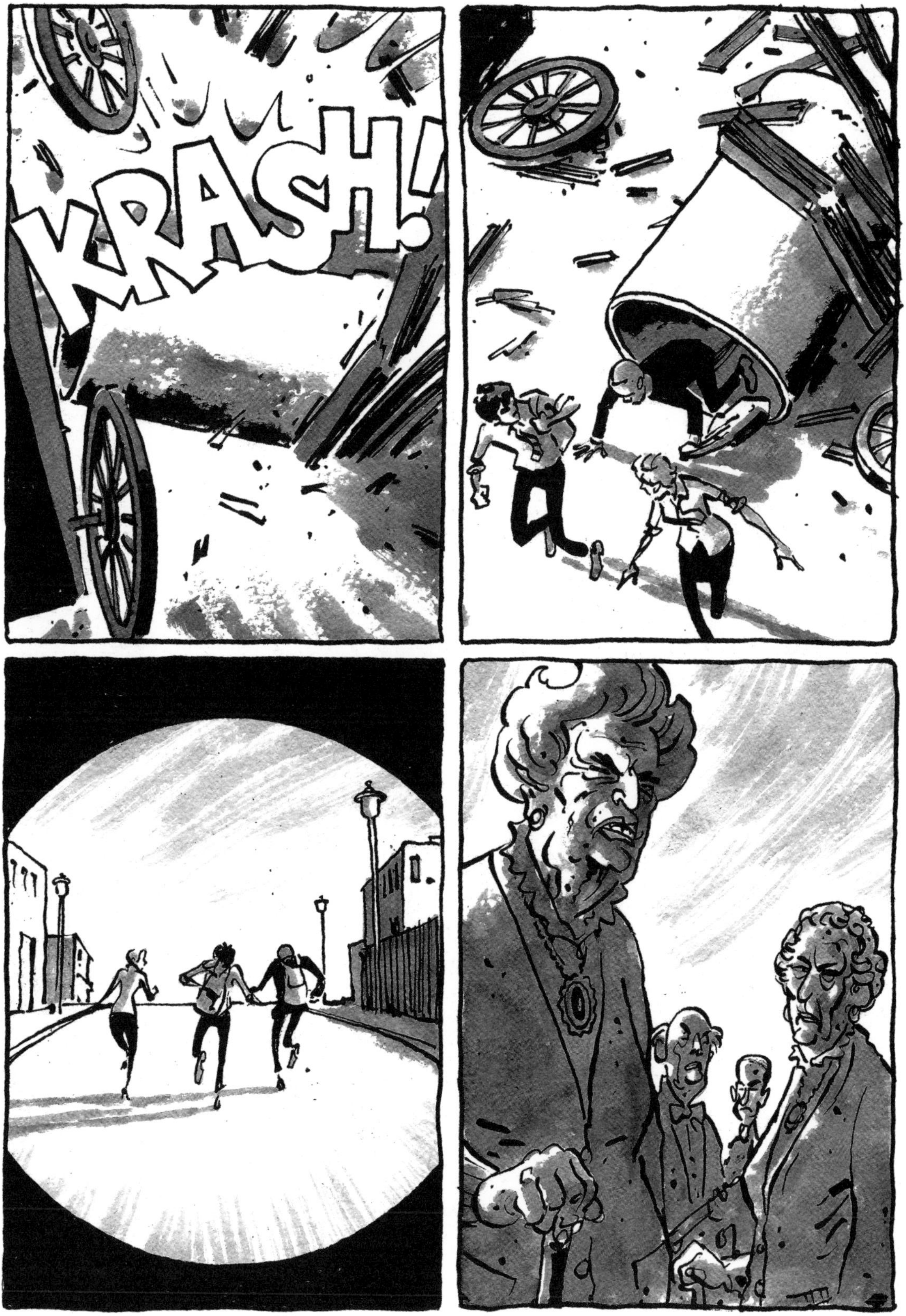
KRASH!

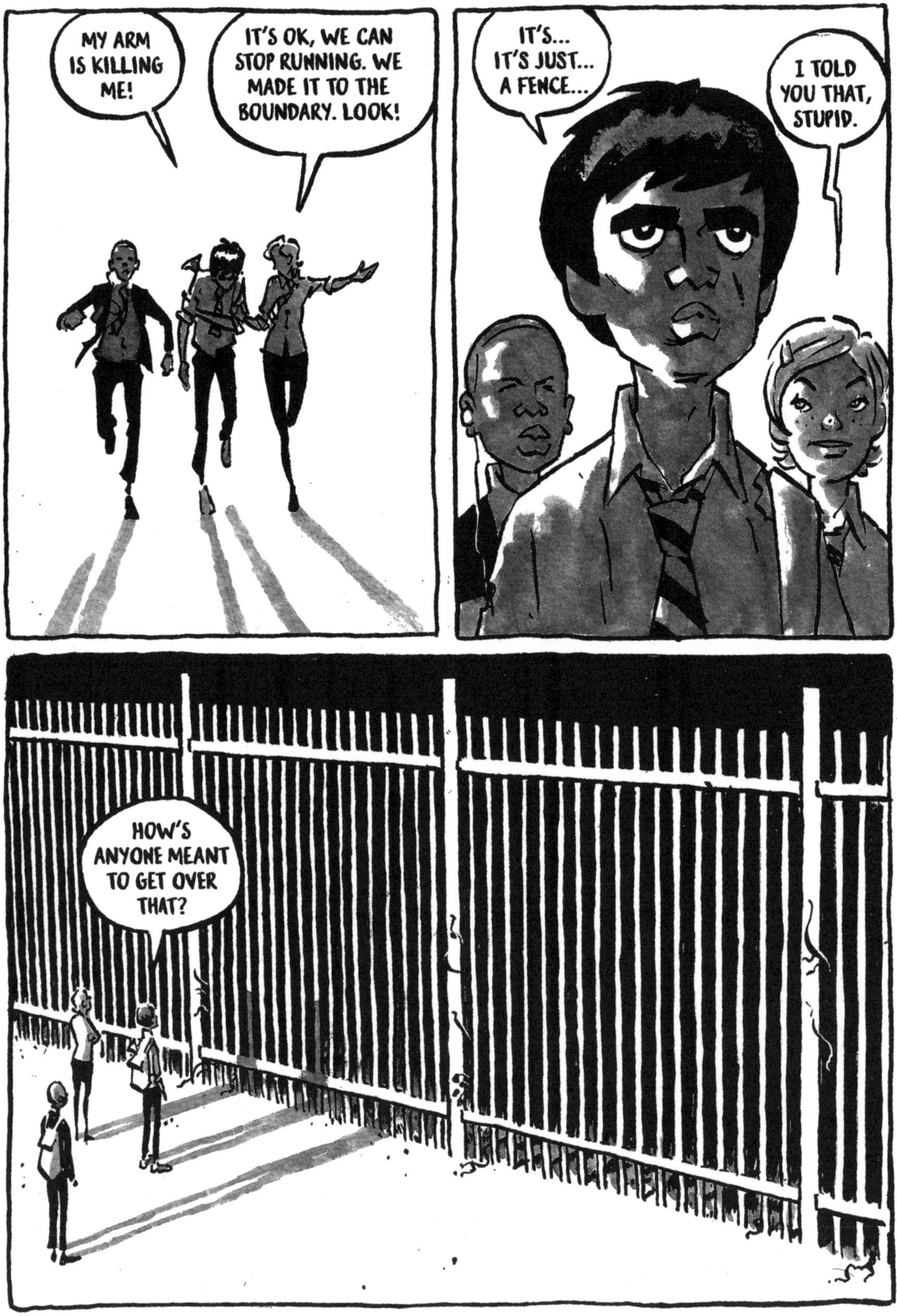
MY ARM IS KILLING ME!
IT'S OK, WE CAN STOP RUNNING. WE MADE IT TO THE BOUNDARY. LOOK!
IT'S... IT'S JUST... A FENCE...
I TOLD YOU THAT, STUPID.
HOW'S ANYONE MEANT TO GET OVER THAT?

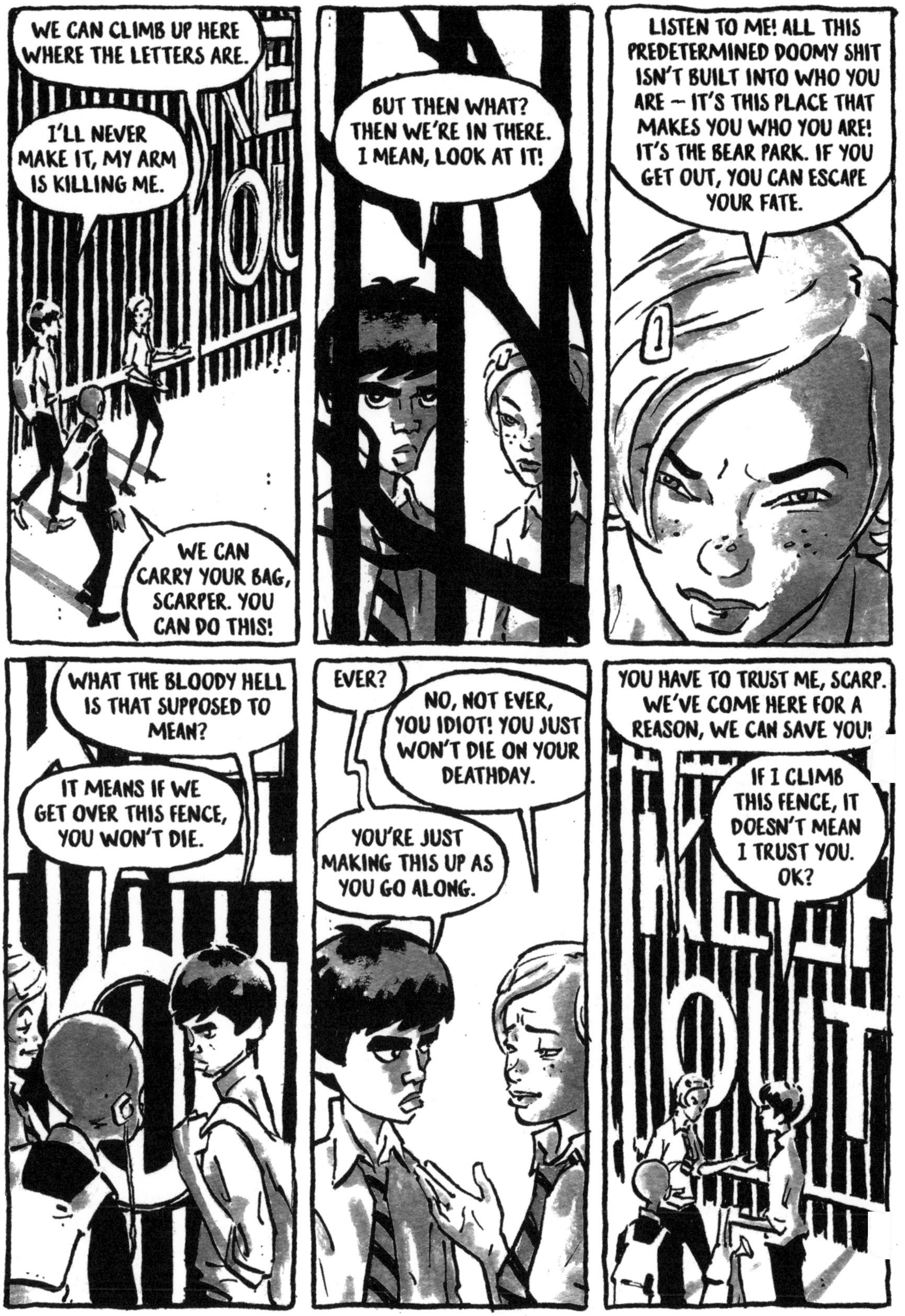
WE CAN CLIMB UP HERE WHERE THE LETTERS ARE.
I'LL NEVER MAKE IT, MY ARM IS KILLING ME.
WE CAN CARRY YOUR BAG, SCARPER. YOU CAN DO THIS!
BUT THEN WHAT? THEN WE'RE IN THERE. I MEAN, LOOK AT IT!
LISTEN TO ME! ALL THIS PREDETERMINED DOOMY SHIT ISN'T BUILT INTO WHO YOU ARE – IT'S THIS PLACE THAT MAKES YOU WHO YOU ARE! IT'S THE BEAR PARK. IF YOU GET OUT, YOU CAN ESCAPE YOUR FATE.
WHAT THE BLOODY HELL IS THAT SUPPOSED TO MEAN?
IT MEANS IF WE GET OVER THIS FENCE, YOU WON'T DIE.
EVER?
NO, NOT EVER, YOU IDIOT! YOU JUST WON'T DIE ON YOUR DEATHDAY.
YOU'RE JUST MAKING THIS UP AS YOU GO ALONG.
YOU HAVE TO TRUST ME, SCARP. WE'VE COME HERE FOR A REASON, WE CAN SAVE YOU!
IF I CLIMB THIS FENCE, IT DOESN'T MEAN I TRUST YOU. OK?

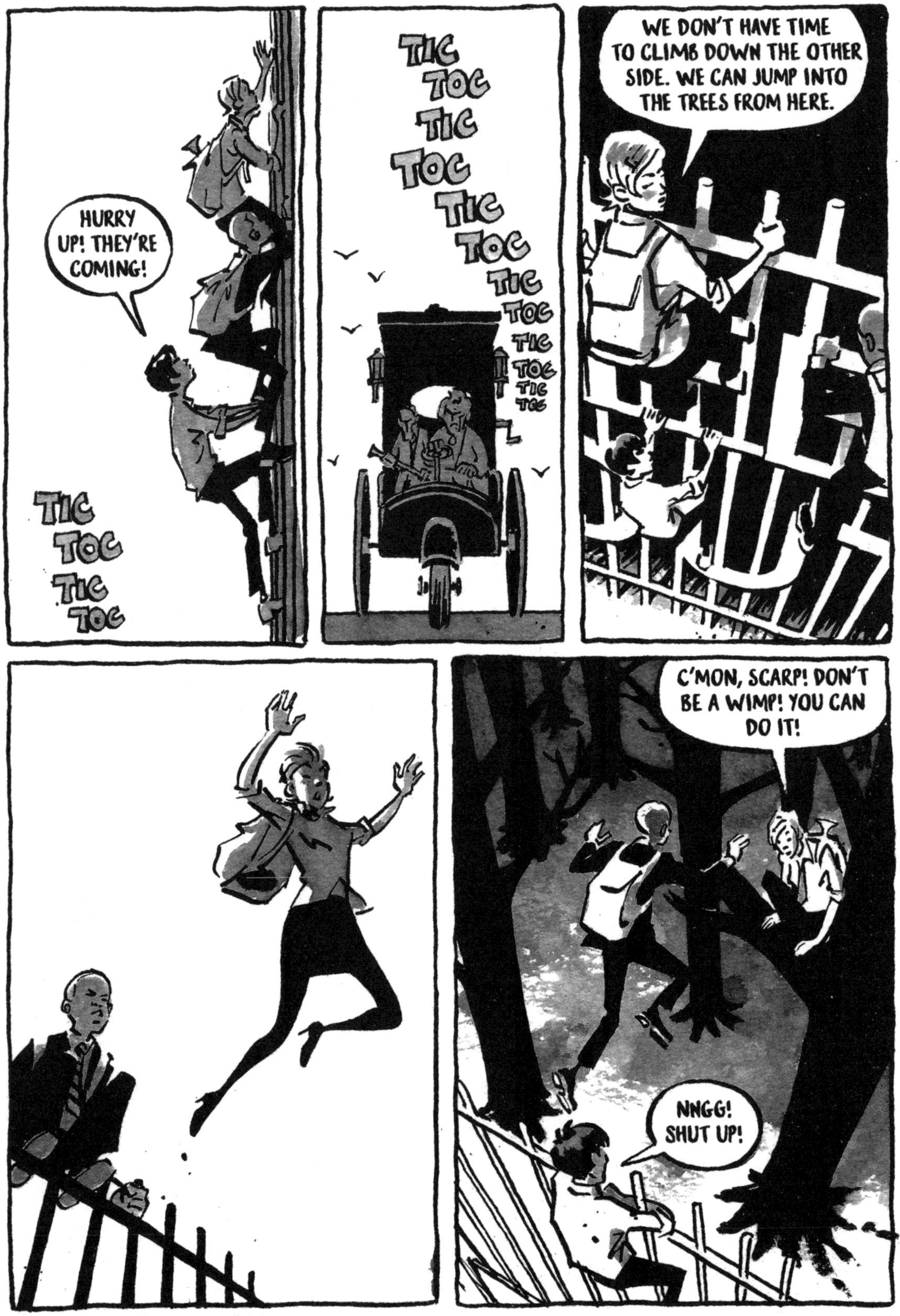
HURRY UP! THEY'RE COMING!
TIC TOC TIC TOC
TIC TOC TIC TOC TIC TOC TIC TOC TIC TOC TIC TOC
WE DON'T HAVE TIME TO CLIMB DOWN THE OTHER SIDE. WE CAN JUMP INTO THE TREES FROM HERE.
C'MON, SCARP! DON'T BE A WIMP! YOU CAN DO IT!
NNGG! SHUT UP!

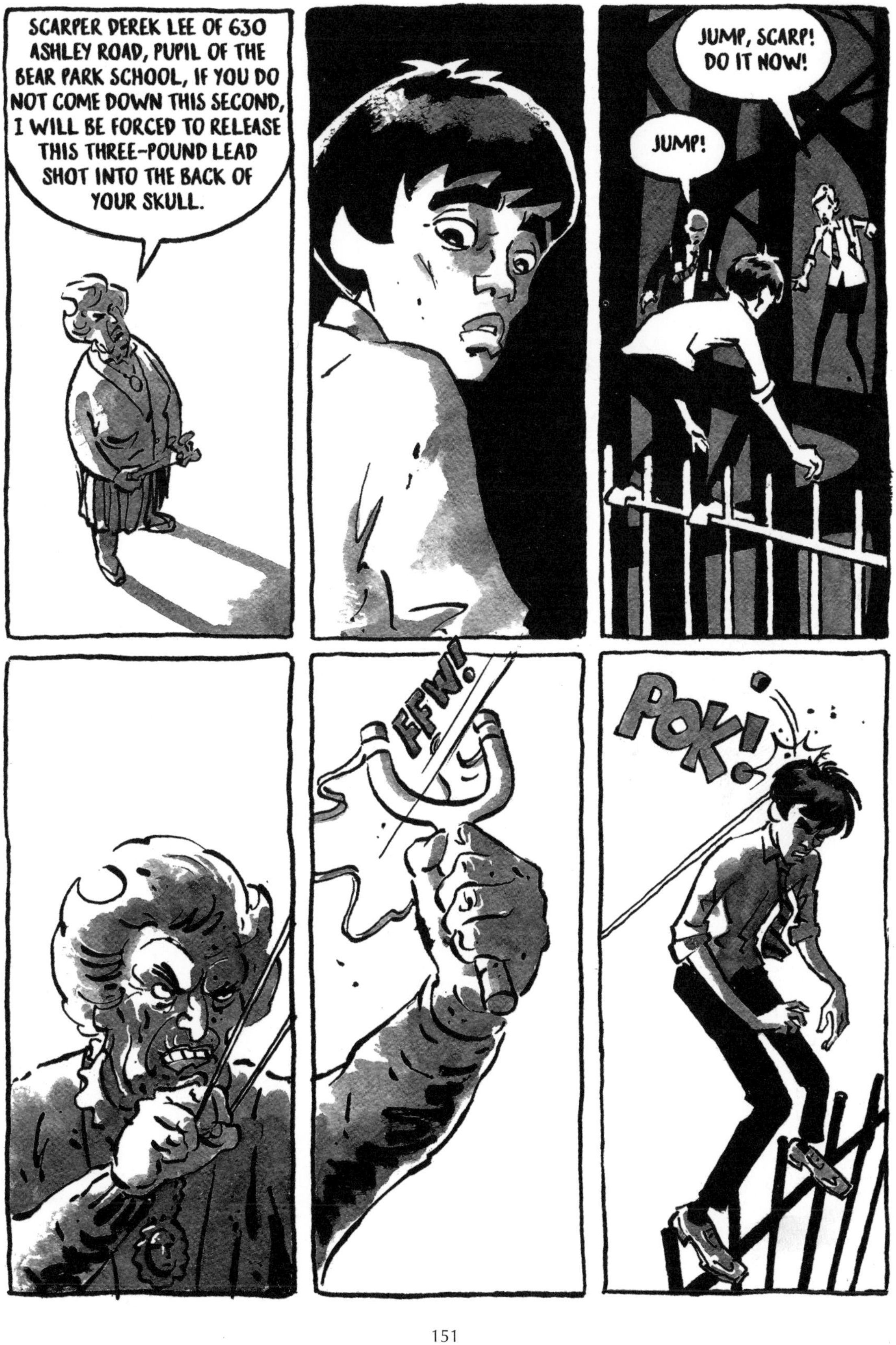
SCARPER DEREK LEE OF 630 ASHLEY ROAD, PUPIL OF THE BEAR PARK SCHOOL, IF YOU DO NOT COME DOWN THIS SECOND, I WILL BE FORCED TO RELEASE THIS THREE-POUND LEAD SHOT INTO THE BACK OF YOUR SKULL.
JUMP, SCARP! DO IT NOW!
JUMP!
FFW!
POK!

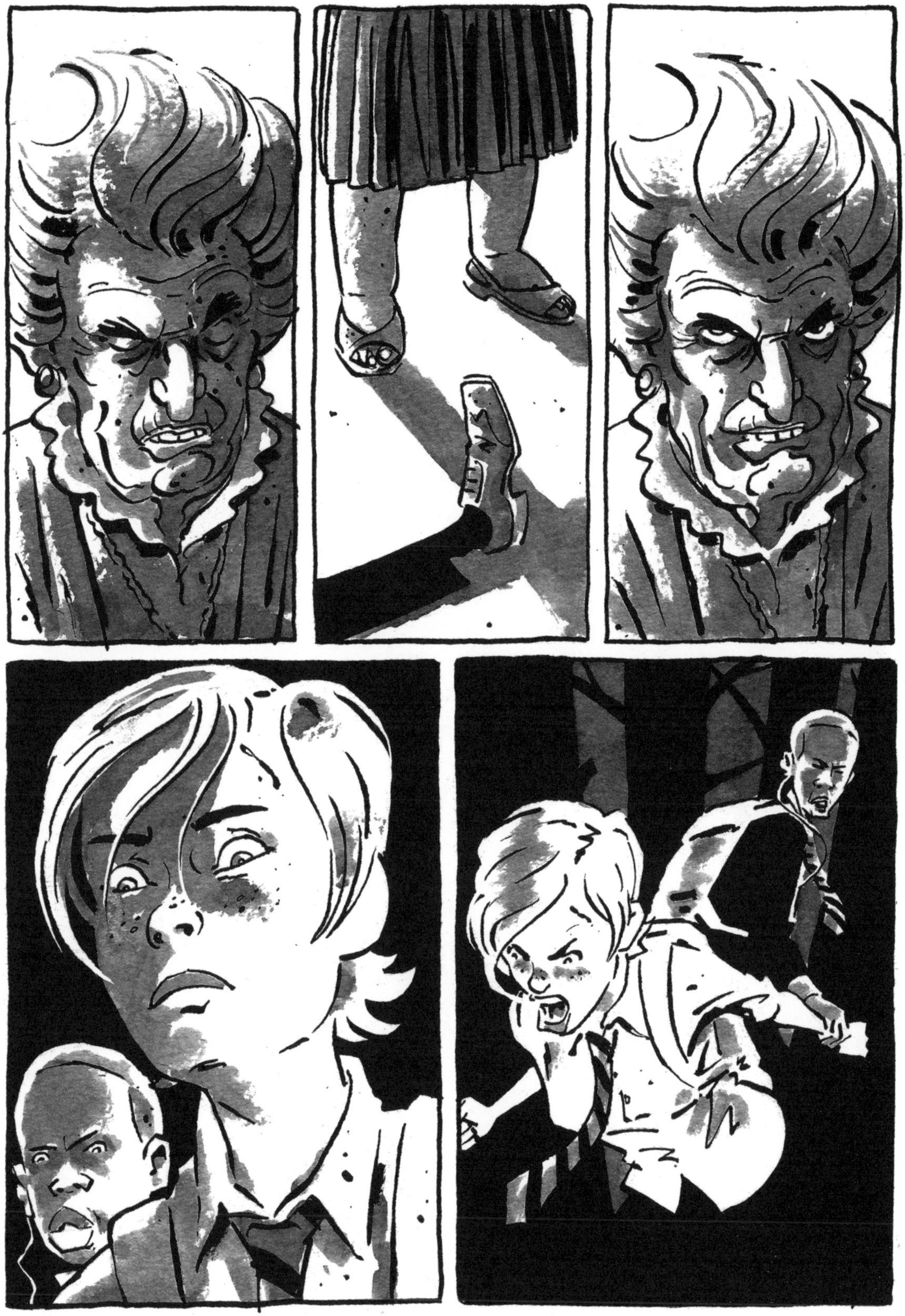

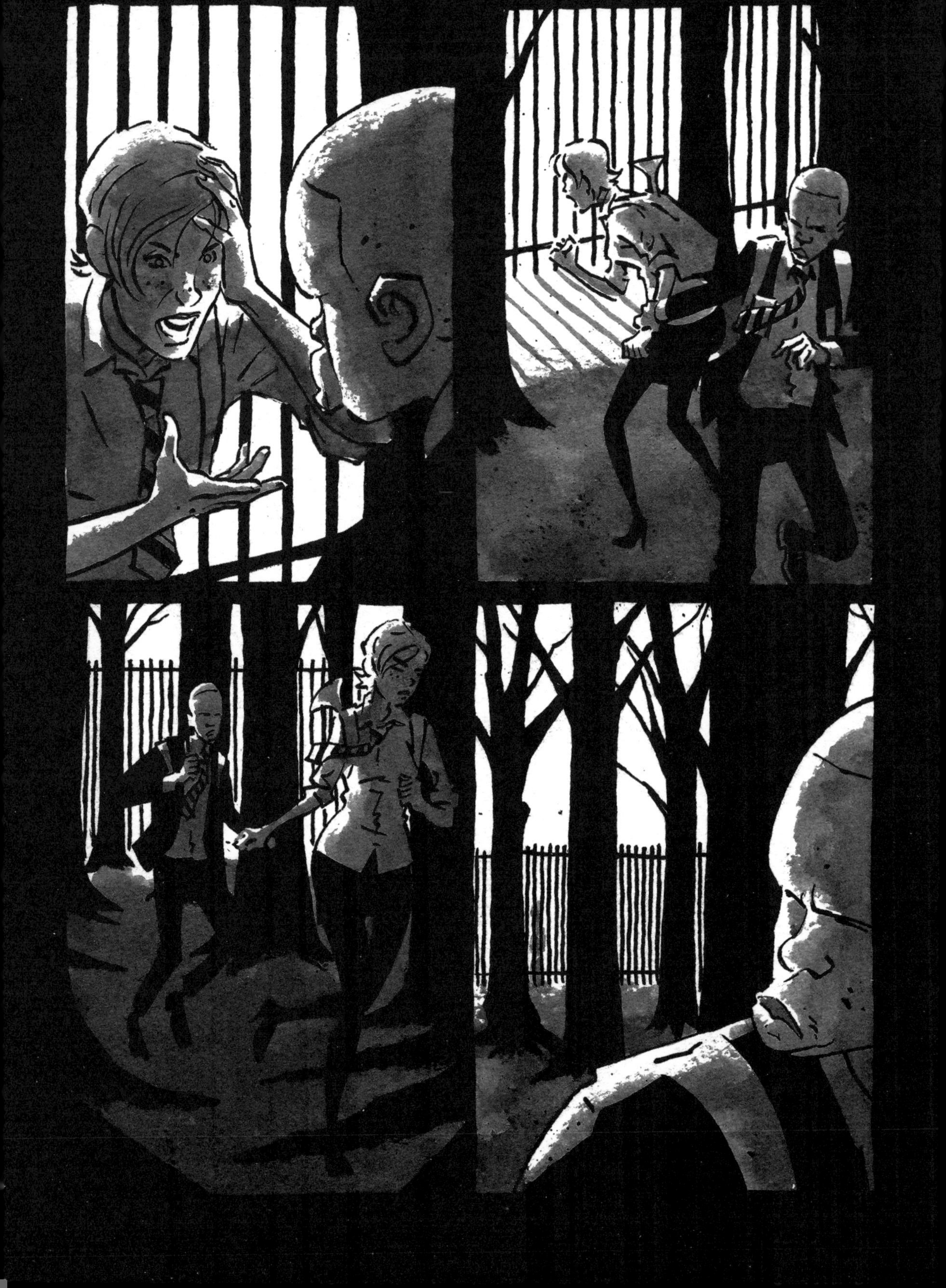

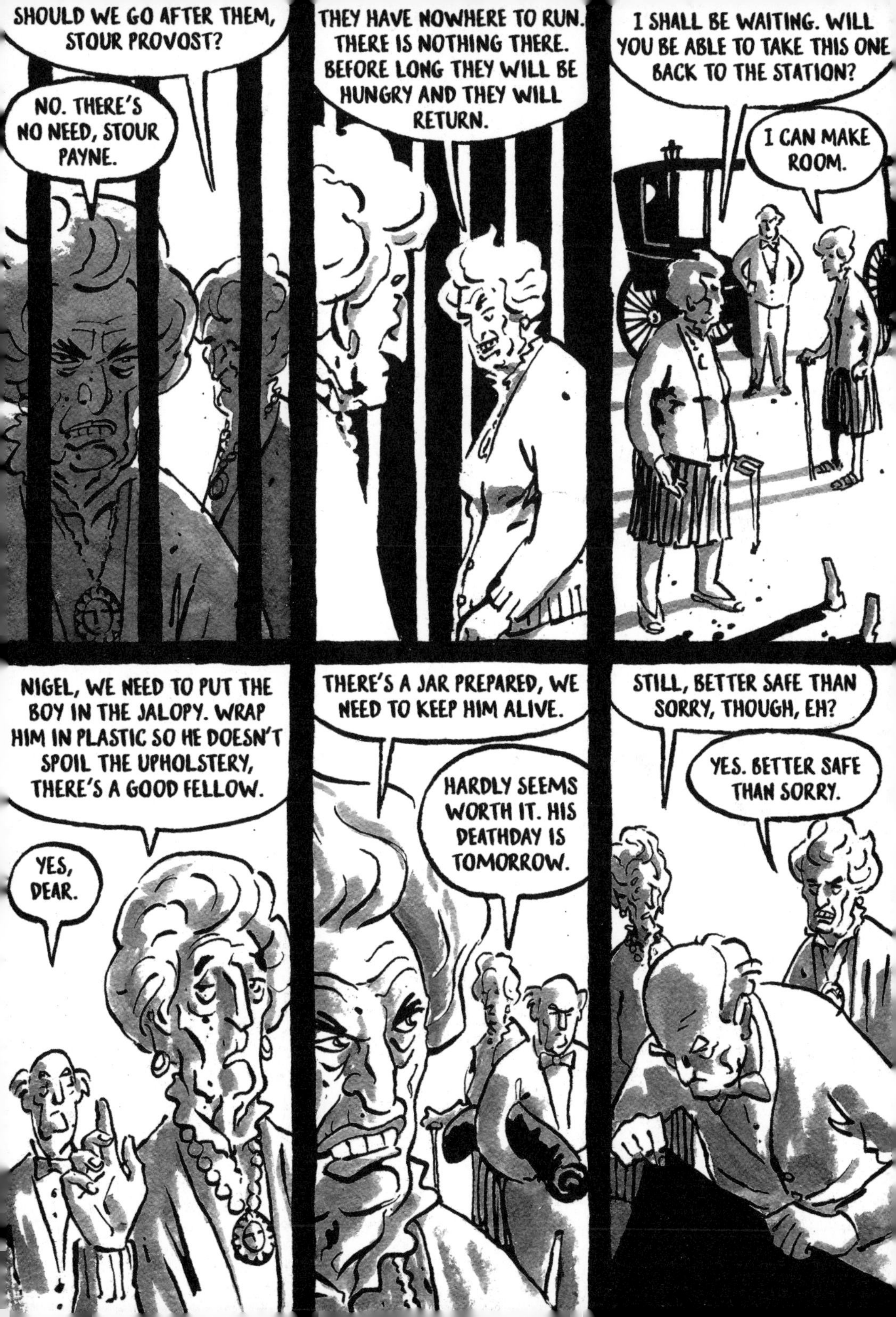
SHOULD WE GO AFTER THEM, STOUR PROVOST?
NO. THERE'S NO NEED, STOUR PAYNE.
THEY HAVE NOWHERE TO RUN. THERE IS NOTHING THERE. BEFORE LONG THEY WILL BE HUNGRY AND THEY WILL RETURN.
I SHALL BE WAITING. WILL YOU BE ABLE TO TAKE THIS ONE BACK TO THE STATION?
I CAN MAKE ROOM.
NIGEL, WE NEED TO PUT THE BOY IN THE JALOPY. WRAP HIM IN PLASTIC SO HE DOESN'T SPOIL THE UPHOLSTERY, THERE'S A GOOD FELLOW.
YES, DEAR.
THERE'S A JAR PREPARED, WE NEED TO KEEP HIM ALIVE.
HARDLY SEEMS WORTH IT. HIS DEATHDAY IS TOMORROW.
STILL, BETTER SAFE THAN SORRY, THOUGH, EH?
YES. BETTER SAFE THAN SORRY.

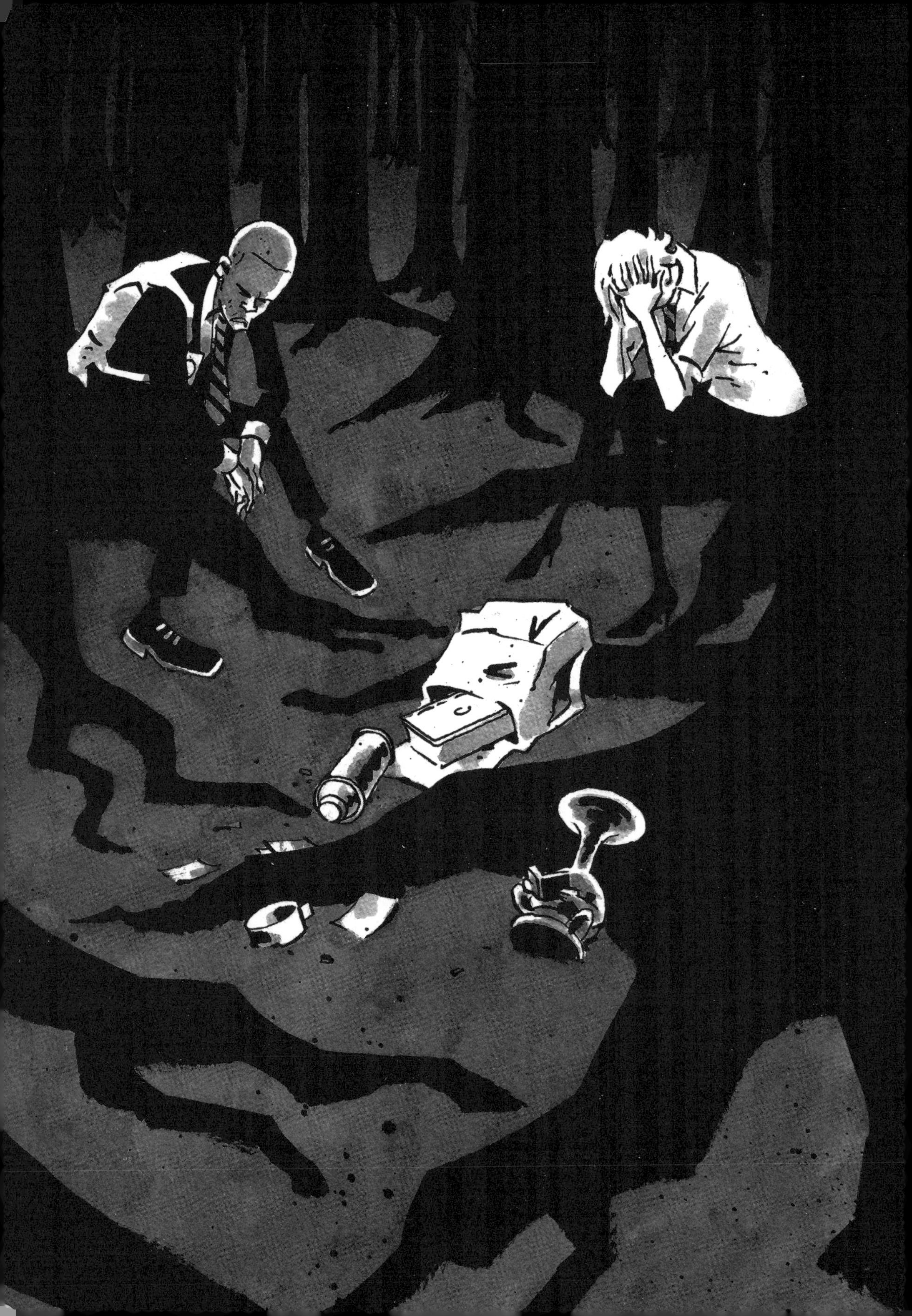

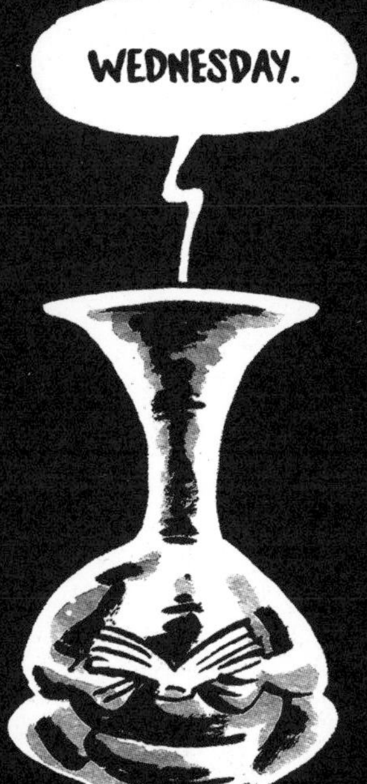
WEDNESDAY.

First published 2014
by SelfMadeHero
139-141 Pancras Road
London NW1 1UN
www.selfmadehero.com

© 2014 Rob Davis

Written and Illustrated by Rob Davis
Edited by Dan Lockwood
Typeface created by Dan Berry

Lyrics from *Alibi Lullaby* by Ernest Berry used with permission.

Publishing Assistant: Guillaume Rater
Editorial & Production Manager: Lizzie Kaye
Sales & Marketing Manager: Sam Humphrey
Publishing Director: Emma Hayley
With thanks to: Jane Laporte

A CIP record for this book is available from the British Library

ISBN: 978-1-906838-81-2

10 9 8 7 6 5 4 3 2 1

Printed and bound in China